AGAMBEN'S
PHILOSOPHICAL LINEAGE

AGAMBEN'S PHILOSOPHICAL LINEAGE

Edited by Adam Kotsko and Carlo Salzani

EDINBURGH
University Press

Edinburgh University Press is one of the leading university presses in the UK. We publish academic books and journals in our selected subject areas across the humanities and social sciences, combining cutting-edge scholarship with high editorial and production values to produce academic works of lasting importance. For more information visit our website: edinburghuniversitypress.com

© editorial matter and organisation Adam Kotsko and Carlo Salzani, 2017
© the chapters their several authors, 2017

Edinburgh University Press Ltd
The Tun – Holyrood Road, 12(2f) Jackson's Entry, Edinburgh EH8 8PJ

Typeset in 10.5/13 Sabon by
Servis Filmsetting Ltd, Stockport, Cheshire

A CIP record for this book is available from the British Library

ISBN 978 1 4744 2363 2 (hardback)
ISBN 978 1 4744 2365 6 (webready PDF)
ISBN 978 1 4744 2364 9 (paperback)
ISBN 978 1 4744 2366 3 (epub)

The right of Adam Kotsko and Carlo Salzani to be identified as the editors of this work has been asserted in accordance with the Copyright, Designs and Patents Act 1988, and the Copyright and Related Rights Regulations 2003 (SI No. 2498).

Contents

List of Abbreviations	viii
Introduction: Agamben as a Reader *Adam Kotsko and Carlo Salzani*	1

Part I Primary Interlocutors

1. Aristotle *Jussi Backman*	15
2. Walter Benjamin *Carlo Salzani*	27
3. Guy Debord *Dave Mesing*	39
4. Michel Foucault *Vanessa Lemm*	51
5. Martin Heidegger *Mathew Abbott*	63
6. Paul the Apostle *Ted Jennings*	76
7. Carl Schmitt *Sergei Prozorov*	87

Part II Points of Reference

8. Hannah Arendt *John Grumley*	101

9. Georges Bataille — 109
   Nadine Hartmann

10. Émile Benveniste — 117
    Henrik Wilberg

11. Dante Alighieri — 125
    Paolo Bartoloni

12. Gilles Deleuze — 131
    Claire Colebrook

13. Georg Wilhelm Friedrich Hegel — 138
    Alysia Garrison

14. Friedrich Hölderlin — 146
    Henrik Wilberg

15. Franz Kafka — 154
    Anke Snoek

16. Immanuel Kant — 162
    Susan Brophy

17. Friedrich Nietzsche — 171
    Vanessa Lemm

18. Plato — 178
    Mika Ojakangas

19. Plotinus — 186
    Mårten Björk

20. Marquis de Sade — 193
    Christian Grünnagel

21. Baruch Spinoza — 201
    Jeffrey A. Bernstein

22. Aby Warburg — 208
    Adi Efal-Lautenschläger

Part III Submerged Dialogues

23. Theodor W. Adorno — 219
    Colby Dickinson

24. Jacques Derrida — 230
    Virgil W. Brower

25.	Sigmund Freud *Virgil W. Brower*	242
26.	Jacques Lacan *Frances L. Restuccia*	252
27.	Karl Marx *Jessica Whyte*	262
28.	Antonio Negri *Ingrid Diran*	272
29.	Gershom Scholem *Julia Ng*	282
30.	Simone Weil *Beatrice Marovich*	292
	Conclusion: Agamben as a Reader of Agamben *Adam Kotsko*	303

Contributors 314
Index 318

Abbreviations

References to the work of Agamben are made parenthetically in the text according to the following conventions.

	Italian	English translation
AV	*L'avventura*. Rome: Nottetempo, 2015.	
CC	*La comunità che viene*. Turin: Einaudi, 1990.	*The Coming Community*. Trans. Michael Hardt. Minneapolis: University of Minnesota Press, 1993.
CF	*Che cos'è la filosofia?* Macerata: Quodlibet, 2016.	
CR	*La Chiesa e il Regno*. Rome: Nottetempo, 2010.	*The Church and the Kingdom*. Trans. Leland de la Durantaye. London: Seagull Books, 2012.
CRM	*Che cos'è il reale? La scomparsa di Majorana*. Vicenza: Neri Pozza, 2016.	
EP	*Categorie italiane. Studi di poetica*. Venice: Marsilio, 1996.	*The End of the Poem: Studies in Poetics*. Trans. Daniel Heller-Roazen. Stanford: Stanford University Press, 1999.
FR	*Il fuoco e il racconto*. Rome: Nottetempo, 2014.	
GU	*Gusto*. Macerata: Quodlibet, 2015.	
HP	*Altissima povertà. Regole monastiche e forma di vita*. Vicenza: Neri Pozza, 2011.	*The Highest Poverty: Monastic Rules and Form-of-Life*. Trans. Adam Kotsko. Stanford: Stanford University Press, 2013.
HS	*Homo sacer. Il potere sovrano e la nuda vita*. Turin: Einaudi, 1995.	*Homo Sacer: Sovereign Power and Bare Life*. Trans. Daniel Heller-Roazen. Stanford: Stanford University Press, 1998.

	Italian	English translation
IH	*Infanzia e storia. Distruzione dell'esperienza e origine della storia.* Turin: Einaudi 1978.	*Infancy and History: On the Destruction of Experience.* Trans. Liz Heron. London: Verso, 1996.
IP	*Idea della prosa.* Milan: Feltrinelli, 1985; new edn, Macerata: Quodlibet, 2002.	*Idea of Prose.* Trans. Sam Whitsitt and Michael Sullivan. Albany, NY: SUNY Press, 1995.
KG	*Il Regno e la Gloria. Per una genealogia teologica dell'economia e del governo.* Vicenza: Neri Pozza, 2007; repr., Turin: Bollati Boringhieri, 2009.	*The Kingdom and the Glory: For a Theological Genealogy of Economy and Government.* Trans. Lorenzo Chiesa (with Matteo Mandarini). Stanford: Stanford University Press, 2011.
LD	*Il linguaggio e la morte. Un seminario sul luogo della negatività.* Turin: Einaudi, 1982.	*Language and Death: The Place of Negativity.* Trans. Karen Pinkus and Michael Hardt. Minneapolis: University of Minnesota Press, 1991.
MC	*L'uomo senza contenuto.* Milan: Rizzoli, 1970; repr., Macerata: Quodlibet, 1994.	*The Man Without Content.* Trans. Georgia Albert. Stanford: Stanford University Press, 1999.
ME	*Mezzi senza fine. Note sulla politica.* Turin: Bollati Boringhieri, 1996.	*Means Without End: Notes on Politics.* Trans. Vincenzo Binetti and Cesare Casarino. Minneapolis: University of Minnesota Press, 2000.
MM	*Il mistero del male. Benedetto XVI e la fine dei tempi.* Rome–Bari: Laterza, 2013.	
NI	*Ninfe,* Turin: Bollati Boringhieri, 2007.	*Nymphs.* Trans. Amanda Minervini. London: Seagull Books, 2013.
NU	*Nudità.* Rome: Nottetempo, 2009.	*Nudities.* Trans. David Kishik and Stefan Pedatella. Stanford: Stanford University Press, 2011.
O	*L'aperto. L'uomo e l'animale.* Turin: Bollati Boringhieri, 2002.	*The Open: Man and Animal.* Trans. Kevin Attell. Stanford: Stanford University Press, 2004.
OD	*Opus Dei. Archeologia dell'ufficio.* Turin: Bollati Boringhieri, 2012.	*Opus Dei: An Archaeology of Duty.* Trans. Adam Kotsko. Stanford: Stanford University Press, 2013.
PJ	*Pilato e Gesù.* Rome: Nottetempo, 2013.	*Pilate and Jesus.* Trans. Adam Kotsko. Stanford: Stanford University Press, 2015.
PO	*La potenza del pensiero. Saggi e conferenze.* Vicenza: Neri Pozza, 2005.	*Potentialities: Collected Essays in Philosophy.* Trans. Daniel Heller-Roazen. Stanford: Stanford University Press, 1999.

	Italian	English translation
PR	*Profanazioni*. Rome: Nottetempo, 2005.	*Profanations*. Trans. Jeff Fort. New York: Zone Books, 2007.
PU	*Pulcinella ovvero divertimento per li regazzi in quattro scene*. Rome: Nottetempo, 2015.	
RA	*Quel che resta di Auschwitz. L'archivio e il testimone*. Turin: Bollati Boringhieri, 1998.	*Remnants of Auschwitz: The Witness and the Archive*. Trans. Daniel Heller-Roazen. New York: Zone Books, 1999.
S	*Stanze. La parola e il fantasma nella cultura occidentale*. Turin: Einaudi, 1977.	*Stanzas: Word and Phantasm in Western Culture*. Trans. Ronald L. Martinez. Minneapolis: University of Minnesota Press, 1993.
SE	*Stato di eccezione*. Turin: Bollati Boringhieri, 2003.	*State of Exception*. Trans. Kevin Attell. Chicago: University of Chicago Press, 2005.
SL	*Il sacramento del linguaggio. Archeologia del giuramento*. Rome–Bari: Laterza, 2008.	*The Sacrament of Language: An Archaeology of the Oath*. Trans. Adam Kotsko. Cambridge: Polity Press, 2011.
ST	*Signatura rerum. Sul metodo.* Turin: Bollati Boringhieri, 2008.	*The Signature of All Things: On Method*. Trans. Luca di Santo and Kevin Attell. New York: Zone Books, 2009.
STA	*Stasis. La guerra civile come paradigma politico*. Turin: Bollati Boringhieri, 2015.	*Stasis: Civil War as a Political Paradigm*. Trans. Nicholas Heron. Stanford: Stanford University Press, 2015.
TR	*Il tempo che resta. Un commento alla "Lettera ai romani"*. Turin: Bollati Boringhieri, 2000.	*The Time that Remains: A Commentary on the Letter to the Romans*. Trans. Patricia Dailey. Stanford: Stanford University Press, 2005.
UB	*L'uso dei corpi*. Vicenza: Neri Pozza, 2014.	*The Use of Bodies*. Trans. Adam Kotsko. Stanford: Stanford University Press, 2016.
UG	(con Monica Ferrando) *La ragazza indicibile. Mito e mistero di Kore.* Milan: Mondadori Electa, 2010.	(with Monica Ferrando) *The Unspeakable Girl: The Myth and Mystery of Kore*. Trans. Leland de la Durantaye. London: Seagull Books, 2014.
WA	*Che cos'è un dispositivo?* Rome: Nottetempo, 2006.	*What is an Apparatus?, and Other Essays*. Trans. David Kishik and Stefan Pedatella. Stanford: Stanford University Press, 2009.

Introduction: Agamben as a Reader

ADAM KOTSKO AND CARLO SALZANI

One of the greatest challenges Giorgio Agamben presents to his readers is the vast and often bewildering range of sources that he draws upon in his work. His books, written in an elegant and refined style that is also extremely dense and almost elliptical, venture into fields as diverse as aesthetics, religion, politics, law and ethics, with an uncommon erudition that ranges from ancient sources to medieval, modern and contemporary works in various disciplines and fields. Moreover, his peculiar 'Italian' style often plays with the 'unsaid' and practises the Benjaminian art of 'quoting without quotation marks', so that the reader is confronted not only by a wide range of sources, but also by a subtle and not always transparent use of them.

The present volume aims to guide the reader through the maze of Agamben's sources, rendering explicit what remains implicit and providing a reliable guide to his reading of the many figures he draws from. Yet a preliminary task is required, namely that of unpacking Agamben's own idiosyncratic 'style' as a reader, his philological/philosophical method of approaching a text, and the peculiar 'use' he puts his sources to. This is no minor task, since not only are Agamben's style and method extremely idiosyncratic, often challenging the norms of traditional philosophical writing, but they are also indissolubly intertwined with the 'content' of his writings, and are as such an essential component of his philosophical proposal.

Given the very limited space available to us in this introduction, we have decided to organise this short attempt around four main concepts, which constitute, as it were, the backbone and the rationale of his reading practices: tradition, study, citation and *Entwicklungsfähigkeit*. In Agamben's philosophy, these concepts exceed the realm of mere methodology and trespass into that of philosophy proper: they are no mere 'tools' of interpretation, but rather flow together into the broad definition of what philosophy is and how philosophical practice is supposed to work.

TRADITION

Reading a text is a cultural act embedded within a centuries-old tradition, which presupposes a set of norms and practices and a cultural heritage to draw from. From his very beginnings as a philosopher in the late 1960s, Agamben inserted himself into a philosophical lineage of *critique* of the Western cultural heritage – and hence also of its cultural practices of transmission and reception. His first book, *The Man Without Content*, is in this sense paradigmatic: the critique of the present predicament is construed as an investigation (later called 'genealogy' or 'archaeology') of its conceptual and ideological roots. Moreover, the critique of apparently circumscribed phenomena (here aesthetics) partakes in a much wider critique of Western 'metaphysics' as a whole, considered from its very inception. Finally, if the present is experienced as 'crisis', as the extreme and decisive limit of an 'alienating' course ('metaphysics'), the overcoming of the crisis is neither sought in a regressive return to more 'authentic' historical-cultural stages, nor in a complete rupture that would cast off all traits of the present, but rather in a full and conscious assumption of this present as one's 'own'.

For our purposes, it is not important that in *The Man Without Content* this methodology is still 'incomplete' (since the strongly Heideggerian approach still leads Agamben to postulate modernity as a radical rupture to be overcome in order to regain a more 'original' condition); what is important is rather the fact that the critique of metaphysical 'nihilism' ends up in a critique of tradition and of the possibility of transmissibility itself. This is a sort of general 'pattern' that Agamben's subsequent works will follow point-by-point. Beginning with *Stanzas*, however, the gap that separates tradition from its transmissibility will be extended from modernity to the 'original' structure of metaphysics itself. In *Stanzas*, the gap is that between knowledge itself and its object, which, in the fourth and last 'stanza' on semiology, is declined as the metaphysical (and thus 'originary') fracture between signifier and signified (S 135–58). Here Agamben's strategy vis-à-vis this crisis of tradition and transmissibility is identified with 'critique': the project of bridging this gap through a word and a knowledge which merge – and thus deactivate the separation between – philosophy and poetry, knowledge, possession and enjoyment, towards a 'liberated' approach – and 'use' – of knowledge and tradition.

The last essay of *Infancy and History*, 'Project for a Review', connects with the last chapter of *The Man Without Content* and with the project of *Stanzas* by calling for a '"destruction" of literary historiography' (*IH* 143). Confronted with the irreparable fracture between the cultural heritage and its transmission, the task of the never-published review (and of the 'coming philosophy') would be to perform a philological *Aufhebung* of mythology and transform it into a 'critical mythology', an 'interdisciplinary discipline' assimilated to 'critique', into which all human sciences would converge and whose goal would be a 'general science of the human' (*IH* 146–7). More generally, the thread holding together the essays collected in *Infancy and History* is precisely to confront the modern 'destruction of experience' – that is, of a fecund relation to tradition and cultural heritage – while trying to prepare a 'likely ground' in which the 'germinating seed of future experience' can mature (*IH* 15). The reflections about the loss of experience are an extension of those about the crisis of tradition, and the whole theory of 'infancy' connects with the previous – and subsequent – attempts to rethink language beyond the deadlock of Western metaphysics.

Language and Death does not depart from this pattern, since the whole analysis of the metaphysical link that binds language (that is, Western tradition) and 'negativity' (or death) aims at an overcoming of this 'original' structure – and thus of Western tradition as such – towards a liberated 'post-historical humanity' (*LD* 104). The final excursus is particularly important insofar as it sketches and contains *in nuce* the core problems of what, a decade later, will become Agamben's ambitious political project, and also anticipates its innovative and ground-breaking vocabulary: the problem with Western tradition is that its 'original', metaphysical 'negativity', its 'groundlessness' (*LD* xiii), entails a 'sacrificial' self-grounding, a foundation in sacrifice, and thus a paradigmatic *sacrum facere* that is intrinsically violent and leads to the 'inclusionary exclusion' of the *homo sacer* and to the sacrifice of 'bare life'. The task of the coming philosophy is thus to overcome the *sacer*, the negative and ineffable foundation, and to invent a praxis and a speech 'transparent to themselves' (*LD* 106). At this stage – and throughout the 1980s – Agamben's project focuses on a 'linguistic' critique and a 'linguistic' project of overcoming of Western tradition, and through various essays (some of which were later collected in the first part of *Potentialities*, but also in the literary-poetic studies of *The End of the Poem*) and philosophical 'experiments' on and with language (the most important and 'successful' being *Idea of Prose*) he will consistently carry on the critique begun with *The Man Without Content*.

The transition to the more overtly 'political' project that began in the 1990s is not so much a rupture as an extension and a widening of the scope of critique: a critique and an overcoming of metaphysics through language, which is never left behind, opens a space for, and almost 'naturally' leads to, a quest for a new concept of ethics and a new concept of politics. This transition is worked out through a series of short essays at the end of the 1980s, epitomised by 'Experimentum Linguae', which tellingly concludes:

> if the most appropriate expression of wonderment at the existence of the world is the existence of language, what then is the correct expression for the existence of language? The only possible answer to this question is: human life, as *ethos*, as ethical way. The search for a *polis* and an *oikia* befitting this void and unpresupposable community is the *infantile* task of future generations. (*IH* 9–10)

In its essence, Agamben's 'political' project is a critique of the whole Western tradition and of its deepest structures, whereby language, aesthetics, ethics, politics and ontology all merge in an all-encompassing 'deactivation' of tradition.

This is precisely the point of the archaeological (or genealogical) method which results from the 'graft' of the Foucauldian method on to Agamben's own practice: archaeology searches tradition for the 'moment of a phenomenon's arising' (*ST* 89) by confronting itself with the sources and by deactivating the paradigms through which tradition conditions and regulates access to them. Archaeology thus consists precisely in the deactivation of tradition and of its sedimented structures and apparatuses, a deactivation that simultaneously transforms the archaeologist himself: 'It is never the emergence of the fact without at the same time being the emergence of the knowing subject itself: the operation on the origin is at the same time an operation on the subject' (*ST* 89).

It is against this background that we have to read Agamben's interpretations, uses and 'bending' of his sources. His philosophical lineage is not merely a reservoir from which he draws, but it is rather a tradition turned against itself, a tradition that, being itself alienated and 'intransmissible', is further disavowed, betrayed, warped, 'deactivated' and put to a new 'use'.

STUDY

Reading as a cultural act – and especially as a philosophical practice – culminates in study. Study is a learned set of techniques and strategies implemented in order to acquire and master a given knowledge in a given discipline, and is a highly defined and regulated practice. But it is also an 'idea' and 'ideal', which has defined for centuries the aims and scope of Western culture, so much so that in the Middle Ages the term *studium* defined the university itself. Agamben almost epitomises the classical idea of the traditional 'scholar', the archetypical 'man of learning', extraordinarily erudite (even in comparison to his peers) and versed in many different disciplines. However, in his case, study does not remain at the descriptive, utilitarian level of a set of techniques and methodologies, but is problematised together with the relation to tradition and transmissibility and enters his specific philosophical vocabulary, becoming a pillar of his soteriological proposal.

The valence and importance of study in Agamben's philosophy is condensed in the extremely compressed and almost elliptical elaboration of one of the 'ideas' of *Idea of Prose*, 'The Idea of Study' (*IP* 63–5). Here Agamben connects to this 'idea' a whole set of notions ('messianism', 'potentiality', 'completion', 'inoperativity') which constitute the core of his soteriology and at the same time epitomise his own idea of philosophy and of philosophical work. The short text begins with a historical overview of the circumstances leading to the enthronement of study at the core of Judaism (*Talmud* in Hebrew means 'study'): first the Babylonian exile and then the second destruction of the Temple by the Romans forced Judaism to make the Talmud the 'real temple of Israel' and led to a transformation at the heart of Judaism itself, rendering it 'a religion which does not engage in worship but makes it an object of study'. Study therefore acquires a messianic connotation, insofar as at issue in it is redemption, and thus its goal is salvation itself.

This messianic connotation, however, entails a 'polarity', because study is, by definition, interminable: study is, as such, a labyrinthine pursuit, since every passage and fragment opens up new, divergent paths of investigation, which not only hinder a proper 'termination', but make it also undesirable. The person immersed in study is therefore lost in an interminable maze of stimuli, which renders the comparison with the labyrinth less accurate and makes us rather think of the Baudelarian–Benjaminian modern metropolis. And in fact Agamben refers then to the etymology of *studium* – from the root *st-* or *sp-*, indicating an impact or collision and the deriving shock – which it shares with 'stupefy' but also with 'stupid': lost, stupefied and stunned, the *studioso* remains unable to grasp and absorb the amazing amount of stimuli that are striking him, and is at the same time unwilling to take leave of them. On the other hand, the messianic nature of study incessantly drives it towards completion, towards *parousia*, and this polarity between interminability and completion constitutes the 'rhythm' of study: a succession of stupor and lucidity, discovery and bewilderment, passion and action.

This is the very condition, Agamben argues, which Aristotle named 'potential': on the one hand *potentia passiva*, passivity, pure and virtually infinite passion, and on the other *potentia activa*, relentless tension towards completion, incessant drive to 'actuality'. The scholar's long dwelling in potential explains a trait that has been attributed to them at least since Aristotle's *Problemata* (XXX, 953a) and that Agamben names *melancholia philologica*, borrowing the definition from the Italian classical philologist Giorgio Pasquali.[1] And there is no doubt that, if he surmises that Pasquali intended this definition for himself while feigning to attribute it to Theodor Mommsen, Agamben himself uses this whole 'idea' as a (thinly) disguised self-portrait as much as a personal *discours de la méthode*. All these traits that he attributes to study, however, are not so much a description of the great philologist or the 'saintly scholar', but rather of a figure pitted against traditional, 'sanctified' scholarship (and against tradition as a whole): the student, such as he appears in the writings of Kafka and Robert Walser, and whose extreme exemplar is to be found in Melville's scrivener Bartleby. Unlike the classical figure of the 'saintly scholar' lionised by tradition, these students are 'failures', and as such they undermine the whole construct of cultural transmission and legitimacy. In Bartleby, however, there occurs the messianic reversal, whereby the messianic polarity of study is surpassed, or better deactivated: Bartleby, who for Agamben represents 'pure potentiality' (*PO* 259), is a scrivener who has ceased to write, and thus his gesture represents a potential that does not precede but follows its act. This 'liberated' potential frees study of its melancholy and returns it to its truest nature, which is not the work, but rather inspiration, 'the self-nourishment of the soul'.

Bartleby and the students of Kafka and Walser represent a study released both from the *oikonomia* of the Western cultural tradition and from that of its Christian heritage, impassive before, and freed from, divine judgement and socio-cultural imperatives. This form of study goes far beyond a simple relation to texts, taking on a messianic charge that comes to epitomise a fundamental operation in Agamben's soteriology: deactivation. In opposition to action and performance, study brings about a standstill in the workings of cultural apparatuses; it 'jams' the cultural machine, as it were, and opens it up to a new 'use'. As such, it also becomes an important component of the *pars construens* of Agamben's project, and is usually linked to interpretations of Kafka.[2]

This idea derives in fact from Benjamin, who, in his 1934 essay on Kafka (and in his correspondence with Scholem), emphasised the messianic charge of study, and in his short reading of Kafka's 'The New Advocate' compared Bucephalus's renunciation of the practice of the law in order to immerse himself in its study to an opening up of a way towards justice. Agamben famously took up this interpretation in *State of Exception* in order to identify the task of the coming philosophy: not a destruction (of law, of tradition, of the cultural heritage) followed by a proactive new foundation, but rather its *deactivation*. 'What opens a passage toward justice', he writes, 'is not the erasure of law, but its deactivation and inactivity [*inoperosità*] – that is, another use of the law' (*SE* 64). The same point is made in 'K.', where Agamben briefly rehearses his famous interpretation of Kafka's 'Before the Law' in *Homo Sacer* (*HS* 49–57), adding, however, an unexpected twist: here what is at stake is not the study of the law, but rather 'the long study of its doorkeeper' in which the man from the country was immersed throughout his long sojourn before the law. 'It is thanks to this study, to this new Talmud', Agamben writes, 'that the man from the country – in opposition to Josef K. – was able to live to the very end outside the trial' (*NU* 31). And it is from the 'trial' of tradition that this new Talmud releases the scholar of the coming philosophy.

CITATION

This new Talmud jams the workings of the cultural machine in a number of ways, and one of its peculiar strategic tools is a disruptive theory of citation. Agamben has often struck his (mostly Anglo-American) readers as not always complying to the strict rules of academic citation, not always citing his sources explicitly or properly, declining at times to name them altogether, and leaving it to the reader to figure them out for themselves. However, in Agamben this is not the snobbish sloppiness of the esoteric 'saintly scholar' who clouds in obscurity a wisdom reserved to the 'initiated' (a still quite common practice in Italian academia), but rather a specific strategy of disruption of this very authoritative tradition.

The last chapter of *The Man Without Content* opens with a theory of citation that refers back to Benjamin's own idiosyncratic citation style – *without citing it properly*. Agamben starts the chapter with a quotation from Benjamin's *One-Way Street*: 'Quotations in my work are like wayside robbers who leap out, armed, and relieve the idle stroller of his conviction' (*MC* 104). Benjamin's theory, Agamben glosses, did not subscribe to the traditional aims of citation ('to transmit [the] past and allow the reader to relive it'), but was rather based on the idea of *Entfremdung*, whereby alienating a fragment of the past from its historical context 'makes it lose its character of authentic testimony and invests it with an alienating power that constitutes its unmistakable aggressive force'. The true 'authority' of a quotation rests precisely on the 'destruction of the authority that is attributed to a certain text by its situation in the history of culture', and its 'true content' emerges precisely from this violent alienation (*MC* 104).

Subscribing to Benjamin's theory, Agamben aims at disrupting what in *Stanzas* he calls the 'vicious circle of authority and citation (the authority is the source of the citation but the citation is the source of authority)', which has transformed cultural transmission (and contemporary academia) into an '"authoritarian" counterfeit' (*S* 74). Throughout his career he has waged a war against 'academic prose' because it shelters itself behind a normative blandness, thereby distancing itself from an authentic experience of language, and in the 1980s he attempted a series of experiments with language that renounced the whole apparatus of traditional philosophical prose and that are exemplified by the complete absence of references in *Idea of Prose*. In an interview that he gave for the publication of this book he said:

> Precisely because poetry, just like philosophy, is essentially an experience of language, nay an experience of language 'as such', of what is at issue for man in the very fact of speaking, the place in which the speaking subject positions itself must be extremely clear. Footnotes, quotation marks, bibliographical references, 'cf.', they all refer to a subject of knowledge sheltered like a ventriloquist behind the speaking subject, as if it were possible to speak from two places at the same time. This is why current academic prose is so often unfortunate, torn as it is between an authentic experience of speech, which cannot have anything to say before measuring itself against speech, and its defensive castling into a position of knowledge.[3]

Adopting the 'art of citing without quotation marks', Agamben thus challenges the automatic support of a tradition turned into a 'fortress of knowledge' and vindicates an anti-authoritarian experience of language which measures its truth value only against its own merits.

At the end of *The Time that Remains* Agamben again explicitly refers to Benjamin's theory of citation in order to argue that, in the theses 'On the Concept of History', Benjamin quoted Paul's messianism 'without quotation marks', and that it is Paul whom one has to see in the figure of the hidden, 'theological' dwarf of the first thesis (*TR* 139–40). Here, however, he makes another important point about a theory of 'reading' as such, and thus also about his own reading practice. In his unveiling of the 'textual [. . .] and not mere conceptual correspondence' (*TR*

144) between Benjamin's theses and Paul's letters, he draws attention to the identical structure of Benjamin's 'dialectical image' and Paul's concept of *typos*: both signify a temporal structure 'wherein an instant of the past and an instant of the present are united in a constellation where the present is able to recognize the meaning of the past and the past therein finds its meaning and fulfilment' – and the messianic *kairos* is precisely this 'typological relation' (*TR* 142). However, this relation depends on a 'historical index', whereby the image and the *typos* become 'legible' and 'knowable' only at a certain time, which Benjamin called 'the now of legibility (or knowability)': every text 'contains a historical index which indicates both its belonging to a determinate epoch, as well as its only coming forth to full legibility at a determinate historical moment' (*TR* 145). This thesis constitutes a true 'theory of reading' that Benjamin proposed and refined throughout his life, and by concluding *The Time that Remains* on this note, Agamben also reveals something about his own 'theory of reading': his reading (and citing) practice obeys a logic of 'legibility' (and 'citability') which, by wrenching its source from its historical context, 'actualises' it – as Benjamin would say – by transforming it into something of his own.

ENTWICKLUNGSFÄHIGKEIT

What Benjamin called 'actualisation' is inflected by Agamben through a peculiar term that he derives from Ludwig Feuerbach: *Entwicklungsfähigkeit*, 'capacity for elaboration'. In the preface to his *Darstellung, Entwicklung und Kritik der Leibnitz'schen Philosophie* (*Presentation, Development and Critique of Leibniz's Philosophy*, 1837), Feuerbach called the 'essential' task of philosophy that of 'immanent elaboration', which makes of the 'capacity for elaboration [*Entwicklungsfähigkeit*] the very mark of what philosophy is'. The elaboration is, for Feuerbach, the 'decipherment of the true *meaning* of a philosophy, the unveiling of what is *positive* in it, the *presentation* of its *idea* within the historically determined and finite conditions which have defined this idea'; therefore '[t]he possibility of elaboration is the idea itself'.[4] This is why, for example, unlike Leibniz's, Locke's philosophy does not possess this capacity for elaboration, because in it everything is already stated and self-contained.

Agamben cites Feuerbach's thesis in various interviews and in the preface to *The Signature of All Things* precisely to define his relation to the authors who have marked his life and career. The point of this relation lies in something the source has left 'unsaid': this is 'the germ, what has been left unsaid and can thus be developed, resumed. I have always followed this line.'[5] This 'germ' is the 'potentiality' of a work that, while present, remains unstated and undeveloped, and thus is left for others to unveil and elaborate in different ways. It is also, as for Feuerbach, what marks and distinguishes the true 'idea' of a work (*ST* 7–8).

This, however, leads to a relation and interaction between the philosopher and his sources that borders on a commingling: as Agamben again states in the preface to *The Signature of All Things*, '[i]t is precisely when one follows such a principle that the difference between what belongs to the author of a work and what is attributable to the interpreter becomes as essential as it is difficult to grasp' (*ST* 8). The philosophical 'idea', which lies *in potentia* in a work, can be taken in directions unforeseen – and perhaps undesired – by the author, and thus transformed into something no longer attributable to them. This point marks many of the controversial 'corrections' of other philosophers' ideas that Agamben has proposed in his career (most [in]famously of Foucault, but also of Benjamin, Heidegger and others). But, to return to Feuerbach, this is precisely the true task of philosophy: 'Elaboration is difficult, whereas critique is easy. [. . .] True critique lies in elaboration itself, because the latter is possible only through the separation of the essential from the accidental, of the necessary from the contingent, of the objective from the subjective.'[6]

Finally, Agamben also applies this practice to his own works and ideas: archaeology, he writes, 'must retrace its own trajectory back to the point where something remains obscure and unthematized. Only a thought that does not conceal its own unsaid – but constantly takes it up and elaborates it – may eventually lay claim to originality' (*ST* 8). Each completed work – including the author's own – contains within itself something left 'unsaid' which demands to be further elaborated and taken up, perhaps by someone else. It is therefore telling that Agamben warns the readers of the final volume of the *Homo Sacer* series that they will not find a 'conclusion' in this book: his twenty-year-long investigation, 'like every work of poetry and of thought, cannot be concluded but only abandoned (and perhaps continued by others)' (*UB* xiii). This is a quotation from the Swiss artist Alberto Giacometti that Agamben had been repeating in interviews, conferences and seminars during the years leading up to the publication of *The Use of Bodies*.[7] The 'potentiality' of a work is not exhausted by the last brushstroke or the last word – in fact, it can never be exhausted, and its true philosophical 'idea' lies precisely in its inexhaustible potential which traverses epochs and generations. If, as Agamben states, 'philosophy does not have a content purely of its own',[8] then this Feuerbachian 'idea' is perhaps the true 'idea of philosophy'.

THE STRUCTURE OF THIS VOLUME

Each chapter of the present volume provides an overview of the most important passages in which Agamben addresses the source in question, then discusses any ways in which Agamben's reading is unique or distinctive. The work is divided into three broad sections: the first, 'Primary Interlocutors', features more lengthy essays on Agamben's most important sources; the second, 'Points of Reference', includes figures who are discussed in a more occasional or secondary way; the third, 'Submerged Dialogues', focuses on figures who seem to be lurking in the background of Agamben's arguments even though he mentions them only fleetingly, if at all.

Yet a final remark is in order, namely about the rationale that led us to include and, more importantly, exclude some of Agamben's sources. While we hope that few readers of Agamben would dispute the figures included in the first section, the second (or even the third) section of this volume could have included any number of other figures: for example, Augustine, Averroës, Maurice Blanchot, Odo Casel, Hobbes, Furio Jesi, Max Kommerell, Lévi-Strauss, Emmanuel Levinas, Nicole Loraux, Erik Peterson, Rilke, Jacob Taubes, Yan Thomas, Wittgenstein, to name only a few possibilities. We would have liked to include many more figures, but felt that we had to balance inclusiveness with the need to prevent the volume from becoming unwieldy.

There is no one answer as to why any given figure was left aside in favour of another. In some cases, the decision came down to the contingencies of the editors' academic networks: there were times when we simply could not find someone who was both able to address a certain figure and able to produce the chapter within a reasonable amount of time. Yet that consideration only came up for figures we viewed as less essential – if we could not have found a suitable author to cover Aristotle or Schmitt, for example, we simply would not have pursued this project at all – and several factors contributed to that determination. For instance, while recognising that this distinction is often blurred, we did not generally commission chapters about figures whom Agamben treats primarily as scholars rather than as philosophical interlocutors. In some cases, this standard seemed easy to apply (Casel, Thomas), while in others it was more difficult to decide (Loraux, Peterson). We also tended to cut figures whose influence was limited to only one or two of Agamben's works (e.g., Kommerel, Levinas or

Taubes) or who seemed to be important only for one particular concept or motif (e.g., Wittgenstein and 'form-of-life'). In some cases, we left a figure aside if their influence was somehow subsumed by another – for instance, Hobbes's place in Agamben's work is heavily determined by Schmitt, and Rilke is primarily a foil for Hölderlin. And finally, we did not generally pursue figures who have had a profound personal impact on Agamben but seldom if ever appear directly in his texts (e.g., Pasolini or Elsa Morante).

We understand that this explanation will not satisfy every reader who believes a crucial interlocutor has been omitted. But we believe that everyone who has read Agamben with understanding will recognise that any true work of commentary on Agamben can never be completed, but only abandoned – and perhaps taken up by others.

NOTES

1. Giorgio Pasquali, 'Il testamento di Teodoro Mommsen' (1951), in *Pagine stravaganti di un filologo*, vol. II, ed. Carlo Ferdinando Russo (Florence: Le Lettere, 1994), pp. 383–96.
2. And in fact 'The Idea of Study' was reprinted, one year after the publication of *Idea of Prose*, as the fourth of the 'Quattro glosse a Kafka' ['Four Glosses on Kafka'], under the title 'The Students'; cf. Giorgio Agamben, 'Quattro glosse a Kafka', *Rivista di estetica* 26 (1986): 37–44, here pp. 42–4.
3. Adriano Sofri, 'Un'idea di Giorgio Agamben', an interview with Giorgio Agamben, *Reporter*, 9–10 November 1985, p. 32.
4. Ludwig Feuerbach, *Darstellung, Entwicklung und Kritik der Leibnitz'schen Philosophie*, in *Gesammelte Werke*, vol. 3: *Geschichte der neuern Philosophie*, part 2, ed. Werner Schuffenhauer (Berlin: Akademische Verlag, 1969), pp. 3, 4 (emphases in the original).
5. Roberto Andreotti and Federico de Melis, 'I ricordi per favore no', an interview with Giorgio Agamben, *Atlas* 420 (9 September 2006): 2.
6. Feuerbach, *Darstellung, Entwicklung und Kritik der Leibnitz'schen Philosophie*, p. 4.
7. See, for example, the interview by Juliette Cerf of 10 March 2012, 'Le philosophe Giorgio Agamben: "La pensée, c'est le courage du désespoir"', http://www.telerama.fr/idees/le-philosophe-giorgio-agamben-la-pensee-c-est-le-courage-du-desespoir,78653.php (accessed 24 April 2017). Giacometti repeated this statement on several occasions, for example in the film interview with Jean-Marie Drot, *Un homme parmi les hommes: Alberto Giacometti* (1963).
8. Gianluca Sacco, 'Intervista a Giorgio Agamben: dalla teologia politica alla teologia economica', 8 March 2004, qtd. in Leland de la Durantaye, *Giorgio Agamben: A Critical Introduction* (Stanford: Stanford University Press, 2009), p. 9.

PART I
Primary Interlocutors

1 *Aristotle*

JUSSI BACKMAN

Homo Sacer, Giorgio Agamben's transformative twenty-year project in political ontology, is framed at its very outset in terms of Aristotelian philosophy – read, as we will see, from a strongly medieval, Heideggerian and Arendtian perspective. As a *locus classicus* of the juxtaposition of the two Greek terms for life, *zōē* ('the simple fact of living common to all living beings') and *bios* ('the form or way of living proper to an individual or a group'), Agamben (*HS* 1–2) cites a passage in Aristotle's *Politics* that notes that there is a certain 'natural delight (*euēmeria*) and sweetness' in the 'mere fact of being alive itself' (*to zēn auto monon*), which makes human beings hold on to it for its own sake, provided that the mode of life (*bios*) that this being-alive amounts to is not fraught with excessive difficulty.[1]

The complicated interlacing of *zōē* and *bios* defines the fundamental parameters of Agamben's magnum opus. We will use them here as the starting point for a brief discussion of Agamben's engagement, throughout the *Homo Sacer* series, with the Aristotelian foundations of Western political thought and its basic strategy of 'dividing the factical experience and pushing down to the origin – that is, excluding – one half of it in order then to rearticulate it to the other by including it as foundation' (*UB* 265). This strategy is particularly visible in the two Aristotelian conceptual divisions whose political consequences *Homo Sacer* never ceases to address: that between 'bare' and politically qualified life, and that between potential and act, *dynamis* and *energeia*. We will see that Agamben's concept of 'form-of-life' (*forma-di-vita*), introduced in *Homo Sacer* (*HS* 188), is designed to deconstruct or 'deactivate' both of these interlocking oppositions.

BEING-ALIVE SAID IN MANY WAYS: *zēn/eu zēn*

We should, however, begin our discussion with a caveat. Contrary to what Agamben seems to suggest (*HS* 11), *zōē* and *bios* are in no way contrasted in the passage cited above. Characterising their relationship as an 'opposition' (*HS* 66), as a 'fundamental categorial pair of Western politics' (*HS* 8), or as a 'classical distinction' (*HS* 187) gives rise to certain interpretative and philological objections, such as those put forward by J. G. Finlayson.[2] Finlayson shows that Agamben starts out from Hannah Arendt's somewhat simplifying account of the 'specifically human life' as the narrated and biographical '*bios* as distinguished from mere *zōē*'.[3] Such a distinction does occasionally appear in late antiquity, but in Aristotle and in other classical texts, *zōē* and *bios* are not opposed in this way.[4] They simply differ in sense: whereas *zōē* is the simple fact and process of being alive, *bios* is the 'mode of life' enacted by a living being in and through this process. What is essential to *bios* is temporal extension: while *zōē* is what is going on at every given instant of being alive, *bios* is the characteristic life-project that this being alive amounts to over an extended period of time, or the entire biographical 'span of life' reaching all the way from birth to death and fully visible only in retrospect.[5] The reason for the fact, noted by Agamben (*HS* 2), that the verb *bioō* is in classical texts almost never found in the present tense is that it does not have a primarily presential sense of an ongoing process, but rather the perfective sense of 'having passed or constituted one's life in a certain manner (over a span of time)'.[6] This sense of completeness and limitation inherent in *bios* also explains why Aristotle does not ascribe a *bios* to the 'continuous and everlasting being-alive' (*zōē synechēs kai aidios*) of the metaphysical divinity.[7]

It follows that *bios* is neither an alternative to *zōē* nor something over and above it. By virtue of the fact of being alive, one cannot fail, over time, to realise some kind of *bios*.[8] A political mode of life, *bios politikos*, is one such possible life-project, as is the life of contemplation (*bios theōrētikos*), but even the life of enjoyment (*bios apolaustikos*), which Aristotle disdainfully regards as a mode of life 'fit for cattle', constitutes a *bios*.[9] Even though the *bioi* that primarily interest the philosophers are those of free human beings, they by no means limit *bios* to humans: animals and even plants implement their particular *bioi*.[10] Moreover, as Agamben is well aware (*UB* 200–6), even though Aristotle may be the first to use *zōē* as an abstract term for that which separates animate from inanimate things, in *De anima* he explicitly denies that there is such a thing as generic being alive that would be shared in a univocal sense by plants, animals and human beings.[11] Being alive (*zēn*) is 'said in many ways (*pleonachōs*)' and the soul (*psychē*), the animating principle of vital functions, is analogous to a polygon in that, just as there is no abstract polygon apart from determinate types such as triangles and squares, no generic soul exists apart from the three basic types: the vegetative (*threptikon*) vitality of plants, consisting merely in the intake of nutrition and organic growth; the sensory and mobile vitality of non-human animals; and the discursive-rational vitality of humans.[12]

To be sure, vegetative life is the most elementary form of *zēn* in that it is capable of separate existence in plants and is 'contained' in the more complex levels, since animals and humans are also capable of nourishment and growth, but only as potentially (*dynamei*), not actually, separable.[13] No separate layer of 'bare life' can be extracted intact from the human soul. For beings endowed with a human soul, life is always already irreducibly human: in it, the 'inferior' vital functions have always already been qualitatively transformed in their seamless fusion with the discursive being alive of humans. Nonetheless, differentiating vitality into its different component faculties is possible conceptually (*logō*), and Agamben will insist (*UB* 202–6) that precisely this conceptual, potential divisibility is the basis for the political 'exclusive inclusion' of that which is in reality inseparable, of 'bare' life.[14] This political exclusion begins with Aristotle's own exclusion of vegetative life from human virtue (*aretē*), discursive reason (*logos*) and flourishing (*eudaimonia*), and culminates in the modern techniques for actually sustaining 'bare' vital functions through resuscitation or for producing 'bare life' in the figure of the *Muselmann* of the Nazi concentration camps (*RA* 41–86; *UB* 204).[15]

In the case of Aristotle, the *zōē/bios* distinction thus boils down to that between two kinds of *zōē*, between mere survival and 'living well' (*eu zēn*). It is initially for the sake of the former, Aristotle maintains, that human beings form more and more complex communities and finally come to live in a politically structured community. However, even when material survival has been secured by the economic, military and judicial framework of the *polis*, the political community persists as a teleological project, since it further allows humans to pursue a life of fulfilment and flourishing as human beings.[16] The *polis* 'comes to be [*ginomenē*] for the sake of living [*zēn*] but is [*ousa*] for the sake of living well [*eu zēn*]'.[17] The latter cannot consist in any sense of being alive that is not unique to free human beings: there can be no *polis* of slaves or non-human animals, whose life is subject to the external compulsion of commands and instincts and deprived of the rational self-determination and self-sufficiency (*autarkeia*) that constitutes 'accomplished' being alive (*zōē teleia*).[18] Such complete *zōē* is one that constitutes a temporally extended span of life (*bios teleios*) consisting in the accomplishment of the 'work' or function (*ergon*) proper to the human being: the activity or 'being-at-work' (*energeia*) of the human soul (*psychē*) in terms of the supreme virtues or excellences (*aretai*) of its properly human – that is, discursive (*meta logou*) – aspects.[19] Aristotle stresses the importance of the actual use or employment (*chrēsis*) of virtue, as opposed to merely having virtue as a potential (*dynamis*), as a habit/disposition (*hexis*) or possession (*ktēsis*).[20] On the other hand, as 'habits', virtues – unlike natural or innate capacities, in which the potential precedes the activity – are only acquired through a prior exercise (*energein*) in the form of instruction (*didaskalia*) or habituation (*ethos*).[21]

THE INCAPACITY OF CAPACITY: *dynamis/energeia*

From these considerations, we see to what extent the Aristotelian hierarchy of life is pervaded by the dialectic of potential and act. In *Homo Sacer*, Agamben notes that reconsidering the problem of constituent and constituted power and their subjugation to the concept of sovereign power

> opens the way for a new articulation of the relation between potential [*potenza*] and act [*atto*]. [...] Until a new and coherent ontology of potential [...] has replaced the ontology founded on the primacy of act and its relation to potential, a political theory freed from the aporias of sovereignty remains unthinkable. (*HS* 44; translation modified)

This task of a new ontology of potentiality, emancipated from the primacy of act, frames Agamben's discussion of *dynamis* and *energeia*; among his precursors in this project he mentions Spinoza, Schelling, Nietzsche and Heidegger (*HS* 44, 48). Indeed, his reading of the Aristotelian *dynamis* is decisively influenced by Heidegger's 1931 lecture course on Aristotle's *Metaphysics*, Book Theta (see *PO* 201).[22] The reappropriation of *dynamis* in Heideggerian fundamental ontology, for which 'higher than actuality [*Wirklichkeit*] stands *possibility* [*Möglichkeit*]', is clearly an orienting template for Agamben's attempt to think power and life beyond the classical Aristotelian hierarchies.[23]

Aristotle's distinction between potential and act is motivated by his quest to conceptually grasp movement, change and transition, *kinēsis* and *metabolē*. *Kinēsis* is the principal context for understanding potential and act, and the primary sense of *dynamis* is to be a principle (*archē*) of transition in another entity, or in the same entity *qua* other: the doctor is capable of treating herself, but only to the extent that she is also a patient.[24] Every transition thus involves two capacities, the capacity to produce (*poiein*) a process and the capacity to undergo (*paschein*) it. This distinction is the key to Aristotle's statement – a focal point of Agamben's attention (CC 34; HS 45–6; PO 181–3, 201, 215, 245; OD 94–5; UB 59, 276) – that since 'to the extent that something is constituted as one [*sympephyken*], it does not itself undergo [*paschei*; any transition produced] by itself', every capacity (*dynamis*) is, by consequence, also 'an incapacity [*adynamia*] of the same [activity] and in the same respect'.[25] This seemingly paradoxical statement is clarified by Aristotle's remark, in *De anima*, that the faculty of sensory perception is incapable of perceiving itself without access to a separate sensory object, just as the combustible is incapable of igniting itself without access to heat: the capacity to produce or to undergo a process is incapable of carrying out the process by itself.[26] The two corresponding *dynameis* must come into contact before *energeia* is initiated. However, as opposed to purely mechanical capacities, this contact alone is not sufficient in the case of the discursive capacities of rational beings, oriented to conceptually determinate ends – a desire (*orexis*) or preference (*proairesis*) to act for the end, rather than not, is also required.[27]

'Capable [*dynaton*] is that which, whenever the activity [*energeia*] to which it is said to have the capacity [*dynamin*] becomes present [*hyparxē*] in it, will not be incapable [*adynaton*] in any respect.'[28] Heidegger and Agamben (HS 45–6; PO 183, 264) both emphasise that in spite of its seeming triviality – what is capable of something is not incapable of it – this articulation is highly significant when we understand it in light of the incapacity inherent in *dynamis*.[29] Until the conditions for the commencement of the activity are met, a potential always retains an impotential that is only surrendered in the process of actualisation – either once and for all, as in an action (*praxis*) such as contemplating that is at once its own end and complete (*entelecheia*), or gradually, as in an 'incomplete' *energeia* or *kinēsis*, a process such as construction that is a production (*poiēsis*) of an end external to the process itself.[30] Capacity-for-*x* is the point of departure for the process in which its inherent incapacity-for-*x* is expelled by the coming-to-be of *x* itself.

Agamben stresses (CC 35; HS 46; PO 184; UB 267) that this is well captured in a passage of *De anima* that notes that undergoing a process through which an inherent potential is actualised is not really an alteration (*alloiōsis*) so much as a 'preservation' (*sōtēria*) of what is potentially (*dynamei*) by what is completely (*entelecheia*). Rather than an alteration, this is an 'increase [*epidosis*] to itself [*eis hauto*] and to completeness [*entelecheian*]'.[31] However, contrary to what Agamben suggests, what is 'preserved' in the transition from potentiality to actuality is clearly not potentiality as such – Aristotle makes it clear that the move is 'from a potential being [*ek dynamei ontos*] to completeness'[32] – but rather the being that is potentially, such as the house under construction, whose identity or 'selfhood' as a house is preserved and intensified in the transition.[33] Being in act (*energeia on*) is determined by the extent to which it has cast off the incapacity and the negative capacity inherent in potential being.[34] Actual being is prior to potential being in terms of the substantial beingness (*ousia*) of the entity in question: a finished house is more of a house than one still being built or one that is merely being planned, in the sense of 'less incapable of being a house'.[35] In Aristotle's ontological hierarchy, the most accomplished manifestation of being is necessary and everlasting actuality, which has shed all potentiality and, with it, all incompleteness, transience and contingency, all impotential and potential-not-to-be.[36]

Even though Agamben claims that 'it is never clear [...] whether Book Theta of the *Metaphysics* in fact gives primacy to act or to potential' (*HS* 47; translation modified), the ontological primacy of *energeia* in Aristotle thus seems beyond dispute, even though it can only be determined in opposition to *dynamis* as the 'other' way of being, as the 'not incapable'.[37] Agamben is thinking in the direction of the later Aristotelian tradition, of the scholastic distinction between God's absolute power (*potentia absoluta*) and his ordained power (*potentia ordinata*), which provides the theological background for Abbé Sieyès's distinction between constituent and constituted power (*PO* 253–5; *KG* 104–8; *UB* 266–7).[38] Whereas God's omnipotence was conceived by the scholastics as the absolutely sovereign source of all normativity, and the created order of nature as ultimately contingent in the sense that it is based on the divine will alone and dictated by no other necessity, the fact that God has willed the existing order commits and ordains divine power not to conflict with the initial decision of the creator. God's absolute or constituent potential thus becomes the ontological source of all inherently contingent, created actuality – and, at the same time, a merely retrospective legitimation of the existing order, subordinated to what actually exists in the sense that it has suspended its capacity for negating the actual and manifests it only in 'states of exception'. In this context, potential and act are indeed 'only two aspects of the process of the sovereign autoconstitution of being [*essere*]' in which act presupposes itself as a potential that is merely a suspended act, and, on the other hand, act is only a 'preservation' of what already potentially was (*UB* 267; translation modified).

It is this medieval model of divine power that underlies the theological paradigm of divine 'economy' or 'administration' of the world, studied in *The Kingdom and the Glory* (KG 53–108), as well as the theological transformation of the *ergon* of human *energeia* into divinely operated liturgical 'offices' or 'duties' studied in *Opus Dei* (OD 42–64, 89–129), both of which Agamben shows to profoundly inform the modern concept of government.[39] It is within this framework that we should understand the task of an 'ontology of potentiality' that the *Homo Sacer* project assigns to itself, that of thinking a potential without any relation to being in act (HS 47), a purely 'destituent' (*destituente*) potential set free from the logic of sovereignty and constitution (UB 268). Agamben's abiding fascination with Melville's 'Bartleby, the Scrivener' (1853) should be situated in this context. Bartleby is the clerk who refuses to actualise his *ergon*, his function, office, or duty, simply because he 'prefers not to', thus withholding the *proairesis* or preference determined by Aristotle to be prerequisite for the actualisation of a rational capacity, which is always also a 'capacity not to'. In stubbornly vindicating this negative aspect of his *dynamis*, in refusing to ordain his constituent power into any constituted power and thereby rendering it de-constituent or destituent, Bartleby is 'the strongest objection against the principle of sovereignty' (HS 48; cf. CC 34–6; PO 243–71).[40]

USE, HABIT AND FORM-OF-LIFE: *chrēsis* AND *hexis*

We find Agamben's hitherto most sustained attempt to articulate an ontology of destituent potential in the concluding volume of the *Homo Sacer* series, *The Use of Bodies*. Here, Agamben's strategy is to deconstruct both the *zōē/bios* (or, rather, *zēn/eu zēn*) and the *dynamis/energeia* distinctions, and to flesh out his concept of 'form-of-life' with the help of the concept of use (*uso*). Already in *The Highest Poverty*, Agamben had suggested that, had it been properly articulated, the Franciscan notion of non-appropriative use 'could have been configured as a *tertium* with respect to law and life, potential and act' (HP 141). This suggestion is reiterated more forcefully in *The Use of Bodies*:

> [W]hat if use [. . .] implied, with respect to potential, a relationship other than *energeia*? [. . .] What if use in fact implied an ontology irreducible to the Aristotelian duality of potential and act that, through its historical translations, still governs Western culture? (UB 48, original italics)

The Use of Bodies sets out from the Aristotelian concept of use or employment (*chrēsis*), which, Agamben notes, Aristotle tends to use as a synonym of act, *energeia*: to use a capacity is to put a potential to work, to make it serve its function or purpose (*ergon*; UB 5–7). Thus, in the case of capacities whose employment constitutes an activity (*praxis*) that is its own end, such as seeing, the employment itself is the ultimate *ergon*, but in the case of production (*poiēsis*), the employment of one's capacity is an instrumental process towards the *ergon* (*UB* 12–13).[41] From this perspective, Agamben shows (*UB* 3–23), Aristotle's account of the work (*ergon*) of the slave as the 'use of the body' (*hē tou sōmatos chrēsis*) is an interesting anomaly.[42] While Aristotle regards hypothetical 'natural' slaves as human beings, they are clearly a limiting case or, as Agamben would have it, a 'threshold': they belong to the community (*koinōnein*) of human *logos* insofar as they are able to 'perceive' or 'grasp' discursive reason (they understand commands and their rationale), but just as they do not belong to themselves but to another, they do not possess (*echein*) reason as an independent faculty at their disposal, lacking rational deliberation and initiative.[43] Thus, the 'work' of slaves *qua* slaves cannot be that of human beings in general – the free activity of the discursive faculties of the soul – but consists simply in making use of their bodies as animate instruments and in being used to uphold the autarchy of their master's 'way of life' (*bios*) by liberating it from the necessities of survival.[44] As an instrument of the master's *bios*, the activity of the slave is thus, Agamben notes (*UB* 18–21), a very peculiar 'work' or 'function', in that it is neither *praxis* nor *poiēsis*, neither an end in itself nor a process towards an end. It is a sheer routine of toil and labour, devoid of intrinsic purposiveness. The work (*ergon*) through which slaves constitute themselves as slaves thus lies beyond the teleological matrix of the *dynamis/energeia* distinction; it represents a 'paradigm of another human activity [. . .] for which we lack names' (*UB* 78).

Through studies of the polysemy of the Greek verb *chrēsthai* and the Latin *uti* as well as their medial and passive voices, of the affinity between 'use' and 'care', of the Heideggerian understanding of the use of the world, and of the Stoic concept of 'use of oneself', Agamben delineates a Foucauldian understanding of use as a 'constitution of the self' in relation to what is other than the self: '*The self is nothing other than use-of-oneself* [*uso di sé*]' (*UB* 54, original italics). This brings him back to the Aristotelian concept of habit (*hexis*), the capacity acquired through usage and exercise, custom and habituation, in a word, through self-constitution. What is at stake is to rescue this concept from the Aristotelian template of potential and act: to think being-in-use (*essere-in-uso*) as distinct from being-in-act, as 'habitual use' (*uso abituale*) that is always already in use, habitually, and does not presuppose a potential that must at a certain point pass into the act. Habitual use is 'a potential that is never separate from act, which never needs to be put to work' (*UB* 58).

The negative aspect of the conceptual task proposed to us by Agamben is that of ceasing to think habit as a potential put into use and exercised through a sovereign act of the will or decision – that is, ceasing to think habit (literally, 'having', *hexis*) as something 'had' by a subject, which, as Aristotle himself notes, would amount to an infinite regression of the having of having (*UB* 58–65, 276–7).[45] The positive aspect of the task is to think habit *as* use, as usage or custom (*ethos*), that is, as a manner of constituting oneself as a subject by habitually making use of oneself and the world in a certain way: as a form-of-life. '*Use, as habit, is a form-of-life and not the knowledge or faculty of a subject*' (*UB* 62, original italics). Only by thus 'deactivating' the traditional split of habitual use into potential (habit) and act (use) will we be able to come to terms with the aporetic nature of Aristotle's account of *hexis* as, on the one hand, a disposition (*diathesis*) for acting in a certain way that is, in itself, only constituted through previous activity and exercise (*OD* 92–9).[46]

This Foucault-inspired ontology of habit, of identities constituted through usage and practice and constantly retaining the 'destituent' capacity to undo themselves, captures the sense of the Apostle Paul's experience of a messianic time in which ordained powers, norms and identities have been 'rendered inoperative' (*katargein*) by the advent of the messiah and in which what remains is to make use (*chrēsai*) of them for radically new purposes (*UB* 56–7, 273–4).[47] This ontology extends itself towards the Heidegger-inspired 'modal' ontology, delineated in the second part of *The Use of Bodies*, that no longer sees identities in terms of Aristotelian stable and determinate substances (*ousiai*) but as 'hypostases', as ceaseless (re)configurations of a dynamic and self-constituent process (*UB* 111–91). We are thus offered an 'inoperative' (*argon*) model of human life without any single preordained function or work – a possibility considered and immediately abandoned by Aristotle in the *Nicomachean Ethics* (*UB* 5) – a life that 'lives only in use-of-itself, lives only (its) livability' (*UB* 63).[48] Agamben's name for the self-constituting, self-destituting and self-reconfiguring process of inoperative living is form-of-life, that is,

> a life [. . .] in which singular modes, acts, and processes of living are never simply *facts* but always and above all *possibilities* of life, always and above all potential. And potential, insofar as it is nothing other than the essence or nature of each being, can be suspended and contemplated but never absolutely divided from the act. The habit of a potential is the habitual use of it and the form-of-life of this use. The form of human living is never prescribed by a specific biological vocation nor assigned by any necessity whatsoever, but even though it is customary, repeated, and socially obligatory, it always preserves its character as a real possibility. (*UB* 207–8)

We see that the *Homo Sacer* project has thus rewound to its point of departure, *zōē* and *bios*. In asserting their inseparability as form-of-life, a life that is never 'bare' or pre-political but always constitutes and reconstitutes itself into some form or mode of life or other and is thus always already qualified and political, the conclusion of the project also, in a sense, retrieves the 'originary' concept of *bios*, which, as we have seen, is by no means an opposite of *zōē* or separable from it, but rather simply the form invariably assumed over time by the process of being alive.

NOTES

1. Aristotle, *Politics* (*Politica*), ed. W. D. Ross (Oxford: Clarendon Press, 1957), 3.6.1278b23–30.
2. James Gordon Finlayson, '"Bare Life" and Politics in Agamben's Reading of Aristotle', *The Review of Politics* 72.1 (2010): 97–126.
3. Finlayson, '"Bare Life" and Politics', p. 102; Hannah Arendt, *The Human Condition* (Chicago: University of Chicago Press, 2nd edn, 1998), p. 97.
4. In a fragment from a third-century treatise, Porphyry of Tyre notes that the Stoics understand *bios* exclusively as discursive-rational life (*logikē zōē*), while Plato uses the term also for the life of non-discursive animals; Porphyry, *On What Is in Our Power*, cited in Joannes Stobaeus, *Anthologium*, vol. 2, ed. Kurt Wachsmuth (Berlin: Weidmann, 1884), 2.8.39. A work on synonyms attributed to the fourth-century scholar Ammonius Grammaticus (possibly an epitome of a first-century work by Philo of Byblos) defines *bios* as limited to humans and *zōē* as applying even to irrational animals, and mistakenly attributes to Aristotle the definition of *bios* as discursive *zōē*; Ammonius, *Ammonii qui dicitur liber de adfinium vocabulorum differentia*, ed. Klaus Nickau (Leipzig: Teubner, 1966), pp. 100–2.
5. This sense is particularly tangible in Heraclitus' pun on the words *bíos* 'life' and *biós* 'bow': 'The name of the bow [*toxou*] is *bios*, but its work [*ergon*] is death.' Heraclitus, DK 22 B 48; Heinrich Diels and Walter Kranz, *Die Fragmente der Vorsokratiker*, vol. 1 (Berlin: Weidmann, 6th edn, 1951).
6. This is illustrated by a passage in Plato's *Laches*, where Nicias points out that anyone facing Socrates in discussion cannot avoid giving an account of 'the manner in which he is now living [*zē*] and of the manner in which he has passed his life hitherto [*bion bebiōken*]'; Plato, *Laches*, in *Platonis opera*, vol. 3, ed. John Burnet (Oxford: Clarendon Press, 1903), 187e10–188a2.
7. Aristotle, *Metaphysics*, vol. 2, ed. W. D. Ross (Oxford: Clarendon Press, 1924), 12.7.1072b28–30. Cf. Hans Hübner, 'Leben II', in Joachim Ritter and Karlfried Gründer (eds), *Historisches Wörterbuch der Philosophie*, vol. 5 (Basel: Schwabe, 1980), pp. 56–9.

8. In Plotinus' *Enneads* we find an attempt to define time (*chronos*) as 'the being-alive [*zōēn*] of a soul in movement, changing from one mode of life [*bion*] to another'; Plotinus, *Enneads* (*Enneades*), in *Plotini opera*, vol. 1, ed. Paul Henry and Hans-Rudolf Schwyzer (Leiden: Brill, 1951), 3.7.11.43–5.
9. Aristotle, *Nicomachean Ethics* (*Ethica Nicomachea*), ed. Ingram Bywater (Oxford: Clarendon Press, 1894), 1.5.1095b14–22.
10. See Plato, *Laws* (*Leges*), in *Platonis opera*, vol. 5, ed. John Burnet (Oxford: Clarendon Press, 1907), 5.733d2–e6. Cf. Aristotle, *On the Generation of Animals* (*De generatione animalium*), ed. Hendrik Joan Drossaart Lulofs (Oxford: Clarendon Press, 1965), 2.3.736b13.
11. Aristotle, *On the Soul* (*De anima*), ed. David Ross (Oxford: Clarendon Press, 1956), 2.2.413a20–b32, 2.3.414b20–415a13.
12. Aristotle, *On the Soul* 2.2.413a22–5, 2.3.414b25–8.
13. Aristotle, *On the Soul* 2.3.414b28–32.
14. Aristotle, *On the Soul* 2.2.413b29–32.
15. Aristotle, *Nicomachean Ethics* 1.7.1097b33–1098a1, 1.13.1102a32–b12, 29–30.
16. Aristotle, *Politics* 1.1.1252b27–1253a1.
17. Aristotle, *Politics* 1.2.1252b29–30.
18. Aristotle, *Politics* 3.9.1280a31–b5, 29–35; *Nicomachean Ethics* 1.7.1097b6–16.
19. Aristotle, *Nicomachean Ethics* 1.7.1098a7–20.
20. Aristotle, *Nicomachean Ethics* 1.8.1098b21–1099a7.
21. Aristotle, *Nicomachean Ethics* 2.1.1103a14–b25.
22. Martin Heidegger, *Gesamtausgabe*, vol. 33: *Aristoteles, Metaphysik Θ 1–3: Von Wesen und Wirklichkeit der Kraft* [1931], ed. Heinrich Hüni (Frankfurt am Main: Klostermann, 2nd edn, 1990); *Aristotle's Metaphysics Θ 1–3: On the Essence and Actuality of Force*, trans. Walter Brogan and Peter Warnek (Bloomington: Indiana University Press, 1995).
23. Martin Heidegger, *Sein und Zeit* [1927] (Tübingen: Niemeyer, 18th edn, 2001), p. 38, cf. p. 262; *Being and Time*, trans. Joan Stambaugh, rev. Dennis J. Schmidt (Albany: SUNY Press, 2010), p. 36, cf. p. 251.
24. Aristotle, *Metaphysics* 9.1.1045b35–1046a2, 10–11.
25. Aristotle, *Metaphysics* 9.1.1046a28–30. Both Heidegger and Agamben reject the emendation, adopted in William of Moerbeke's thirteenth-century Latin translation of the *Metaphysics* but not found in the best manuscripts, of the word *adynamia* to a dative form, which would alter the passage to say 'every capacity corresponds to an incapacity of the same' – although, as Agamben (*OD* 94–5) notes, this does not greatly affect its sense. See Heidegger, *Gesamtausgabe*, vol. 33, p. 110; *Aristotle's Metaphysics Θ 1–3*, p. 93. However, Agamben does not specify how he precisely understands *adynamia* in this context. For a critique of Agamben's interpretation of *dynamis*, see Johannes Fritsche, 'Agamben

on Aristotle, Hegel, Kant, and National Socialism', *Constellations* 19.3 (2012): 437–41.
26. Aristotle, *On the Soul* 2.5.417a2–9.
27. Aristotle, *Metaphysics* 9.5.1047b35–1048a24, 9.8.1050b30–4.
28. Aristotle, *Metaphysics* 9.3.1047a24–6.
29. Heidegger, *Gesamtausgabe*, vol. 33, pp. 219–22; *Aristotle's Metaphysics Θ 1–3*, pp. 188–91.
30. Aristotle, *Metaphysics* 9.6.1048b18–36; *Physics*, ed. W. D. Ross (Oxford: Clarendon Press, 1936), 3.1.201a10–b15, 3.2.201b31–2.
31. Aristotle, *On the Soul* 2.5.417b2–7.
32. Aristotle, *On the Soul* 2.5.417b10.
33. In this context, *epidosis* does not seem to signify a 'giving oneself', in Agamben's sense of potentiality 'giving itself' over to actuality, but rather simply a 'giving in addition', an increase in the being of the entity in question in the sense of the transformation of potentiality into actuality. Cf. Fritsche, 'Agamben on Aristotle', pp. 439–41.
34. Aristotle, *Metaphysics* 9.6.1048a30–b36.
35. Aristotle, *Metaphysics* 9.8.1050a4–b6.
36. Aristotle, *Metaphysics* 9.8.1050b6–1051a3.
37. Aristotle, *Metaphysics* 9.6.1048a30–b9.
38. Cf. David Bleeden, 'One Paradigm, Two Potentialities: Freedom, Sovereignty and Foucault in Agamben's Reading of Aristotle's *dynamis*', *Foucault Studies* 10 (2010): 68–84. On the distinction between absolute and ordained power, see William J. Courtenay, 'Potentia absoluta/ordinata', in Joachim Ritter and Karlfried Gründer (eds), *Historisches Wörterbuch der Philosophie*, vol. 7 (Basel: Schwabe, 1989), pp. 1157–62.
39. Cf. Daniel McLoughlin, 'On Political and Economic Theology: Agamben, Peterson, and Aristotle', *Angelaki* 20.4 (2015): 53–69.
40. Cf. Jessica Whyte, '"I Would Prefer Not To": Giorgio Agamben, Bartleby and the Potentiality of the Law', *Law and Critique* 20.3 (2009): 309–24.
41. Aristotle, *Metaphysics* 9.8.1050a21–b2.
42. Aristotle, *Politics* 1.5.1254b16–20.
43. Aristotle, *Politics* 1.4.1254a14–17, 1.5.1254b20–4, 1.13.1260a12.
44. Aristotle, *Politics* 1.4.1253b32–3, 1254a7–8, 1.5.1254b24–6.
45. Aristotle, *Metaphysics* 5.20.1022b8–10.
46. Aristotle, *Metaphysics* 5.20.1022b10–14; *Nicomachean Ethics* 2.1.1103b21–5, 2.2.1104a27–b3, 2.5.1105b25–8.
47. 1 Cor. 7:21, 15:24, Rom. 7:6; *Novum Testamentum Graece*, 27th edn, ed. Barbara Aland et al. (Stuttgart: Deutsche Bibelgesellschaft, 1993).
48. Aristotle, *Nicomachean Ethics* 1.7.1097b28–33.

2 *Walter Benjamin*

CARLO SALZANI

ON BIOGRAPHY, STYLE AND METHOD

In a 1985 interview with Adriano Sofri, Agamben says of his encounter with Benjamin:

> I read him for the first time in the 1960s, in the Italian translation of the *Angelus Novus* edited by Renato Solmi. He immediately made the strongest impression on me: for no other author have I felt such an unsettling affinity. To me happened what Benjamin narrates about his own encounter with Aragon's *Paysan de Paris*: that after a very short while he had to close the book because it made his heart thump.[1]

For Agamben, this encounter with Benjamin proved to be 'decisive'[2] and would mark his entire career, as much as meeting Heidegger in person at the end of the 1960s. Of these two first philosophical 'masters' he would often say, quite enigmatically, that for him the two philosophers worked 'each one as antidote for the other',[3] or more precisely: 'Every great work contains a shadowy and poisonous part, against which it does not provide the antidote. Benjamin has been for me this antidote, which helped me to survive Heidegger.'[4] The nature of Heidegger's poison and of Benjamin's antidote is not very clear; what is clear, however, is that this early encounter with Benjamin shaped Agamben's own encounter with philosophy itself, and would exert an enduring influence (perhaps 'the single most important influence')[5] on his entire *oeuvre*.

This influence was decisive also from a biographical point of view. During the 1970s Agamben thoroughly worked through and with Benjamin's *oeuvre* at a textual and philological level, and in 1981 he made an important discovery: looking for traces of Benjamin in Georges Bataille's correspondence, he found a letter from Bataille to the custodian of the Bibliothèque Nationale in Paris, asking him to recover an envelope containing some manuscripts that Benjamin had left in storage during the war. After a few months of research, Agamben found five large envelopes in the private depository of Bataille's widow containing, among other things, the original typescript of *Berlin Childhood*, that of the essay 'The Storyteller', some sonnets written after the death of Benjamin's friend Christoph Friedrich Heinle, and a large number of notes for the unfinished book on Baudelaire.[6] In another, unspecified circumstance, Agamben also found in Paris the original typescript of *On the Concept of History* – which is still in his possession.[7] The same year he was thus entrusted by the Italian publisher Einaudi (where he was already working as an advisor thanks to Italo Calvino) with the editorship of the Italian translation of Benjamin's collected works, and between 1981 and 1994 he published five volumes. In 1994 Einaudi was bought by Silvio Berlusconi's Mondadori group, and Agamben violently objected to the new editorial demands that he substantially modify the edition of the new volume he was working on (about Benjamin's writings on Baudelaire at the end of the 1930s, which included part of the manuscripts he had found). In 1996, since he refused to modify the volume, he was removed from his position as editor, and he published an angry open letter to Giulio Einaudi, founder of the publishing house, in the Italian newspaper *La Repubblica*, breaking all relations with the publisher.[8] Only in 2012, once the translation rights of Benjamin's works had expired, was he able to publish the volume he had been preparing for Einaudi twenty years before.[9]

Agamben's knowledge of Benjamin's work is therefore not only extremely vast and thorough, but also philologically intimate and precise. On at least two occasions he even contested and corrected the interpretation of the German editors of Benjamin's *Gesammelte Schriften*: in *State of Exception*, he shows that the emendation by the German editors of the phrase *Es gibt eine barocke Eschatologie* ('there is a Baroque eschatology') to *Es gibt keine barocke Eschatologie* ('there is no Baroque eschatology') goes contrary to Benjamin's actual argument (*SE* 56). And in *The Time that Remains* he corrects the interpretation of a metaphor by analysing in depth Benjamin's notoriously difficult handwriting: describing the division between the before and the after of an historical event, in a passage of the *Arcades Project* Benjamin describes it as being *wie eine Strecke, die nach dem apoll(i)nischen Schnitt geteilt wird* ('like a line divided by the Apollonian incision'); Agamben points out that this makes no sense, since in Greek mythology there is no reference to any 'Apollonian incision', and so he proposes to read *apell(i)nischen* instead of *apoll(i)nischen*, where 'Apelles' – and not Apollo's – incision' would refer to the account by Pliny the Elder of how the Greek painter Apelles divided in two an incredibly fine line drawn by his colleague Protogenes (*TR* 50).

Such an intimate knowledge of Benjamin's *oeuvre* reflects on Agamben's own work in a process that Colby Dickinson deems to 'go beyond mere resemblance and into the territory of assimilation'.[10] There is no doubt that, from a stylistic perspective, Agamben aspires to the extreme elegance and compression of Benjamin's prose, to the point of adopting Benjamin's 'art of citing without quotation marks'[11] (and his whole theory of citation) and his marked tendency towards abstraction. Thematically, the vast interdisciplinary range of Benjamin's work clearly inspired Agamben's own extremely broad choice of topics and is certainly one of the main reasons for Agamben's tendency to foray into fields as different as theology, philosophy, politics, linguistics and economy. Finally, Agamben's own method is explicitly indebted to Benjamin's attention to philological details and to the 'assertion of a nearly material relation to texts, to objects', to the 'materiality of the past';[12] more strongly, Alex Murray argues that Benjamin's work, and in particular *The Origin of German Tragic Drama* (1928), exerted a crucial (and explicitly acknowledged) influence upon Agamben's own critical method and the task of his critical philosophy.[13]

Given such an intimate relationship, any account of Benjamin's 'presence' in Agamben's work will be reductive. In this brief essay, I will focus on this presence in the major themes which build up the cornerstones of Agamben's philosophical project: history and language; violence and law; and the messianic.

ON HISTORY AND LANGUAGE

Agamben started to write about Benjamin in the late 1960s and early 1970s, at a time when Benjamin's work was not yet universally known (the publication of his *Gesammelte Schriften* in German started only in 1972). In this early phase (and almost until the 'political' writings of the 1990s), Benjamin's influence can be located mainly in – though certainly not reduced to – two thematic areas: the philosophy of history and the philosophy of language. This is already evident in Agamben's first book, *The Man Without Content* (1970), where the last chapter frames the question of aesthetics within the coordinates of Benjamin's philosophy of history: the crisis of Western tradition is analysed through the lenses of Benjamin's critique of historicism and of the commodification and museification of culture, of which the 'angel of history' of thesis IX of Benjamin's *On the Concept of History* (1940) becomes the emblem (*MC* 104–18). In Agamben's second book, *Stanzas* (1977),

Benjamin's presence is perhaps less evident and mostly implicit, but a number of themes (explored especially in the second part, 'In the World of Odradek', *S* 30–61), such as melancholy, commodity fetishism, the Universal Exposition, Baudelaire's poetry and the loss of the aura, are authentically Benjaminian.

It is, however, Agamben's third book, *Infancy and History* (1978), where Benjamin's influence is more strongly felt: this is perhaps Agamben's most 'Benjaminian' book, not only because the essays composing the volume draw their inspiration (more or less explicitly) from texts by, and ideas coming from, Benjamin, but most importantly because the very project of the book – to establish the possibility of a new experience of history, time and language – is wholly Benjaminian.[14] In this book Agamben develops ideas and concepts to which he will incessantly return to redefine and specify their meaning and importance, and he establishes a (Benjaminian) vocabulary which will inform his future projects. The eponymous first essay, 'Infancy and History', takes its cue from Benjamin's 1934 essay 'Experience and Poverty', whose main thesis is that 'experience has fallen in value',[15] but then unfolds as a follow-up and development of another Benjaminian essay, 'On the Program of the Coming Philosophy' (1918),[16] which called for a reinvention of experience beyond the constraints of the Kantian model. In particular, Benjamin suggested that the question of language was essential for this 'reinvention' of experience, and it is this specific strain that Agamben elaborates on and develops: a new experience of time and history must be grounded on a new experience of language. The other essays of the volume develop these questions, focusing in particular on Benjamin's notion of history as catastrophe and on historical action as 'interruption'. Implicit – though fundamental for the intention of the book – remains Benjamin's influence on the question of infancy and childhood: nowhere does Agamben mention Benjamin's many writings on these issues, but they are beyond doubt a strong inspiration for his line of questioning.

In the following book, *Language and Death* (1982), Agamben proceeds on a mostly Heideggerian route, but the question of language here developed is accompanied throughout the 1980s by a series of essays on Benjamin, such as 'Walter Benjamin and the Demonic: Happiness and Historical Redemption' (1982) or 'Language and History: Linguistic and Historical Categories in Benjamin's Thought' (1983) (both later collected in *Potentialities*, *PO* 138–58, 48–61), where Agamben explores Benjamin's philosophy of language, its connection with the problem of history and its messianic intention. These essays show that Agamben's philosophy of language, though it is certainly construed upon in-depth analyses of ancient, medieval and modern linguistics, culminating in attentive and insightful readings of Benveniste, nonetheless draws its fundamental inspiration from Benjamin's elaborations and cannot be understood without them. These writings are thus fundamental to understanding Agamben's own work on language throughout the 1980s, and in particular *Idea of Prose* (1985): not only does this book constitute a series of experiments which attempt to develop Benjamin's view on language and challenge its limits beyond traditional philosophical prose, but its very title comes from a preparatory note for *On the Concept of History*, where the language in the messianic world is precisely defined as 'the idea of prose itself' (quoted in *PO* 48).

The works of the 1970s and 1980s on history and language constitute the backbone of Agamben's future projects and the foundations on which the 'political' writings of the 1990s (and beyond) will be erected. Though one cannot reduce these 'foundations' to a single influence, Benjamin's share is no doubt preponderant, as is also the case with the *Homo Sacer* project.

ON SACREDNESS, VIOLENCE AND LAW

One Benjaminian text would take a particular importance in Agamben's best-known book, *Homo Sacer* (1995), and in the twenty-year-long project of the same name that arose from it: the extremely dense and difficult 'Critique of Violence' (1921). Despite the diffuse presence of Benjamin's writings in Agamben's works, one can safely argue that this text is the single most important reference in his project. This text had a peculiar trajectory in the reception of Benjamin, coming to the forefront of philosophical debates only in the late 1980s,[17] but Agamben had focused on it as early as 1970 when he published the short article 'On the Limits of Violence'.[18] Agamben did not return to 'Critique of Violence' during the 1970s, but in the 1980s he started to refer to it implicitly by using a vocabulary derived from it, which would become the cornerstone of *Homo Sacer*. In the final excursus of *Language and Death* (1982), Agamben begins an analysis of violence and society that will slowly lead to *Homo Sacer*, and he uses the syntagm '*nuda vita*' for the first time (*LD* 106).[19] The syntagm then appears twice in *The Coming Community* (1990) (*CC* 64–5, 86), the book that established the philosophical-political coordinates on which *Homo Sacer* would be constructed, and subsequently in a series of preparatory studies published in the early 1990s (e.g., 'Beyond Human Rights' [1993], later included in *Means Without End* [1996], *ME* 20).

Where these coordinates are made explicit is in the first 'Threshold' of *Homo Sacer* (1995) (*HS* 63–7), which separates the first from the second part of the book and proposes an extremely compressed reading of 'Critique of Violence': this threshold not only finally reveals the origins of the idiosyncratic vocabulary Agamben uses, but also lays out the conceptual and problematic groundwork of the book and of the project as a whole. If the problem of the Western political tradition (presented in the first part of the book) is the indissoluble link that binds together sovereignty, law and violence and reduces life to its 'bareness', then Benjamin's essay not only unveils and makes explicit this link, but also posits the necessity of its interruption: law dialectically oscillates between the two poles of law-positing and law-preserving violence, and only the de-position (*Ent-setzung*) of this cycle will lead to an overcoming of violence, a liberation of life, and thus to a 'new historical epoch'.[20] Benjamin enigmatically bestows the task of this deposition on what he calls 'pure' or 'divine violence': his ambiguity with regard to this term has led to the most diverse and contrasting interpretations, from Derrida's juxtaposing it with the Nazi 'Final Solution'[21] to Žižek's equating it to the Latin adage *vox populi, vox dei*;[22] Agamben reads it instead as the deposition of the link that binds together law and violence, and this 'deposition' will become the cornerstone of his soteriology, more often under the name of *désoeuvrement*.

At the end of 'Critique of Violence', Benjamin links the notion of mere life to that of 'sacred life' and states that 'it might be worthwhile to track down the origin of the dogma of the sacredness of life'.[23] As some commentators have perceptively noted, not only the book entitled *Homo Sacer*, but Agamben's entire project could be read as but a follow-up and a vindication of this sentence.[24] In the course of this vindication, other Benjaminian texts become fundamental, like his 1934 essay on Kafka, whose analysis of law, violence and life partially rehearses (with a different vocabulary) the arguments of 'Critique of Violence';[25] and the correspondence between Benjamin and his friend Gershom Scholem about this essay and other Kafka-related issues,[26] from which Agamben derives one of his crucial definitions of the law in the sovereign ban: 'being in force without significance' (*HS* 51). Another important text related to 'Critique of Violence' is undoubtedly *The Origin of German Tragic Drama*,[27] where Benjamin transfers on to the term *Kreatur* ('creature') the features that identified 'mere life' in 'Critique of Violence', but also, quoting Carl Schmitt's *Political Theology* (1922), refutes and deactivates the latter's theory of sovereignty in a manner that will be fundamental for Agamben's own critique of Schmitt.

In fact, the confrontation between Benjamin and Schmitt is precisely the point of the reading of 'Critique of Violence' in *Homo Sacer*, and is absolutely central to Agamben's whole project, insofar as he uses Benjamin to expose and confute Schmitt's notion of sovereignty (which for Agamben is sovereignty *tout court* and constitutes the heart of the predicament of Western politics).[28] This confrontation is explored and analysed in detail in a central chapter of *State of Exception* (2003) titled 'Gigantomachy Concerning a Void', where Agamben rehearses and refines his reading of 'Critique of Violence' in contraposition to Schmitt and even proposes a bold hypothesis: that Schmitt knew 'Critique of Violence' and had written *Political Theology* to confute its argument (SE 52–64). To the constellation of 'Critique of Violence' and of the confrontation with Schmitt also belongs another fundamental text, thesis VIII of Benjamin's *On the Concept of History*, which (implicitly) refutes Schmitt's theory of sovereignty by pointing out that, today, 'the "state of emergency" in which we live is not the exception but the rule', and assigns to historical materialism the task 'to bring about a real [*wirklich*] state of emergency'.[29] This argument is fundamental for Agamben insofar as it allows him not only to link Schmitt's theory of sovereignty (whereby bare life is banished to the limits of the political space as 'exception') to Foucault's concept of biopolitics (for which the management of life becomes, in modernity, the main issue of politics), but also to put forward his original proposal to overcome the deadlock of Western politics: there is no way back to the old, pre-biopolitical coordinates (since Western politics is, essentially and from its very origins, biopolitics), so that the only way forward is to embrace our predicament and push it towards an *euporic* resolution of the *aporias* of the West (i.e., the 'real' state of emergency).

A MESSIANIC VOCABULARY

It was Catherine Mills (among others) who underlined Benjamin's role in providing Agamben 'with the tools for the *euporic* overcoming of the *aporias* that he diagnoses'.[30] In effect, a distinctive gesture of Agamben's argumentative style is to follow and develop a line of analysis which, especially – but not only – in the earlier works, draws heavily from Heidegger (but then also from Aristotle, Debord, Foucault, Schmitt, Arendt and others), in order then, in the final instance, to turn towards Benjamin for the *euporic*, messianic resolution. This is a gesture that marks many an Agambenian work, from his first book, *The Man Without Content*, where the strongly Heideggerian approach to the question of aesthetics and the work of art gives way, in the final chapter, to a Benjaminian reframing of the question within the (messianic) coordinates of history and transmissibility (MC 104–18), to *The Open* (2002), where the last few chapters on *désoeuvrement* use Benjamin's work in order to propose a messianic way out from the analysis of the human/animal divide developed earlier along strongly Heideggerian lines (O 81–8), to, finally, the concluding volume of the *Homo Sacer* series, *The Use of Bodies* (2014), in which a chapter on Benjamin's notion of the 'inappropriable' crowns and concludes the whole first part on the theory of 'use' (UB 80–94).

In fact, Benjamin provides Agamben not only with a philosophical *modus* and style and with a thematic framework, but also – and especially – with a soteriological, messianic *intention* and with the whole messianic vocabulary that goes with it. From early on, Agamben takes on the expression 'coming' to characterise the task of (his own) philosophy and politics (the most obvious example being *The Coming Community* [1990], though the term recurs thereafter almost as a philosophical 'brand'), and this derives from Benjamin's 1918 essay 'On the Program of the Coming Philosophy', emphasising the messianic frame of the investigation (in the Judaeo-Christian tradition, 'the Coming One' is the messiah).[31] A Benjaminian figure, among others, could be taken to represent this intention and frame: the 'messianic reversal'. Benjamin identified this 'reversal' (*Umkehr*) as being the central messianic category at work in Kafka's *oeuvre*,[32] and Agamben not only picks it up in his own readings of Kafka,[33] but rather adopts it from the very beginning as his methodological guiding principle, together with the (strongly related) Hölderlinian-Heideggerian motto of looking for redemption where the predicament is most extreme.[34] Moreover, in this reversal, as shown by the examples above, it is precisely Benjamin's work that provides the messianic impulse. Even when, from *The Time that Remains* (2000) onwards, he turns to Paul's theology, Agamben reads it, as it were, almost as an 'early matrix' for Benjamin's messianism, which the latter supposedly quoted 'without quotation marks' (cf. TR 138–45).[35]

The example of Paul is telling, since it reveals that it is rather Benjamin's messianism that, from the beginning, constitutes the 'matrix' of Agamben's soteriology and provides it with a messianic vocabulary. Paul's *katargesis* (TR 95–9), for instance, can be read but as a further translation (together with *désoeuvrement*, deactivation, inoperativity, etc.) of Benjamin's *Ent-setzung* (de-position) – the 'pure violence' of 'Critique of Violence'. Another fundamental concept originating from this text is that of 'pure means' or 'means without end' (whence the title of Agamben's 1996 collection of essays), a means emancipated from its relation to ends and that, as such, exhibits its 'mediality': for Agamben, this defines nothing less than *politics* as such, which is *'the exhibition of a mediality: it is the act of making a means visible as such'*, and thus is *'the sphere of pure means'* (ME 115–16, 60, original italics; cf. also PR 86ff.). An exemplary 'pure means' for Agamben is 'gesture', another Benjaminian concept central for his interpretation, among others, of Kafka and Brecht, which Agamben rearticulates along political and linguistic lines (cf. 'Notes on Gesture', ME 49–60; 'Kommerel, or On Gesture', PO 77–85; 'The Author as Gesture', PR 61–72). Also belonging to this messianic constellation are two important Benjaminian concepts, 'play' and 'study', present, again, in Benjamin's reading of Kafka, and that Agamben adopts as early as *Infancy and History* ('In Playland', IH 65–88), transposing them later into the political field of 'pure means' (SE 63–4; PR 75–6). Even the concept of 'profanation', progressively more and more central in the last phase of the *Homo Sacer* project, though not explicitly derived from Benjamin, originates from the latter's emphasis on the notion of 'profane' and the profaneness of the ideas of happiness and redemption.[36]

This messianic vocabulary is obviously also subjected to a number of other influences that modify, distort, bend and finally transform it into something different from its original Benjaminian form, into something that becomes Agamben's *own*. And this is the case, of course, for all kind of influences, but perhaps even more so when the relationship is so intimate and pervasive as to become almost invisible to the author himself; and even more so with an author like Agamben, whose *originality* and true philosophical *innovation* lay not in repeating and adapting his sources to his own philosophical project, but rather in developing them and their 'obscure' and 'undeveloped' sides into something *new*. As he consciously posits in *The Signature of All Things* while explaining his methodological principles,

> the genuine philosophical element in every work, whether it be a work of art, of science, or of thought, is its capacity for elaboration, which Ludwig Feuerbach defined as *Entwicklungsfähigkeit*. It is precisely when one follows such a principle that the difference between what belongs to the author of a work and what is attributable to the interpreter becomes as essential as it is difficult to grasp. (ST 7–8)

This is what finally happened, I would conclude, with Benjamin's presence in Agamben's work: it is so pervasive, so diffused, so intimate as to transcend philological exegesis and conscious reading or misreading, and to become an integral part of his own philosophy.

NOTES

1. Adriano Sofri, 'Un'idea di Giorgio Agamben', *Reporter*, 9–10 November 1985, p. 32. The translation Agamben mentions is Walter Benjamin, *Angelus Novus. Saggi e frammenti*, trans. Renato Solmi (Turin: Einaudi, 1962), the volume which introduced Benjamin to the Italian public (only the Artwork essay had been previously translated). Benjamin's statement about Louis Aragon's *Le Paysan de Paris* (1926) comes from a letter to Theodor W. Adorno from 31 May 1935, where Benjamin writes: '*Le Paysan de Paris*, of which I could never read more than two or three pages in bed at night before my heart started to beat so strongly that I had to lay the book aside'; *The Correspondence of Walter Benjamin 1910–1940*, trans. Manfred R. Jacobson and Evelyn M. Jacobson (Chicago: University of Chicago Press, 1994), p. 438.
2. Sofri, 'Un'idea di Giorgio Agamben', p. 32.
3. Roberto Andreotti and Federico De Melis, 'I ricordi per favore no', an interview with Giorgio Agamben, *Alias* 35 (9 September 2006): 2.
4. Jean-Baptiste Marongiu, 'Agamben, le chercheur d'homme', an interview with Giorgio Agamben, *Libération*, 1 April 1999, p. ii. But it works also the other way around: 'the two [philosophers] work to one another as poison and antidote. Benjamin saved me from Heidegger's poison, and the same is true viceversa'; Hannah Leitgeb and Cornelia Vismann, 'Das unheilige Leben. Ein Gespräch mit dem italienischen Philosophen Giorgio Agamben', *Litteraturen* 2.1 (2001): 18.
5. Adam Kotsko, 'Reading the "Critique of Violence"', in Colby Dickinson and Adam Kotsko, *Agamben's Coming Philosophy: Finding a New Use for Theology* (Lanham, MD: Rowman & Littlefield, 2015), p. 41. Cf. also, in the same volume, Colby Dickinson, 'On the "Coming Philosophy"', pp. 22–3.
6. For the complete list, see Giorgio Agamben, 'Un importante ritrovamento di manoscritti di Walter Benjamin', *Aut-aut: rivista di filosofia e cultura* 189–90 (1982): 4–6.
7. Cf. also Sofri, 'Un'idea di Giorgio Agamben', p. 33.
8. Giorgio Agamben, 'Caro Giulio che tristezza questa Einaudi', open letter to Giulio Einaudi, *La Repubblica*, 13 November 1996, p. 31.
9. Cf. Walter Benjamin, *Charles Baudelaire. Un poeta lirico nell'età del capitalismo avanzato*, ed. Giorgio Agamben, Barbara Chitussi and Clemens-Carl Härle (Vicenza: Neri Pozza, 2012).
10. Dickinson, 'On the "Coming Philosophy"', p. 23.
11. Benjamin talks about this 'art' in a note for the *Arcades Project* (N1,10), where it is related to 'montage' and is taken as stylistic cornerstone for the never-written book on the Parisian arcades. Cf. Walter Benjamin, *The Arcades Project*, trans. Howard Eiland and Kevin McLaughlin (Cambridge, MA: The Belknap Press of Harvard University Press, 1999), p. 458.

12. Agamben in Andreotti and De Melis, 'I ricordi per favore no', p. 3.
13. Alex Murray, *Giorgio Agamben* (London: Routledge, 2010), p. 37. Murray argues that '[t]his form of "true" criticism thus enacts rather than explains, represents rather than presents. This idea of an immanent representation should be kept in mind for the reader who approaches Agamben's body of work' (p. 39).
14. Heidegger's presence in the book is not to be underestimated, and in fact the points of contact between Heidegger's and Benjamin's philosophical projects (at least with regard to the themes mentioned above) are important; this notwithstanding, the language, the structure and the 'tone' of *Infancy and History* remain essentially Benjaminian.
15. Walter Benjamin, 'Experience and Poverty', in *Selected Writings*, 4 volumes, ed. Michael W. Jennings et al. (Cambridge, MA: The Belknap Press of Harvard University Press, 1996–2003), vol. 2, pp 731–6.
16. Walter Benjamin, 'On the Program of the Coming Philosophy', *Selected Writings*, vol. 1, pp. 100–10.
17. For a brief history of the reception of this text, and in particular for Agamben's readings of it, see Brendan Moran and Carlo Salzani, 'On the *Actuality* of "Critique of Violence"', introduction to Brendan Moran and Carlo Salzani (eds), *Towards the Critique of Violence: Walter Benjamin and Giorgio Agamben* (London: Bloomsbury Academic, 2015), pp. 1–15.
18. Cf. Giorgio Agamben, 'On the Limits of Violence' (1970), trans. Elisabeth Fay, *diacritics* 39.4 (2009): 103–11, reprinted in Moran and Salzani (eds), *Towards the Critique of Violence*, pp. 231–8.
19. This syntagm will enter the philosophical debate in the form given to it by Daniel Heller-Roazen in his translations of Agamben's books, 'bare life', but here is still rendered as 'naked life'.
20. Walter Benjamin, 'Critique of Violence', *Selected Writings*, vol. 1, pp. 236–52, here pp. 251–2.
21. Jacques Derrida, 'Force de loi: Le "fondement mystique de l'autorité"' / 'Force of Law: The "Mystical Foundation of Authority"', trans. Mary Quaintance, *Cardozo Law Review* 11.5–6 (1990): 919–1045.
22. Slavoj Žižek, *Violence* (New York: Picador, 2008), especially the last chapter, 'Divine Violence', pp. 178–205.
23. Benjamin, 'Critique of Violence', p. 251.
24. Kotsko, 'Reading the "Critique of Violence"', pp. 41–2; Leland de la Durantaye, *Giorgio Agamben: A Critical Introduction* (Stanford: Stanford University Press, 2009), p. 354; cf. also Anselm Haverkamp, 'Anagrammatics of Violence: The Benjaminian Ground of *Homo Sacer*', in Andrew Norris (ed.), *Politics, Metaphysics, and Death: Essays on Giorgio Agamben's* Homo Sacer (Durham, NC: Duke University Press, 2005), pp. 135–44.
25. Walter Benjamin, 'Franz Kafka: On the Tenth Anniversary of His Death', *Selected Writings*, vol. 2, pp. 794–818.
26. *The Correspondence of Walter Benjamin and Gershom Scholem,*

1932–1940, ed. Gershom Scholem, trans. Gary Smith and Andre Lefevere (Cambridge, MA: Harvard University Press, 1980).
27. Walter Benjamin, *The Origin of German Tragic Drama*, trans. John Osborne (London: Verso, 1998).
28. For some commentators, this move renders Benjamin's arguments too dependent on a Schmittian mould, forcing them, in a sense, to 'fit' the latter's theory. Cf. Kotsko, 'Reading the "Critique of Violence"', and also, partially, Carlo Salzani, 'From Benjamin's *bloßes Leben* to Agamben's *Nuda Vita*: A Genealogy', in Moran and Salzani (eds), *Towards the Critique of Violence*, pp. 109–23.
29. Walter Benjamin, 'On the Concept of History', *Selected Writings*, vol. 4, p. 392.
30. Catherine Mills, *The Philosophy of Agamben* (Stocksfield: Acumen, 2008), p. 6 and *passim*.
31. For example, 'Blessed is he who comes in the name of the Lord!' (Ps. 118:26); 'Are You the coming One, or are we to look for another?' (Matt. 11:3; Luke 7:19).
32. On 11 August 1934 he wrote to Scholem apropos of his essay on Kafka: 'Kafka's messianic category is the "reversal" or the "studying"' (*The Correspondence of Walter Benjamin and Gershom Scholem*, p. 135).
33. 'One of the peculiar traits of the Kafkian allegories', he writes in *Homo Sacer*, 'is that they contain right at the end a possibility of reversal which overturns completely their meaning' (*HS* 58).
34. The incipit of Hölderlin's poem *Patmos* reads: '*Wo aber Gefahr ist, wächst/ Das Rettende auch*' ('But where there is danger/ A rescuing element grows as well'); *Poems of Friedrich Hölderlin*, ed. and trans. James Mitchell (San Francisco: Ithuriel's Spear, 2004), p. 39. Heidegger often quoted these verses and made them a guiding principle of his philosophical inquiry, which Agamben replicates right from *The Man Without Content*, merging it with the Kafkian-Benjaminian messianic reversal and showing how intertwined and inseparable are the influences of Heidegger and Benjamin on his *oeuvre*.
35. The theology of Benjamin's first thesis in *On the Concept of History* that 'today [...] is small and ugly and has to keep out of sight' (*Selected Writings*, vol. 4, p. 399) would then be that of Paul (cf. *TR* 141). This reading, according to some commentators, tends/risks 'Christianising' Jewish messianism in general and the interpretation of Benjamin in particular: cf., for example, Colby Dickinson, 'Canon as an Act of Creation: Giorgio Agamben and the Extended Logic of the Messianic', *Bijdragen: International Journal in Philosophy and Theology* 71.2 (2010): 132–58.
36. On this topic, see Leland de la Durantaye, '*Homo profanus*: Giorgio Agamben's Profane Philosophy', *boundary 2* 35.3 (2008): 27–62.

3 Guy Debord

DAVE MESING

THE DEBORD–AGAMBEN RELATION

Posing the question of the Debord–Agamben relation immediately presents us with a series of problems, particular to Debord as well as Agamben. In terms of Debord, we must decide how to position ourselves towards his work in order to understand its place on Agamben's philosophical path. Such a decision has to be taken in several senses. As Agamben himself reports in a lecture on Debord's films, 'Once, when I was tempted (as I still am) to consider Guy Debord a philosopher, he told me: I'm not a philosopher, I'm a strategist.'[1] Bracketing the *Holzweg* of the disciplinary specificity of philosophy, what this quote opens up is the occasional rather than systematic character of Debord's interventions, insofar as the stakes for Debord, and with them the marshalling of his own philosophical lineage, are bound up with a certain political and aesthetic practice and not the production of thoughts that will stand the test of time.

Of course, we can observe that Agamben's own production does not stand in stark contrast to this heuristic distinction, which is further testified to by the fact that only two of the other primary interlocutors under consideration here, Aristotle and Heidegger, fit the standard image of canonical, even if not necessarily systematic, philosophical figures. Agamben's engagement with Debord runs throughout his entire published work, from the recent, nearly memorialising prologue to *The Use of Bodies*, to an important stylistic remark in his first book, *The Man Without Content*. As reflected in some later works, Agamben would develop a friendship with Debord, but his first encounter with Debord's thought took place during the seminar with Heidegger that he attended in 1968 at Le Thor.[2] Agamben's remark in *The Man Without Content* – that *détournement* and plagiarism play the same role of interrupting the authority of context in Debord as citation does in Benjamin (*MC* 128–9) – serves as a kind of watchword for the fleeting but no less fundamental or pervasive appearance of Debord throughout his work. While Agamben never explicitly resolves his relation to Debord as strategist or philosopher, both the character of his references to Debord and the non-systematic output of his overall production bear the imprints of this Debordian heritage.

A second and related sense of deciding how to position ourselves towards Debord concerns his status as a singular figure within the Situationist International. While Agamben deploys Debord in an individual way, taking up concepts from his solo-authored works and making reference to him either by name or by referencing such concepts (spectacle, spectacular society, *détournement*), it is worth noting that Debord's intellectual production and the complex history of his role in the SI further differentiate him from typical theoretical interlocutors. Agamben does nod to this wider theoretical lineage, and problem, such as when he cites the definition of a situation from the first issue of the *Internationale Situationniste* in the text that offers perhaps his most sustained treatment of Debord (*ME* 78).

Such a settling of accounts is less pressing for clarifying the Agamben side of the Debord–Agamben relation, but Debord's heterogeneity as a singular strategist and/or stand-in strategist for the SI spills over into a more explicit aspect of this relation. In addition to theoretical texts such as *Society of the Spectacle*, Debord wrote and directed several films.[3] As noted above, Agamben relays Debord's preference for being called a strategist in the context of a lecture on his films. In the next two sections, I restrict my focus to key concepts in Agamben which are developed through Debord, and specifically two solo-authored texts by Debord, but Debord's political and aesthetic context, especially as a filmmaker, is well worth pursuing further in relation to Agamben's reading and use of him.[4]

If we shift our attention to the other side of the hyphen in the Debord–Agamben relation, we find similar diversity in terms of genre and approach. Agamben's theoretical production is thoroughly solo-authored and text-driven, but the way in which Debord appears along his philosophical path varies, and we can characterise these appearances in at least four ways. First, there are direct and standard references to Debord's name or concepts, such as the footnote from *The Man Without Content* discussed above, or quick references such as those in *Homo Sacer* (*HS* 10), *The Kingdom and the Glory* (*KG* 255–6, 259),[5] and *Il fuoco e il racconto* (*FR* 124). Then, as also noted above, there is the almost memorialising, repeated reference to Debord by his first name in the prologue to *The Use of Bodies*. Third, we have Agamben's dedication to the collection *Means Without End*, probably his most overtly interventionist and directly political work. *Means Without End* includes Agamben's preface to an Italian translation of *Comments on the Society of the Spectacle*, which points towards a fourth style of approach towards Debord in Agamben, the marginal. The marginal references are more situation-driven, involving newspaper articles, translation introductions and projects or collections beyond Agamben's own work, even if the marginalia are sometimes repurposed there.[6]

Indeed, the idea of marginalia, or marginal notes (*glosse in margine*), to borrow from Agamben's preface to the translation of *Comments on the Society of the Spectacle*, is precisely what characterises the Debord–Agamben relation. In that text, Agamben writes that Debord's books 'do not need clarifications, praises, or, least of all, prefaces. At most it might be possible to suggest here a few glosses in the margins, much like those signs that the medieval copyists traced alongside of the most noteworthy passages' (*ME* 73). Even the direct and 'standard' references are marginal in the sense that Agamben quickly moves past them into another aspect of his work. Yet the marginal and fleeting references to Debord are pervasive along Agamben's philosophical path, and my aim here has been to catalogue such capacious ephemerality, posing the Debord–Agamben relation in its actuality. In order to further draw out the theoretical lineage along this path, I will turn first to the traces of Debord in two central concepts for Agamben: language and life. I will follow this with an analysis of Agamben's relation to *Society of the Spectacle* and *Comments on the Society of the Spectacle* in order to parse his claim that the society of the spectacle is 'the politics we live in' (*la politica in cui viviamo*) (*ME* 82/67; *CC* 80/64).

LANGUAGE AND LIFE

In two works from the *Homo Sacer* project where Agamben pursues the concepts of language and life at length, *The Sacrament of Language* and *The Highest Poverty*, no references to Debord or Debordian concepts occur.[7] Yet while these concepts pervade Agamben's work and extend beyond Debord's influence, a passage in the opening paragraphs of the prologue to *The Use of Bodies* succinctly recapitulates Agamben's reading of their co-implication in Debord. Agamben indicates Debord's awareness that there is something important in private life, which, although otherwise insufficient and insignificant, demands public communication. For Debord and also Agamben, a certain 'intransmissable clandestinity' stands at the heart of a central contradiction: 'the obscure, unavowed awareness that the genuinely political element consists precisely in this incommunicable, almost ridiculous clandestinity of private life' (*UB* xv). Agamben takes up and avows this surreptitiousness, and a closer look at his most sustained treatment of Debord, 'Marginal Notes on *Commentaries on the Society of the Spectacle*', helps situate key aspects in his understanding of the concepts of language and life.

We can focus on three important aspects in this text in order to turn initially to language, which is closely tied up with fundamental aspects of contemporary life for both thinkers. First, Agamben adopts the centrality of commodity fetishism to Debord's concept of the spectacle. Clearly, commodity fetishism has no direct relation to the concept of language, but it establishes a comprehensive challenge at the root of any attempt to construct community in the present. Agamben references commodity fetishism at the outset of the version of the Shekhinah chapter in *The Coming Community* (*CC* 79), but spells out its importance more fully in the 'Marginal Notes' text: 'The "becoming-image" of capital is nothing more than the commodity's last metamorphosis, in which exchange value has completely eclipsed use value and can now achieve the status of absolute and irresponsible sovereignty over life in its entirety, after having falsified the entire social production' (*ME* 76). Debord glosses this comprehensiveness by referring to the struggle between commodities as an epic poem 'that no fall of Troy can bring to an end'.[8] What interests Agamben most is the extremity of this claim, a simultaneously transparent and phantasmagoric present in the commodity form itself.

A second detail in the 'Marginal Notes' text takes us to one of Agamben's most direct statements on Debord, as well as language itself. Comparing Debord to Karl Kraus, Agamben claims that in both, 'language presents itself as the image and place of justice' (*ME* 77). We can read this statement in the context of Agamben's retrieval of commodity fetishism: language presenting itself as the image of justice should be read as an extension of the becoming-image of capital. Agamben does not seek to reduce capital to language or vice versa. Rather, it is language which renders the image-character of capital (as a social relation, not simply a static image)[9] visible. Agamben finds this vision in Debord's texts, and reproduces it throughout the Shekhinah and Tiananmen sections of the essay, which are reprinted with slight alterations in *The Coming Community*. Put most starkly, the vision is of nothing. In the society of the spectacle, 'language is not only constituted in an autonomous sphere, but also no longer ever reveals anything – or better, it reveals the nothingness of all things' (*ME* 84; *CC* 82).

Turning to some passages in *Society of the Spectacle* will help frame the Debordian context even further, but we should briefly linger over a third detail in the 'Marginal Notes' text. Agamben identifies gesture as 'the other side of the commodity' (*ME* 80). Again, gesture moves beyond Agamben's understanding of language, but gesture completes his analysis here in the sense that it names the way in which the nothingness revealed by language is traversed. Agamben notes that gestures are visible in the constructed situations of the SI, which deliberately and concretely aim at the collective organisation of a milieu, not in order to aestheticise, but rather to render a point of indifference manifest (*ME* 78). Gesture, then, 'is not the actuation of a power but the liberation of an ulterior power' (*ME* 80). Taken together, the phantasmagoric present of the commodity form, language as the image and place of justice, and the gestural, ambivalent opening possible amid the nihilism of contemporary life each gravitate around a Debordian heritage which drives Agamben's speculation about language.

These aspects underlie Agamben's synthetic and broad-sweeping claims, such as when he writes that 'the era in which we live is also that in which for the first time it is possible for humans to experience their own linguistic being – not this or that content of language, but language itself, not this or that true proposition, but the very fact that one speaks' (*ME* 85; *CC* 83). The idea of 'linguistic being' (*essenza linguistica*), as well as some implicit claims within the three aspects we have focused on, draw out something confirmed by some passages in *Society of the Spectacle*: for Agamben as well as Debord, language and life are co-implicative. For example, the phantasmagoric present of the commodity form is sovereign *over life*, and gesture draws out an ulterior power at the intersection between 'life and art, act and power, general and particular, text and education' (*ME* 80). Debord provides a similar account of the co-implication of language and life, the latter understood not merely in general, but more pointedly as life in contemporary societies where the capitalist mode of production prevails.

He does so in two steps. First, he argues for a relation between types of political power and types of time: distinguishing from cyclical time which he thinks correlates with a type of non-political power characterised by kinship ties, Debord claims that the birth of political power coincides with a conception of irreversible time, measured by dynasties: 'This irreversible time is the time of those who rule, and the dynasty is its first unit of measurement. Writing is the rulers' weapon. In writing, language attains its complete independence as a mediation between consciousnesses.'[10] Second, Debord underscores the incoherence and deficiency of this relation in spectacular society: 'The reality of time has been replaced by the *publicity* [*publicité*] of time.'[11] Insofar as the passing of time is presented to society as separate, there is no longer an experience of succession. 'What is really lived', Debord writes, 'has no relation to the society's official version of irreversible time, and conflicts with the pseudo-cyclical rhythm of that time's consumable by-products.'[12] One way to read this set of claims in our context is as a further explication of the phantasmagoric present in the commodity form, here glossed more in terms of life than what hangs over the vision of nothingness made possible in language.

The concepts of language and life in Agamben, then, and their knotted imbrication take their point of departure from similar assumptions in Debord. Both Debord and Agamben present these points in synthetic and enigmatic statements. Continuing on from the passage quoted above, Debord concludes: 'This individual experience of a disconnected everyday life remains without language, without concepts, and without critical access to its own past, which has nowhere been recorded.'[13] Agamben seizes upon this context, reconfiguring its ambivalences in a more positive way than Debord:

> what drives the nations of the earth toward a single common destiny is the alienation from linguistic being, the uprooting of all peoples from their vital dwelling in language. [. . .] Only those who succeed in carrying [this devastating *experimentum linguae*] to completion – without allowing what reveals to remain veiled in the nothingness that reveals, but bringing language itself to language, will be the first citizens of a community with neither presuppositions nor a State. (CC 83)

Understanding Debord as a *point of departure* for such claims is useful insofar as we can draw out their iteration in another context in order to then render their implications and assumptions – not only for language and life, but here also, history, time and experience – more explicit. While the claims we have examined from Debord and Agamben around the concepts of language and life are plainly articulated in a political sense, Agamben's main conceptual debt to Debord lies in his repeated invocation of terms such as spectacular society, spectacular politics and other variants. Agamben's use of Debord forces us to reckon with what he means when he writes that the society of the spectacle is the politics we live in, which *conditions* his other claims, especially those around the passages in the 'Marginal Notes' text and *The Coming Community* we have tarried with here. It is to this problem that we can now turn.

'THE POLITICS WE LIVE IN'

When we outlined the marginalia characteristic of Debord's presence in Agamben's work, we noted that the Shekhinah and Tiananmen chapters, which conclude *The Coming Community*, appear in a slightly reworked form in the 'Marginal Notes' text. Careful attention to an important shift in Agamben's presentation of the Debordian lineage between *The Coming Community* and the 'Marginal Notes' essay helps to focus on the specificity of what Agamben retrieves from Debord when he claims that the society of the spectacle is the politics we live in. Agamben opens the Shekhinah chapter of *The Coming Community* by writing: 'When Guy Debord published *Society of the Spectacle* in November 1967, the transformation of all social life into a spectacular phantasmagoria had not yet reached the extreme form that today has become completely familiar' (*ME* 79). Here Agamben signals the sweeping claims behind the phantasmagoric present in the commodity form we outlined above, but does not mention Debord's follow-up to *Society of the Spectacle*, *Comments on Society of the Spectacle*, which was published in 1988 and translated into Italian in 1990, occasioning Agamben's 'Marginal Notes' text as an introduction for Italian audiences.

Agamben's shift in focus, although he retains a total reverence for Debord's analysis, partially occludes the fact that Debord's *Comments* provides the direct context for the claim that the society of the spectacle is the politics we live in. Agamben notes the importance of Debord's later text in a section entitled 'Auschwitz/Timisoara', which is not present in the other versions:[14]

> Probably the most disquieting aspect of Debord's books is the fact that history seems to have committed itself to relentlessly confirm their analyses. Twenty years after *The Society of the Spectacle*, the *Commentaries* (1988) registered the precision of the diagnosis and expectations of that previous book in every aspect. (*ME* 80)

Agamben's words echo Debord's own stark introductory remarks in *Comments*:

> the society of the spectacle has continued to advance. [. . .] Proving this point has more than academic value, because it is undoubtedly indispensable to have understood the spectacle's unity and articulation as an active force in order to examine the directions in which this force has since been able to travel. These questions are of great interest, for it is under such conditions that the next stage of social conflict will necessarily be played out. [. . .] I am going to outline certain *practical consequences*, still little known, of the spectacle's rapid extension over the last twenty years. I have no intention of entering into polemics on any aspect of this question; these are now too easy, and too useless. Nor will I try to convince. The present comments are not concerned with moralising. They do not propose what is desirable, or merely preferable. They simply record what is.[15]

While Agamben's writings do not linger over practical consequences, they do proceed with a similar direct claim on recording what is. Moreover, the indispensability of an understanding of spectacular society for the next stages of social struggle provides further background for Agamben's presentation of a future community predicated on a co-belonging without any representable condition of belonging. What the attention to Debord's later work brings out most specifically, however, is the relevance of three particular historical categories of the spectacle: the concentrated, diffuse and, original to *Comments*, integrated spectacle.

Debord establishes the categories of concentrated and diffuse spectacle in sections 63–6 of *Society of the Spectacle*. He identifies the concentrated spectacle with bureaucratic capitalism: property is concentrated such that individual bureaucrats can take part in the entire economy only by means of mediation through the community of bureaucrats. The production of commodities in these societies is structured around this point. They are 'concentrated' because the bureaucracy, as the centre of control, retains a sovereign position relative to the rest of society: 'The commodity the bureaucracy appropriates is the total social labor, and what it sells back to the society is that society's wholesale survival.'[16] By contrast, the diffuse spectacle characterises societies in which there is an abundance of commodities, unhindered by any bureaucratic mediation. In these societies, 'each individual commodity is justified in the name of the grandeur of the total commodity production, of which the spectacle is a laudatory catalogue'.[17] They are 'diffuse' because no single type of commodity stands in for the survival or satisfaction of society; commodities proliferate such that consumers access them only as successions of fragments.

In *Comments*, Debord suggests that twentieth-century Russia and Germany helped form the concentrated spectacle, while the United States did the same for the diffuse spectacle.[18] However, he adds a new, even more important category that he sees as having emerged between the publication of *Society of the Spectacle* and *Comments*: the integrated spectacle. The integrated spectacle is the 'single detail' Debord thinks must be added to his theoretical analysis, a detail with 'far-reaching consequences'.[19] The integrated spectacle is a combination of the concentrated and diffuse spectacle, in terms of the diffuse spectacle, which Debord judges as generally victorious. It takes from the concentrated spectacle a 'controlling centre' that is occult, never occupied by a clear leader or ideology. It owes to the diffuse an unprecedented extension of the spectacle to 'almost the full range of socially produced behaviour and objects':

For the final sense of the integrated spectacle is this – that it has integrated itself into reality to the same extent that it was describing it, and that it was reconstructing it as it was describing it. As a result, this reality no longer confronts the integrated spectacle as something alien. When the spectacle was concentrated, the greater part of surrounding society escaped it; when diffuse, a small part; today, no part. The spectacle has spread itself to the point where it now permeates all reality.[20]

The integrated spectacle is thus Debord's analysis as to what will condition future social struggles. It is more explicitly universalising, and establishes a framework for the similarly universalising claims Agamben makes as a result of the society of the spectacle being the politics we live in.

Agamben does pick up on the analysis of the integrated spectacle as a unification of the concentrated and diffuse spectacles in the Auschwitz/Timisoara section of the 'Marginal Notes' essay. Writing in 1990, he regards this unification, which he claims appeared paradoxical when *Comments* was published in 1988, as 'trivial evidence' (*ME* 80). He does not analyse it in depth, but this brief section prior to the Shekhinah and Tiananmen sections underscores what he draws from Debord in more detail than the nearly identical invocation at the conclusion of *The Coming Community*. Most forcefully, the integrated spectacle demonstrates the historical conditions around Agamben's matter of fact proclamation that the society of the spectacle is the politics we live in. Certainly both Debord's concepts and Agamben's deployment of them involve assumptions about philosophy of history beyond our scope here,[21] but Debord's integrated spectacle gives Agamben's use of him more structure in terms of what problems Agamben sees the coming politics as facing. It is in this sense that we can situate Agamben's claims regarding the alienation of linguistic being returning to us and the spectacle as 'the pure form of separation' (*CC* 79): these are encountered from within the integrated spectacle. The practical consequences of the integrated spectacle which Debord lists – 'incessant technological renewal, integration of state and economy, generalised secrecy, unanswerable lies, [and] an eternal present'[22] – further specify Agamben's political task of carrying the accomplished nihilism in language and life outlined above to completion.

These details around language, life and politics demonstrate the Debord–Agamben relation. When we posed this relation at the outset, we noted its pervasive yet marginal character. Having established some form to this marginality by means of these three concepts, we can perhaps take leave of our treatment of Debord's place on Agamben's theoretical path by noting an endeavour common to both 'sides' of the Debord–Agamben relation: a rejection of spectacular conditions as determining the possible social relations of current politics. Towards the beginning of *Comments*, Debord writes, starkly, 'To be known outside spectacular relations is already to be known as an enemy of society.'[23] Agamben's most pointed marginal gloss on Debord is his rewriting of this conclusion at the end of *The Coming Community*: 'Whatever singularity, which wants to appropriate belonging itself, its own being-in-language, and thus rejects all identity and every condition of belonging, is the principal enemy of the State' (*CC* 87). The marginal refutation of spectacular society that Agamben shares with Debord points us towards an exit from this path, under the injunction to seek out new forms of separation from the integrated spectacle in common.[24]

NOTES

1. Giorgio Agamben, 'Difference and Repetition: On Guy Debord's Films', in Tom McDonough, *Guy Debord and the Situationist International: Texts and Documents* (Cambridge, MA: MIT Press, 2002), p. 313. I owe this reference to Jason Smith, who explores the problem of strategy in the context of Debord's thought further in his essay, 'Strategy and the Passions: Guy Debord's Ruses', in Mark Potocnik, Frank Ruda and Jan Völker (eds), *Beyond Potentialities? Politics between the Possible and the Impossible* (Zurich: diaphanes, 2011), pp. 169–82.
2. See Hannah Leitgeb and Cornelia Vismann, 'Das unheilige Leben. Ein Gespräch mit dem italienischen Philosophen Giorgio Agamben', *Litteraturen* 2.1 (2001): 16–22.
3. The history of these films is quite complex. Useful information can be found at Ken Knabb's Bureau of Public Secrets website (http://www.bopsecrets.org/SI/debord.films/, accessed 24 April 2017). Debord made six films, and had plans for several more. The films that Debord did make were withdrawn from circulation until after his death following the assassination of the films' producer (and publisher of *The Society of the Spectacle*) Gérard Lebovici in 1984. A third notable type of theoretical production, which Debord took quite seriously, was that of board games. See Alexander R. Galloway, 'Debord's Nostalgic Algorithm', *Culture Machine* 10 (2009): 131–56. I mention these details not so much as biographical anecdotes but rather to further flesh out Debord's heterogeneity as part of Agamben's theoretical lineage and to indicate some further paths that might be taken up in light of Debord's oblique rejection of philosophy for strategy, which Agamben occasionally gestures towards (*ME* 74).
4. Alex Murray takes up several of these issues in relation to Agamben's poetics; see 'Beyond Spectacle', in Justin Clemens, Nicholas Heron and Alex Williams (eds), *The Work of Giorgio Agamben: Law, Literature, Life* (Edinburgh: Edinburgh University Press, 2008), pp. 164–80. Evan

Calder Williams provides a more expansive account of Debord's films as theoretical than I can explore here, concluding that Agamben misses the mark in his interpretation of Debord's films, relying too heavily on montage and comparing Debord too closely with Godard. See Evan Calder Williams, 'Pseudo-Cinema', *World Picture* 8 (2013), http://www.worldpicturejournal.com/WP_8/Williams.html (accessed 24 April 2017).

5. It is deceptive to pass over *The Kingdom and the Glory* so quickly in relation to Debord, as both Mathew Abbott and Daniel McLoughlin have demonstrated well. See Mathew Abbott, 'Glory, Spectacle and in Operativity: Agamben's Praxis of Theoria', and Daniel McLoughlin, 'Liturgical Labour: Agamben on the Post-Fordist Spectacle', both in Daniel McLoughlin (ed.), *Agamben and Radical Politics* (Edinburgh: Edinburgh University Press, 2016), pp. 27–48 and 91–114. Jessica Whyte also provides a nuanced and wide-ranging discussion of Debord vis-à-vis Agamben in her excellent *Catastrophe and Redemption: The Political Thought of Giorgio Agamben* (Albany: SUNY Press, 2013), pp. 123–57.
6. Material relevant to Agamben's work on Debord appears in slightly reworked form across three different texts: the 'Marginal Notes' essay in *Means Without End*, the concluding sections of *The Coming Community*, and the essay 'Violenza e speranza nell'ultimo spettacolo', in *I Situazionisti* (Roma: manifestolibri, 1991), pp. 11–18. Parts of the latter essay originally appeared as a newspaper article: 'Violenza e speranza nell'ultimo spettacolo: Dal maggio francese a piazza Tian An Men', *Il Manifesto*, 6 July 1989.
7. I have pursued the concepts of language and life more broadly in Agamben's thought, as they relate to Debord and also a similar conceptual apparatus in the work of Paolo Virno, in 'Debordian Strategists: Agamben and Virno on the Coming Politics', *Russian Journal of Philosophy & Humanities* 2.1 (2017): 155–72.
8. Guy Debord, *Society of the Spectacle*, trans. Ken Knabb (London: Rebel Press, 2004), p. 32.
9. 'The spectacle is not a collection of images; it is a social relation between people that is mediated by images', Debord, *Society of the Spectacle*, p. 7.
10. Debord, *Society of the Spectacle*, p. 76.
11. Debord, *Society of the Spectacle*, p. 89.
12. Debord, *Society of the Spectacle*, p. 90.
13. Debord, *Society of the Spectacle*, p. 90.
14. 'Violenza e speranza nell'ultimo spettacolo' does not include distinct section titles, but Agamben does briefly tarry with the same content regarding the diffuse, concentrated and integrated spectacle. He also references the experience of Italian politics as a self-evident confirmation of Debord's analysis, especially insofar as Debord presents France and Italy as the laboratory of the integrated spectacle. See Agamben, 'Violenza e speranza', pp. 12–14.

15. Guy Debord, *Comments on the Society of the Spectacle*, trans. Malcolm Imrie (London: Verso, 1998), pp. 4–5.
16. Debord, *Society of the Spectacle*, p. 31.
17. Debord, *Society of the Spectacle*, p. 32.
18. Debord, *Comments*, p. 8.
19. Debord, *Comments*, p. 8.
20. Debord, *Comments*, p. 9.
21. Although we should note that there is some tension between Agamben's general retrieval of Debord and certain elements in Debord (such as when he writes, in *Society of the Spectacle*, that 'the formulation and communication of the type of theory envisaged here is already inconceivable without a rigorous practice' [p. 112]), we should resist the tired song in critiquing Agamben that he has no historical nuance and simply reifies philosophical categories in arranging and rearranging the history of Western metaphysics. On the one hand, Agamben will often identify and explicitly adopt practical currents in contemporary politics when pressed. See '"I am sure that you are more pessimistic than I am . . .": An Interview with Giorgio Agamben', trans. Jason E. Smith, *Rethinking Marxism* 16:2 (2004): 115–24. On the other hand, Justin Clemens has recently provided a decisive contribution to issues usually involved in this debate in an account of Agamben's methodology with special attention to the way in which he deploys categories at a different level than Foucault, even while refusing to repudiate Foucault's various objects. See Justin Clemens, 'An Alogical Space of Genetic Reintrication: Notes on an Element of Giorgio Agamben's Method', in Daniel McLoughlin (ed.), *Agamben and Radical Politics* (Edinburgh: Edinburgh University Press, 2016), pp. 115–40.
22. Debord, *Comments*, pp. 11–12.
23. Debord, *Comments*, p. 18.
24. While we would need to think through questions and contemporary forms of power in much more detail, the following quote from Debord provides some general orientation for this injunction and the overall sense of the Debordian markings on Agamben's path. On the challenges of environmental problems and nuclear power specifically, Debord writes, 'It is indeed quite unfortunate that human society should encounter such burning problems just when it has become materially impossible to make heard the least objection to the language of the commodity; just when power – quite rightly because it is shielded by the spectacle from any response to its piecemeal and delirious decisions and justifications – *believes that it no longer needs to think*; and indeed can no longer think' (Debord, *Comments*, p. 38).

4 Michel Foucault

VANESSA LEMM

Michel Foucault begins to play a major role in Giorgio Agamben's work starting with his book *Homo Sacer*. Agamben's thinking about biopolitics, sovereignty, governmentality and form-of-life is deeply influenced by the work of Foucault, as evidenced by his sustained engagement with Foucault's texts throughout the entire *Homo Sacer* series. One commentator notes that the trajectory of Agamben's work since the mid-1990s 'makes evident that it is proceeding by an ongoing interpretation of the thought of Michel Foucault'.[1] But Agamben's debt to Foucault does not end here. With *The Signature of All Things*, Agamben also shows that his research methods arise from reflections on Foucault's use of archaeology and genealogy in his studies of discourse formation. As Agamben remarked in an interview from 2004, 'I see my work as closer to no one than to Foucault.'[2] It is therefore not surprising that Foucault has been referred to as the 'single most decisive influence on Agamben's later works'.[3]

HOMO SACER: BIOPOLITICS AND SOVEREIGNTY

Without doubt the most important concept Agamben takes from Foucault is that of biopolitics. Foucault scholars would agree that there is no one single meaning of the term in Foucault's work, but at least three different ones.[4] Late in his career, Foucault discovered a major paradigm shift in the conception of power at the turn of the seventeenth/eighteenth century, reflected in the rise of a new *episteme* characterised by an unprecedented interrelation between the new science of biology and the human sciences. When Foucault first employs the term biopolitics in the first volume of *The History of Sexuality*, he uses it to identify a new kind of power reflected in technologies and discourses of security that take the life of populations as their object, and play a central role in the emergence of modern state racism.[5] However, in his lecture series on *The Birth of Biopolitics*, Foucault also connects biopolitics to the kind of political rationality characteristic of the liberal and neoliberal forms of government and governance.[6] Biopolitics then refers not only to technologies of security but also to technologies of self. This has led to a study of the relation between biopolitics and what Foucault calls governmentality. Lastly, there is in Foucault a third use of biopolitics referring to the possibility that life itself may function as a source of critique and resistance to biopolitics: 'it is not that life has been totally integrated into techniques that govern and administer it; it constantly escapes them'.[7] Agamben takes up the different meanings of biopolitics in Foucault by questioning, developing, complementing and correcting them in multiple, sometimes controversial ways that have been much debated in both Agamben and Foucault scholarship.[8] Agamben takes Foucault's thought on biopolitics in new and unexpected directions, giving it new relevance and significance in an age that more than any other is confronted with the urgent need to invent a new politics beyond biopolitics (*HS* 11). As such, Agamben has provided by far one of the most original and influential readings of Foucault in the twenty-first century.

In a 2001 interview, Agamben noted that he first began to understand the figure of *homo sacer*, the protagonist of the first book in the *Homo Sacer* series, after he read Foucault's texts on biopolitics.[9] Agamben's acknowledgement of Foucault's influence on his coming to terms with the riddle of *homo sacer* relativises the otherwise rather critical assessment of the limits of Foucault's concept of biopolitics put forward by Agamben in the much commented-on introduction to *Homo Sacer* (*HS* 3–6).[10] Here Agamben regrets that Foucault did not build on Hannah Arendt's *The Human Condition*, which twenty years before the publication of Foucault's *The History of Sexuality* had already fully articulated 'the process that brings *homo laborans* – and with it, biological life as such – gradually to occupy the very centre of the political scene of modernity' (*HS* 3). Moreover, Agamben remarks that Foucault did not pay sufficient attention to 'the exemplary places of modern biopolitics: the concentration camp and the structure of the great totalitarian states of the twentieth century' (*HS* 4). Agamben sets out to address these 'blind spots' in Foucault's work (*HS* 6). *Homo Sacer* has renewed research in the field of biopolitics in three major ways: first, by extending the historical horizon of Foucault's inquiry into biopolitics to the Ancients; second, by re-articulating the intimate link between sovereign power and bio-power; and third, by initiating a highly influential shift in the study of biopolitics towards law[11] and theology, disciplines that Foucault, according to Agamben, 'left out of account'.[12] As such, Agamben understands his own work as a correction, or at least a completion, of Foucault's conception of biopolitics (*HS* 9).[13]

In contrast to Foucault, who identifies biopolitics essentially as a phenomenon of modern politics, Agamben seeks to show that the Greek and Roman experience of politics must also be investigated from the perspective of biopolitics. Foucault claimed that 'for millennia, man remained what he was for Aristotle: a living animal with the additional capacity for a political existence; modern man is an animal whose politics places his existence as a living being in question'.[14] Agamben also returns to Aristotle, but this time to show that, for the Greeks, there are two different meanings of the word 'life' and that this dualism already contains the seeds of biopolitics. Agamben distinguishes between *zoè*, which designates 'the simple fact of living common to all living beings (animals, men or gods)' and pertains to the sphere of the household (*oikos*), on the one hand, and *bios*, which designates 'the form or way of living proper to an individual or a group' and pertains to the sphere of the *polis*, on the other (*HS* 1). Against Foucault, Agamben holds that 'what characterizes modern politics is not so much the inclusion of *zoè* in the *polis* – which is, in itself, absolutely ancient – nor simply the fact that life as such becomes the principal object of the projections and calculations of state power' (*HS* 9). Instead, relying on Carl Schmitt's theory of sovereignty, Agamben argues that the crucial feature of modern politics is 'the state of exception' in which *zoè* and *bios* enter into a 'zone of irreducible indistinction' (*HS* 9). As such, for Agamben the sovereign decision is always already a biopolitical decision and sovereign power is always already intimately linked to (power over) life. This is also why Agamben believes that the camp is 'the fundamental biopolitical paradigm of the West' (*HS* 181). Catherine Mills nicely sums up this point of difference between Agamben and Foucault: 'Against Foucault, Agamben suggests that the definitional formula of biopower is not "to make live or let die", but rather, to make survive, that is, to produce bare life as life reduced to survival through the separation of the human from the inhuman, or the speaking being from the living being.'[15]

For Agamben, the rise of biopolitics does not reflect a shift from sovereign to disciplinary power as Foucault had thought. Rather the sovereign power of life and death stands at the centre of the inclusive/exclusive logic inherent to biopolitics.[16] Agamben traces the notion of sovereignty back to its roots in Roman law where he discovers the enigmatic figure of the *homo sacer*, the sacred man, '*who may be killed and yet not sacrificed*' (*HS* 8, original italics). Agamben is interested in the mysterious mechanism by which *homo sacer* is stripped of all the distinguishing features of a way of living to such an extent that nothing remains except its 'bare life' that can be killed without committing a crime. Agamben advances the controversial thesis that *homo sacer* constitutes 'the first paradigm of the political realm in the West' (*HS* 9). From this perspective, 'the fundamental activity of sovereign power is the production of bare life' (*HS* 181).

METHODS: PARADIGMS, GENEALOGY AND ARCHAEOLOGY

There is one particular thesis that Agamben puts forward in *Homo Sacer* that deserves further attention, namely the much-contested claim that the camp is 'the fundamental biopolitical paradigm of the West' (*HS* 181). As we shall see, the key point of this thesis is not so much related to the question of Agamben's conception of biopolitics in its relation to Foucault, but to the question of Agamben's method. In a 2004 interview, Agamben explained that when he referred to the camp as the biopolitical paradigm of the West, he applied the same genealogical and paradigmatic method that Foucault employed.[17] The importance of Foucault's methodology for Agamben figures prominently in *The Signature of All Things*, with three chapters dedicated to Foucault's idea of the paradigm, his theory of the signature[18] and his conception of philosophical archaeology. In the preface to the book, Agamben acknowledges the similarity of his approach to that of Foucault: 'The astute reader will be able to determine what in the three essays can be attributed to Foucault, to the author, or to both' (*ST* 7).

On the question of the camp as a paradigm for modern politics, de la Durantaye notes that it is difficult to assess whether and how Agamben's use of the term 'paradigm' differs from the use made by Foucault, since Foucault has not offered a definition. De la Durantaye, who is one of the few Agamben scholars to have dedicated close attention to his method,[19] shows how the meaning of paradigm in Foucault can be deduced from Foucault's method and his famous reference to the paradigm of the panopticon in *Discipline and Punish*.[20] De la Durantaye remarks that, for Foucault, the use of paradigms entails viewing history in terms other than those of traditional historical causality. It is in this sense noteworthy that neither Foucault nor Agamben understand themselves as historians.[21] In line with Nietzsche's genealogical method, both Foucault and Agamben operate with a different conception of *arché*, one that contests the homogeneity of the past. For them, 'all historical inquiry involves the identification of a fringe or of a heterogeneous stratum that is not placed in the position of a chronological origin but is qualitatively other' (*ST* 84). Agamben remarks that the goal of a paradigm 'is to render intelligible a series of phenomena whose relationship to one another has escaped, or might escape, the historian's gaze' (*ST* 33). Just as the panopticon in Foucault becomes 'a paradigm for the entire governmental mode, a manner of conceiving how best to regulate citizens',[22] the camp in Agamben becomes a paradigm for an entire governmental mode, a manner of conceiving of how best to produce bare life.

Agamben writes that 'the paradigm is a singular case that is isolated from the context to which it belongs only to the extent that by exploiting its singularity it renders a new group of phenomena intelligible whose homogeneity the paradigm itself constitutes' (*ST* 20). From these formulations, it is also evident that Agamben employs a Platonic conception of the paradigm, which is synonymous with the idea that saves the phenomena (*IP*; *UB* 259). Paradigms are examples that draw on historical developments over time (past) which are concretised in a specific moment in time (present), but are directed towards the future in view of overcoming the present. As such, the way in which Foucault and Agamben make use of paradigmatic figures can be inscribed in the tradition of critical theory that goes back to Nietzsche's genealogy and to what he referred to as untimeliness in his reflections on the advantages and disadvantages of history.[23] Here the goal is not to bring back the past, but to increase our understanding of the present. For Agamben, 'the camp is a concrete historical fact that at the same time serves as a paradigm, making it possible to understand the present situation',[24] and I would add that this new understanding is not aimed at maintaining the present but at overcoming it. In *The Signature of All Things*, Agamben articulates this idea of overcoming the past and present in the concept of the future anterior. It is 'that which will become accessible and present, only when the archaeological operation will have completed its operation' (*ST* 105–6). Again, Agamben is here parsing Foucault's idea of a 'genealogy of the present' with a Benjaminian conception of the task of history as *apokatastasis* of the past into the present that interrupts its empty progression and allows for a radical novelty.

THE KINGDOM AND THE GLORY: ECONOMY AND THEOLOGY

In his careful review of the *Homo Sacer* series, Jeffrey Bussolini points out that throughout the series Agamben revisits and revises some of his earlier accounts of Foucault in *Homo Sacer* which were largely based on Foucault's *The History of Sexuality*. In *Remnants of Auschwitz* and *State of Exception*, Agamben acknowledges Foucault's biopolitical considerations on the concentration camp and the Nazi state, and Bussolini holds that this is largely due to Agamben's exposure to Foucault's lecture series *Society Must be Defended*.[25] But it is not until *The Kingdom and the Glory* that Agamben takes up in a more systematic way Foucault's concept of governmentality. Foucault defines governmentality in terms of the problem of leading or conducting the conduct of individuals. This reflexive expression, 'the conduct of conduct', is intended to highlight the central feature of governmentality, namely, that the subject who is governed is also at the same time the subject who governs. In the opening pages of the book, Agamben locates his singular articulation of the Trinitarian model as the meeting point between transcendent authority and the administrative management of populations 'in the wake of Michel Foucault's investigation into the genealogy of governmentality' (*KG* xi). Whereas *Homo Sacer* draws out the differences between Agamben's and Foucault's conceptions of biopolitics, by the time of *The Kingdom and the Glory* these differences seem to have become a minor issue for Agamben: 'it is merely a question of the length of the historical shadow'.[26]

In his genealogy of governmentality, Foucault claims that the ideal of pastoral government found in early Christianity is taken up and transformed in the late sixteenth century into the police/policy sciences (*Polizeiwissenschaften*) that lead to biopolitical governmentality in the seventeenth and eighteenth centuries.[27] Foucault defines pastoral power as 'an art of conducting, directing, leading, guiding, taking in hand, and manipulating men, an art of monitoring them and urging them step by step, an art with the function of taking charge of men collectively and individually throughout their life and at every single moment of their existence'.[28] In pastoral politics, the human being's existence as a living being is at stake in two ways. First, the human being's biological existence is totalised into the life of a species – every single human being as a living being is subsumed under the totality of the species. Second, the human being's existence as a living being is particularised into separate, isolated, individual subjects. According to Foucault, when pastoral power becomes modern biopolitics, its 'inevitable effects are both individualization and totalization': the political rationality of the modern biopolitical state is both 'individualizing and totalitarian'.[29]

Agamben maintains that the historical horizon of the emergence of biopolitical governmentality should be pushed back further to 'the early centuries of Christian theology, which witness the first, tentative elaboration of the Trinitarian doctrine in the form of an *oikonomia*' (*KG* xi).[30] Agamben argues that 'the very secularization of the world becomes the mark that identifies it as belonging to a divine *oikonomia*' (*KG* 4). As such *The Kingdom and the Glory* can be read as a continuation and development of Foucault's genealogy of governmentality, but departs from Foucault's investigation of the genealogy of government insofar as it locates the concept of an 'economic' government of things already back in the second and third century of Christian thought on the 'economy' of divine dispensation in history.[31] *The Kingdom and the Glory* devotes attention to a tradition that Foucault, according to Agamben, did not sufficiently consider, and also provides an account of divine economy that sheds light on the relationship between the government of the soul and the political government of men in Foucault's conception of pastoral power and the art of government. Agamben here does not seem to take into consideration Foucault's last volume on *The Government of Self and of Others*, which discusses these issues at length.[32] For Agamben, the theological implications of the notion of economy in Gregory of Nazianzus's doctrine of the Holy Trinity are crucial for an understanding of the centrality of economy in the art of government from the pastoral to liberal and neoliberal forms of governmentality, and Agamben argues that Foucault failed to complete his genealogy of governmentality (*KG* xi, 109–13).

Agamben follows Foucault on pastoral power understood as an economy of power that reveals the introduction of economy into political practice as one of the main features of governmentality. However, Agamben regrets that Foucault 'seems to ignore completely the theological implications of the term *oikonomia*' (*KG* 110). Foucault also does not provide an analysis of providence in his conception of pastoral power. Agamben understands government as synonymous with providence and explains that providence, or what he also refers to as the providential machine, is God's government of the world through the nexus of secondary causes that give direction to all living beings. In the end, the differences between Agamben and Foucault on Christian pastoral power repeat their disagreement with respect to the relationship between sovereignty and government: whereas, for Foucault, these denote distinct forms of power, Agamben understands them to have a dialectical relation. By drawing sovereignty into the sphere of God the Father, Christian theology sought from the beginning to relinquish the government of the world to God the Son, representative of a non-sovereign, 'economic' management of things that he links with liberal political economy through a theological reading of Adam Smith's 'invisible hand' (*KG* 273–7).[33]

THE USE OF BODIES: ETHICS AND ONTOLOGY

In *The Use of Bodies*, the last volume of the *Homo Sacer* series, Agamben pursues his engagement with Foucault in a way that is comparable to Foucault's own trajectory. In his late work, Foucault turns to Greek philosophy in search of alternative technologies of the self that may provide an answer to the problems of biopolitics and governmentality. In *The Hermeneutics of the Self* and his lecture series on *The Government of Self and of Others*, Foucault is looking for a different way of conducting oneself, for forms of 'counter-conducts' that resist the grasp of political power over life.[34] Despite the distinctly political motivation of Foucault's investigations into Greek philosophy, this new direction in Foucault's work has often been understood as a turn towards ethics and centred on an exploration of what Foucault called an aesthetics of existence.[35]

In *The Use of Bodies*, Agamben pursues a similar project with a clear orientation towards ethics and ontology, seeking to further determine the concept of a 'form-of-life' that 'names the mode in which a singularity bears witness to itself in being and being expresses itself in the singular body' (*UB* 233). In one of the Intermezzos in *The Use of Bodies*, Agamben provides a careful reading of Foucault's idea of style of life and aesthetic of existence that rectifies Pierre Hadot's misconception of this idea in Foucault (*UB* 95–108). According to Agamben, Foucault had already developed an interest in the idea of an art of existence at the beginning of the 1980s, as evidenced by his growing attention to practices through which human beings seek to modify themselves and to make their own life something like a work of art (*UB* 97). Following his survey of the places where Foucault makes use of the expression 'aesthetics of existence', Agamben argues that this expression should not be attributed to Foucault's final conception of philosophy, as Hadot does, but is situated in the ethical sphere (*UB* 97–8). Furthermore, Agamben shows that, contrary to Hadot's understanding of style of life in Foucault as a form of cultivation of the self, what Foucault tries to articulate through the idea of life as a work of art are the transformations of the self, the becoming other of the self (*UB* 99). Against Hadot's understanding of ethics in Foucault, Agamben stresses that Foucault seeks to conceive of an ethics that is detached from a conception of the subject as transcendent with respect to its life and actions. In a remark that is equally applicable to his own thinking, Agamben recalls that when Foucault speaks of the work of art, what he has in mind is Nietzsche's idea of the artwork without an artist (*UB* 100): 'The very idea of the life as work of art derives from his conception of a subject that can no longer be separated out into an originary constituent position' (*UB* 100). In Foucault's terms, there is no subject but only a process of subjectification (*UB* 101). For Agamben, '[t]his is the paradox of the care of the self that Hadot does not manage to understand' (*UB* 101).

Agamben also elaborates on Foucault's last lecture series at the Collège de France, *The Courage of Truth*, where Foucault presented the theme of the philosophical life as the true life in the context of a reading of the Cynics which he explicitly links to the paradigm of the artist in modernity, whose life, 'in the very form it takes, should constitute some kind of testimony of what art is in its truth' (qtd. in *UB* 103). Agamben is interested in further exploring the 'peculiar ontological status of this subject that is constituted through the practice of the self' by drawing an analogy with the categories of constituent and constituted power (*UB* 104). In both cases, these categories stand in an indissoluble immanent relation to each other to the extent that 'ethics is not the experience in which a subject holds itself behind, above, or beneath its own life but that whose subject constitutes and transforms itself in indissoluble immanent relation to its life, by living its life' (*UB* 104).

But according to Agamben, the theory of the subject also entails an ontological problem, where we find the aporias that have marked from the very beginning its status in first philosophy (*UB* 105–6). Agamben remarks that although Foucault seems to have been aware of the 'ontological adequation of the self to the relationship', he did not unfold all of its implications (*UB* 108). Agamben speculates that Foucault may have had good reasons to 'constantly avoid the direct confrontation with the history of ontology that Heidegger had laid out as a preliminary task' (*UB* 108). Against this background, Agamben's *Use of Bodies* can be read as a continuation of Foucault's conception of ethics towards an ontology of style (*UB* 224–33). Its task is '[t]o bring to light – beyond every vitalism – the intimate interweaving of being and living: this is today certainly the task of thought (and of politics)' (*UB* xix). For Agamben, the challenge is to think beyond the idea of the subject as a free subject:

> What Foucault does not seem to see, despite the fact that antiquity would seem to offer an example in some way, is the possibility of a relation with the self and of a form of life that never assumes the figure of a free subject – which is to say, if power relations necessarily refer to a subject, of a zone of ethics entirely subtracted from strategic relationships, of an Ungovernable that is situated beyond states of domination and power relations. (*UB* 108)

The Use of Bodies seeks to delineate the contours of a form-of-life and a common use of bodies that no longer stand in need of 'liberation'.

NOTES

1. Jeffrey Bussolini, 'Critical Encounter Between Giorgio Agamben and Michel Foucault', *Foucault Studies* 10 (2010): 108–43, here p. 108.
2. 'Dalla teologia politica alla teologia economica: Un'intervista a Giorgio Agamben su un lavoro in corso', interview conducted by Gianluca Sacco, 8 March 2004, http://www.lavocedifiore.org/SPIP/article.php3?id_article=1209 (accessed 24 April 2017).
3. Leland de la Durantaye, *Giorgio Agamben: A Critical Introduction* (Stanford: Stanford University Press, 2009), p. 208.
4. On the three different uses of biopolitics in Foucault, see Thomas Lemke, *Biopolitik zur Einführung* (Hamburg: Junius Verlag, 2007), pp. 49–67. For a more extended discussion of the different meanings of biopolitics in Foucault, see Vanessa Lemm and Miguel Vatter, 'Michel Foucault's Perspective on Biopolitics', in Steven A. Peterson (ed.), *Handbook of Biology and Politics* (London: Edward Elgar, 2017), chapter 4.
5. Michel Foucault, *The History of Sexuality. Vol. 1*, trans. Robert Hurley (New York: Vintage Books, 1990).
6. Michel Foucault, *The Birth of Biopolitics*, trans. Graham Burchell (New York: Palgrave Macmillan, 2008).
7. Foucault, *History of Sexuality*, p. 143. Tom Frost puts forward the interesting thesis that Foucault's law can also be construed as the site of resistance, 'with the law reacting to resistance and therefore always opening to political possibilities. Resistance thus becomes the driving force behind the law and the operations of power'; Tom Frost, 'Agamben's Sovereign Legalization of Foucault', *Oxford Journal of Legal Studies* 30.3 (2010): 545–77, here p. 563. The meaning of biopolitics as resistance is articulated by Agamben in *The Coming Community* in the concept of a 'whatever singularity'.
8. On the the differences between Agamben's and Foucault's approach to biopolitics, see Paul Patton, 'Agamben and Foucault on Biopower and Biopolitics', in Matthew Calarco and Steven DeCaroli (eds), *Giorgio Agamben: Sovereignty and Life* (Stanford: Stanford University Press, 2007), pp. 203–18; Mike Ojakangas, 'Impossible Dialogue on Bio-power: Agamben and Foucault', *Foucault Studies* 2 (2005): 5–28; Katia Genel, 'Le biopouvoir chez Foucault et Agamben', *Methodos: Savoirs et textes* 4 (2004), http://methodos.revues.org/131 (accessed 24 April 2017). On the question of 'Completing Foucault', see also Peter Fitzpatrick, 'Bare Sovereignty: Homo Sacer and the Insistence of Law', in Andrew Norris (ed.), *Politics, Metaphysics, and Death: Essays on Giorgio Agamben's Homo Sacer* (Durham, NC: Duke University Press, 2005), pp. 49–73, in particular pp. 56–8.

9. Hannah Leitgeb and Cornelia Vismann, 'Das unheilige Leben: Ein Gespräch mit dem italienischen Philosophen Giorgio Agamben', *Literaturen* 2.1 (2001): 16–21.
10. Agamben's earlier remarks on Foucault in the introduction to *Homo Sacer* have led scholars to insist on the differences between Foucault and Agamben, without sufficiently acknowledging their points of agreement. Bussolini has pointed out that some of the earlier (mis)speculations about the relation between the two thinkers have since then been clarified (Bussolini, 'Critical Encounter', p. 108). Sarasin's reading of Agamben's *Homo Sacer* as a '*todesfixierter Mystizismus der Souveränität*' may provide an example of such a misconceived reading; Philipp Sarasin, 'Agamben – oder doch Foucault?', *Deutsche Zeitschrift für Philosophie* 51 (2003): 348–53, here p. 353.
11. Agamben's controversial account of the position of law in Foucault has been much debated among scholars as Agamben's 'Expulsion Thesis', i.e., the 'decisive abandonment of the traditional approach to the problem of power, which is based on juridico-institutional models (the definition of sovereignty, the theory of the State), in favour of an unprejudiced analysis of the concrete ways in which power penetrates subjects' very bodies and forms of life' (*HS* 5). Tom Frost contests Agamben's view that Foucault excluded the law from his formulations of power and argues that his attempt to formulate a critique of Foucault in *Homo Sacer* reflects in many ways a mis-characterisation of Foucault ('Agamben's Sovereign Legalization').
12. Sacco, 'Dalla teologia politica alla teologia economica'.
13. See also de la Durantaye, *Giorgio Agamben*, pp. 207–11.
14. Foucault, *History of Sexuality*, p. 143.
15. Catherine Mills, 'Linguistic Survival and Ethicality: Biopolitics, Subjectification, and Testimony in *Remnants of Auschwitz*', in Norris (ed.), *Politics, Metaphysics, and Death*, pp. 198–221, here p. 202.
16. Agamben will hold on to this thesis also in *The Kingdom and the Glory*, where he takes up Foucault's interpretation of Rousseau in his lecture series *Security, Territory, Population* in order to show that sovereign power does not disappear with the emergence of the modern art of governing, but on the contrary becomes reinforced (*KG* 273–5).
17. Sacco, 'Dalla teologia politica alla teologia economica'.
18. On the differences between Foucault and Agamben on method, see also what Agamben calls signatures in his genealogy of government in *The Kingdom and the Glory*, where he puts forward his reading of *oikonomia*, *ordo* and *gubernatio* as signatures characteristic of God's government of the world and thus key elements in a theory of government.
19. See also Bussolini, 'Critical Encounter', pp. 131–43.
20. Michel Foucault, *Discipline and Punish: The Birth of the Prison*, trans. Alan Sheridan (New York: Vintage Books, 1995). For an extensive discussion of Agamben's paradigmatic method and its reception, see de la Durantaye, *Giorgio Agamben*, pp. 214–17 and 219–26.

21. See Leitgeb and Vismann, 'Das unheilige Leben', p. 19, and Ulrich Rauff, 'An Interview with Giorgio Agamben', *German Law Journal* 5 (2004): 609–14.
22. de la Durantaye, *Giorgio Agamben*, p. 216.
23. See Friedrich Nietzsche, *Untimely Meditations*, trans. R. J. Hollingdale (Cambridge: Cambridge University Press, 1997), p. 60.
24. Leitgeb and Vismann, 'Das unheilige Leben', p. 19.
25. Michel Foucault, *Society Must Be Defended: Lectures at the Collège de France, 1975–1976*, trans. David Macey (London: Penguin Books, 2003). See also Bussolini, 'Critical Encounter', p. 110.
26. 'Der Papst ist ein weltlicher Priester', interview with Abu Bakr Rieger, *Literaturen* 6 (2005): 21–5, here p. 23.
27. Michel Foucault, *Security, Territory, Population. Lectures at the Collège de France 1977–1978*, trans. Graham Burchell (New York: Palgrave Macmillan, 2007), pp. 115–90; Michel Foucault, 'Omnes et Singulatim: Toward a Critique of Political Reason', in James Faubion (ed.), *Power: Essential Works of Foucault, 1954–1984. Vol. 3* (New York: The New Press, 2000), pp. 298–327.
28. Foucault, *Security, Territory, Population*, p. 165.
29. Foucault, 'Omnes et Singulatim', p. 325.
30. For an extensive discussion of this thesis in Agamben, see Dotan Leshem, 'Embedding Agamben's Critique of Foucault: The Theological and Pastoral Origins of Governmentality', *Theory, Culture & Society* 32.3 (2015): 93–113.
31. See Mitchell Dean, 'Governmentality Meets Theology: "The King Reigns, but He Does Not Govern"', *Theory, Culture & Society* 29.3 (2012): 145–58.
32. See Michel Foucault, *The Government of Self and Others: Lectures at the Collège de France, 1982–1983*, trans. Graham Burchell (New York: Palgrave Macmillan, 2010); and *The Courage of Truth. The Government of Self and Others II. Lectures at the Collège de France, 1983–1984*, trans. Graham Burchell (New York: Palgrave Macmillan, 2012).
33. For a discussion of sovereignty and government in Agamben, Foucault and Rousseau, see Jessica Whyte, '"The King Reigns, but He Doesn't Govern": Thinking Sovereignty and Government with Agamben, Foucault and Rousseau', in Tom Frost (ed.), *Giorgio Agamben: Legal, Political and Philosophical Perspectives* (New York: Routledge, 2013), pp. 143–61.
34. Michel Foucault, *The Hermeneutics of the Subject, Lectures at the Collège de France 1981–82*, trans. Graham Burchell (New York: Picador, 2005).
35. See Michel Foucault, 'What is Critique', in Sylvère Lotringer (ed.), *The Politics of Truth* (Los Angeles: Semiotext(e), 1997), pp. 41–81; and Michel Foucault, 'On the Genealogy of Ethics', in Paul Rabinow (ed.), *Ethics: Subjectivity, and Truth: Essential Works of Foucault 1954–1984. Vol. 1* (New York: The New Press, 1994), pp. 253–80.

5 *Martin Heidegger*

MATHEW ABBOTT

It would be hard to overstate the importance of Martin Heidegger's philosophy for Giorgio Agamben's thinking. It is not simply that the Italian philosopher turns at various points in his work to texts and themes from early and later Heidegger, as important as this obviously is. As well as abiding interests in problems of ontology, finitude, facticity and authenticity, Agamben inherits from Heidegger a philosophical programme. That programme is the critique of Western metaphysics: the tradition founded on the neglect, forgetting and oblivion of being, and which – for Agamben as for Heidegger – has reached a point of crisis in modernity after a long historical genesis. Understanding Agamben's debt to the Heideggerian critique of metaphysics is important for grasping the basic problematic of the *Homo Sacer* project, for comprehending its grounds and ultimate stakes, and for getting a clearer sense of the positive political philosophy to which he gestures at crucial moments in the series.

The influence of Heidegger, in other words, runs right to the heart of Agamben's thought. At the same time, however, Agamben's absorption of Heideggerian philosophy is marked by a profound ambivalence: so profound that, on more than one occasion, we find him remarking that the thought of Walter Benjamin functioned for him as a kind of 'antidote'[1] to Heidegger. To understand Agamben's philosophy, then, we not only have to understand the deep influence of Heidegger on it. We also have to understand what it was in Heidegger that Agamben found poisonous, and how he seeks to resist it. To that end I turn here to Agamben's concept of inoperativity, arguing that it may be a reply to Heidegger's notion of *Ereignis* and his associated ideas of appropriation and destiny. Agamben extends the Heideggerian critique of metaphysics, transposing it into a political register with the concept of bare life, but he sees that completing this critique means abandoning the idea that humanity has historical tasks, determined by the epochal dispensation of being with which it finds itself confronted. For Agamben, overcoming metaphysics would mean appropriating not our destiny but our inoperativity: the fact that humanity has no vocation, calling or mission. This thought was not foreign to Heidegger, but Agamben thinks he failed to grasp it properly: a failure that saw him become the 'last philosopher to believe in good faith that the place of the *polis* [. . .] was still practicable, and that it was still possible for men, for a people [. . .] to find their own proper historical destiny' (O 75).

EARLY ENCOUNTERS

In 1966 a 24-year-old Giorgio Agamben was one of a small group of scholars and thinkers invited to attend a seminar at Le Thor led by Martin Heidegger. Though he had just completed studies in law and philosophy at the University of Rome, Agamben has stated that it wasn't until the Le Thor seminars that 'philosophy became possible' for him.[2]

The first two meetings of the 1966 seminar focused on Parmenides and were not recorded by their participants; protocols were kept of three of the remaining five meetings, in which the participants spoke about Heraclitus. The 5 September seminar began with a discussion of the role of λόγος [*logos*] in Fragment 1. Heidegger calls it 'the foremost fundamental word of all the fundamental words', reading it as naming 'beings in their being'.[3] The 8 September seminar opened with a discussion of Fragment 2, where Heraclitus reflects on how the multitude live with their own private opinions of the *logos*, despite the fact that it is ξυνόν. Instead of translating this term as 'universal', Heidegger suggests that we hear in it 'a going together, the coming of one to the other'.[4] Resisting the traditional reading of a central thought of Heraclitus in terms of a unifying coincidence of opposites, Heidegger takes it instead in terms of a co-belonging of contraries, in which each one lets the other 'reciprocally come forth' into its own.[5] The 9 September seminar concluded with remarks that indicate the nature of Heidegger's interest in Heraclitus: the fragments of the pre-Socratic point the way to a mode of thinking fundamentally different from the one ordering our 'age of world impoverishment'.[6] 'I have risked speaking of the "destiny of being" as it first addressed itself to Greek thinking at the beginning of our world', Heidegger says, going on to wonder if we will 'someday be in the position to think this on its own terms'.[7]

The 1968 seminars turned to Hegel and specifically his *Differenzschrift*. The first session was held on 30 August, when the participants discussed an issue in Hegel's text which resonates with the notion of co-belonging Heidegger drew out of Heraclitus: the concept of 'conjoining'.[8] The 31 August session turned to self-consciousness and the scission between subject and object, which Heidegger claims did not hold in the world of Greek thought, emerging as a result of the 'quest for absolute certainty' characteristic of post-Cartesian philosophy.[9] Heidegger also discussed a quotation from Hegel to which he would return in the remaining seminars: 'When the power of conjoining vanishes from the life of men and the opposites lose their living connection [. . .] the need of philosophy arises.'[10] In Hegel's notion of the need of philosophy, Heidegger argued in the remaining sessions, we see traces of an attempt at approaching the question of being.

In *The Man Without Content* Agamben describes an instance of opposites losing their living connection, and which stand in need of sublation through philosophical conjoining: the scission that enters art in modernity, which splits the disinterested experience of the judging spectator from the creative activity of the artist, 'leaving on the one side the aesthetic judgment and on the other artistic subjectivity without content, the pure creative principle' (*MC* 37). Agamben treats Hegel's argument that art is no longer the primary means by which Spirit can encounter itself in the sensuous world, and hence that it 'remains for us a thing of the past' (qtd. in *MC* 52). Although his book contains only a handful of references to Heidegger, the notions of nihilism and metaphysics developed in the German philosopher's later works play a fundamental role in *The Man Without Content*, as when Agamben links Hegel with Heidegger on the destiny of art, arguing that the latter's work 'on the relationship between art and philosophy' shows we 'have good reason not to take Hegel's word on the destiny of art too lightly' (*MC* 53).

IMMANENT CRITIQUE

Developing accounts of concepts that would become fundamental to the *Homo Sacer* series, 1982's *Language and Death* is Agamben's most systematic work, and hence perhaps the most important for understanding his philosophy. It turns on an engagement with the status of language and death in Hegel and Heidegger, staking out similarities and differences between the two thinkers, linking their thought with issues in structural linguistics, and outlining subtle but incisive critiques of both of them.

The book carries out a thematic investigation of the 'essential relationship' (qtd. in *LD* xi) that Heidegger posited between language and death, 'guided by the conviction that we may approach a crucial outer limit in Heidegger's thought – perhaps the very limit about which he told his students, in a seminar conducted in Le Thor during the summer of 1968: "You can see it, I cannot"' (*LD* xi). In his next book, Agamben would describe this moment in more detail, connecting this remark from Heidegger's seminar on Hegel with the idea of inspiration, which he describes in terms of a hiddenness that must be maintained 'in order that there be disclosure' (*IP* 59). This reverberates with Heidegger's understanding of truth as *alētheia*, and the connection he posited between concealment and unconcealment, such that '[c]oncealment deprives *alētheia* of disclosure' while simultaneously 'preserv[ing] what is most proper to *alētheia* as its own'.[11] Nevertheless Agamben goes on to complicate this: 'But this hiddenness is also the infernal core around which the obscurity of character and of destiny thickens; the non-said, growing in thought, precipitates into madness' (*IP* 59). On the first page of *Language and Death*, then, we get a glimpse not only of Agamben's profound debt to Heidegger, but also of his ambivalence. He will come back to the issue of destiny in the book's conclusion.

As the introduction continues, Agamben indicates that his thematic investigation of the relation between language and death will lead him to an attempt at redefining nihilism. He achieves this by recasting the key Heideggerian category of ontotheology. For Heidegger, 'ontotheology' names the tendency, fundamental to the development of Western metaphysics, to conceive of being as a universal ground and cause of beings.[12] Extending this idea, Agamben argues that ontotheology is at work not only in the positive and constructive metaphysical projects pursued by the Western philosophers who came before Heidegger, but also in the negative projects pursued by recent critics of that tradition. If metaphysics was characterised historically by attempts at grounding human being by giving it a foundation in ontotheology, then it cannot be overcome simply through showing that human being lacks a foundation, because this would merely represent the revelation of the negativity that ontotheology has worked to cover over, and which was therefore always at its heart: the 'devastating arrival of its final negative ground [. . .] *nihilism*' (*LD* xiii). This is why, in the book's sixth chapter, we find Agamben critiquing Heidegger's account in *What is Metaphysics?* of the mood of anxiety, where the experience of being is figured in terms of a 'Voice that calls without saying anything' (*LD* 60). Because it is framed in terms of an abyssal encounter with nothingness, Agamben argues, Heidegger's account 'falls back inside' (*LD* 61) metaphysics, as he 'seems to reach a limit that he is unable to overcome' (*LD* 58).

In the book's conclusion, Agamben develops his critique of Heidegger, bringing it to bear on one of the most important concepts of his work after *Being and Time*: *Ereignis*. Sometimes translated as 'enowning' (Emid and Maly), sometimes as 'event' (Rojcewicz and Rojcewicz Vallega-Neu), and sometimes as 'event of appropriation' or 'appropriating event' (Polt),[13] *Ereignis* names a moment of vision in which human being is given over to the truth of being, and vice versa. In *Ereignis*, humanity comes face to face with temporality, experiencing its own historical nature through an experience of the finitude and thus the essential historicity of being as such. Using language that resonates with that of Heidegger's Le Thor seminars, Agamben describes the term as picking out the 'co-belonging of Being and time', a reciprocal relationship of contraries that conveys each of them 'in their proper existence' (*LD* 101). He cites Heidegger's statements that, with *Ereignis*, he attempted to 'think being without regard to the entity': something he took to be equivalent to thinking being 'not in the manner of metaphysics' (qtd. in *LD* 102). Linking the concept with Hegel's Absolute, Agamben argues that this means that *Ereignis* carries with it a sense of historical completion. *Ereignis* is humanity's chance to overcome the nihilism constitutive of metaphysics through an appropriation of its own historicity: an event that must mark the end of the history of being. If metaphysics is 'the history of the self-withdrawal of what is sending in favour of the destinies' (qtd. in *LD* 102), then *Ereignis* should dissolve human destinies by disclosing what sends them. There is no paradox here: as with Hegel's Absolute, the idea is that human history reaches a kind of consummation when humanity can own the fact that it is essentially historical.

Despite all this, Agamben contends, Heidegger's concept remains caught in ontotheology. Drawing on Heidegger's claim that '[w]e can never represent Ereignis' and his statement that 'Ereignis does not exist nor does it present itself' (qtd. in *LD* 102), Agamben argues that – as with the concept of anxiety developed in *What is Metaphysics?* – *Ereignis* betrays negativity, and so remains nihilistic. He makes a crucial (and perhaps surprising) link here between the notions of nihilism and destiny, arguing that even in *Ereignis*, humanity is unable to shake off destiny, because the event of the truth of being remains in thrall to negativity. Once again, the air of paradox here is only that: the claim is that destiny is nihilistic because it represents a failure to come to terms with negativity, the result of an attempt at covering it over. *Ereignis* 'does not seem to be entirely liberated from negativity or the unspeakable' (*LD* 102), so even here 'some possibilities of unveiling remain that thought cannot exhaust and, thus, there are still some historical destinies' (*LD* 104). In Heidegger's later thought, in other words, 'the lineaments of a truly absolved, truly appropriated humanity – one that is wholly without destiny' (*LD* 104) remain obscure.

In *The Coming Community*, Agamben presents accounts of community, ethics, language and the state that clarify these lineaments. In an important passage, he links humanity's status as wholly without destiny to ethics:

> The fact that must constitute the point of departure for any discourse on ethics is that there is no essence, no historical or spiritual vocation, no biological destiny that humans must enact or realize. This is the only reason why something like an ethics can exist, because it is clear that if humans were or had to be this or that substance, this or that destiny, no ethical experience would be possible – there would only be tasks to be done. (*CC* 42)

As Agamben goes on, he works to distinguish this notion of humanity's poverty of historical tasks from nihilism, arguing that it does not entail that human beings are 'simply consigned to nothingness' (*CC* 42). Instead, Agamben indicates, this absolution from destiny is also an absolution from negativity. In the terms of *Language and Death*, this is an experience of 'ethos, the proper dwelling of humanity' (*LD* 53); in the language Agamben would go on to develop, it is an experience of inoperativity. In these moments, Agamben is working to articulate a notion of groundlessness that is not simply a lack of ground, but a form of potentiality: 'the simple fact of one's own existence as possibility' (*CC* 42). This is how Agamben will carry out his immanent critique of Heidegger.

HEIDEGGER REFIGURED

With its emphasis on an obliviation that acts as a negative foundation for the development of Western politics, the *zoè/bios* schema interrogated throughout the *Homo Sacer* series is deeply indebted to Heidegger's critique of metaphysics, and his claim that it is founded on the forgetting of being, which leaves it unable to think the difference between being and beings as the co-belonging of contraries. Indeed the very opposition between *zoè* and *bios* may be a transposition of the ontological difference, where *zoè* – as the fact of life as such – is mapped on to being as such, and *bios* – as the multiplicity of ways of life – is mapped on to the multiplicity of beings. This would explain Agamben's links throughout the book between the nihilistic trajectory of Western politics and the nihilistic trajectory of Western metaphysics, and his repeated comparisons between the contemporary political situation and the 'epochal situation of metaphysics' (*HS* 188): the oblivion of being and the exclusion of *zoè* are two aspects of a single tendency. In the *Homo Sacer* series, Agamben recasts the central problematic of *Language and Death*, with politics now figured as 'the fundamental structure of Western metaphysics', and the political predicament of capitalist modernity rendered in terms of a crisis in 'the essential structure of the metaphysical tradition' (*HS* 8).

With the crucial category of bare life – which, as life stripped of all features save the mere capacity to be killed, is 'certainly as indeterminate and impenetrable' (*HS* 182) as the metaphysical category of pure being without content – Agamben gives political purchase to the notion of negativity that was so important in *Language and Death*. As the form that *zoè* assumes in modernity, when it is captured by the biopolitical apparatuses that Michel Foucault tracked in his research, the arrival of bare life on the political scene is the flipside of the 'devastating arrival' (*LD* xiii) of negativity as nihilism in the twilight of Western metaphysics. Just as with negativity, bare life was held at bay in the history of being, but has emerged as a problem in modernity and forced a crisis in that history. As Agamben frames the problem in the final section of the book: 'Pure Being, bare life – what is contained in these two concepts, such that both the metaphysics and the politics of the West find their foundation and sense in them and in them alone?' (*HS* 182) As for the Agamben of *Homo Sacer*, for the Agamben of *Language and Death* 'that which is excluded from the community is, in reality, that on which the entire life of the community is founded', as this originary act of exclusion 'simply abandons the naked natural life to its own violence and its own unspeakableness, in order to ground in them every cultural rule and all language' (*LD* 105). *Zoè* is to bare life as negativity is to nihilism. Because of the deep connection Agamben identifies between life and politics, this analogy allows him to cash out the political implications of the Heideggerian critique of metaphysics.

The Kingdom and the Glory develops a genealogy of an 'economic paradigm' (*KG* 44) in Western thought, which Agamben contrasts with the paradigm of sovereignty he traced in *Homo Sacer*. He argues that the tension between the two consists in how economy is forced somehow to function both as the foundation of and as a supplement to sovereign power, just as natural life is both excluded from yet constitutive of the *polis*. As in *Homo Sacer*, Agamben draws on Foucault, but argues that the French thinker's research 'failed to be completed' because he did not grasp the deep historical origins of his problematic. As such, Agamben argues, Foucault's genealogy of governmentality must be 'extended and moved back in time' (*KG* 110), and specifically to early Trinitarian thought, which grappled with problems of economy handed down to it from the classical world. As Agamben develops his argument, he connects it to Heidegger's account of the history of being, describing a 'nexus that links the theological problem of *oikonomia* [...] to the problem of ontology and, in particular, to Heidegger's reading of the ontological difference and of the "epochal" structure of the history of being' (*KG* 64).

This can help explain Agamben's conviction that, to understand the economic paradigm and the forms of governmentality for which it provides the conceptual foundation, we should note its genesis in Ancient Greece, for 'without this being one of his aims, Aristotle transmitted to Western politics the paradigm of the divine regime of the world as a double system' (*KG* 84). It can also help explain the book's focus on the problem of providence, which produces puzzles that are importantly similar to the ones with which Heidegger wrestled in his work on *Ereignis*, history and destiny. Further, the conceptual heart of the book – the notion that sovereignty and government form two halves of a 'bipolar machine, whose unity always runs the risk of collapsing' (*KG* 62) – again repeats the basic problematic of the conjoining of contraries that Heidegger and his students worked through at Le Thor. But the book clarifies that problematic in such a way that it starts to move beyond its provenance in Heidegger. Instead of figuring the problem in terms of conjoining the ontic and the ontological, Agamben works to figure it in terms of a connective separation, such that the task is not to bring together two contraries, but to expose the 'inoperative disarticulation of both *bios* and *zoè*' (*KG* 259). This is not incidental to Agamben's critique of Heidegger's notion of destiny, because the latter conceived it precisely in terms of a relation between the ontic and the ontological, where ontological dispensation sets up for us an ontic historical mission, such that being *as such* is taken on as a task.

As this point indicates, while Heidegger's account of the development of Western metaphysics is crucial to the genealogy presented in *The Kingdom and the Glory*, the book also presents a powerful critique of Heidegger, which echoes the one Agamben developed through the 1980s. In particular he turns to Heidegger's 'decision to pose the problem of technology as the ultimate problem of metaphysics' (*KG* 252). The significance of this problem, Agamben claims, can be grasped in light of the genealogy presented in *The Kingdom and the Glory*, but that genealogy will also 'reveal its limits' (*KG* 252). On the one hand, Agamben argues that his account shows that the notion of *Gestell* – which Heidegger defined as the violent form of ordering at the heart of modern technology, which reveals entities in their capacity for exploitation – 'is nothing other than that which, from within the horizon of our investigation, appears as *oikonomia*' (*KG* 252). On the other hand, he argues that Heidegger's 'attempt to resolve the problem of technology' (*KG* 252) failed because of his insistence that 'it is not something that can be decided by men' (*KG* 252). It failed, in other words, because of his commitment to a notion of destiny, and his fixation on the idea that human action is not adequate to the problem of metaphysics, because resolving it would depend not on humanity but on the possibility of a new dispensation of being. As Charles Guignon argues, for Heidegger '[h]umans are participants in this "destining" of being but are not its sole agents'.[14] This commitment is part of what drove Heidegger's thinking during the 1930s and 1940s, when he produced a number of politically fraught, indeed chauvinistic works on the particular historical task of the German people. Importantly, however, it also led him to the quietism to which he retreated after the war. After all, if in his post-war works Heidegger retreats from ontic politics, then he does not fully retreat from the notion of destiny. Rather than abandon the idea of a people seizing its historical mission in the history of being, he just relinquishes the idea that the time for such seizure is ripe. In the words of James Phillips, 'Heidegger *defers* the emergence of the Volk'.[15] Hence in his final works Heidegger's philosophy 'appears to pass into religion', as he falls back on a notion of salvation that 'does not signify an action but a bringing back into the essence, a guarding, a preserving' (*KG* 253).

In *Opus Dei*, Agamben returns to Heidegger's philosophy of technology, granting it an important place in his archaeological account of the concept of duty. Tracing the development of the concept through the history of Christian liturgy and its re-emergence in new guises in modern philosophy, Agamben addresses Heidegger's account of the transformation in ontology effected in the Roman period (and carried forward by the scholastics), when Aristotelian and Neoplatonic notions of being as *energeia* gave way to the metaphysical image of being as *actualitas*. For Heidegger, the paradigm that made this transformation possible was the Christian idea of creation, which he placed 'at the center of his reconstruction of the history of being', defining 'the central trait of modern metaphysics as a working in the sense of a causing and producing' (*OD* 60). Effectively identifying *actualitas* with causality, modern metaphysics in turn 'renders possible the transformation of truth into certainty, in which the human being [. . .] secures its unconditional dominion over the world by means of techniques' (*OD* 61). If this allowed Heidegger to 'think the essence of technology as production and disposition' through the figure of *Gestell*, however, then it also saw him fail to grasp the 'more refined and diffuse form of management' (*OD* 61) at work in the liturgical paradigm, which exceeds concepts of causal production. This claim forms the basis of a deeper critique of Heidegger, which builds on the ones developed in Agamben's other works: because *Dasein* finds itself forced to 'assume its own being thrown into facticity' (*OD* 61), it remains under the spell of work and liturgy. Thus Heidegger's ontology 'is more in solidarity with the paradigm of operativity that he intends to critique than is commonly believed' (*OD* 61), as we find him figuring the relationship between *Sein* and *Dasein* as 'something like a liturgy' (*OD* 62).

The profound influence of Heidegger on Agamben's thought is particularly evident in *The Use of Bodies*, which turns to him repeatedly throughout its three sections. In the first Agamben develops accounts of use and selfhood before engaging at length with the early Heidegger's concepts of care and equipmentality. This provides the grounds for another confrontation with him on technology, as Agamben develops *Opus Dei*'s claim that he failed to grasp its liturgical character. Connecting the role of technology in modernity to the status of the slave in the classical world, Agamben argues that, in 'liberating human beings from necessity', both provide conditions for the possibility of anthropogenesis: 'the becoming fully human of the living human being' (*UB* 78). Because Heidegger failed to see the nature of the technological instrument, Agamben argues, he was not equipped to engage the metaphysical machine that works to produce the human being. The second section develops a Foucauldian account of the historical a priori that has clear debts to Heidegger, but which breaks with him by insisting that ontological change depends not on destiny but on modifications in 'the complex of possibilities that the articulation between language and world' (*UB* 111) discloses as human history. It argues that only a modal ontology can 'resolve the aporias' (*UB* 145) of Heidegger's thought (*UB* 174). This leads Agamben to deepen further his critique of Heidegger on destiny and *Ereignis*, as he works to show that the notion of a 'task or a test that the human being must take up and endure' (*UB* 177) is really a repetition of the founding gesture of Western metaphysics, in which 'an animality or non-humanity' is passed over as the negative foundation of the 'truly human' (*UB* 181). He fleshes out this claim with another account of his time with Heidegger at Le Thor, telling a story about watching him motionlessly behold Montagne Sainte-Victoire, 'as though struck dead' before it: 'Perhaps [...] he still sought to assume the "there," to remain in the clearing of Being, in suspended animality' (*UB* 188). If the political was always opaque to Heidegger, Agamben implies, it is because he was unable to grasp life, and its intimate relation to being and ontology.

The third section is Agamben's most extended treatment of the crucial concept of form-of-life, or a life that is inseparable from its form, which is meant to jam the metaphysical machine that drives the presupposition, exclusion, inclusion and domination of bare life, and which Agamben accuses Heidegger of unknowingly sustaining. Because 'life is the political declension of being', Agamben argues, it will be impossible to deactivate the biopolitical machine without also deactivating 'the ontological apparatus' (*UB* 205). To act politically in Agamben's sense means to 'neutralize the bipolar *zoè/bios* apparatus' (*UB* 225) by demonstrating that 'there is never anything like a bare life' (*UB* 228); to carry out thought is to become receptive to 'the mode in which a singularity bears witness to itself in being and being expresses itself in the singular body' (*UB* 233). In both cases, we find ourselves 'deactivating the opposites and rendering them inoperative', situated 'beyond the Heideggerian perspective [. . .] at the center of the ontologico-political machine': the very point at which it 'can no longer function' (*UB* 239). As in *The Kingdom and the Glory*, the strategy is not one of conjoining but of 'the exposition of the central void, of the gap that separates' (*UB* 265).[16]

Against Heidegger, then, Agamben is asking us to own up to our inoperativity, which is what shipwrecks any attempt to take on bare life or being as political or historical tasks. For Agamben, the history of being is just the history of our failures to grasp this: failures that have not resulted from some external agency at work in the epochal determination of being, but from our attempts to refuse its contingency and gratuity, and the impossibility of grounding our action in it. The history of being is not the history of its dispensations but 'an errancy [. . .] that seems interminable' (*UB* 272). Contra Heidegger, then, the resolution of the problem of technology – and so of nihilism – does not require that we prepare for the coming of a new god, but that we render it inoperative through political praxis. Standing Heidegger on his feet in this way, Agamben is able to rescue a notion of agency from his destruction of the history of being, refusing his equation of action with the metaphysics of subjectivity. This is the heart of the difference between the two thinkers, which Agamben has established through his reading of Benjamin, in whose work he finds the outlines of a notion of 'anomic human action' (*SE* 54) that could jam the ordering machine of economy, and neutralise the violence of sovereign power. In other words, the antidote to Heidegger is communism. Yet this is a communism that has passed through his critique of metaphysics, emerging out of the collapse of that critique as its very completion: a politics of inoperativity conceived 'as a properly human praxis' (*KG* 251). What would communism look like if it gave up the 'ingenuous emphasis on productivity and labor that has long prevented modernity from accessing politics as man's most proper dimension' (*KG* xiii)? Agamben thinks it must depart from an appropriation of our lack of destiny: the fact that there is nothing we must do or be, no tasks for us to complete, and so no work for us to carry out. That this is not nihilism is one of his most significant discoveries.

NOTES

1. See the discussions of these remarks in Leland de la Durantaye, *Giorgio Agamben: A Critical Introduction* (Stanford: Stanford University Press, 2009), pp. 53–4 and 303–13.
2. Qtd. in de la Durantaye, *Giorgio Agamben*, p. 2.
3. Martin Heidegger, *Four Seminars: Le Thor 1966, 1968, 1969, Zähringen 1973*, trans. Andrew Mitchell and François Raffoul (Bloomington: Indiana University Press, 2003), p. 2.
4. Heidegger, *Four Seminars*, p. 4.
5. Heidegger, *Four Seminars*, p. 5.
6. Heidegger, *Four Seminars*, p. 9.
7. Heidegger, *Four Seminars*, p. 9.
8. Heidegger, *Four Seminars*, p. 12.
9. Heidegger, *Four Seminars*, p. 13.
10. Heidegger, *Four Seminars*, p. 14.
11. Martin Heidegger, 'On the Essence of Truth', in *Basic Writings*, trans. David Farrell Krell (San Francisco: HarperCollins, 1993), p. 130.
12. Martin Heidegger, 'The Onto-Theo-Logical Constitution of Metaphysics', in *Identity and Difference*, trans. Joan Stambaugh (New York: Harper & Row, 1957), p. 57.
13. See Martin Heidegger, *Contributions to Philosophy (From Enowning)*, trans. Parvis Emid and Kenneth Maly (Bloomington: Indiana University Press, 2000); *Contributions to Philosophy (Of the Event)*, trans. Richard Rojcewicz and Daniela Vallega-Neu (Bloomington: Indiana University Press, 2012); Richard Polt, *The Emergency of Being: On Heidegger's "Contributions to Philosophy"* (Ithaca, NY: Cornell University Press, 2006).
14. Charles Guignon, 'The History of Being', in Hubert L. Dreyfus and Mark Wrathall (eds), *A Companion to Heidegger* (Malden, MA: Blackwell, 2005), p. 393.
15. James Phillips, *Heidegger's Volk: Between National Socialism and Poetry* (Stanford: Stanford University Press, 2005), p. 23 (emphasis added). It should be said that Phillips argues that in his post-war writings Heidegger recasts the notion of Volk so as to encompass not simply the German people and their historical destiny, but the mission of the West more generally (see p. 219).

16. With its account of how the notion of the soul that is developed in the final pages of the *Republic* figures the fact that *zoè* and *bios* are 'neither separate nor coincident' (*UB* 262), the final chapter of *The Use of Bodies* also consolidates another of Agamben's differences from Heidegger: his apparent belief that it was not the work of Plato but that of Aristotle which first bequeathed nihilistic metaphysics to humanity.

6 Paul the Apostle

TED JENNINGS

By far the majority of Agamben's books (about 23) make reference to Paul's letters, often at key points in discussions of concepts that he finds important for his own work as a thinker of the political. This reliance upon Paul in the context of political philosophy goes back to Spinoza (and we should recall that Agamben has held the Baruch Spinoza chair at the European Graduate School). In his *Theological-Political Treatise* of 1670 Spinoza identified Paul as the most philosophical of the biblical writers and made use of Paul's thought to advance a view of the constitution of a liberal or secular republic. Agamben also makes significant use of Paul, but this time as the major thinker of a messianic politics, a thinking with which Agamben identifies his own work.

While in his reading of Paul Agamben occasionally refers to modern theologians such as Barth and Moltmann, as well as modern biblical scholars, the most important intellectual context within which he reads Paul is provided, on the one hand, by Carl Schmitt with his reflections on political theology and, on the other, by Walter Benjamin, especially the latter's theses 'On the Concept of History'.

At one point or another in Agamben's work all the texts traditionally attributed to Paul make an appearance. In academic circles of Pauline scholarship it has become customary to separate seven 'authentic' letters (Romans, 1 and 2 Corinthians, Galatians, Philippians, Philemon and 1 Thessalonians) from 'deutero-Pauline' letters (Ephesians, Colossians and 2 Thessalonians) believed to be strongly influenced by Pauline thought. In addition, the 'pastoral epistles' (1 and 2 Timothy and Titus) are placed in a category of their own, reflecting a much later attempt to domesticate and institutionalise Paul while still claiming his authority. Moreover, there is the odd case of Hebrews which by broad consensus is not a letter and certainly not by 'Paul'.

In keeping with the culture of Catholicism within which these distinctions are often ignored in favour of the traditional attribution of all these texts to Paul (save perhaps for Hebrews), Agamben seems to accept Pauline attribution at face value. We may recall here the use of 2 Thessalonians by Heidegger in his *Phenomenology of Religious Life* as offering (with Galatians and 1 Thessalonians) decisive insight into the comportment of early Pauline Christians.

With this in mind, we can ask which texts seem to be decisive for Agamben's reading of Paul. Of course, Romans leaps immediately to mind, since Agamben has written a book subtitled a 'Commentary on Romans'. In that as well as other texts, passages from 1 Corinthians also play a prominent role. In addition, we should notice his significant use of Galatians and of 2 Corinthians. In contrast, Agamben makes little use of Philippians, 1 Thessalonians and Philemon. Of the deutero-Pauline texts, Agamben makes some use of Ephesians and Colossians but very significant use of 2 Thessalonians. References to the pastoral epistles generally occur when Agamben seems to be using a concordance to make sure all the relevant Pauline passages are noted (e.g., *KG* 166, 244; *HP* 94). In general, this means that these references are incidental and play no material role in the development of Agamben's thought. The case of Hebrews is more complex. It plays a significant role in some discussions (*KG* 239–40; *OD* 7) but it is sometimes difficult to determine whether Agamben regards this as a Pauline text or not.

In what follows I will attempt to show the Pauline passages that play a regular and decisive role in Agamben's thought. This will include both 'authentic' as well as 'deutero-' Pauline texts.

THE LAW (GRACE)

The relation to the law is the theme in Pauline literature to which Agamben gives the most attention. Already in *Homo Sacer*, referring to Kafka, he writes: 'the Messiah is the figure in which the great monotheistic religions sought to master the problem of law [. . .], in Judaism, as in Christianity or Shiite Islam, the Messiah's arrival signifies the fulfilment and complete consummation of the Law', and he refers explicitly to Sabbateanism and to Paul's letter to the Romans (*HS* 56). The stakes of this issue are clarified when he again refers to the three monotheistic traditions and the messianic overcoming of the law and contrasts this with Christianity having 'struck with the law a lasting compromise', thereby renouncing its messianic vocation (*ME* 133). This notion of Christianity having lost its messianic vocation will return in the discussion of the *katechon* below.

In his commentary on Romans, *The Time that Remains*, Agamben sets out, as he says, 'to restore Paul's Letters to the status of the fundamental messianic text for the Western tradition' (*TR* 1). However, we have to wait until the fifth 'day' (of six) of the seminar to grapple with what he has identified as the most important issue, the law. He notes that early commentators from the time of Origen recognised the 'aporetic' character of Paul's approach to the law. On the one hand, Paul appears to oppose the law as that which brings sin and death, but on the other hand, he can claim the law is 'holy, just and good'. How is this to be understood? Agamben proposes his own solution which has the advantage of seeming to be based in the text itself. It has to do with Paul's use of the term *katargein* or *katargeo*. Agamben claims to have made the discovery of the significance of this term (*TR* 95), which he takes to mean to deactivate, to render inoperative, or to suspend the efficacy of something, in this case the law. On the one hand, this does not mean to destroy or abolish. On the other hand, it also does not permit its object to remain as it was, in force or operative. Thus, with respect to the law and its works, it does not simply negate or annihilate them, but renders them 'no-longer-at-work' (*TR* 97). In this way, he understands the law to be fulfilled (Rom. 13:8–10) on the basis of its first having been deactivated: 'The messianic is not the destruction but the deactivation of the law, rendering the law inexecutable' (*TR* 98). At the same time this is to be understood as preserving or fulfilling the law: 'Justice without law is not the negation of the law, but the realization and fulfilment, the *pleroma*, of the law' (*TR* 107).

Agamben returns to this question in *State of Exception* (2003), published four years after the lectures in *The Time that Remains*. Here he notes the assertion of Walter Benjamin, whom he had previously identified as one whose thinking is decisively influenced by Paul (*TR* 138–45), to the effect that the law that is studied but no longer practised is the gate to justice (*SE* 64). He notes that this 'deposition' of the law is an issue that concerns both primitive Christianity and the Marxian tradition (in the latter case he is referring to the well-known question in Marxist thought about what happens to the state once the revolution has succeeded). Referring again to Benjamin, Agamben maintains that the path to justice (which is not yet justice itself) is not the erasure of the law but its deactivation. But in what consists this deactivation or deposition? It is a law that no longer has force or application. This is even more clearly stated when he asserts that 'the only truly political action is that which severs the nexus between violence and the law' (*SE* 88).

Thus far we have the deactivation of the law as that which disconnects law from the threatened or actual violence of its application or enforcement. It is this which will make it available for other uses, here, most especially, study. But if, as Agamben insists following Benjamin, the deactivation of the law which makes it an object of study but not enforcement is the gate that leads to but is not justice itself, what positive indicator do we have concerning the 'content' or character of justice into which this gate opens? As is well known, Paul proposes that it is love of one's neighbour that accomplishes or fulfils the law. Agamben certainly knows and seems to endorse this indication. He makes reference to this text in *Remnants of Auschwitz* (*RA* 69), and even earlier he had maintained that '[t]he punishment for those who go away from love is to be handed over to the power of judgment: they will have to judge one another' (*ME* 133). Agamben does not give us much in the way of reflection on the meaning of this 'love' that fulfils law and accomplishes justice (Paul famously does so in 1 Corinthians 13, but Agamben does not favour us with extended comment on this passage). His later reflections on 'form-of-life' may be construed as at least a formal indication of the manner in which this love may make itself concrete.

Agamben had mentioned judgement as that to which we are consigned if we 'go away from love'. In a later text on the trial of Jesus, he will return to this question. After noting Karl Barth's development of the significance of Jesus' being 'handed over', first by Judas to the judgement of the Judaean authorities and then by the latter to the judgement of Pilate, Agamben notes that the resultant crucifixion of Jesus 'has abolished and realized all traditions' (*PJ* 29). This echoes what he had said of the law earlier. But here he notes, rightly I think, that it is the cross itself which occasions the severing of the law from the mechanisms of enforcement and so of violence. He also recalls that 'the radical critique of every judgment is an essential part of Jesus' teaching' (*PJ* 37) and notes that this is paralleled in Rom. 14:3. Indeed, even though he knows that the Gospel accounts were written after Paul, he supposes that Paul may have been aware of some of the traditions concerning Jesus' trial (and perhaps of his teaching) so that '[j]ust as the law cannot justify anyone, so also can it judge no one' (*PJ* 52).

That the law can no longer judge is also brought to expression in a different argument that Agamben explores in *The Sacrament of Language* in connection with the relation between oath and curse. He asserts: 'The Pauline argument – and therefore the very meaning of redemption – can be understood only if it is situated in the context of mutual belonging, in a juridical and not only religious sense, of law and curse' (*SL* 38). Here he refers to Gal. 3:10–13 in contrast to Deut. 21:23, and suggests that not only is the abolition of curse important for

Paul, but that this may be connected to the abolition of oath as well, citing Jas. 5:12 and Matt. 5:33–7 (*SL* 42, 44).

As is clear from the foregoing, the deactivation of the law is extended by Agamben to include the acts of judgement (which enforce the law) and the more general connection of oath to curse. This entails an extension of the theme of deactivation to all that wields power. In *The Kingdom and the Glory*, the text that contains the most diverse citation of Pauline texts, Agamben notes that Paul uses this terminology of *katargeo* to indicate the messianic rendering inoperative of all superhuman principalities and powers (*KG* 165–6). Although he notes that for Aquinas and others these powers (thrones, dominions and so on), are 'angelic or heavenly powers' (*KG* 159), they may also be understood as those more mundane powers that determine or govern human existence. Thus the terms employed, for example in Col. 2:15 and Eph. 6:12, are 'commonly used in the Greek of that time as a way of indicating human powers in a generic way' (*KG* 166) This would also mean therefore social, political and economic institutions that govern human life; 'the ultimate and glorious telos of the law and the angelic powers, as well as the profane powers, is to be deactivated and made inoperative' (*KG* 166). (Oddly Agamben does not seem to attend much to Phil. 2:8–11 in this regard.)

We might pursue this line of thinking if we were to ask what becomes of economics when it is loosed from its connection to the telos of acquisition and the law of the market, or what would become of globalisation should it be deactivated from its connection to hegemony and imperialism. These are questions which some had hoped would be at the forefront of discussion in the concluding volume of the *Homo Sacer* series, *The Use of Bodies*, but this was not to be. Agamben notes that this deactivation is even said to be true of the messiah himself when he is called the head of the body (Col. 1:18; Eph. 5:23), in that the consummation entails that 'there will no longer be any distinction between the head and the body, because God will be all in all' (*STA* 63).

'AS IF NOT' (*hōs mē*)

We have thus far focused on deactivation that leads to another use at the level of law and state, at the level of force and the application of the 'or else' of the powers that seem external or 'objective'. But Agamben also deploys this figure with respect to what might be termed the subjective side of messianic existence.

The crucial passage here is 1 Corinthians 7, to which Agamben devotes considerable attention on the 'second day' of his seminar/

commentary on Romans. Following up on a suggestion made by Heidegger in his *Phenomenology of Religious Life* (*TR* 33–4), where he had indicated an 'appropriation' (or a taking on) of the situation, Agamben will insist instead on its alternative use (*TR* 34). It is the combination of 'as if not' (the suspension of the given condition) and its 'use' that will together constitute the characteristic comportment of the messianic relative to the given conditions of existence.

The 'as if not' is most clearly found in 1 Cor. 7:29–31: 'I mean, brethren, the appointed time has grown very short; from now on let those who have wives live as though they had none [. . .] for the form of this world is passing away.' This 'as if not' is then retroactively used to interpret what Paul has to say about circumcision and uncircumcision, slave and free, beginning with 'Let everyone lead the life which the Lord has assigned to him and in which God has called him' (1 Cor. 7:17). The point that Agamben makes in reading Paul is that the given social or religious structures in which one finds oneself do not themselves need to be changed; rather, what is changed is one's relation to them. In this way, like the law, they are rendered inoperative, no longer determinative of messianic existence. But they are an object of a new use. Thus more is at stake here than a simple stoic detachment, for all is related to the messianic 'use'. (Here Agamben makes brief reference to the transformation of the situation of Onesimus as slave in Paul's letter to Philemon, a transformation that would warrant further exploration from this perspective.)

Already in this text Agamben refers to 'the Franciscan claim to a *usus* opposed to property' in which 'what mattered was to create a space that escaped the grasp of power and its laws, without entering into conflict with them yet rendering them inoperative' (*TR* 27). This became the theme of Agamben's later work on the Franciscans, in which he would maintain that they should have made use of this Pauline passage which contains 'hints of a theory of use' (*HP* 139). Agamben will return to this theme at the end of the *Homo Sacer* series, when he will maintain that 'the factical and juridico-political conditions in which each one finds himself must be neither hypostasized nor simply changed. The messianic call does not confer a new substantial identity but consists first of all in the capacity to "use" the factical conditions in which each one finds himself' (*UB* 56). In the Epilogue to this book Agamben returns to this figure all the more clearly, connecting it to the idea of the rendering inoperative of the law: 'The "as not" is a deposition without abdication. Living in the form of the "as not" means rendering destitute all juridical and social ownership without this deposition founding a new identity' (*UB* 274).

One of the ways that Agamben makes clear that no new identity is constituted for the messianic community is through his reflection on the Pauline *pistis*. He insists that this is not to be understood as belief in relation to doctrine or dogma, but rather as loyalty (TR 91, 114–18). This loyalty is oriented towards the messianic word, a word that has the character of promise (and as such also rupture).

'THE NOW TIME' (*ho nyn kairos*)

The 'now time', which Agamben will elaborate in connection with Paul, is first introduced in connection with Benjamin in the very early 1978 *Infancy and History* (IH 110, 165). Two decades later it becomes one of the main emphases of his reflections on Romans.

Time as generally represented is a line that passes from past to present to future. This is called *chronos*, time that is extended. On such a representation, the 'end' is situated at the far end of the line that stretches towards the future. In contrast to this, there is what may be termed *kairos*, which is the decisive or significant moment. It is contracted *chronos*. In this discussion Agamben sharply distinguishes messianic time from eschatological time, where the latter is a representation of the end of time at the end of the timeline (TR 62). In a later text, Agamben will conflate eschatology with messianic time while still retaining its distinction from apocalyptic as the depiction of the end. This move corresponds to that of Barth and Bultmann and perhaps to Moltmann, to whom he also refers (MM 37).

The contraction of time in the now time is reflected in the way in which the past is given a present significance in the Pauline notions of typos and recapitulation. In the former, what has happened in the past (for example, Adam) becomes a type or prefiguration of the messianic now. And that messianic now recapitulates the past as it is thrust forward into the messianic now. On the other hand, the *parousia* or appearance of the messiah no longer pertains to a postponed future but presses upon the present (see WA 53 and NU 18, which reproduce the same essay). Although Agamben does not directly say this, it seems to work out in Paul as a certain scrambling of temporal codes in which the future has already taken place, or is taking place in the present and the past (the resurrection of the messiah in the past is also both our immediate future and our present). In this connection he cites Benjamin's notion that every moment is a door through which the messiah may enter (TR 71). This now time or messianic time is precisely that contraction of time in which the law is rendered inoperative and the messianic community lives as if not determined by the structures of the world that is 'passing away'. Agamben illustrates the character of messianic time with a complex reflection on poetry and, in particular, on rhymed poetry. He maintains 'that rhyme issues from Christian poetry as a metrical-linguistic transcodification of messianic time and is structured according to the play of typological relations and recapitulations evoked by Paul' (*TR* 85). He even notes the ways in which this rhyming tendency is already directly present in Paul in 1 Cor. 7:29–31 and 15:42–4 (*TR* 86–7). He concludes by suggesting that 'rhyme, understood in the broad sense of the term as the articulation of a difference between semiotic series and semantic series is the messianic heritage that Paul leaves to modern poetry' (*TR* 87).

THE RESTRAINER (*katechon*)

Like Heidegger before him, Agamben takes 2 Thessalonians to be a letter from Paul. Unlike Heidegger, however, Agamben focuses his attention on 2 Thess. 2:3–9, which deals with a quasi-apocalyptic narrative concerning the messiah, the man of lawlessness and the *katechon* or restrainer. This third figure restrains the outbreak of lawlessness or chaos for a time before being overwhelmed by the man of lawlessness, who is then overcome by the messiah. The *katechon* had been regularly associated with the state from the time of Tertullian through Hobbes, and Carl Schmitt had maintained that it was the basis for any Christian understanding of the state (*TR* 109).

Reflection on this passage and this figure has a significant history in the writings of Agamben. He first makes use of it, not in relation to the theory of the state, but in relation to a sort of theory of poetry. He suggests that the poem is that which 'slows and delays the advent of the messiah' (*EP* 114). This brief allusion indicates the main direction of Agamben's reading of the text. A 'naive' reading of the text would suggest that the *katechon* delays, not the coming of the messiah, but rather the outbreak of chaos associated with the 'man of lawlessness'. When this delay fails, then the messiah arrives to overcome the man of lawlessness. Thus, characteristic of traditional interpretation is not the delay of the messiah as such, but the restraint of chaos/violence associated with the mysterious man of lawlessness. Agamben's reading tends to elide the figure of the man of lawlessness to arrive at a simple delay of the *parousia*. In this way Agamben's interpretation diminishes the apocalyptic features of the text (a 'history of the future') in order to stage a direct confrontation between the *katechon* and the messiah. This erasure of the man of lawlessness depends upon a sort of conflation between the messianic abolition of the law and the power of the man of *anomos* (*TR* 111).

Agamben returns to this view of the *katechon* as that which 'defers or eliminates concrete eschatology' (*KG* 8) and associates this with Troeltsch's famous saying that Christianity has closed its eschatological office or bureau, a reopening of which Agamben attributes to Benjamin, Moltmann and Dodd (later Barth and even von Balthasar will also be adduced [*MM* 37]). In a 2009 lecture in Notre Dame Cathedral, Agamben wonders whether the Church will 'finally grasp the historical occasion and recover its messianic vocation' (*CR* 41).

Subsequently Agamben returns to this last question in two related addresses to the Church, in which he reflects on the significance of the abdication of Pope Benedict XVI. In the first of these, Agamben returns to his question about a return of the Church to its messianic vocation. Here he will add interesting twists to his interpretation of the *katechon*. Taking account of suggestions by the fourth-century Donatist Tychonius, he understands the Church as divided between the antichrist and the messiah. The former is then associated with 'economy', while the latter refers to eschatology (*MM* 16). But here we also get a sort of ambiguation of the man of lawlessness, who, while in certain respects like the Christian (referring to 1 Cor. 9:21), is also 'the unveiling of the lawlessness that today defines every constituted power within which State and terrorism form a single system' (*MM* 35). It is not altogether clear how the relation between the lawlessness of the messianic and the lawlessness of the 'system' is to be untangled. It is clear that Agamben thinks the Church should renounce the role of restraining the messianic. Perhaps this means confronting, like the messiah, the lawlessness of the system, whether political or ecclesiastical, in our own *kairos*, rather than temporising like the *katechon* with that system.

In this text and later in *Stasis*, Agamben refers not only to 2 Thessalonians, but also to the contrasting reflection of Paul in 1 Thessalonians, where we are told that the messiah will arrive unexpectedly in a time of peace and quiet like a thief in the night (*STA* 68). It is the contrast between this last image and the rather lurid apocalypticism of 2 Thessalonians 2 that leads many scholars to dispute the authenticity of 2 Thessalonians. In that respect, 1 Thessalonians seems more compatible with Agamben's focus on the now time in Paul.

OTHER THEMES

We may briefly mention additional themes that Agamben derives from Paul. The first is his reflection on the remnant, dependent on Rom. 9:6–29. While many commentators on Paul have sought to interpret this figure in a non-dialectical way as simply referring to a fragment or fraction of the whole (of Israel), Agamben notices that it is paradoxically related to the Pauline assertion in Rom. 11:26 that 'all Israel will be saved'. Earlier Agamben had deployed this figure: 'in the end the remnant appears as a redemptive machine allowing for the salvation of the very whole whose division and loss it had signified' (*RA* 163). This reference is elaborated on the 'third day' of the commentary on Romans, which is devoted to the notion of separation. At first this separation is related to Paul himself (as one separated), but then to the presumed division between Jew and gentile which he maintains is itself cut or divided through the messianic announcement. This then raises the question of the remnant as a possible figure of Judaism divided between those who respond to the messianic announcement and those who do not, a separation that has served to disqualify actually existing Judaism from salvation. It is this anti-Judaic and supercessionist logic that Agamben overturns by connecting it to Romans 11 (*TR* 53–8): 'the remnant is not so much the object of salvation as its instrument, that which properly makes salvation possible' (*TR* 56). Conceived in this way, the remnant 'only concerns messianic time and only exists therein', which is to say the 'now time' (*TR* 56). In secular, or rather – as Agamben would later insist – profane, terms then, 'the remnant is the figure, or the substantiality assumed by a people in a decisive moment, and as such is the only real political subject' (*TR* 57). That is, it is only that which is constituted as a fragment, as left over or left out, that can point to and propel towards a whole that exceeds any actually existing totality, that is, towards salvation.

In an earlier text Agamben follows Paul in considering an even wider frame for messianic salvation. This is found in Romans 8 which points towards the salvation not only of the human world, but of the world as such. In *The Open*, Agamben enters into discussion with Heidegger precisely about the relation of the human and the animal. Like Heidegger, he also refers to Rom. 8:19. But from this he will draw a different conclusion, namely that the human and the animal share a common destiny towards salvation. In this, Agamben refers to 'the brilliant exegesis' of the gnostic Basilides (although he might have referred as well to Gregory of Nyssa), which links the human and the whole of creation in the yearning towards redemption. Agamben wonders: 'perhaps there is still a way in which living beings can sit at the messianic banquet of the righteous without taking on a historical task and without setting the anthropological machine into action', and refers to this as the 'Shabatt of both animal and man' (*O* 92), an allusion to the insistence of Judaism that not only the human but the (domestic) animals as well participate in the rest of the Sabbath.

A Pauline term that is not taken from Romans but from 1 Corinthians is that of glossolalia, which Agamben deploys in his wrestling with language. In a 1982 essay later published in *Potentialities*, Agamben wonders whether 'what is at issue here is a language that while remaining human and alive, dwells in itself – a language no longer destined to grammatical and historical transmission, a language that, as the universal and novel language of redeemed humanity, coincides without residue with human activity and praxis' (*PO* 127). This reflection is further developed in *Remnants of Auschwitz* (*RA* 114–15), where he also notes Paul's reserve with respect to this phenomenon in 1 Corinthians 14.

Although there are other topics that might be developed in this discussion, I will content myself with mentioning the figure of 'glory'. After discussing the intra-Trinitarian use of this figure derived from the Gospel of John, Agamben notes correctly that in Pauline texts this refers to 'the radiation of glory by the Father onto the Son and to the members of the messianic community. At the heart of Paul's gospel lies not the Trinitarian economy but messianic redemption' (*KG* 204). Surprisingly, he does not pursue the co-implication of abjection and glory in Philippians or 2 Corinthians that echoes the relation of power and weakness that we find in the Corinthian correspondence.

CONCLUSION

How might we understand Agamben's relation to Paul as the inaugurator of a messianic political thinking? He does not mean simply to repeat Paul, but rather to use Paul to think a new messianic politics. One is tempted to think of a secularisation following on from Carl Schmitt's saying that political concepts are secularised theological concepts. Agamben distances himself from this Schmittian position by insisting that what is properly at stake is not secularisation but 'profanation', which does not leave power intact but 'deactivates the apparatuses of power and returns to common use the spaces that power had seized' (*PR* 77). Certainly the Pauline corpus is one that has been taken hold of by structures of political and religious power. It is Agamben's task to return these texts to a common use, as a prod to thinking and acting differently in a world that, like Paul's, is passing away.

7 Carl Schmitt

SERGEI PROZOROV

The work of Carl Schmitt has been a key influence on Agamben's work, particularly his more political writings. Especially in the Anglo-American context, the discovery of Agamben's work after the publication of the first volume of *Homo Sacer* coincided with a major revival of interest in Schmitt, both of which were partly motivated by the exceptionalist tendencies in US domestic and foreign policy in the aftermath of the 9/11 attacks. At least in the first wave of reception of Agamben's writings,[1] his reinterpretation of Schmitt's theory of sovereignty in the Foucauldian biopolitical key was the best-known and most controversial aspect of his work.

And yet Schmitt has been a strange kind of influence. His work hardly influenced Agamben philosophically, as Heidegger's and Benjamin's did on the level of ontology or method. Agamben did not try to 'correct or complete' Schmitt the way he did with Foucault's work on biopolitics and government. Finally, Agamben did not really debate with or criticise Schmitt's theories the way he did with Derrida. While Schmitt's political thought was certainly *employed* in a variety of ways after *Homo Sacer*, Schmitt was not really *engaged* with as a philosophical interlocutor. Instead, I suggest that the use of Schmitt in Agamben's *oeuvre* has been *paradigmatic* in the rigorous methodological sense that Agamben later developed (*ST* 9–30). Schmitt's theory offered Agamben the most elaborate and most explicit example of the ontopolitical apparatus of sovereign power. Furthermore, Schmitt did not merely provide the best insight into how sovereign power works, but was also a paradigmatic *defender* of this apparatus, whose interpretation in katechontic terms was central to his political theology.

The second reason why Schmitt's influence on Agamben is somewhat strange is that it clearly begins to wane in Agamben's late work, so that *The Use of Bodies*, the final volume of the *Homo Sacer* project, contains no reference to the author who was so central to the first volume. We shall argue that this gradual disappearance of Schmitt from Agamben's set of philosophical references has to do precisely with the paradigmatic status of Schmitt's work. Since its primary use for Agamben was in exemplifying the apparatus he sought to render inoperative, the shift from the critical reconstruction of that apparatus to the more affirmative engagement of what lies beyond it must evidently entail much lesser utility of the Schmittian paradigm. We shall conclude that this mode of engagement with Schmitt actually succeeds in overcoming Schmitt's logic much more effectively than its frontal negation.

THE UNIVERSAL LOGIC OF THE EXCEPTION

Schmitt enters Agamben's political philosophy in *Homo Sacer* as a means of 'correcting and completing' Foucault's theory of biopolitics. Agamben's revision of Foucault's diagnosis is twofold: 'the inclusion of bare life in the political realm constitutes the original – if concealed – nucleus of sovereign power. *It can even be said that the production of a biopolitical body is the original activity of sovereign power.* In this sense, biopolitics is at least as old as sovereign power' (*HS* 6, original italics). Thus, biopolitics is neither substantively *different* from sovereignty nor temporally *successive* to it. This means that Foucault's infamous hostility to theories of sovereignty is no longer helpful for the analysis of biopolitics.

It is therefore not surprising that in *Homo Sacer* Agamben revisits and elaborates Schmitt's theory of sovereignty, though it is hardly a coincidence that he chooses Schmitt's notion specifically. For Schmitt, 'sovereign is he who decides on the exception'[2] or, in more contemporary juridical language, who has the power to institute a state of exception or emergency, suspending the existing juridico-political order. This means that the sovereign is simultaneously *inside* the legal order and *outside* it, since its power remains effective even when the validity of the existing legal or constitutional norms is suspended. Insofar as the sovereign's power extends to suspending the very order that it constitutes and sustains, it follows that the sovereign decision could never be subsumed under any positive law, norm or rule. Yet this exteriority remains essential for the very existence of the interiority of order: 'The rule applies to the exception in no longer applying, in withdrawing from it. The state of exception is thus not the chaos that precedes order but rather the situation that results from its suspension' (*HS* 17–18).

Paradoxically, it is only through the construction of the zone of *anomie* at the heart of the legal order that this order may establish its connection to the life that it governs (*SE* 51). Agamben uses Jean-Luc Nancy's term 'ban' to describe this relationship of inclusive exclusion that defines the sovereign exception.³ What is caught up in the ban is life itself, which is never 'let be' as irrelevant to power but is rather abandoned to its continuing force, yet stripped of the protections that its positive norms may have afforded (*HS* 28). This is precisely the situation in which life *becomes bare*, exposed to the governmental violence that strips it of its form. Schmitt's theory of sovereignty is thus interpreted by Agamben as inherently biopolitical, since sovereign power is ultimately about life not law, or, more precisely, it is about taking hold of life by emptying out the law. This is why the somewhat obscure figure of *homo sacer* in Roman law becomes for Agamben the paradigm of the object of sovereignty: a criminal whose killing constitutes neither sacrifice nor homicide is only included in the political order through its potentiality to be killed, and functions as the 'purest' object of sovereign power as well as the symmetrical obverse of the sovereign itself: 'the sovereign is the one with respect to whom all men are potentially *homines sacri*, [while] *homo sacer* is the one to whom all men act as sovereign' (*HS* 84). *Homo sacer* is precisely the biopolitical body whose production is the key activity of sovereign power, and it has been producing such bodies in various forms from time immemorial, and keeps doing so today.

It is important to note that Schmitt's theory is deployed as a paradigm of sovereign power not because it best captures its meaning or function, but because its formal logic ensures its fundamental stability and even immutability throughout history and its relative independence from all ideological and institutional variations in political regimes and forms of government. The actual *homo sacer* may be a long-forgotten judicial curiosity, but the logic of sovereignty, which links law and life through the suspension of the former and the capture of the latter in the state of exception, persists from the *polis* through the Empire, the Middle Ages, absolute monarchies and parliamentary democracies. Other, more historically attuned theories of sovereignty would not be able to support Agamben's claim about the extremely ancient character of sovereignty and biopolitics, which for him are ultimately as old as human language. In fact, the *only* theory that could support such a claim is a strictly formal one, which brackets off the substantive differences between forms of government and social order and focuses only on the paradox of the institution of the rule. In any political order whatsoever there must be an instance that does not merely have supreme authority within the system but also the power to suspend the content of the system itself, and only this power of suspension spares the normative order from being a lifeless abstraction. No order can entirely remove the possibility of the exception from its normative edifice and hence dispense with the need for the instance of decision that could not possibly be subsumed under the norm itself. No matter whether the order in question is a monarchy or a republic, a tyranny or a democracy, it will always have some sovereign instance that decides on the exception, suspending the law and thereby linking itself to life, producing, at least virtually, new versions of *homo sacer*.

While mainstream political theory in the post-Second World War period ignored or dismissed Schmitt's theory of sovereignty as hopelessly antiquated in its decisionist authoritarianism and entirely inadequate for contemporary liberal democracies, in the first volume of *Homo Sacer* Agamben takes an opposite view and even fortifies Schmitt's argument by tracing similar structures in logic (HS 24–5) and even ontology (HS 59-60): the ban is no longer the outlandish concept of a former Nazi jurist, but the ontopolitical principle of the Western tradition as a whole.

This is something that much of the reception of both Schmitt and Agamben in political and international relations theory in the aftermath of 9/11 has missed. Similarly to Schmitt, though admittedly for different reasons, Agamben did not interpret exceptional measures as an unfortunate remnant of, or relapse into, authoritarian rule in modern democracies, but rather as a constitutive principle that sustains these democracies themselves. Contrary to the critics of the US government after 9/11 who demanded the return to normal, domestic or international law-based governance, Agamben argued that the hope of any such 'return' was illusory, since the normal is constituted and sustained by the exception, which remains at work within it. The Patriot Act, Guantanamo and other apparently 'exceptionalist' responses to 9/11 are entirely unexceptional as examples of the constitutive role of the exception in politics. Thus, the formal logic of Schmitt's theory permits Agamben to raise the stakes of his diagnosis of Western politics far beyond Foucault's original idea: biopolitics now appears not only lethal but also practically immortal, a deathless power of death. Any confrontation with this power can therefore never rely on this-worldly resources alone and its overcoming will understandably become a matter of messianic power. As we shall show in the following section, in this 'gigantomachy' (SE 52) Agamben also deploys Schmitt as a paradigmatic opponent.

THE KATECHONTIC FAITH

Of course, Schmitt's theory of sovereignty was not merely an exercise in conceptual logic, but, in accordance with Schmitt's own sociology of concepts, reflected important metaphysical and theological commitments. Yet there remains some ambiguity regarding what these commitments actually are. If we extend Schmitt's notion of political theology beyond his own limited realm of application and pose the question of what exactly was 'theological' or theologised in Schmitt's work, the answer is as follows: the political itself, the sovereign power that decides on the exception, distinguishes between friends and enemies and maintains order by periodically tapping into anomie. Agamben finds this theologisation of the political in Schmitt's use of the notion of the *katechon*, a figure from Paul's Second Letter to the Thessalonians that withholds the *parousia* by keeping at bay the antichrist whose reign precedes it (2 Thess. 2:6–8).

In his *Nomos of the Earth*, Schmitt follows the tradition begun by Tertullian of identifying the *katechon* with the Roman Empire. For Schmitt, the understanding of the Empire as the *katechon* provided a link between the eschatological promise of Christianity and the concrete experience of history, explaining the delay of *parousia* and giving meaning to historical and political action, which the imminence of *parousia* would devalue:

> I do not believe that any historical concept other than katechon would have been possible for the original Christian faith. The belief that a restrainer holds back the end of the world provides the only bridge between the notion of an eschatological paralysis of all human events and a tremendous historical monolith like that of the Christian empire of the German kings.[4]

The *katechon* is so important for Schmitt that it functions not simply as an artful device to endow history with meaning in the context of the Christian faith, but rather as an article of faith in its own right: 'I believe in the katechon; for me he is the sole possibility for a Christian to understand history and find it meaningful.'[5] Yet what does it mean to *believe* in the *katechon* and how does this belief relate to the rather more familiar belief in God? In Agamben's argument, the belief in the *katechon* characterises every theory of the state, 'which thinks of it as a power destined to block or delay catastrophe' (TR 110). While the concepts of both the state and the catastrophe in question may be completely secularised, in Agamben's reading secularisation 'leaves intact the forces it deals with by simply moving them from one place to another' (PR 77). The *katechon* now refers to any constituted authority whose function is to delay the undoing of the social bond while simultaneously withholding any radical redemption. Yet how does this delaying power work? As a form of sovereign authority, the *katechon* necessarily places itself both inside and outside the order it protects, periodically tapping into the very anomie whose advent it delays. The *katechon* is only able to withhold the real state of exception (the reign of the antichrist) by producing its fictive versions that serve to sustain rather than undermine order. It is this katechontic disposition that is at stake in the esoteric Benjamin–Schmitt debate that Agamben reconstructs in *State of Exception*. Whereas Benjamin persistently sought to theorise an experience of power not tied to either law or order (the real state of exception, divine violence, weak messianic power), Schmitt ventured to reinscribe this excess back into the orbit of law and order, so that anomie never threatened the order in question but rather served as the instrument of its perpetuation (*SE* 52–64).

It is clear that Agamben takes Benjamin's side in this debate. In *The Time that Remains* he elaborates the contrast between the katechontic and the messianic dispositions by a reinterpretation of Paul's passage on the *katechon* in the Second Letter to the Thessalonians. Agamben argues that, rather than grounding anything like a Christian 'doctrine of State power', this passage harbours no positive valuation of the *katechon* whatsoever, especially since the term could not possibly have referred to Christian 'state power'. Indeed, in the letter the *katechon* is something that is to be 'removed' or taken 'out of the way' in order to reveal the 'mystery of anomie' that is 'already at work' (2 Thess. 2:6–8). In Agamben's reading of Paul, anomie refers to the suspension of the law in the messianic state of exception (*katargesis*), whereby the law is rendered inoperative and remains in force without significance (*TR* 95–101). Insofar as this *katargesis* is not something perpetually to come but is 'already at work', the *katechon* as a structure of constituted authority originally represented by the Roman Empire merely defers the ultimate unveiling of the 'absence of law': 'The unveiling of this mystery entails bringing to light the inoperativity of the law and the substantial illegitimacy of each and every power in messianic time' (*TR* 111).

Similarly to his enfolding of Hobbes's state of nature back into the order of the commonwealth in the mode of the state of exception in *Homo Sacer* (*HS* 35–6, 105), Agamben's reading of Paul highlights the way anomie is always already at work within the order of constituted power, which appropriates it and limits its use to the sovereign alone. Yet if all power is illegitimate, then it is impossible to distinguish the *katechon* as a power that restrains anomie from the figure of the *anomos* that is conventionally held to refer to the antichrist. Agamben proposes to conceive of the two figures as two aspects of one single power before and after the unveiling of the 'mystery of anomie': 'Profane power – albeit of the Roman empire or any other power – is the semblance that covers up the substantial lawlessness of messianic time. In solving the "mystery", semblance is cast out and power assumes the figure of the *anomos*, of that which is the absolute outlaw' (*TR* 111). Simply put, for Agamben, the *katechon* does not delay the advent of the antichrist; it *is* the antichrist that perpetuates its reign by concealing the fact of its long having arrived and pretending, as a 'lesser evil', to ward off its own advent. The idea of the *katechon* is an artful device by which 'substantially illegitimate' power perpetuates its reign, diverting the quest for redemption to the preoccupation with protection against the 'greater evil' that requires obedience to the 'lesser' evil of constituted authority.

In *Stasis*, Agamben makes the same argument even more forcefully in his decidedly anti-Schmittian reinterpretation of Hobbes's *Leviathan*: 'The end of time can take place at any instance and the State not only does not act as a katechon, but in fact coincides with the very eschatological beast which must be annihilated at the end of time' (*STA* 52). The katechontic faith is thus to be opposed with a genuinely messianic disposition, for whom the only connection between the Leviathan and the Kingdom of God is that 'the first will necessarily have to disappear when the second is realized' (*STA* 52). Sovereign power cannot protect us from the antichrist that it is, nor can it bring about salvation from itself. It is simply that which must be rendered inoperative for human life and praxis to be restored to themselves in the real state of exception. Only as that which is to be removed can sovereignty assist precisely 'through being profane, the coming of the Messianic Kingdom. The profane, although not itself a category of this Kingdom, is a decisive category of its quietest approach.'[6] In the final section, we shall trace the way this inoperativity is theorised in Agamben's later writings, in which the influence of Schmitt gradually wanes.

TAKING LEAVE OF SCHMITT

This paradigmatic use of Schmitt is relatively short-lived. After *Homo Sacer*, *State of Exception* and *The Time that Remains*, Schmitt plays a rather less important role in Agamben's work, all but disappearing in the latest texts, including the final volume of the *Homo Sacer* series, *The Use of Bodies*. This disappearance is in part self-evident in the case of the more specialised texts, such as *The Sacrament of Language* or *The Highest Poverty*, which deal with topics that Schmitt simply never addressed. A more important reason is the shift of theoretical focus from sovereignty to government in the key 'middle' volume of the *Homo Sacer* series, *The Kingdom and the Glory*. While Schmitt is certainly a major presence in that book, he is so largely as part of the opposition between sovereignty and government, political theology and economic theology.

Taking his point of departure from the debate between Schmitt and Erik Peterson on the possibility of political theology, Agamben quickly moves beyond that particular controversy to outline a fundamental split in Western ontology between two dimensions: 'being and praxis, transcendent and immanent good, theology and oikonomia' (KG 140). Typically for Agamben's line of reasoning, this split simultaneously forms an articulation, the bipolar machine of Kingdom–Government, in which Schmitt's logic of sovereignty and political theology occupies the first, 'theological' dimension of Kingdom. However, Agamben's own interest is now clearly captured by the second, immanent 'economic' dimension of Government, which he reconstitutes starting from the Trinitarian dogma all the way up to contemporary political and sociological theories. Moreover, in the course of the study Agamben makes it clear that the two poles of the 'machine' are not functionally equivalent: in fact, the Kingdom serves as the ultimately fictive foundation of Government, the locus of ineffectual being at once excluded and included from effective praxis. 'God's impotence functions to make possible a righteous government of the world' (KG 106).

The ostensibly absolute power of the sovereign that should logically exceed the governmental power that derives from it ends up wholly sustained by the latter and in fact only exists as the necessary presupposition for the effects produced by it. Just as God's glory is ultimately the product of our practices of glorification, the splendour of the sovereign is nothing but a shadow cast by the tedious workings of the myriad of bureaucrats, the angels of government. The king only reigns because he does not govern, though, to be fair, government can only govern by presupposing a transcendent figure that only reigns. Thus, Agamben concludes the inquiry with the following statement: 'the real problem, the central mystery of politics is not sovereignty, but government; it is not God, but the angel; it is not the king, but ministry; it is not the law but the police – that is to say, the governmental machine that they form and support' (KG 276). The logic of sovereignty that Schmitt's theory was the paradigm of recedes into the background as the condition of possibility of the governmental machine, about which Schmitt had little to say. While Agamben continues to refer to Schmitt in his discussion of acclamation rituals in modern states (KG 253–9), he no longer appears to be the paradigmatic target of Agamben's critique.

Yet even this downgrading of the problematic of sovereignty in favour of government does not prepare us for the complete absence of references to Schmitt in the final volume, *The Use of Bodies*. The diagnosis of the first volume regarding the logic of sovereignty remains the same, yet is now generalised beyond politics to a variety of apparatuses, which all exemplify the presuppositional logic of negative foundation, whereby a phenomenon is split into two aspects, one of which constitutes the other by being excluded from it: 'The city is founded on the division of life into bare life and politically qualified life, the human is defined by the exclusion-inclusion of the animal, the law by the exception of anomie, governance through the exclusion of inoperativity and its capture in the form of glory' (*UB* 265–6).

What distinguishes *The Use of Bodies* from other volumes in the series is the much more extensive and detailed treatment of the way the presuppositional logic governing these various apparatuses can be rendered inoperative. Just as in *Homo Sacer*, the most detailed elaboration unfolds on the ontological level, where Agamben develops an elaborate modal ontology devoid of the presuppositional principle. Rejecting both the Aristotelian presupposition of existence as the condition of essence and the (neo-)Platonist presupposition of essence as the condition of singular existences, Agamben offers the image of

> mode as a vortex in the flux of being. It has no substance other than that of the one being, but, with respect to the latter, it has a figure, a manner and a movement that belong to it on its own. The modes are eddies in the boundless field of the substance that, by sinking and whirling into itself, disseminates and expresses itself in singularities. (*UB* 174)

In this ontology, strongly indebted to Spinoza, 'singularity bears witness to itself in being and being expresses itself in the singular body' (*UB* 223). Essence and existence become indeterminate in myriad modes, into which being is fully and irrevocably dispersed.

On the basis of this ontological operation, Agamben finally redeems the promise made in the first volume of *Homo Sacer* of theorising biopolitics in an affirmative key, as a '*bios* that is only its own *zoè*' (*HS* 188). Whereas the Schmittian sovereign ban included unqualified life (*zoè*) into a political form (*bios*) as a negative foundation in the form of 'bare life' exposed to violence, in the form-of-life, *bios* is nothing other than the perpetual modification of *zoè* itself. Since forms of life emerge and proliferate in the very activity of living, there is no need for the violence of founding exclusion that produced the figure of *homo sacer*. Life does not have a form that it must attain by sacrificing living itself, it always already *is* a form that it takes up by living. Life and form are inseparable just as a being and its being, only expressible in a certain mode. In the epilogue of the book, the same deactivating operation is applied to the concept of power. While Schmitt is not addressed explicitly in this epilogue, Agamben's notion of 'destituent potential' (*UB* 266–74) follows the above-discussed Benjaminian messianic logic that rejects Schmitt's subsumption of power under the order it either sustains or constitutes. Destituent potential does not exhaust itself in what it constitutes but rather unworks, makes destitute every work of constitution in its every act.

Modal ontology, form-of-life and destituent potential are all variations on the same theme of deactivating the presuppositional logic and thereby rendering indeterminate what sovereignty keeps in a paradoxical relation of inclusive exclusion: essence and existence, life and form, potentiality and actuality. It is important to emphasise that Agamben does not simply affirm potentiality *over* actuality or life *against* form, which would only serve to sustain the Schmittian logic in an inverted form. Instead, he ventures to define a mode of praxis in which both are present *at once*: an act that retains and manifests its potentiality not to be, a form wholly contained in living itself, a constitutive practice that fully brings into its act its own destituent potential. The sole explicit example of the operation of destituent potential in the political sphere that Agamben provides, the Nocturnal Council in Plato's *Laws* (*UB* 278–9), is somewhat controversial, since it has also been analysed in Plato studies as a form of power not constrained by any laws, an informal counterpart to the proper authorities of the city that might well be its true sovereign in the Schmittian sense.[7] Nonetheless, Agamben's logic of rendering the Schmittian apparatus inoperative is clear. The power of decision and distinction, of cutting up being into ordered regions, can only be deactivated by the affirmation of indistinction and indetermination as ontologically, ethically and politically primary. When being is wholly dispersed into modes, it can no longer 'constitute itself sovereignly' (*HS* 46) by negating its own potentiality not to be. When life is only the form that living takes, it cannot be stripped from its form or have a new form imposed on it. When constitution and destitution coincide in every act, it is no longer possible to decide on the exception or distinguish friends and enemies, since every such decision or distinction must undo itself immediately. Lifestyles, habits and manners, which become Agamben's new focus in *The Use of Bodies*, are too ephemeral and irresolute for their norms to be anything but exceptional and their exceptions to be anything but normal.

It is for this reason that Schmitt is absent from the pages of *The Use of Bodies* and other late texts: for this new domain of practices the Schmittian paradigm is remarkably ill-fitting. Schmitt himself famously argued in *Political Theology* that 'the metaphysical image that a definite epoch forges of the world has the same structure as what the world immediately understands to be appropriate as a form of its political organization'.[8] By this criterion, Agamben's deactivation of presuppositional ontology by modal ontology should make Schmitt's logic of sovereignty inappropriate as a form of our political organisation. The inappropriateness in question here goes further than moral or practical objections. In the world of myriad modes in which being is disseminated and forms of life perpetually constitute and deconstruct themselves, both the decision on the exception and the distinction of friends and enemies become almost inconceivable: no form of life can ever acquire stability and determinacy to such an extent that it could function as a norm, let alone a predicate of identity, in terms of which friends and enemies could be designated. Similarly to Benjamin's notion of baroque sovereignty,[9] things are simply already too exceptional in this picture for any decision on the exception to be even possible (cf. SE 55–7).

With the final volume of the *Homo Sacer* series, Agamben has therefore ventured to take leave of Schmitt's ontopolitical logic in an authentic way. While Schmitt's political theory has been criticised from all possible perspectives throughout the twentieth century, it has proven surprisingly resilient, bouncing back from disrepute and even surprising its critics by lodging itself in their very argumentation. There is actually nothing more Schmittian than declaring Schmitt an enemy and building up an alternative edifice through a frontal opposition to his approach, replacing exception by norm, enemy by friend and so on – all as a matter of one's own sovereign decision. Schmitt will beckon at the end of any attempt to negate the decision by deciding on the negation or to annul the political by making of it an enemy. Instead, in full accordance with Schmitt's own view, Agamben wagers on deactivating his political apparatus together with the metaphysical one that renders it intelligible and 'appropriate'. It is by no means guaranteed that the new ontopolitical arrangement will be a happy one: we might well end up missing Schmitt with his ordering, if itself disorderly, power of the scission of being. It is also possible, however, that the change in the metaphysical image of our epoch that Agamben strives to attain will lead to our true overcoming of Schmitt – not by opposition but by oblivion.

NOTES

1. See, for example, Andrew Norris (ed.), *Politics, Metaphysics and Death: Essays on Giorgio Agamben's* Homo Sacer (Durham, NC: Duke University Press 2005); Matthew Calarco and Steven DeCaroli (eds), *Giorgio Agamben: Sovereignty and Life* (Stanford: Stanford University Press, 2007).

2. Carl Schmitt, *Political Theology: Four Chapters on the Concept of Sovereignty*, trans. George Schwab (Cambridge, MA: MIT Press, 1985), p. 1.
3. Jean-Luc Nancy, 'Abandoned Being', in *The Birth to Presence*, trans. Brian Holmes et al. (Stanford: Stanford University Press, 1993), pp. 43–4.
4. Carl Schmitt, *The Nomos of the Earth in the International Public Law of the Jus Publicum Europaeum*, trans. G. L. Ulmen (New York: Telos Press, 2003), p. 60.
5. Schmitt cited in Heinrich Meier, *The Lesson of Carl Schmitt: Four Chapters on the Distinction between Political Theology and Political Philosophy*, trans. Marcus Brainard (Chicago: University of Chicago Press, 1998), p. 162.
6. Walter Benjamin, 'Theologico-Political Frangment', in *Reflections* (New York: Schocken Books, 1978), p. 312.
7. George Klosko, 'The Nocturnal Council in Plato's *Laws*', *Political Studies* 26 (1988): 74–88. See also Sergei Prozorov, 'Living à la Mode: Form-of-Life and Democratic Biopolitics in Giorgio Agamben's *Use of Bodies*', *Philosophy and Social Criticism* 43.2 (2017): 144–63.
8. Schmitt, *Political Theology*, p. 46.
9. Cf. Walter Benjamin, *The Origin of German Tragic Drama*, trans. John Osborne (London: Verso, 2003).

PART II

Points of Reference

8 Hannah Arendt

JOHN GRUMLEY

I

In his fine introduction to Agamben's philosophical world,[1] Leland de la Durantaye draws our attention to the very early contact between Agamben and Arendt in 1970, when the former was a young man only just finding his own theoretical voice. In a personal letter, the then unknown Italian scholar writes to Arendt expressing both admiration and gratitude for what he judges to be a 'decisive experience' – not just the experience of historical rupture, but also the unexpected possibility of change accompanying this loss.[2] The disruption of tradition is both emancipatory and a burden: it provides meaning but also clouds and limits present possibilities. In tune with Agamben's messianic temperament and his critique of the Western tradition, he is primarily interested in the critical potential of the moment of rupture and its emancipatory possibilities.

Yet Agamben's more public acknowledgement of Arendt's theoretical inspiration comes in his most famous work, *Homo Sacer*, which begins from an iconoclastic reading of the concentration and death camps. He radicalises her view in the *Origins of Totalitarianism* by asserting that the 'camp' is not only the central institution of mid-century totalitarian societies but also of contemporary liberal democratic societies. This intentionally provocative claim is meant to immediately raise the stakes by expunging the differences that separate the liberal democratic regimes of the post-war period from their totalitarian precursors, problematising the whole Western tradition of political thought and pointing to the unacknowledged dark prospects of the anticipated future.[3] To fill out Agamben's claims here we need to more fully explore Arendt's interpretation of totalitarianism, its historical distinctiveness and how Agamben stands in relation to these propositions.

II

Agamben endorses Arendt's claim for the historical distinctiveness of totalitarianism. This is a novel regime that in its preference for terror as a means is historically unprecedented. The totalitarian leaders viewed themselves primarily as instruments of higher historical laws to be assisted with extreme violence. The refinement of the use of terror only vindicates her claim that the guiding social ideal of these societies were the camps, which represent an entirely new world of unrestrained, absolute power. In such extremity, human nature became infinitely malleable. The widespread appearance of the *Muselmann* (the living dead), according to Arendt, attests to the brutal efficiency of this process of human deconstruction.[4]

For Arendt, such a system renders human beings superfluous.[5] It expresses the 'experiences of the modern masses in their superfluity on the over-crowded earth'.[6] The camps form an experimental microcosm annihilating the best in human nature. As she puts it: 'human nature is only human in so far as it opens up the possibility of man becoming something unnatural'.[7] The totalitarian movement aims to refashion the infinite plurality of human beings into just one big individual.[8]

Arendt's account becomes most compelling for Agamben when she finds an essential logic threatening to outlive the totalitarian regime. The attack on human spontaneity, creation, action and plurality is a permanent challenge that lies deep within the interstices of modernity. The bourgeois reliance on utilitarianism and instrumentality not only created the conditions that make totalitarian movements possible, but continues to play an ongoing role in producing the 'spiritual and social rootlessness' characteristic of the modern condition.

However, it is really when Arendt unpacks this threat to the post-totalitarian modern world that we begin to see the starkest differences that distinguish her standpoint from Agamben's. She focuses on the Christian notion of sovereignty, modelled on the idea of a divine will that commands and expects obedience. By contrast, the ancient *polis* taught the irreducible opinionated character of the political and the need for plural perspectives and individual initiative. In Arendt's political vocabulary, sovereignty is opposed to freedom: man is born free but not sovereign. The latter requires violation of the freedom of others and the death of plurality. Agamben shares Arendt's negative estimation of the concept of sovereignty; however, for him sovereign decision remains the inescapable foundation of politics in the Western tradition. This judgement goes against the deepest impulses of Arendt's political thought. Her celebration of plurality and legitimate constituent power demands their priority over the concept of sovereignty. She calls for the revival of republican politics, not its condemnation as a vehicle of violence.[9]

This call, so foreign to Agamben, is perhaps Arendt's key positive insight. Political institutions are manifestations of the living power of the people:[10] they are never the property of individuals but of collectives acting in concert.[11] The idea of being 'in power' implies public support that empowers leaders to act on its behalf.[12] This is nowhere more clearly seen than when power suddenly evaporates, as we have seen repeatedly in recent times from 1989 to the Arab Spring. This reveals how deceptive the appearance of power can be: power is not primarily a means but an end that derives from the free character of the initial concert.[13]

Arendt moves the notion of 'natality' into the centre of her conception of politics. Human beings come into the world as new beginnings, unique, unrepeatable and with the capacity for creation and regeneration. Agamben shares Arendt's anthropological optimism, but in her case it is tempered by an acknowledgement that biological potential is not itself freedom. While birth individuates biologically, it does not do so existentially. The potential uniqueness of birth must be actualised through a 'second birth', where potentiality assumes a definite shape in action. Natality is the gift of a natural freedom but it does not make humanity free. It remains, in Benjamin's sense, a 'weak messianic force' for which there is neither certainty nor inevitability, but only hope. Such exposure of action to historical conditions is also the very opposite of the sovereign power that finds its model in divine fabrication. Design is the ultimate model of closure which is incompatible with the spontaneity and open-endedness that is so crucial to Arendt's understanding of the human potential of politics. For Arendt, individual and collective political activity is the messianic ingredient of democratic politics. This can only be restored with the political understanding of the concept of freedom as collective political action. For her, freedom is not one among the many problems of politics, but the very reason why human beings live together at all.[14]

III

Agamben is fond of the lines from Hölderlin: 'Where there is danger, there grows the saving power.' This provides a key insight into his philosophical personality. Belief in the immediate proximity of crisis and solution compels him to pursue only the most radical theoretical and political options. His rereading of Foucault's biopolitical narrative becomes the basis for the most damning critique of the present. Biopolitics signifies the reorientation of politics away from questions of law to those of life, death and work and the strength of the state in general (*ME* 7). But this Foucauldian move was already anticipated in Arendt with her critique of the priority accorded to the concept of life in modern politics. Echoing this, Agamben judges the entry of unadorned 'bare life' into the domain of the political as the decisive event of modernity (*HS* 4). The apparent triumph of democracy over all its adversaries at the end of the twentieth century is illusory. The more profound interpretation is of modern democracy's increasing decadence, its gradual convergence with totalitarianism in what he calls post-democratic spectacular society (*HS* 10). This society is the completion/decomposition of the nation state. The constitutive elements of the earlier nation state – territory, birth and order – no longer functioned in the new epoch of biopolitics. The camp, which was initially an exceptional measure, has now become an indispensable, but unacknowledged, fourth element and pillar of governance. Internationally, Agamben foresees a global movement towards the constitution of a kind of supra-national police state that abrogates both the balance of power and all the norms of international law (*ME* 86). This is an index of the biopolitical system's inability to function without turning itself into a lethal machine (*ME* 43). Internally, the society of the spectacle substitutes the sham electoral machine of majority rule and media control over public opinion for real freedom of thought and communication. Democratic civil life is simply hollowed out by commodification and the hegemony of mass media politics. Once the manipulation of bare life becomes the principal political concern, the question of which political form is best suited to this task is reduced to a secondary strategic issue (*HS* 122). The will of totalitarian politics to total self-possession can be achieved either by the logic of total exclusion of the other or by unrestrained falsification and consumption (*ME* 97). The techniques and institutions first honed in the totalitarian systems of the 1920s and 1930s easily migrate to become central props of the new post-democratic convergence.

Unlike totalitarian societies, liberal democratic ones attribute to their citizens inalienable human rights. However, Agamben is not interested in democracy's self-interpretation nor in Arendt's view of its political potential. All this, for him, ignores the key moments of violence and exclusion inscribed in the modern understanding of political legitimacy. Hobbes promoted the fiction that rights were a function of nature or birth rather than political inclusion. This critical insight takes Agamben into the very heart of the Western political tradition. Until the twentieth century the immediate identification of rights with birth was unquestioned. However, political denationalisation and displacement of mass populations after the First World War finally exposed the essential link between the sovereign nation state and the fate of human rights. From this time the refugee increasingly becomes the representative individual of modern politics and exposes the crisis of the nation-state system (*ME* 134).

It is especially telling that from this point Agamben chooses Carl Schmitt over Arendt. Following Schmitt's response to the Weimar constitutional crisis, Agamben asserts the priority of the sovereign tie over that of positive rule or the social pact. The former is also a ban which both produces and excludes 'bare life' (*HS* 90). In the starkest contrast to Arendt, Agamben views sovereign decision as the secret centre of democratic politics. To endorse it means affirming a killing machine responsible for the manufacture of bare life. In the early decades of the twentieth century, the biopolitical fracture assumed an especially implacable form. Race legislation facilitated the grey zone of exclusion that culminated in the reduction of camp inmates to 'bare life'. Agamben rejects Arendt's explanation that these measures were a product of the totalitarian project alone and its aspiration to transform human nature. For him, they are a necessary product of the Western theological-political tradition and its logic of sovereign decision. The ancient prerogative of the sovereign to kill and to let live in the new era now assumes a specific biopolitical shape (*RA* 82–3). Agamben underscores that the notion of a life 'worthy of being lived' is not an ethical but an essentially political judgement connected, in the final analysis, to sovereign decision. Although in the present biopolitical horizon this task is increasingly allocated to the physician and the scientist, we should not doubt its essentially political character (*HS* 159). The *Muselmann* was only the first instalment of the excluded other that will grow when the future biopolitical task concerns the survival of the species and a habitable world.

IV

The foregoing comparison between Arendt and Agamben has revealed a key point of convergence. Both refuse to limit their analysis to the conventional philosophical terrain of the actual in the quest for a human potential promising a new beginning. They share a deep scepticism towards progressive, liberal incremental politics. The wait for indefinite salvation is displaced by a call to action, to grasp the full potential of the present.

Beyond this point, however, agreements end and we began to see the fractures that emanate from fundamental differences. Arendt has a much less suspicious attitude to the past. She views herself as a Benjaminian 'pearl diver' who recovers 'treasures' of the past that simply need to be resuscitated. Key episodes of the Western political tradition provide foundational ideas that can be appropriated positively as both models of freedom and deep truths about the nature of the political. Agamben, by contrast, detaches his utopian will to emancipation from almost all historical contamination; no achievements of past struggle can stand if they compromise future possibility.[15] He traces the seeds of sovereign domination back to the sources of Western politics and the founding distinctions that underwrite political qualification but also legitimate contemporary exclusions. Agamben's messianism demands disassociation from these systemic crimes.

Here we broach a fundamental question. Agamben claims to offer a philosophy of immanence, yet the standpoint of 'bare life' wants nothing to do with the contemporary institutional machinery of politics. Formal politics requires compromise, while informality allows the flexibility and the clarity of the margin. However, in a democratic society, at some point these supposed virtues have to be translated into concrete demands acceptable to majorities. Ultimately Agamben's messianic seems more like an ethical claim that threatens to tip over into the apocalyptic that he otherwise repudiates. Nothing can be rescued from the labour of the Western political tradition, nothing has escaped the theological-political net of domination. For him, the question of sovereignty is the originary political question: politics is governed by conflict and the necessity of inclusive exclusion.[16] But this is mere assertion engendered by an ethical aspiration that spurns all compromises. It is perfectly possible to reconcile legal constitutionalism with decisionist elements like high courts and executive officers. But Agamben ignores such options: for him the critique of the actual from the standpoint of potential assumes the shape of ontological truth.

By contrast Arendt's 'love of the world' is evident not just in her political commitment to the republican tradition, but also in the shape she gives to her messianic moment. Arendt's messianic is anchored in natality and the future. However, she does not wager everything on mere potential. Real freedom requires public, foundational institutions and therefore is essentially captive to historical conditions. For Arendt, new beginnings are an ontological gift but still subject to conditions of historical realisation.

Arendt is also wary of political compromise and wants to elevate the political beyond interests. However, these preferences rest uneasily with other key elements in her vision that are closer to associational politics, which falls on the historical memory of free collective action and pluralist creativity. For her, these latter elements are the real substance of the political domain, ancient or modern. From this perspective comes her stinging critique of the concept of sovereignty. The democratic tradition theoretically subsumes sovereignty as an expression of popular self-definition: it expresses the living power of the people acting in concert. She allows that emergencies do happen and that final political decisions must be made. However, *contra* Schmitt, emergency provisions can always be accommodated within constitutional arrangements that allow the will of the people to express itself even in a dire situation. On Arendt's reading, there need be no privileged link or exclusive connection between emergency powers and an allegedly 'original' political will.

Agamben's scathing critique of liberal democracy is the core of his diagnosis of contemporary modernity. However, this only gained real purchase in the now largely discredited political reaction to 9/11 and the increasing mobility of mass populations fleeing political oppression and economic disadvantage. Precipitate recourse to harsh security legislation, increased border surveillance and extraterritorial camps require reinforced sovereign power and the extension of the security state. But are these developments really the secret truth of liberal democracy? Or were they the first expression of crisis thinking, the consequence of excessive and regrettable political and policy failures that we are, to some extent, still living with? Even such populist explosions, lamentable as they are, hardly prove that democracy and sovereign power are one and the same. For Agamben, this response is simply too comfortable and accommodating; it signifies complicity in all the sovereign crimes of exclusion. This is an ethical rebuke that no democrat can ignore and packs an even more powerful punch in the light of contemporary efforts in Europe to stem the flood of Syrian refugees. Critics of contemporary liberal democracies are right to repudiate ethical complacency. The demand for more tolerance, inclusiveness and generosity must be constantly renewed. However, this does not mean that liberal democratic politics can be reduced to Agamben's grey zone in which every privilege is built on suffering and exclusion. It is certainly true that politics necessitates choices and, more often than not, even hard choices between evils: compromising between ethics and *Realpolitik*, between existing interests and the promise of the new, eking out minor victories while confronting abuses of power. On this terrain, the hopes, determination and aspirations that inspired the contemporary call for the messianic still exist but less abstractly. Within the fabric of everyday life, in both formal and informal politics, they persist as momentary flashes of inspiration and unexpected advances amid the Sisyphean political labour that Max Weber once described as 'boring holes in hard boards'.

NOTES

1. Leland de la Durantaye, *Giorgio Agamben: A Critical Introduction* (Stanford: Stanford University Press, 2009).
2. de la Durantaye, *Giorgio Agamben*, p. 41.
3. de la Durantaye, *Giorgio Agamben*, p. 241.
4. Hannah Arendt, *The Origins of Totalitarianism* (New York: Schocken Books, 2004), p. 455.
5. Arendt, *The Origins of Totalitarianism*, p. 457.
6. Arendt, *The Origins of Totalitarianism*, p. 457.
7. Arendt, *The Origins of Totalitarianism*, p. 455.
8. Arendt, *The Origins of Totalitarianism*, p. 238.
9. Hannah Arendt, 'On Violence', in *Crisis of the Republic* (New York: Harcourt Brace Jovanovich, 1969), p. 151.
10. Arendt, 'On Violence', p. 140.
11. Arendt, 'On Violence', p. 141.
12. Arendt, 'On Violence', p. 143.
13. Arendt, 'On Violence', p. 151.
14. Hannah Arendt, *Between Past and Future* (London: Faber & Faber, 1958), p. 149.
15. But whether this is ultimately a viable theoretical strategy is thrown in doubt by Agamben's deployment of Franciscan ethical models in one of his more recent works, *The Highest Poverty*.
16. George Schwab, 'Introduction', in Carl Schmitt, *Political Theology: Four Chapters on the Concept of Sovereignty*, trans. George Schwab (Chicago: University of Chicago Press, 2005), p. xvi.

9 Georges Bataille

NADINE HARTMANN

I

Throughout his *oeuvre*, Giorgio Agamben makes numerous references to Georges Bataille. Already in the 1977 *Stanzas*, Bataille's general economy is afforded one of the scholia of the chapter 'The Appropriation of Unreality' and scolded for its alleged simplification of Marcel Mauss's account of the gift. A brief discussion of the letters that Bataille and Alexandre Kojève exchanged in 1937 is contained in Agamben's 1982 *Language and Death* and picked up again in 2002's *The Open: Man and Animal*. The only text that exclusively deals with Bataille, however, is Agamben's 1987 essay 'Bataille e il paradosso della sovranità'. By the time Agamben begins the *Homo Sacer* project (1995), and in particular in *Means Without End* (1996), Bataille has been banished into unambiguously dismissive footnotes or 'thresholds' in which Agamben distances himself from Bataille's definitions of the sacred, sacrifice and sovereignty. Thus, unlike Carl Schmitt, Martin Heidegger, Walter Benjamin or Michel Foucault, Bataille not only cannot be considered one of Agamben's main informants, but receives all but marginal attention from him – and this despite the fact that Bataille is generally held to be one of the crucial thinkers of the sacred and of sovereignty.

I am starting from the assumption that this persistent downplaying of Bataille's thought in Agamben's mature project is itself symptomatic, and that a closer look at the segments of Agamben's texts that mention Bataille can contribute to an interpretation, or at least an appreciation, of the somewhat intricate relationship between the two thinkers' definitions of the terms 'sacred' and 'sovereignty'.

II

Just as in *Stanzas* Agamben had marshalled Mauss against Bataille, in *Language and Death* he praises the superior wisdom of another of Bataille's elders, in this case Kojève. Agamben recalls the conflict between Bataille and Kojève concerning their differing readings of Hegel's conception of the master–slave dialectic. In this instance, Agamben sides with Kojève, stating that 'any thought that wishes to think beyond Hegelianism cannot truly find a foundation, against the negative dialectic and its discourse, in the experience (mystical and, if coherent, necessarily mute) of disengaged negativity' (*LD* 53). With this formulation – 'the experience of disengaged negativity' – Agamben is clearly, albeit somewhat obliquely, referring to Bataille's conception of a *'negativité sans emploi'*, a construction with which Bataille aims beyond dialectics – refusing to charge the concept of negativity with the meaning provided through *Aufhebung* or sublation. Whereas in Hegel negativity remains subservient to the conceptions of totality and absolute knowledge, Bataille insists on an unemployed negativity which would resist precisely this incorporation. With history having come to an end – the very premise of the Hegel interpretation that Kojève presented at the École pratique des hautes études in the 1930s with Bataille in the audience – meaningful historical action is no longer possible for mankind. Bataille insists in his letter to Kojève that what remains in this scenario is an a-relational negativity of which he gives his own existence as an example. Foucault, in his 'Preface to Transgression', explains the specifics of this curious form of negativity:

> Transgression contains nothing negative [...] Transgression opens onto a scintillating and constantly affirmed world, a world without shadow or twilight, without that serpentine 'no' that bites into fruits and lodges their contradictions at their core. It is the solar inversion of satanic denial.[1]

While Foucault attempts to discern in Bataille a complete renunciation of the Hegelian vocabulary, Derrida may be more faithful to Bataille's strategy, which could be described as operating 'with Hegel against Hegel':

> The blind spot of Hegelianism, around which can be organized the representation of meaning, is the point at which destruction, suppression, death and sacrifice constitute so irreversible an expenditure, so radical a negativity – here we would have to say an expenditure and a *negativity without reserve* – that they can no longer be determined as negativity in a process or a system. In discourse (the unity of process and system) negativity is always the underside and accomplice of positivity. Negativity cannot be spoken of, nor has it ever been except in this *fabric of meaning*. Now,

the sovereign operation, *the point of nonreserve*, is neither positive nor negative.²

It is important to keep the distance in mind that is measured in these two interpretations (or extensions) of Bataille's unemployed negativity, as we turn to Agamben's precarious relation to Bataille. I would maintain that the conception of unemployed negativity constitutes a core of Bataille's philosophy – certainly more so than the overused and almost always misleading formula spun out of his concept of transgression.

III

Agamben's 'Bataille e il paradosso della sovranità', not yet translated into English, proves surprisingly sympathetic to Bataille's theories, particularly in light of Agamben's later dismissals. In addressing *Acéphale*, the secret society founded by members of the Collège de Sociologie (among them Bataille, Pierre Klossowski and, on occasion, Walter Benjamin), Agamben relates to a then contemporary discourse on Bataille, namely Maurice Blanchot and Jean-Luc Nancy's works on *Acéphale* and the political promises of a 'negative community'. He quickly moves on to what would become the primary preoccupation of his writings of the 1990s, that is, the question of sovereignty. Here Agamben accurately depicts the topological analogy between the account of sovereignty offered by Carl Schmitt and Bataille's paradox of sovereignty. He begins by summarising the former in almost the same way as he would later do in *Homo Sacer*:

> 'the sovereign is at once outside and inside the juridical order'. The specification 'at once' is not insignificant: the sovereign, having the *legitimate* power to suspend the validity of the law, *legally places himself outside the law*. This means that the paradox can also be formulated this way: 'the law is outside itself, it is outside the law'.³

He approaches the problem of sovereignty in a schematic fashion, quoting Schmitt: 'The exception is that which cannot be subsumed' (qtd. in *HS* 15). Schmitt articulates a paradox – or the dialectic, if you will – that can be classified as strictly Pauline:

> The exception is more interesting than the regular case. The latter proves nothing; the exception proves everything. The exception does not only confirm the rule; the rule as such lives off the exception alone. (qtd. in *HS* 16)

Agamben adheres to this logic in his reflections about the rule/law and the exception. Taking up this topological determination, the analogy with Bataille's theory of the limit/rule and the transgression becomes visible. The fact that transgression remains bound to the limit is also the focus of Foucault's interest in his text about Bataille. To again quote Foucault:

> The limit and transgression depend on each other for whatever density of being they possess: a limit could not exist if it were absolutely uncrossable and, reciprocally, transgression would be pointless if it merely crossed a limit composed of illusions and shadows.[4]

IV

'Sovereignty' is another key term of the Bataillean *oeuvre*, one which proves at the same time to be the most complex. Bataille's theory is grounded in a general organisation of human experience according to a fundamental dichotomy. The occurrences and practices of the everyday dictated by utility and capital accumulation belong to the sphere of the profane. The sphere of the sacred is characterised by exceptional states of excess and wastefulness in which alone the subject has the chance to experience its own sovereignty. In accordance with his general loathing of any kind of utility and means–end calculation, Bataille thus defines sovereignty as follows: 'The sovereignty *I* speak of has little to do with the sovereignty of States, as international law defines it. I speak in general of an aspect that is opposed to the servile and the subordinate.'[5]

Inasmuch as the sovereign of the state is bound by political and economic interests, deliberations and calculations – which is true even of the Hobbesian or 'absolute' sovereign – he cannot be truly sovereign in the Bataillean sense. For Bataille, on the contrary, 'sovereignty' means ridding oneself of any desire for power, accumulation and self-preservation, and ultimately, of the fear of death. It should be clear that this sovereignty can never be pursued in a consistent fashion, let alone ultimately realised, but that it is attained only momentarily in states of ecstatic experience. Agamben concludes his 1987 essay on Bataille:

> If this is the paradox of sovereignty, can we then say that Bataille succeeded in breaking its circle in his passionate attempt to think community? In attempting to think beyond the subject, in attempting to think the *ecstasy* of the subject, he essentially only thought its [the subject's] inner limit, its constitutive antinomy, the *sovereignty of the subject*.[6]

Agamben here takes a decidedly Heideggerian line of attack: Bataille's polemical appropriation of the term sovereignty might expose its fundamental paradox, but can only do so by restricting itself to a crypto-Cartesian inquiry into the condition of the subject. Agamben thereby certainly touches upon an aspect of Bataille's thought system, namely his shift of focus from communal to inner experience, from a horizontal to a vertical level of analysis. Questions of community certainly become less relevant in Bataille's post-war texts, and practices of mysticism are more important to the inner experience that Bataille seems now to be pursuing.

V

Interestingly, however, in *Homo Sacer*, Agamben picks up on the subject of mysticism when the question of negation arises in his topological elaborations:

> The exception is to positive law what negative theology is to positive theology. While the latter affirms and predicates determinate qualities of God, negative (or mystical) theology, with its 'neither ... nor ...', negates and suspends the attribution to God of any predicate whatsoever. Yet negative theology is not outside theology and can actually be shown to function as the principle grounding the possibility in general of anything like a theology. Only because it has been negatively presupposed as what subsists outside any possible predicate can divinity become the subject of a predication. (*HS* 17)

As we learned earlier from Foucault, Bataille's negation is not to be confused with a 'satanic denial' – Satanism does nothing more than to invert the cross, and it therefore ultimately affirms a decidedly Christian system of reference. Bataille, however, does embrace the practice of negative theology in constituting his practice of 'atheology'. God is defined by that which he is not, his absence is the object of all prayer. Yet Bataille rids himself of this signifier – that is, God – altogether, centring 'absence' alone in his atheology, which he describes as the science of not-knowing.

Famously, Bataille found an expression of this ecstatic experience, in which pleasure and pain can no longer be clearly distinguished, in the photograph of a man undergoing *Lingchi*, the 'death by a thousand cuts'. In this Chinese form of execution, a man is tied to a pole and then has large pieces of flesh cut from his body. Bataille was fascinated with this image because he believed he saw not an expression of agony in the victim's face, but rather one of ecstasy. The photograph remained an 'object of meditation' for Bataille which he kept above his desk, a practice that seems analogous to the mystics' contemplation of the dying Christ or the saints' accessorising with skulls and other *memento mori*. But of course, Bataille's meditation does not serve a Christian self-mortification or *imitatio*. Rather, in looking at the Chinese torture, he attempted to grasp the experience of ecstasy in the face of death. In this connection, Agamben does not acknowledge the particular definition of 'sovereignty' that Bataille tries to establish, and criticises the latter in *Homo Sacer* accordingly:

> Yet what Bataille is unable to master is precisely (as is shown by his interest in the pictures of the young Chinese torture victim, which he discusses in *The Tears of Eros*) the bare life of *homo sacer*, which the conceptual apparatus of sacrifice and eroticism cannot grasp. (*HS* 113)

It is true that Bataille views the picture of the Chinese torture victim as detached from any social or historical context of the pictured event. Yet what follows from this is not at all what Noys denounces – only slightly varying the overused Benjaminian formula – as an 'aestheticization of violence', but is on the contrary an attempt to gain access to an otherwise inaccessible reality. Bataille sees in the image the possibility for an intense communication, one that might involve what others would identify as aesthetic registers or issues of representation, but that traverses and undercuts any such assignation.

> The young and seductive Chinese man of whom I have spoken, left to the work of the executioner – I loved him with a love in which the sadistic instinct played no part: he communicated his pain to me or perhaps the excessive nature of his pain, and it was precisely that which I was seeking, not so as to take pleasure in it, but in order to ruin in me that which is opposed to him.[7]

Of course this communication must always remain limited; it carries the impossibility of communication with it, the impossibility of truly knowing what another subject experiences, as Amy Hollywood states:

> The photograph is always double, however, always capable of being read either as a support for the myth of total presence or as a sign of the past's 'pastness'. The photograph, not surprisingly, shares the ambiguity of the fetish, marking both the reality of castration and loss *and* their disavowal.[8]

VI

While at this point in time Bataille's thoughts on sovereignty focus on a subjective inner experience, he can indeed be taken to have addressed the issue of 'bare life' in his discussion of fascism and base materialism. It is in those writings that the core of confusion resulting from Agamben's and Bataille's conflicting definitions of the sacred becomes visible. Bataille avails himself of the line of modern anthropological and early sociological thought that defines the sacred as a phenomenon qualified by ambiguity. On the contrary, Agamben's position, by the time he publishes *Homo Sacer* in 1995, has hardened into a wholesale dismissal of this view. Following Robertson Smith, Durkheim and Mauss, Bataille is downright fascinated with the idea that the lowest, dirtiest being would have to be considered the most valued. In the world of political subjects, this logic would seem to pick out those who are, in Marxian terms, members of the *Lumpenproletariat*, that is, a part of society which cannot be controlled and does not have the power to organise itself, and thus, as opposed to the proletariat, lacks (revolutionary) agency.[9] Whereas Marx stigmatises and excludes the *Lumpenproletariat* from his theory of class struggle, Bataille is explicitly concerned with these remnants of society and relates them to his concept of 'base materialism'. 'Base materialism' – or as Bataille would later come to call it, 'heterology' – denotes a thought system he developed, once again, as a response to the very closure of Hegel's dialectical system.[10] His conception centres on the rejects of reason, on that which has to be excluded from everyday experience in order to maintain the capitalist business of instrumentalisation and accumulation. In a deliberate hyperbole of Marx's inversion of Hegel, Bataille claims that the 'ideal' cannot be thought of without considering the 'base' on which it is constituted. Indeed, this variation of Hegelian schemata could appear to be – in particular to English readers – a radicalisation of the Marxian theory of an economic 'base' that serves as a determinant for the intellectual, religious and cultural 'superstructure'. But while the 'base' of this materialism is extracted from the Marxist talk of a *'base matérielle'*, Bataille once again undercuts dialectical closure, in this case by dropping the 'e' and turning the *'base matérielle'* into a *'bas matérialisme'*, mobilising the 'low' against a class identity grounded in a notion of employment and hence labour. As he puts it in his 1933 'The Psychological Structure of Fascism':

> [T]he lowest strata of society can equally be described as heterogeneous, those who generally provoke repulsion and can in no case be assimilated by the whole of mankind. In India, these impoverished classes are considered *untouchable,* meaning that they are characterized by the prohibition of contact analogous to that applied to sacred things.[11]

In his 1993 'Form-of-Life', the opening essay of *Means Without End*, Agamben dismisses this interest in the pariah and the concomitant ambivalence of the sacred in the harshest words he ever found for Bataille: 'To have mistaken such a naked life separate from its form, in its abjection, for a superior principle – sovereignty or the sacred – is the limit of Bataille's thought, which makes it useless to us' (*ME* 7). This noticeable change of course regarding Bataille's theory may become more comprehensible when we remember that Agamben himself still followed this typically 'modern' definition of the sacred in *Language and Death:* '[T]he sacred is necessarily an ambiguous and circular concept. In Latin *sacer* means vile, ignominious, and also august, reserved for the gods' (*LD* 105). When Agamben comes to vigorously reject the idea of an originary ambivalence of the sacred in order to push his newly developed agenda in *Homo Sacer*, Bataille thus effectively – and somewhat ironically – becomes the scapegoat for this operation.

NOTES

1. Michel Foucault, 'A Preface to Transgression', in *Language, Counter-Memory and Practice: Selected Essays and Interviews*, trans. Donald Bouchard and Sherry Simon (Ithaca, NY: Cornell University Press, 1980), pp. 34–6.
2. Jacques Derrida, 'From Restricted to General Economy', in *Writing and Difference*, trans. Alan Bass (London: Routledge, 1978), p. 327 (original italics).
3. Giorgio Agamben, 'Bataille e il paradosso della sovranità', in Jacqueline Risset (ed.), *Georges Bataille: Il politico e il sacro* (Naples: Liguori Editore, 1987), p. 117.
4. Foucault, 'Preface to Transgression', p. 34.
5. Georges Bataille, *The Accursed Share. An Essay on General Economy*, vol. 2: *The History of Eroticism and Sovereignty*, trans. Robert Hurley (New York: Zone Books, 1991), p. 197.
6. Agamben, 'Bataille e il paradosso della sovranità', p. 117 (original italics).
7. Georges Bataille, *Inner Experience*, trans. Stuart Kendall (Albany: SUNY Press, 1988), p. 120.
8. Amy Hollywood, *Sensible Ecstasy, Mysticism, Sexual Difference, and the Demands of History* (Chicago: University of Chicago Press, 2002), p. 94.
9. Cf. Gavin Grindon, 'Alchemist of the Revolution: The Affective Materialism of Georges Bataille', *Third Text* 24.3 (2010): 307.
10. Cf. Georges Bataille, *Visions of Excess. Selected Writings 1927–1939*, ed. Allan Stoekl (Minneapolis: University of Minnesota Press, 1985), pp. 45–52.
11. Bataille, *Visions of Excess*, p. 144.

10 Émile Benveniste

HENRIK WILBERG

THE EXPERIENCE OF LANGUAGE

Émile Benveniste was a French linguist of Sephardic descent, born in 1902 in Aleppo in what was then the Ottoman Empire. A specialist in comparative Indo-European grammar and, in the interwar years, a student of Ferdinand de Saussure's follower Antoine Meillet at the École pratique des hautes études in Paris, he held the chair of linguistics at the Collège de France from 1937 to 1970.[1] Having published widely since 1935, Benveniste came to prominence outside the field of linguistics in 1956, when he contributed a famous article on the function of language in Freud to the first issue of Jacques Lacan's early journal, *La psychanalyse*.[2] From 1960 onwards, at the height of structuralism's influence, he founded and co-edited another journal, *L'homme*, alongside the anthropologist Claude Lévi-Strauss and the geographer Pierre Gourou.

By quantitative measures alone it can easily be established that Émile Benveniste is the linguist of reference in Giorgio Agamben's *oeuvre*. This is true to such an extent that the name of Benveniste is often synonymous with 'modern' or 'contemporary linguistics', lent further support by the fact that Agamben never exhibits any interest in the developments in linguistics after 1970. While other linguists are sometimes mobilised to advance a particular argument at a particular juncture in the text – in *The Time that Remains* (2000), the work devoted to Paul's letter to the Romans, Gustave Guillaume's concept of operational time is used to develop the notion of messianic time (*TR* 65–8),[3] and in *Language and Death* (1982), the linguist Johannes Lohmann plays a similar role, providing a framework through which to think Heidegger's ontological difference in terms of language (*LD* 26)[4] – the presence of the linguist in Agamben is different in the case of

Benveniste. Not content to count Benveniste as merely a linguist among linguists, Agamben can be seen here as the latest in the twentieth-century tradition to employ the tandem of philosophy and linguistics as a metaphysical exit strategy, not unlike the function of Saussure in Derrida, Roman Jakobson in Lacan, and Louis Hjelmslev for Deleuze and Guattari.[5] In all of these instances, a particular linguist is mobilised to – usually polemically – shift the categories of theoretical inquiry with regard to the place of language. With this shift, crucial to Agamben's use of Benveniste, the place of language is no longer immediately recognisable: language ceases to occupy that stable place that an appeal to the established discipline of linguistics would seem to presuppose.

Agamben's linguistic displacement through Benveniste also serves as an important supplement for his approach to the question of language through the works of Heidegger and Walter Benjamin. In the latter two, Agamben finds an experience of language which is irreducible to logic as well as pragmatic fields of application like linguistics or philology. It is one of Agamben's indisputable innovations, both philological and theoretical, to have united in the notion 'experience of language' the linguistic turn commonly associated with Saussure and the structuralist aftermath with its German-speaking counterpart, articulated simultaneously but contestedly by Heidegger and Benjamin, between phenomenology and poetry. Agamben lays out this programme most clearly in 'Experimentum Linguae', a text first published as the preface to the French edition of *Infancy and History* (1989), and subsequently included in the 1993 English version. Here, Agamben departs (without citation) from Benjamin's attempt to transform Kant's concept of experience to reflect the 'linguistic essence of knowledge' (*IH* 4).[6] In the concept of infancy (also borrowed from Benjamin), Agamben tries to construct such an *experimentum linguae*, 'in which the limits of language are to be found not outside language, in the direction of its referent, but in an experience of language as such' (*IH* 5). Agamben asks:

> How can there be experience not of an object but of language itself? [...] In both my written and unwritten books, I have stubbornly pursued only one train of thought: what is the meaning of 'there is language'; what is the meaning of 'I speak'? (*IH* 5)

This, according to Agamben, is not only the *experimentum* that every thinker has to undertake at least once, but 'it is even possible that what we call thought is purely and simply this *experimentum*' (*IH* 6). This identification of thinking with the experience of language is cemented with Heidegger's notion of 'having an experience with language' (*mit der Sprache eine Erfahrung zu machen*), an experience that can only be had 'where we lack names, where speech breaks on our lips' (*IH* 6).[7] While he shares this radical notion of experience, the task Agamben has set himself in *Infancy and History* is that 'there is an experience of language which is not merely a silence or a deficiency of names, but one whose logic can be indicated, whose site and formula can be designated, at least up to a point' (*IH* 6). It is in the indication of this 'logic' that Agamben turns precisely to Benveniste as the one who led linguistics 'face to face with the supreme aporia, beyond which it cannot advance without its transformation into philosophy', namely the 'difference between language and speech (Saussure's *langue* and *parole* – or rather, in Benveniste's terms, between semiotic and semantic) which cannot be encompassed, and which every reflection on language must confront' (*IH* 6). While Heidegger and Benjamin provide the ultimate orientation of thinking language, it is with Benveniste that language as such is given the necessary contours by way of grasping, as Agamben puts it elsewhere, 'language's point of excess with respect to science' (*PO* 76), and thus paves the way for the coming philosophy.

THE NON-PLACE OF LANGUAGE

There are instances where Agamben goes even further in emphasising the place of linguistics in his works, extending it even to the place of the linguist himself and the linguist's own experience of language. The presence of the linguist himself is required for the displacement of language: whereas the earlier chapters of *Remnants of Auschwitz* are structured around the witness's testimony to a singular experience of survival, the final chapter introduces the theoretical questions posed by the archive in Agamben's archaeological method. The shift, however, takes the form of the following biographical anecdote:

> One evening in 1969, Émile Benveniste, Professor of Linguistics at the Collège de France, suffered an attack on a street in Paris. Without identification papers, he was not recognized. By the time he was identified, he had already suffered a complete and incurable aphasia that lasted until his death in 1972 and kept him from working in any way. (*RA* 137)

A typical example of Agamben's use of textual 'thresholds', this unfortunate episode in the linguist's life pushes the question of testimony and subjective voice into proximity with the linguistic categories involved in its 'archivisation'. Conversely, Benveniste's name is added to those of Primo Levi, Jean Améry and others in the earlier chapters; Benveniste, too, all of a sudden joins the ranks of the paradoxical figures of impossible testimony and of the witness as a remnant, with the paradox given heightened urgency by the fact that this 'complete and incurable aphasia' affected a professor of linguistics. Agamben then points out that in 1972, three years after the incident, his essay 'The Semiology of Language' was published in the journal *Semiotica*: 'At the end of this article, Benveniste outlines a research program that moves beyond Saussurian linguistics, one that was never realized. It is not surprising that the basis for this program lies in the theory of enunciation, which may well constitute Benveniste's most felicitous creation' (*RA* 137). In other words, the valuable theory lost to the linguist's aphasia was the final articulation of Benveniste's theory of enunciation, precisely the 'putting into function of language by an individual act of use' (*un acte individuel d'utilisation*).[8] What Agamben finds so attractive in this anecdote is evidently the coupling of a theory of language use, a theory of its taking place (as opposed to Saussure's notion of *parole*), with a linguist who, like the human beings deprived of their humanity described earlier in *Remnants of Auschwitz*, has taken leave of language altogether.[9] The move beyond Saussure – 'a second-generation semiology', as Benveniste puts it[10] – was based on the realisation of an impasse in the theory of the sign. The final goal articulated by Saussure, the semiology of language, finds itself paradoxically blocked by the conceptual invention that brought the very idea of semiology into being in the first place. According to Benveniste, there is no passage from the sign to the actualised phrasing of language:

> Saussure did not ignore the sentence, but it clearly posed a grave difficulty for him, one that he then referred to the 'parole', which solves nothing; what concerns us is precisely if and how one can pass from the sign to 'parole'. In reality, the world of the sign is closed. From the sign to the sentence there is no transition, neither by syntagmatization nor by any other means. A hiatus separates them.[11]

The world of the sign, and by extension that of Saussurian linguistics, is closed. Thus, for Agamben, Benveniste becomes the paradigmatic figure of the linguist at the threshold, whose final works point towards this non-place of language, the impossibility of constituting or 'having' language at hand as an object of study (which can only be done at the level of the sign as semiotics). At this point, something emerges that is 'of language' but no longer 'linguistic', to which Benveniste's work never ceases to bear witness.

THE ARCHAEOLOGICAL QUESTION

Benveniste remains an important figure for Agamben not just because of these contributions to general linguistics. Especially in the *Homo*

Sacer works, Agamben increasingly makes use of Benveniste's work on comparative Indo-European grammar, and particularly the monumental final work *Le vocabulaire des institutions indo-européennes*, published in two volumes in 1969. Indeed, it seems that the attraction to Benveniste comes in part from what Agamben clearly sees as the latter's double de-struction of linguistics: of general (Saussurian) linguistics on the one hand, and of the nineteenth-century project of comparative grammar on the other. Agamben writes in an essay on Aby Warburg: 'While Benveniste's *Indo-European Language and Society* brought comparative grammar to a limit point at which the very epistemological categories of the historical disciplines seemed to waver, Benveniste's theory of enunciation carried the science of language into the traditional territory of philosophy' (PO 101).[12] In both cases, Benveniste stands for an exhaustion of the paradigm of linguistics, in the structuralist as well as the encyclopaedic nineteenth-century sense. In the preface to the first volume on Indo-European institutions, Benveniste tried to articulate this step beyond the epistemology shared among specialists until then. Most work on Indo-European language had sought to trace the concordances among the known ancient languages and their offshoots, collecting evidence of lexical correspondence in the vocabularies of kinship, livestock, agricultural tools, etc. According to Benveniste, his endeavour is 'entirely different'. Instead of focusing on the commonalities among Indo-European languages, the supposedly shared cultural substrate, Benveniste's study is devoted to the Indo-European vocabulary as specifically institutional terms, lexical entities that often cannot point to such a shared origin. Rather than conceiving of Indo-European as a kind of reservoir of a common culture, Benveniste sees the Indo-European origin as governed by a pattern of institutional dispersal.[13] Here, in Benveniste's notion of the origin not as a point of gathering but as a point of dispersal, Agamben discovers a version of the archaeological method he himself is trying to adopt in the works comprising *Homo Sacer*. In a methodological passage from *The Signature of All Things* (2008), it is this feature of Benveniste's work that Agamben refers to when asking the question of 'how the *archē* that is in question in archaeology is to be understood'. In Benveniste, Indo-European language comes into view as a suspended or an-archic origin, one that can methodologically disregard 'how the epistemological *locus* and historical consistency of something like an "Indo-European institution" was to be understood' (ST 109–10). The limit of Benveniste's method is, however, equally evident, remaining once again at the threshold of Agamben's proposed philosophical archaeology: 'it is quite probable that Benveniste would not have been able to suggest a solution in this regard, even if he had not been struck by a type of total and incurable aphasia' (*ST* 110).

THE USE OF LINGUISTICS

Despite the many occasions when Agamben makes use of arguments from linguistics, as a scientific discipline it is only crucial insofar as it gives shape to the experience of language as such. It can do so precisely by experiencing its own aporetic limits as a threshold to what would be a truly philosophical concept of linguistic experience, and Benveniste is identified as the one linguist, in the aftermath of Saussure, who solicited this aporia in its most radical form. What, one needs to ask, remains of linguistics once this step has been taken? First of all, it should be noted that the encounter with the limits of linguistics does not produce an aphasic effect. It clearly does not prevent Agamben from making direct use of linguistic analyses, and the work of Benveniste in particular, at decisive junctures in the later *Homo Sacer* books. The demonstration of linguistics as an aporetic science in no way diminishes his ability to appeal to Benveniste's authority, in particular on matters of Indo-European grammar and usage.

In conclusion, we may find a possible answer to this question by considering a precedent for such a 'free use' of linguistics: the position taken by Jacques Lacan concerning 'his' representative of linguistics, Roman Jakobson. Lacan articulated his 'final' position vis-à-vis linguistics in his seminar on 19 December 1972. Although not featured among the references to Lacan in *Stanzas*, it nevertheless permeates the conceptual regime of Agamben's text.[14] In Jakobson's (silent) presence, Lacan made it clear that

> [t]he fact that I say that the unconscious is structured like a language is not part and parcel of the field of linguistics. [. . .] [I]f one considers everything that, given the definition of language, follows regarding the foundation of the subject [. . .] – then one must, in order to leave Jakobson his own turf, forge another word. I will call it linguistricks (*linguisterie*).[15]

Taking leave of linguistics in order to articulate an experience of language that is precisely not 'linguistic', 'linguistricks', marks the proper domain of Agamben's use of Benveniste. If this interpretation has anything to it, it would cast a different light upon the 'linguistic' character of some of the fundamental concepts and arguments in *Homo Sacer* in particular. For example, the famous distinction between *bios* and *zoè*, criticised heavily by Jacques Derrida among others, turns out to be not so much a conceptual departure as the expression of an archaeological exigency. This exigency is none other than the need to move beyond the relation Heidegger had developed between being and language in his critique of 'the animal having language', Aristotle's ζῷον λόγον ἔχον. Agamben's Benveniste is therefore not an interdisciplinary use, but a necessary operation in order to capture in the concept of *homo sacer* (between bare life and language) what ultimately eluded Heidegger. It should therefore not surprise us that Agamben, in *The Use of Bodies*, goes so far as to list Benveniste alongside Nietzsche, Benjamin and Foucault as 'those non-professional philosophers' seeking an alternative to the aporias of contemporary thought (*UB* 113).

NOTES

1. Agamben himself engages with the details of Benveniste's studies under Meillet in *The Sacrament of Language* (14).
2. Émile Benveniste, 'Remarques sur la fonction du langage dans la découverte freudienne', in *Problémes de linguistique générale*, vol. 1 (Paris: Gallimard, 1966), pp. 75–87.
3. The work in question is Gustave Guillaume, *Temps et verbe. Théorie des aspects, des modes et des temps* (Paris: Honoré Champion, 1965).
4. Lohmann's study is Johannes Lohmann, 'M. Heideggers "ontologische Differenz" und die Sprache', *Lexis. Studien zur Sprachphilosophie, Sprachgeschichte und Begriffsbestimmung* 1 (1948): 49–106.
5. Most prominently in the section 'Geology of Morals' in Gilles Deleuze and Félix Guattari, *A Thousand Plateaus: Capitalism and Schizophrenia*, trans. Brian Massumi (Minneapolis: University of Minnesota Press, 1987), pp. 39–75.
6. The passage in Benjamin is from *On the Program for the Coming Philosophy*, in *Selected Writings*, ed. Marcus Bullock and Michael W. Jennings, vol. 1 (Cambridge, MA: The Belknap Press of Harvard University Press, 2004), p. 107.
7. The Heidegger text Agamben cites is the first of the lectures published under the title 'Das Wesen der Sprache', in *Unterwegs zur Sprache*, ed. Friedrich Wilhelm von Herrmann, *Gesamtausgabe*, vol. 12 (Frankfurt a.M.: Vittorio Klostermann, 1985), p. 149.
8. Émile Benveniste, 'L'appareil formel de l'énonciation', in *Problèmes de linguistique générale*, vol. 2 (Paris: Gallimard, 1974), p. 80.
9. Agamben places such an importance on this conjuncture that he inaccurately brings forward the publication date of Benveniste's essay: 'The Semiology of Language' was published in 1969, that is, prior to its author's descent into aphasia. See Émile Benveniste, 'Sémiologie de la langue', *Semiotica* 1 (1969): 1–12. Furthermore, Benveniste did not die in 1972, but lived until 1976.

10. Émile Benveniste, 'Sémiologie de la langue', in *Problèmes de linguistique générale*, vol. 2, p. 66.
11. Benveniste, 'Sémiologie de la langue', p. 65.
12. Though it should be remembered that the two works of Ferdinand de Saussure that were published during his lifetime were both in comparative Indo-European grammar: *On the Primitive System of Vowels in Indo-European Languages* (1878) and his doctoral thesis *On the Use of the Genitive Absolute in Sanskrit* (1881).
13. See Émile Benveniste, *Le vocabulaire des institutions indo-européennes. 1: Économie, parenté, societé* (Paris, Minuit, 1969), p. 9.
14. At the end of the introduction, we encounter what is almost certainly a reference to *Encore*: 'Only a philosophical topology, analogous to what in mathematics is defined as an *analysis situs* in opposition to *analysis magnitudinis* would be adequate to the *topos outopos*, the placeless place whose Borromean knot we have tried to draw in these pages' (S xviii–xix). Lacan's first publicly available treatment of the Borromean knot is in the session on 22 October 1973. See Jacques Lacan, *The Seminar, Book XX: Encore, On Feminine Sexuality: The Limits of Love and Knowledge*, trans. Bruce Fink (New York: Norton, 1998), pp. 118–36.
15. Lacan, *The Seminar, Book XX*, p. 15.

11 Dante Alighieri

PAOLO BARTOLONI

The Italian poet Dante Alighieri (1265–1321) is invoked several times in the work of Giorgio Agamben, often in passing to stress a point, as when discussing the political relevance of *désoeuvrement* (KG 246); to develop a thought, as in the articulation of the medieval idea of imagination as the medium between body and soul (S, especially 127–9); or to explain an idea, as in the case of the artistic process understood as the meeting of contradictory forces such as inspiration and critical control (FR, especially 48–50). So while Agamben does not engage with Dante systematically, he refers to him constantly, treating the Florentine poet as an *auctoritas* whose presence adds critical rigour and credibility. Identifying and relating the instances of these encounters is useful since they highlight central aspects of Agamben's thought and its development over the years, from the first writings, such as *Stanzas*, to more recent texts, such as *Il fuoco e il racconto* and *The Use of Bodies*. The significance of Agamben's reliance on Dante can be divided into two categories: the aesthetic and the political. The following discussion will address each of these categories separately, but will also emphasise the philosophical continuity that links the discussion of the aesthetic with that of the political. While in the first instance Dante is offered as an example of poetic innovation, especially in relation to the use of language and imagination, in the second he is invoked as a forerunner of new forms of life. Mediality and potentiality are the two pivots connecting the aesthetic and the political.

Stanzas was first published in 1977, and centres on the experience of reality. This is dealt with by tracing the origin of the discussion in antiquity, which often in Agamben equates with the work of Aristotle. As Agamben indicates, by experience of reality Aristotle understood the transformation of the real into a sensible phenomenon. Aristotle described a process that, starting from a thing, turns the thing itself into an image, which is perceived and processed by the senses, and culminates with the experience of not so much the thing but its phantasm. Aristotle's thought was glossed and reinforced by an exemplary philosophical tradition including John Peckham (*Perspectiva communis*) and especially Averroes, who, in *Commentarium magnum in Aristotelis De Anima libros*, emphasised that the act of seeing can be carried out only through a transparent medium. Dante's poetry, Agamben claims, is deeply influenced by Averroes (Agamben calls Dante and Cavalcanti 'Averroistic poets' [*UB* 233]).

Dante, but also Cavalcanti and generally the poetic movement known as *dolce stil novo*, is offered as an example of an aesthetic experience of the threshold, the encounter, in other words, of the subject and object of poetry in the in-between space brought about by the image (the phantasm). In *Stanzas* the image is articulated as the result of the transformative process of the thing itself, but also as the necessary product of imagination, which Agamben, following medieval thought (Boethius's *The Consolation of Philosophy* comes to mind), considers as the medium between body and soul (*S* 127). Image and imagination generate a poetic experience and a language (*la parola poetica*) that abolish the dichotomy between desire and need, and that turn Dante's experience of love into an epiphany of subject/object co-presence. Agamben's claim may appear as a contemporary redressing of Andreas Capellanus's discussion of love in *De amore*. In Capellanus's book, passion was understood as a form of contemplation conceived by the mind from what it saw.[1] Yet there is more to Agamben's argument than the mere rehearsal of medieval conceptualisations. But let us progress chronologically, and one step at a time.

Infancy and History was first published in 1978, one year after *Stanzas*. Although Dante is not mentioned directly, his friend and poetic companion Guido Cavalcanti is the subject of a short chapter. The poetry of Cavalcanti is employed as an umbrella term containing the whole experience of the *dolce stil novo*, including Dante. Agamben argues that by presenting the image as the manifestation of the conjunction of object and subject, their opposition was rendered inoperative in the *dolce stil novo*:

> given the mediating nature of imagination [...] the phantasm is also the subject, not just the object, of Eros. In fact, since love has its only site in imagination, desire never directly encounters the object in its corporeality [...] but an image [...] which is literally the product of desire, within which the boundaries between subjective and objective, corporeal and incorporeal, desire and its object are abolished. (*IH* 25–6)

Putting aside the questionable treatment of Cavalcanti, offered here more as a metonym for *dolce stil novo* than as a poet with his singular voice (recent studies on the love poetry of the *dolce stil novo* stress the continuity but also the significant differences between the various poets belonging to the movement, especially Dante and Cavalcanti – differences that Agamben appears to conveniently disregard),[2] the emphasis on the suspension and halting of binary oppositions such as subject/object, body/spirit and desire/need is strong and striking, and is reminiscent of oppositions such as potentiality/actuality, *zoè/bios* and authenticity/inauthenticity, which Agamben tackles and challenges in subsequent books.

The End of the Poem, originally published in 1996, provides the transition between Agamben's discussion of Dante as a poet and Dante as a political exemplar. In this book, two chapters are devoted to discussing Dante, 'Comedy' and 'The Dream of Language'. The first deals with the notion of guilt and redemption and the second with the double experience of language. In 'Comedy', Agamben proposes an interpretation of the title of Dante's most famous book, *The Divine Comedy*, claiming that Dante's decision to align himself with the comic genre rather than the tragic one, as in the case of his model Virgil, is postulated upon his belief that humans are naturally innocent yet predisposed to sinful acts, and that their earthly journey ought to be marked by a process of redemption from guilt to innocence. In 'The Dream of Language' Dante is presented as an example of bilingualism, in which the language of poetry and love, the vernacular, confronts the grammatical language of politics and power, Latin.

Il fuoco e il racconto and *The Use of Bodies* were both published in 2014. The first collects a series of shorter essays addressing different themes relating to the creative process, and the second is an extended treatise on the relationship between habitus and production or the experience of being and that of doing. By linking the artistic endeavour to modalities of life (*forme-di-vita*), Agamben erects a bridge straddling aesthetic and political philosophy, and Dante is employed instrumentally as one of the several supporting pillars.

While in *Il fuoco e il racconto* Dante is called upon to exemplify the distinction between *creare ex nihilo* and *facere de materia*, thus elucidating an intrinsic poetic preoccupation, in *The Use of Bodies* Dante's writing is gradually extended to include the political dimension of everyday life. Agamben interprets *creare ex nihilo* (inspiration) and *facere de materia* (the bodily act of writing, and thus the creative control brought to bear on the poetic afflatus) as the two main poles of creative production; a successful poetic outcome is the necessary dialectical synthesis of the two. As an example of this conjunction, in *Il fuoco e il racconto* Agamben cites twice (*FR* 14, 48) a line from Dante's *Paradise*, Canto XIII, lines 77–8, where Dante writes that someone who calls himself a poet must have a trembling hand ('l'artista/ c'ha l'abito de l'arte ha man che trema').[3] Essence and existence, *abito* (habitus) and *modo-di-vita* (form-of-life) are the two poles that need to meet and find a balance should one aspire to poetic greatness.

The artistic process is not without analogy to political life for Agamben. He claims that the issue of forms-of-life has emerged in Western thought as an ethical (the way of life of an individual or a group) or an aesthetic (the personal style of an author) problem. Agamben goes on to state that way of life and style can find a productive synthesis if they are considered ontologically, and if aesthetic and ethical problems are tuned into an ontological question or an 'ontology of style' (*UB* 233). Agamben intimates that the only moment at which the ontological dimension has been mobilised in the history of Western philosophy is to be found in the work of Averroes, and especially in the conjunction between the individual (*il singolo*) and what Agamben calls the universal intellect (*l'intelletto unico*). The link between the two terms of the ontological equation, the individual and the group, is provided by imagination.

Agamben argues for an ontological turn which, by combining ethics and aesthetics, becomes the new space of political engagement by going back to the phantasm that he had so closely discussed in *Stanzas*. Dante, as an Averroistic poet, is cited in support of Agamben's argument. It is true, as Agamben argues in *The Use of Bodies* (*UB* 211), that in *De Monarchia*[4] Dante established a link between what he called the 'potential intellect' (*l'intelletto possibile*) and the active intellect (*l'intelleto agente*), the first characterising the individual and the second the multitude. According to this conceptualisation, potentiality and action are conjoined since the human being's praxis is the result of the transformation of the potential aspirations and ideas of the individual into actions brought about by the multitude. In reality, Dante's Averroism is more complicated than Agamben makes us believe. In one of the most famous and central passages of *Purgatory*, Canto XXV, lines 61–75,[5] Dante, through the Roman poet Statius, explains the innate hybrid nature of humans, made partly by divine intervention (the soul) and by nature (the body). These two halves are linked by imagination, which makes it possible to bring to fruition the fullness of sensible and intellectual experience. In the same passage Dante exposes what was believed to be a crucial error in Averroes' philosophy, that is, the separation of soul and potential intellect. Averroes understood the soul as belonging to the sensible dimension and therefore as separate from the potential intellect, which, as a result, could only be activated by the universal or active intellect. Contrary to this belief, and more in tune with the Fathers of the Church, especially St Thomas, Dante affirmed the tangible existence of a potential intellect inspired and guided by the soul. Dante argued that human knowledge is the product of the potential intellect in which sensible forms are received, scanned and understood. The transformation of this particular and singular knowledge into universal and active knowledge requires another form of intelligence, that is, active intellect. The difference is of degrees, but all the same Agamben's treatment of Dante runs the risk of obscuring the religious undertone that marks Dante's writings, reducing him to an uncritical follower of Averroes.

The ontological turn described by Agamben through the combination of ethics and aesthetics has two outcomes, which are not necessarily analogous or co-terminal. In the first instance, as has been already intimated, the singular potentiality of the individual is turned into an active process of political engagement by the multitude:

> but precisely for this reason, the existence of the *multitude* coincides with the generic actualization of the potential to think and, consequently, with politics. If there were only the multiple individual actualizations and their sum, there would not be a politics but only the numerical plurality of activities defined by the variety of particular goals. [. . .] But because the actualization of the generic potential of thought coincides with the existence of a *multitudo*, this latter is immediately political. (*UB* 212–13)

In the second instance potentiality and action are experienced simultaneously rather than as separate moments of a process that sees the contingent (potentiality) turning into the necessary (action). The co-experiencing of potentiality and action, of which Dante is provided as an example through the conflation of subject and object, inspiration and poetic control, is the key moment when, according to Agamben, the apparatus on which Western thought since Aristotle has been based is made inoperative. Yet the suspension of the apparatus is not simply an act of renunciation, but becomes instead a form-of-life, which is, as Agamben claims, 'constitutively destituent' (*UB* 277). Is the multitude a form-of-life that is intimately poised to disconnect political habits or simply a form-of-life? Ultimately, is Dante an example of poetic or political innovation or indeed the first example of an ontology of being to come?

The significance of Dante in the work of Agamben is apparent and stated several times throughout his work. Yet Dante's treatment is akin to a footnote, albeit essential and ever present in consideration of his prestige and status in Western thought and writing. The outcome is impressive, and at times Agamben's discussion of Dante's work generates fascinating philosophical insights. However, it also oversimplifies ideas and thoughts, which although not detracting from the plausibility of Agamben's overall discussion, generates a degree of indeterminacy and ambiguity.

NOTES

1. Capellanus's definition of love, which Agamben quotes word for word in *Stanzas* (S 81), is as follows: '*ex sola cogitatione, quam concipit animus ex eo, quod vidit, passio illa procedit*' ('this passion derives only from the contemplation that the mind conceives from what it saw'). On Capellanus and love, see also Kathleen Andersen-Wyman, *Andreas Capellanus on Love? Desire, Seduction, and Subversion in Twelfth-Century Latin Text* (New York: Palgrave, 2007).
2. See, for instance, Tristan Kay, *Dante's Lyric Redemption: Eros, Salvation, Vernacular Tradition* (Oxford: Oxford University Press, 2016).
3. '[T]he artist who in the practice of his art has a hand that trembles', Dante, *Paradiso*, trans. Charles S. Singleton (Princeton: Princeton University Press, 1975), p. 145.
4. For an English edition and translation of *De Monarchia*, see Dante, *Monarchy*, trans. Prue Shaw (Cambridge: Cambridge University Press, 1996).
5. For the relevant passage in English, see Dante, *Purgatorio*, trans. Charles S. Singleton (Princeton: Princeton University Press, 1973), p. 273.

12 Gilles Deleuze

CLAIRE COLEBROOK

Perhaps the best way to approach the relationship between Deleuze and Agamben is to adopt a method from Deleuze and Guattari's late philosophy: the conceptual persona.[1] Here philosophical proper names do not stand for biographies or persons but for orientations or maps of thinking. Descartes, for example, enables a whole tradition of Cartesian dualism, even for those who neither read nor reference his work. There are some occasions when Agamben's history of thought also considers proper names less as labels for specific historical individuals, and more as markers of a certain style or distribution of thinking. His recent *The Use of Bodies*, for example, sees Spinoza as a way of coming to terms with the relation between essence and existence (between *what* a being is, and *that* a being is) (*UB* 160). The names Agamben draws upon are not so much focused upon for their singular greatness, but because they provide a way for thinking about what Agamben sees as the ongoing problem of the singular existence of an individuated being, and then the way that being is identified in language. One might also think of this as the difference between the simple event *that* something is, and then the identifiable *what* of the thing. In *What is Philosophy?* Deleuze and Guattari treat proper names as conceptual personae, suggesting – as Agamben does – that philosophical problems (and the names that attach to them) are not academic exercises of a specific discipline, but have to do with the very possibility of thinking (in domains well beyond philosophy).

In different ways, both Agamben and Deleuze write as if the proper names of philosophers capture or give form to what is already problematic in thinking. If one wants to think about a world of Ideas, or the essences that have an eternal being regardless of whether they are brought into existence, one thinks of Plato. And if one wants to think – as both Agamben and Deleuze do – of the relation between essences and then the singular event of living beings, one uses the proper names of 'Plato' and 'Aristotle'. Both Deleuze and Agamben write of the relation between Plato and Aristotle not simply as two bodies of work, but as an event that was almost destined to occur in thinking, where there were at once essences posited that would grant the world a timeless order and propriety, and then the life that somehow allows those essences to be brought into being.[2] Proper names are not just ways of organising the history of philosophy but seem to answer a demand, not just for thinking beings but for life. It is as though – again for both Agamben and Deleuze – there is something odd about thought and its relation to life; in comparison to other living beings, thinking creates strange events and odd forms of difference in human beings. When we think about art, science or philosophy we need to acknowledge *both* that such practices emerge from life, but also that they are distinct events that open the question of who 'we' are. To think about artists – such as Proust (for Deleuze)[3] or Titian (for Agamben [O 85]) – is to examine a singular expression of a problem or aporia that is at once grounded in a history of thought, but also emerges from the problem of life. One way to think about Agamben and Deleuze – especially if one deploys the notion of conceptual personae – is to think of Agamben as retrieving the problem of 'man' and language, while Deleuze provided a way for thinking about life beyond humans and language.

Yet another (almost opposing) way to mark out these two figures is to see Agamben as constantly thinking the problem of the threshold between mute life and then its speaking/political formations, while Deleuze and Guattari wrote about art and philosophy almost as though they had broken away from life to become autonomous, operating through the plane of composition or the plane of concepts. For Deleuze and Guattari, conceptual personae mark out possibilities for *philosophical* orientation, as though there might be something like a plane of thought, its history and distributions that could be considered regardless of context. Here one might think of 'Deleuze' as the philosopher of becoming (tied to other concepts, such as difference, schizoanalysis, immanence and – according to Agamben – life). On this same model of conceptual personae Agamben's *homo sacer* would allow for the thought of thresholds, constitutive expulsions, bare life and inoperativity. If one were to take this approach one might see each philosopher as occupying distinct but overlapping planes of immanence (to use Deleuze and Guattari's diction) or paradigms (to follow Agamben). Both would be striving to articulate *thought's* distributions.

It would make quite a difference if one were to use Agamben's (rather than Deleuze and Guattari's) mode of comparison to think about his relation to Deleuze. While both philosophers raise the question of life, and thought's problematic relation to life, and while both are committed to immanence, if one adopts Agamben's approach of considering history in terms of signatures or paradigms then the relation between the two changes. Reading back from what Agamben and Deleuze see as the task of philosophy might help with this distribution. Both thinkers – despite their manifest erudition – are explicit about the *practical* force of thinking (*HS* 8).[4] For Agamben, the history of thinking in all its different formations, or workings, *does something*; it labours over what something is (its identity, essence or name) and then its existence (*this* human here, who is not reducible to a general kind). One might think of this relation as the emergence of relations from something that is absolutely 'in itself and non-relational', or as the difference between God and creation, between law and its exercise or between humans as political forms and their mere life; but in general Agamben thinks of this ongoing operation as something like a machine that produces 'man' as something other than bare life. That operation has distinct political implications, as Agamben's famous example of *homo sacer* makes clear: what counts as a political being (man, the human citizen, the subject of law) is marked off from a life that, without this political naming, is nothing more than bare life, abandoned. The theological history of this separation, difference, threshold, ban or operation seems highly abstract and arcane: how do we think about God whose pure and infinite existence cannot be limited or defined by any single predicate, and then the world of existing things that are all (seemingly) instances *of* divine essences. God creates 'man' in general (essentially) but how do we think about what makes *this* human the singular individuated human that it is? This is the problem of individuation, and its operation, according to Agamben, expresses itself in the history of philosophy. Deleuze, in a somewhat different manner, also sees individuation or the difference of singular beings as the crucial task of thought, and yet does not see the entire history of thought as an ongoing operation around a central aporia. Agamben reads the history of thought as though the operation plays itself out in a series of thinkers, while always producing a structurally similar aporia. If this world and life *are* divine (and not requiring redemption from some transcendent or external source [*IH* 101], if God or the divine are not distinct and other from this world, how *do* we think the existence of this world without seeing it simply as an example or instance of divine essences that could just as easily *not be*?

All of Agamben's work is therefore oriented towards an immanence that renders the distinction between essence and existence *inoperative*, and when he reads Deleuze it is *this* way of reading the problem of life and immanence that he intuits:

> Considered as a simultaneously asyntagmatic and indivisible block, the title 'Immanence: A Life . . .' is therefore something like a diagram condensing the thought of the late Deleuze. At first glance, it already articulates the fundamental character of Deleuzian immanence, that is, its 'not referring to an object' and its 'not belonging to a subject' – in other words, its being immanent only to itself and, nevertheless, in movement. (PO 224)

It is as though Deleuze is one more operation or expression of a problem that is not merely philosophical and that – for Agamben – cannot be captured by philosophy's distinction between what something is (ontology) and the ways we speak about what something is (logic). That division is problematic, and the problem emerges not so much because some philosophers (Plato/Aristotle) simply invented a certain way of speaking. Rather, to be a singular individuated being, to be *me*, is not to be an example of an essence, such that calling myself 'human' would capture who *I* am. Nor does my proper name capture who I am. For both Agamben and Deleuze it is important *not* to think of the world as composed of differences and relations, but of the coming into difference from indifference. If language is important for both of them, and it is, this is not because language is a structure that cuts the world into meaningful units. Language is temporal, and is only possible because the world, life or being is not some stable collection of created things that instantiates essences; essences are the ways in which life comes into being. *What* something is emerges from its coming into being. For Agamben, the importance of rendering the distinction between essence and existence inoperative is political and urgent. It pertains not only to the sense we have of the human – that there is something that we *are* that is then exemplified in life – it is also intertwined with the sovereign paradigm, or the notion of a transcendent, stable, essential and eternally existing Same, that must then (somehow) have a relation to a lesser and created world of life.

To go back to comparing Deleuze and Agamben by way of conceptual personae, we might say that Agamben marks out a way of thinking about the relations among theology (God/creation), sovereignty (law and the life it orders) and life (*what* something is, and *that* something is), and in all cases he attends to the threshold of *indifference*. Deleuze, by contrast, would seem to be *the* philosopher of difference. Rather than a body of work focusing on *the* threshold, his work seems to focus on all the different ways in which difference takes place: in language, in genetics, in genres, in social strata, in bodies, in military formations and so on. A Deleuzian approach would seem to map the two thinkers as bearing quite different orientations, and this would be because, for Deleuze, the history of philosophy is something like a constantly altered plane of the creation of concepts, with the task of philosophy (today) being to confront its singular differential power.

While both Deleuze and Agamben are philosophers of immanence and therefore see a single being or life as the plane from which philosophy, language, humanity and social formations emerge, their method for accounting for the history of philosophy alters how we think about each of them in relation to the other. Both suggest that immanence is almost unthinkable given philosophy's tendencies, and both see a history of philosophy as an ongoing struggle to reach immanence; it is as though life requires philosophy and thinking, and yet what makes thinking possible – its relation to the world – pushes thought into the internal error of thinking of itself (and life) as something fixed, as if essences (or beings) were simply there to be actualised. Both also chart a history of philosophy around this problem, with Agamben suggesting that something 'decisive' occurs with Aristotle that will forever divide being (or what is) from its coming into being, and with Deleuze suggesting that thought has a potentiality towards stupidity (towards not realising its *human* potential).[5] But the *difference* between the two is perhaps best captured by thinking of the different ways in which their thought would map the other. As I have already suggested, Agamben maps the history of thought according to a threshold, and the ways in which philosophers *operate* in order to manage the distinction between what is (essence) and that something is (existence). When he reads Deleuze he situates him as one of the thinkers (after Spinoza and Heidegger) who, like Agamben himself, have almost rendered the distinction inoperative and have done so by articulating the way in which life can only be itself, by recalling itself, by giving itself a linguistic being that somehow captures what it must have been all along (*UB* 165–6).

If one were to consider Agamben from a Deleuzian point of view, two things would change. First, if one begins from Deleuze and Guattari's avowedly pluralist version of expressive philosophy, there would not be 'a' threshold of the emergence of speaking humanity from a being that almost seems to demand human life in order to name itself; such an event would be part of a broader milieu of stratifications:

> We invoke one dualism only in order to challenge another. We employ a dualism of models only in order to arrive at a process that challenges all models. Each time, mental correctives are necessary to undo the dualisms we had no wish to construct but through which we pass. Arrive at the magic

formula we all seek – PLURALISM = MONISM – via all the dualisms that are the enemy, an entirely necessary enemy, the furniture we are forever rearranging.[6]

Rather than a whole series of multiplicities, Agamben's thought focuses more on human and speaking life (especially in its Western mode). Although language is significant in Deleuze's philosophy, this is primarily for what it discloses about the possibility for life to generate distinct planes that are not reducible to organic life. Rather than the end of thought being a rendering inoperative of *the* sovereign paradigm (the paradigm that posits a law of what simply is that must somehow apply to a lawless world), the task would be one of becoming-imperceptible. Rather than see being as something that demands its own naming, there is a striving in Deleuze and Guattari's writing towards the unnameable.[7] Such an 'end' of thought is perhaps close to what Agamben gestures to as the beatitude of 'whatever being, where life might simply be *as it is*, without requiring redemption' (CC 5). But there is a difference of inflection in Deleuze and Guattari's concept of becoming-imperceptible. Yes, it aims to overcome the notion of a subject or a humanity to whom the world is given, and yes, it is part of an expressive philosophy in which the world is nothing other than all the expressions it generates of itself: *but* Deleuze and Guattari find the resources for becoming-imperceptible outside philosophy, and outside humanity – in animals, plants, insects, art objects.

To conclude, Agamben and Deleuze are avowedly philosophers of immanence, and quite explicitly see a modal ontology as the best way of thinking about a life that is not the expression of prior forms and essences, but the expression – each time and with each singular being – of what that life (a life) essentially is. Life is nothing other than its potentiality to give itself forth and distinguish itself. Life *is expression* or a demand to be simply what it is. For both Deleuze and Agamben, *indifference* does not refer to a prior or underlying undifferentiated sameness, but a potentiality for smaller and more refined differences. Instead of thinking the essence of 'man', it would be better to capture the 'being thus' not only of every human, but every mood or predicate. In this respect, both writers are anti-humanists, but not because there is no such essence or thing as the human, but because essences and being human involve *more* rather than fewer differences. Essences, then, are not fixed and stable forms that have the potential to be actualised (as though coming into existence were the simple fulfilment of something that may or may not be). To exist is to have a relation to essence, and essences are nothing outside this relation. This is why, in his sustained discussion of Deleuze, Agamben focuses not only on Deleuze's essay on

'Immanence: A Life', but also on the punctuation: the problem of life is that life never simply exists, but is always *this* life, and *what* any life is comes about through its own demand or desire to be itself:

> 'A life', Deleuze writes, 'contains only virtual entities. It is composed of virtualities, events, singularities. What one calls virtual is not something lacking in reality.' Suspending all syntactic ties, the ellipsis dots nevertheless maintain the term 'life' in relation to its pure determinability and, while carrying it into this virtual field, exclude the possibility that the indefinite article 'a' might (as in Neoplatonism) transcend the Being that follows it. (PO 224)

And so, for Agamben, the naming of life, or life's relation to language – and therefore human life – is at once an ongoing problem, but also a way to think about life that breaks with the operations of philosophy's division. What if we could think of this world, not as one of God's creations that he may or may not have brought into being, but rather as blessed in itself, striving only to be itself and *not* oriented to some proper form that is transcendent or prior to life?

NOTES

1. Gilles Deleuze and Felix Guattari, *What is Philosophy?*, trans. Hugh Tomlinson and Graham Burchell (New York: Columbia Univerity Press, 1994), p. 61.
2. Gilles Deleuze, *Difference and Repetition*, trans. Paul Patton (New York: Columbia University Press, 1994), p. 32.
3. Gilles Deleuze, *Proust and Signs: The Complete Text*, trans. Richard Howard (London: Continuum, 2000).
4. Gilles Deleuze, *Spinoza: Practical Philosophy*, trans. Robert Hurley (San Francisco: City Lights, 1988), p. 29.
5. Deleuze, *Difference and Repetition*, p. 149.
6. Gilles Deleuze and Felix Guattari, *A Thousand Plateaus*, trans. Brian Massumi (Minneapolis: University of Minnesota Press, 1987), pp. 20–1.
7. Deleuze and Guattari, *A Thousand Plateaus*, p. 248.

13 Georg Wilhelm Friedrich Hegel

ALYSIA GARRISON

Though more studies have been dedicated to the place of Kant in Agamben's *oeuvre*, Hegel – that other major Enlightenment philosopher indispensable to modernity – holds an equally formative, if perhaps more subtle, place in his work. From the very earliest to the latest texts, Agamben's work seeks to surpass the horizon of Western metaphysics through a philological engagement with the negative, formed in large part through a complex confrontation with Hegel.

Agamben's grappling with the dialectic in search of its idling is not merely strategic, but as he puts it, 'one of the most urgent tasks today' for a Marxist philosophy shored on its wreckage (*IH* 39). In 'The Discreet Taste of the Dialectic', Antonio Negri claims that the work of Agamben enables a 'discreet dialectical rediscovery' typifying left Hegelianism and the young Marx, resulting not in 'the triumph of the *Aufhebung*', but in 'the heroism of the negative'.[1] Rather than valorising the negative, however, as Agamben painstakingly argues in his early text *Language and Death*, it is precisely the negative structure of the Voice, or, in Hegel's terms, the 'bad infinity' predicted on division, that Agamben's thought seeks to absolve (*LD* 100).

Agamben's aim is no less than to suspend the ontological divisions that undergird language and philosophy, to think such divisions beyond themselves, to render them inoperative and thus to develop an alternative ontology. As part of this effort, Agamben critiques Hegel's dialectic to hollow it out, to unwork it, in order to think what has not yet been thought: the end of metaphysics. Only then, the work suggests, will 'the din of a dialectical machine which, *ad infinitum*, defers its answer to the total social process' be silenced (*IH* 28). Agamben's philological attempts to idle Hegel's dialectic and undo the presuppositions of Western thought consolidate in three conceptual turns that I have entitled for simplicity's sake 'Suspense', 'Circle' and 'Use'.

SUSPENSE

Agamben hints at his critique of the negative foundation of art in Hegel's *Aesthetics* in his first book, *The Man Without Content*. But he explicitly confronts Hegel's negative being in his early book *Infancy and History*. Unlike Kant's transcendental subject, Agamben reminds us, for Hegel consciousness is a dialectical process, an inner doubling of consciousness as self-consciousness (*IH* 34). Because its relation to itself is always a self-sundering, consciousness 'can never grasp itself as an entirety, but is whole only in the total process of its becoming', and thus the negative experience of death 'becomes the very structure of the human being' (*IH* 34). Worryingly for Agamben, the dialectical structure of self-consciousness that subtends Hegel's philosophy expropriates experience as something unattainable except as an abstraction of the total social process, as the 'foam of infinity' in the image from the lines by Schiller that conclude the *Phenomenology* (*IH* 34). Since the dialectic ensures the 'containment and unification of the continuum of negative fleeting instants', it captures human experience and happiness (*IH* 104). Agamben will refer throughout his *oeuvre* to this negative foundation as the 'presuppositional structure' of consciousness, of sense-certainty, of language, and finally of metaphysics itself (*HS* 50; *UB* 150).

Agamben advances and elaborates his critique of Hegel in his next early work, *Language and Death*, a book composed in the context of his seminars from 1979 and 1980. Rather than focusing on time, as he did in *Infancy and History*, the emphasis here falls on language. Agamben seeks to think beyond Hegelianism by locating an experience of speech not presupposed by a negative foundation. He begins with a philological critique of Hegel's dialectic of sense-certainty. As Hegel famously argues, this supposedly immediate knowledge is actually the greatest possible abstraction, a dialectical process that contains within itself a negation (*LD* 11–12). The 'Now' that was night is the 'Now' that is noon, and so, as Hegel points out, 'the Now that is Night is *preserved*' and the 'Now' that is noon proves 'to be something that is not'.[2] Agamben argues that this 'unspeakable' in Hegel is guarded in language by speaking it, by 'grasping it in its negativity'. In other words, as Kojève puts it, 'every point of speech blows the negative breath of *Geist*' (*LD* 13–14).

Not just philosophy but poetry itself experiences the 'originary event of its own word as nothing' (*LD* 74). For Agamben, the poem 'Eleusis' that recounts the Eleusinian mystery, which the young Hegel wrote for his friend Hölderlin in 1796, is indicative not of some ineffable outside of language, but of the negativity always-already inherent in sense-certainty, the moment it attempts to 'take the *This*' (*LD* 15; *TR* 100). Reading Giacomo Leopardi's stunning poem *L'infinito*, Agamben locates the same problem, that the poem's *This*, which is to say its particular, is also 'a Not-this (a universal, a *That*)' (*LD* 76). If both philosophy and poetry seek the lost, inaccessible foundation of the word, both 'finally *demonstrate* this place as *unattainable*' (*LD* 78).

It is, however, from this infinite silence and ungraspable immensity that thought arises, which suspends the distinction between the *This* and the *That*. In Leopardi's poem Agamben finds that thought enacts a comparison between 'this voice' as something alive and immediate and 'that infinite silence'. Agamben writes: 'thought is the movement that, fully experiencing the unattainability of the place of language, seeks to *think*, to hold this unattainability in suspense, to measure its dimensions' (*LD* 80). Thought holds language's unattainability 'in suspense' to think beyond the horizon of the Voice and its negativity. Here *thought*, what Agamben will call 'form-of-life' in his later work *Means Without End* – the inseparable context from which naked life can never be extracted – holds in suspense Hegel's dialectic of sense-certainty predicated on negation (*ME* 8).

A similar paradigm operates with the dialectic of Voice. In Hegel's dialectic of sense-certainty, 'Taking-the-This' expresses the removal of 'That'. Likewise, language expresses the removal of the animal voice, what is at once negated and disclosed as an event of meaning. The young Hegel's Jena lessons from 1803–4 and 1805–6 describe the arrest and preservation of the animal voice as entombment or 'the trace of death' (*LD* 46). Here Hegel aligns the animal voice with desire, as the negative self in the dialectic of master and slave. Bound to meaningful discourse, the master cannot fulfil his enjoyment except as a negative articulation. Bataille, Kojève and his French disciples try to surpass the horizon of Hegel's dialectic by recuperating this desire as 'disengaged negativity'. But Agamben argues that thought cannot think beyond Hegelianism by radicalising negativity (*LD* 49). Unless it finds an experience of speech that does not presuppose any negative foundation, metaphysics will continue to reign 'in its most absolute form' (*LD* 53).

This negative foundation as intractable presupposition operates as a paradigm defined by Agamben in *The Signature of All Things*. The German *Aufheben*, at the heart of Hegel's dialectic, signals both 'to raise' and 'to take away', 'to eliminate' (*ST* 26). Like Aristotle's theory of 'privation', which Hegel develops into his concept of *Aufhebung* at the heart of dialectical method, something is withdrawn but also exposed as such. Likewise, a paradigm, like the voice and the master's enjoyment, is suspended yet exposed in language; it refers to its own form through lack.

So how then does speech awaken from this privative entombment, from this paradigmatic prison-house of death? Agamben excavates in the work of Hegel another experience of language not predicated on an unspeakable foundation. Unlike a donkey braying or a cicada chirping, the human being removes and preserves herself as unspeakable in language (*LD* 84–5). Yet language leaves 'in suspense' the question of whether or not language is yet our voice, as 'chirping is the voice of the cricket' (*LD* 107). To experience a language not marked by negativity and death, one must exist in language without being called there by any Voice (*LD* 96). Holding language in suspense, we 'turn back, untroubled, toward home', the taking place of human praxis (*LD* 108).

CIRCLE

It is at this point of fracture that we glimpse not only language taking place, but also the point of departure for philosophy to absolve this very division. In Hegel the mode of thinking that thinks its own negative foundation is the *Absolute Idea*. The Absolute for Hegel in *Science of Logic* and *Phenomenology of Spirit*, taken up and developed by Agamben in *Language and Death* and *Potentialities*, derives from the verb 'to solve' and the Indo-European root *se (*LD* 92, *PO* 116). As a relation that both unites and separates, *se has the structure of a process. The verb 'to solve' 'indicates the operation of dissolving (*luo*) that leads (or leads back) something to its own *se [. . .] absolving it of every tie or alterity' (*LD* 92). The Absolute is an experience and a return, a result where the beginning is only reached at the end. At the end of his Jena lessons of 1805–6, Hegel refers to the Absolute as a 'restored immediateness' (*LD* 99). It is with Agamben's new use of Hegel's *Absolute* that thought can think a completed foundation of human speech and social praxis.

It is helpful to conceptualise philosophy's task in the figure of the Absolute as a voyage in which thought walks through negative laceration and division in order to return to its beginning without presupposition. To get to 'absolute wisdom' the voyage must pass through 'the marvel of being' and 'the terror of nothing' to return to where it originally was in language, a return to what it never was and that which it never left (*LD* 97–9). Agamben posits this homesickness – this dwelling in division, the pain of return to negative experience in order to reach the beginning, the *ethos* of humanity – as circular. He draws this from Hegel, for whom the Absolute is 'the circle that returns in itself which presupposes its beginning and reaches it only at the end' (*LD* 100).³ In other words, spirit grasps itself as Absolute only at the end of time, as a result that has returned to itself. While the Absolute is necessarily temporal and historical, implying 'a process and a becoming, an alienation and a return', it must finish history, ending time as if its moments are gathered into space like a picture gallery (*PO* 123–4).

For Agamben's rethinking of the Absolute, the circle is the figure of the 'I' of self-consciousness trying to think itself, 'to grasp the **se* of the "I"' by shifting the 'I' to the third person, to think what is 'proper to the subject independent of its "fall"' into speech (*PO* 121). Agamben worries that Hegel's Absolute as fulfilled discourse that has exhausted all of its historical figures merely repeats the negative foundation of the metaphysical tradition as a dead language (*PO* 128). He seeks instead an experience of the Absolute that dwells in itself and 'coincides without residue in human activity and praxis' (*PO* 127). The task is no less than to 'absolve the Voice from its having-been, from its being presupposed as removed', to thus 'think Voice and the foundation as absolute' (*LD* 101).

The Absolute is inseparable from the theme of the end of history taken up by Kojève as well as Marx in their readings of Hegel. Agamben consistently invokes the work of Kojève, usually in relation to his debate with his 'disciple-rival' Bataille about what remains of life beyond the dialectic (*O* 9). Kojève interprets the Hegelian system as a circle, as both 'a point of departure and a point of arrival' at which the notion manifesting its negativity is at work at every point (*LD* 14). At the end of history, work and negation have reached completion, and the human is given back to animal praxis. For Kojève's theme of inoperativity, or *désoeuvrement*, the 'being without work' of humans at the end of history presents the overcoming of work and the end of human struggle.

Bataille's disagreement concerns precisely the animal remnant, a 'negativity with no use' that survives the end of history. For Bataille, the joyful excesses of 'art, love, play' remain 'superhuman, negative, sacred', while for Kojève the state of 'nothing left to do' is pure animal praxis, the absence of work found in figures like Raymond Queneau's 'lazy rascal' (*O* 6; *HS* 61–2). Agamben critiques both readers of Hegel's post-history: Bataille for radicalising negativity as sacred, and Kojève for an inadequately developed notion of inoperativity that leaves the presuppositional structure intact. As Agamben puts it, 'everything depends' on what this inoperativeness means (*HS* 61). It is not simply an absence of work. For Agamben, inoperativity is a mode of potentiality not exhausted in actuality. Kojève's end of history thesis posits a state that survives history by merely maintaining an empty form of sovereignty.

Agamben argues in *The Time that Remains* that the concept of *désoeuvrement* in Kojève as figure for the end of history retains a distinct messianic quality (*TR* 101). Agamben notes that Paul uses the verb *katargeō* throughout the New Testament as part of his messianic vocabulary against normative law to mean 'I make inoperative, I deactivate, I suspend the efficiency' (*TR* 95). While *désoeuvrement* is a 'good translation of Pauline *katargein*', the problem with Kojève's concept is that it flattens the messianic on to the eschatological, confounding messianic time with post-history (*TR* 101). For Agamben, the messianic does not want to destroy the law but deactivate it from within by rendering it inexecutable (*TR* 98). Luther translates the Pauline verb *katargein* as *Aufheben*, the word used by Hegel for the dialectic that harbours the double sense of abolishing and conserving. But unlike Hegel's concept of *Aufhebung*, which lifts and preserves sense-certainty as nothingness, the messianic wants to seize hold of time, making it end rather than infinitely deferring it as zero-degree presence (*TR* 100–1).

While it is no surprise that Hegel's dialectic is the secularisation of Christian theology, the 'messianic weapon' that it contains does not go far enough. Hegel thinks the *pleroma* as 'the final result of a global process' rather than as 'each instant's relation to the Messiah' (*TR* 101). For Agamben, messianic time is the time it takes to achieve a representation of time, a fulfilment in which God will be in all. When the Torah is rendered inoperative, it finds its *pleroma* therein, not through infinite deferment. Agamben describes completed human language in the shape of a ring, with poetry and philosophy thinking one another in the direction of a never-having-been:

> Perhaps only a language in which the pure prose of philosophy would intervene at a certain point to break apart the verse of the poetic word, and in which the verse of poetry would intervene to bend the prose of philosophy into a ring, would be the true human language. (*LD* 78)

USE

Well before the recent publication of *The Use of Bodies*, Agamben theorised a 'new use' for 'use': against 'right' on the one hand, and 'property' on the other. This new use is predicated on remaining in the form of the 'as not': use as 'not to possess', to return use to the free use of men (*TR* 26; *PR* 73). Taking up the Pauline expression *chresai*, or 'to make use', Agamben in *The Time that Remains* invokes Paul's injunction that the messianic vocation is not a right or an identity, but a potentiality that may be used without ownership (*TR* 26). For Paul's definition of messianic life, the slave, in being called to the slave vocation, should use it otherwise, as being free. Rather than remaining in the nothing to which one is called, the slave may revoke his vocational calling through the gesture of the messianic calling: 'the calling of the calling' or *'the revocation of every vocation'* (*TR* 23, original italics). To think this 'free use of the self' against existence as property is to think use as humanity's own *ethos*, the praxis that accompanies it as 'the stowaway of the political' (*CC* 28–9; *UB* xvi). Use is closely tied to Agamben's theory of profanation, to return things to the free use of men from their sacred and commodified status, to convert use into pure means uncoupled from ends (*PR* 73, 87).

The Use of Bodies takes up and elaborates these threads in relation to Hegel's master–slave dialectic and Aristotle's expression 'use of the body' in his *Politics*. Unlike the cobbler or the flute player, the slave's praxis 'is not defined by what he produces but only by the use of the body' (*UB* 15). Aristotle wishes to restore the use of the slave's body to the unproductive mode of praxis independent of an end, to think the 'use' of the slave in relation to the master and the 'community of life' between them. Agamben issues an important cautionary note here about abstracting the slave's body against the sphere of production and the perversions that happen when slavery is constituted as a social institution. Yet he is interested in this point of indifference where the master, in using his own body, is using the slave's body; and the slave, used by the master, puts use in his own body (*UB* 14). Use is redefined as entering into 'a relationship with the self insofar as one is in relationship with another' (*UB* 34). This 'community of life' between master and slave requires a juridical definition of the slave as property that can only register as despotic intimacy (*UB* 36). In Hegel's dialectic, this distinction and undecidability between the master and the slave in Aristotle surfaces again as a kind of anthropogenic operator. But by distinguishing the labour of the slave from the enjoyment of the master, the 'community of life' between them is contained. Even in Hegel's dialectical reversal – when the slave acquires independence through labour and the fleeting enjoyment of the master, and the truth of the master's consciousness emerges as servile consciousness – dialectics are not yet overcome.

Unlike Plato, whose understanding of the dialectical method is an interrogation of 'the thing itself', Aristotle and Hegel fail to challenge the mute presuppositional power of the *logos*. It is through painstaking philological efforts such as these that Agamben's work seeks to free the dialectic from presupposition and put it to a new use in the ethos of human praxis.

NOTES

1. Antonio Negri, 'Giorgio Agamben: The Discreet Taste of the Dialectic', trans. Matteo Mandarini, in Mathew Calarco and Steve DeCaroli (eds), *Giorgio Agamben: Sovereignty and Life* (Stanford: Stanford University Press, 2007), p. 124.
2. G. W. F. Hegel, *Phenomenology of Spirit*, trans. A. V. Miller (Oxford: Oxford University Press, 1977), pp. 59–60.
3. See also *Potentialities*, p. 123, for the diagram of the circle in Hegel's *Phenomenology*.

14 Friedrich Hölderlin

HENRIK WILBERG

In the preface to *Stanzas*, Agamben unambiguously provides the setting for his engagement with Friedrich Hölderlin:

> The name of Hölderlin – of a poet, that is, for whom poetry was above all problematic and who often hoped that it would be raised to the level of *mēchanē* (mechanical instrument) of the ancients so that its procedures could be calculated and taught – and the dialogue that with its utterance engages a thinker who no longer designates his own meditation with the name of 'philosophy' are invoked here to witness the urgency, for our culture, of rediscovering the unity of our fragmented word. (*S* xvii)

Hölderlin is invoked as a poet who occupies a singular position among poets, one for whom poetry was 'above all problematic' – problematic in the sense that it persists as a discourse of recovery with regard to something that is not itself exclusively 'poetic'. In this capacity, the peculiar fracture of poetic discourse in Hölderlin is a 'witness to the urgency' of what is singled out as the main theme of *Stanzas*: the scission, in 'our culture', between poetry and philosophy with regard to objects of experience. Complementing this problematisation of poetry in Hölderlin, however, is the equally problematic discourse of 'a thinker who no longer designates his own meditations with the name of "philosophy"'. The thinker – Martin Heidegger – is not named in this paragraph, but *Stanzas* as a whole is dedicated to his memory (Heidegger had died the year before, in 1976); this name thus governs the entirety of the 'problematic' in question. 'The name of Hölderlin', Agamben insinuates, also necessarily implies 'the name of Heidegger'; so much so, in fact, that 'the thinker' himself need not be named. It is as if with Heidegger *in memoriam*, Hölderlin is no longer accessible as a single figure, but only as indissociably bound up with Heidegger's thought.[1] It is only together that they point to the urgency of *Stanzas*.

The conjunction of Hölderlin and Heidegger names the theoretical point of departure of the book.

Agamben is thus claiming a Heideggerian vanguard of a particular discourse concerning poetry and philosophy. The price, however, of assuming this position is that any direct access to Hölderlin's texts becomes problematic and, to a certain extent, wilfully epigonal. In truth, direct citations of Hölderlin without any ulterior reference to Heidegger have become exceedingly rare already with *Stanzas*. With two notable exceptions, Agamben will not, after *The Man Without Content*, return to a direct engagement with a poetic work of Hölderlin without reference to Heidegger.[2] This peculiar ceding of terrain to Heidegger with regard to Hölderlin distinguishes Agamben's position from other Hölderlin exegetes over the past half-century: prominent readers such as Peter Szondi, Theodor Adorno, Paul de Man, Dieter Henrich and Philippe Lacoue-Labarthe have all, in one form or another, attempted to reclaim the poet from Heidegger's appropriation.

Agamben's engagement with the conjunction of poetry and philosophy in Heidegger's Hölderlin goes at least as far back as his participation in Heidegger's seminars in Le Thor. Organised by the philosopher Jean Beaufret – chief broker of Heidegger's post-war rehabilitation in France, long-time patient of Jacques Lacan, and addressee of Heidegger's *Letter on Humanism* – along with the poet and former *Résistance* member René Char, the first of these seminars in 1966 was devoted to Heraclitus. In these fragments, Heidegger locates an inaugural conjunction in Greek between poetry (*Dichten*) and thought (*Denken*). The final remarks of the year, however, culminate in an appeal to Hölderlin:

> I have risked speaking of the 'destiny of being' as it had first addressed itself to Greek thinking at the beginning of *our* world. The Greeks stand under this destiny just as much as we do. Will we someday be in the position to think this on its own terms, instead of representing history as a succession of events? Therein lies the task of thinking, for which poetry is the 'wholesome danger' [*heilsame Gefahr*]. For poetry has not been unfaithful to the site of an inceptual upsurge [*ursprünglichen Auf-gehens*], while on the contrary the becoming-philosophy of thinking – as well as of the world – determines the course upon which we today find ourselves: 'losing the site' [*verlustig der Stätte*], to adopt a word from Sophocles, however 'well-deserving [indeed] [*voll Verdienst, zwar*]', as Hölderlin says, that we might think of ourselves.[3]

Through Heraclitus, poetry's original proximity and continued fidelity to the Greek 'inceptual upsurge' of what Heidegger calls '*our* world' is mobilised against the technical 'becoming-philosophy of thinking'. Poetry – translating *Dichtung* and not *Poesie* – is where, according to

Heidegger, we might still place ourselves as addressees of the destiny of being. The names of Sophocles and Hölderlin punctuate his concluding remarks as sites where such an original address could still be recovered for thought. The diagnostic 'word from Sophocles' describes 'our' current stance as one of loss. This 'word' is as it happens also a self-citation of Heidegger's translation of the second chorus from Sophocles' *Antigone* (where man is described as 'the uncanniest' of beings).[4] Here, Heidegger's 'losing the site' (*verlustig der Stätte*) translates Sophocles' ἄπολις: the 'losing' in question is a negation of or removal from *polis*, 'the political' in its original and broadest sense. Here, we already discern two facets of a question that is absolutely central to Agamben, one that will emerge fully with the first volume of *Homo Sacer*: the question of the human as one of in- and exclusion from the *polis*, and, second, a notion of the political which is transposed to a question of *site*, a question which in Agamben's work spans from the poetic space of the stanza to the political space of the camps in *Remnants of Auschwitz*.[5]

The same site is marked by Heidegger in Le Thor as the site for the engagement with Hölderlin. After Sophocles, the 'saying' of Hölderlin follows, taken from one of the later poems, '*In lieblicher Bläue*'. A philologically contested text, transmitted to posterity only through Wilhelm Waiblinger's novelistic memoir *Phaeton* (1823), it is a favourite of Heidegger's in his engagement with Hölderlin. The full verse in question also speaks to the peculiar 'site' of man: '*Voll Verdienst, doch dichterisch, wohnet der Mensch auf dieser Erde*';[6] in English it has been rendered: 'Full of acquirements, but poetically, man dwells on this earth'.[7] Heidegger's contraction of the conjunction of poetry and philosophy to these two points – Sophocles' 'losing the site' and Hölderlin's 'dwelling ... poetically', where the 'dwelling' (the poetic fidelity to the destiny of being that Heidegger speaks of) is set up as an response to the a-political 'losing' of the proper site[8] – reprises the question of the nature of the transfer of this task from antiquity to modernity, as well as from Greek to German. This is what makes Hölderlin's work, for Heidegger, a decisive turn in the history not just of poetry but of Western metaphysics in general, and nothing less than the occasion for what Heidegger calls 'the other beginning' of thought.

This turning point is also where Hölderlin enters Agamben's work. In the opening chapter of *The Man Without Content*, Agamben traces the history of a new regime of aesthetics that disrupts the 'classical' paradigm of the observer and the aesthetic object – often caricatured in the 'disinterested pleasure' of a Kantian aesthetic judgement – in favour of one of extreme risk in face of the 'danger' Heidegger attested to in poetry's relation to the destiny of being. In order to invoke this, 'it suffices to quote what Hölderlin wrote on the brink of madness' (*MC* 5). The quotations that follow are: 'Now I fear that I might end like the old Tantalus who received more from the Gods than he could take',[9] and 'so I may say that Apollo has struck me'.[10] Taken from two different letters that Hölderlin wrote to fellow poet Casimir Ulrich Böhlendorff in 1801–2 (one before and one after his psychotic episode in Bordeaux), both describe the poet's overpowering, excessive relation to the gods. Described by Heidegger as a *wholesome* danger, Agamben shows this danger in Hölderlin as a potentially ruinous force. Hölderlin, according to Agamben, extends this notion of peril from the individual being to civilisation as a whole. This, he asserts, is the central conflict in Hölderlin's attempted tragedy *Death of Empedocles*, and is exemplified further in a poetic fragment in the *Homburg Folio Notebook* (*MC* 6):

> *Nämlich sie wollten stiften*
> *Ein Reich der Kunst. Dabei aber ward*
> *Das Vaterländische von ihnen*
> *Versäumet und erbärmlich ging*
> *Das Griechenland, das schönste, zu Grunde.*[11]
> (For they wanted to found
> A kingdom of art. But thereby was
> missed by them that of
> the fatherland and wretchedly went
> Greece, the most beautiful, under.)

The cause of Greece's ruin in this poetic fragment is not just the will to erect a kingdom or *Reich* of art, but an essential neglect: what is missed or neglected in such a kingdom (or Empire, as Agamben translates it as *Impero* in Italian, *MC* 16/6) is that which is truly native, or 'of the fatherland' (*das Vaterländische*). One of the most difficult notions in Hölderlin's work, the 'native' or 'national' stands not for any original acquisition or property at the disposal of those to whom it is given, but paradoxically for something that needs to be learned and appropriated. In the first of the Böhlendorff letters (the only one dated, from 4 December 1801) there is a clear exposition of the native as learning that which is one's own:

> We learn nothing with more difficulty than to freely use the national. [. . .] Yet what is familiar must be learned as well as what is alien. This is why the Greeks are so indispensable for us. It is only that we will not follow them in our own, national [spirit] since, as I said, the *free use of one's own* is the most difficult.[12]

Further underlining the importance of this notion to Agamben, the concluding words of this passage reappear as an epigraph to *The Use of Bodies* (2014). In a section entitled 'The Inappropriable', the same words are assimilated to connect Agamben's concepts of use and form-of-life, presenting Hölderlin's use of the proper (*das Eigene*) as 'his supreme thought' and the ultimate task:

> To inhabit with oneself, to inhabit-oneself, therefore names the fundamental trait of human existence: the form of life of the human being is, in the words of Hölderlin, an 'inhabiting life' (*Wenn in die Ferne geht der Menschen wohnend Leben*...). But precisely for this reason, in the letter to Böhlendorff of December 4, 1801, in which Hölderlin formulated his supreme thought, use appears as always already divided into 'proper' and 'foreign', and the decisive thesis reads: 'the free use of the proper [*der freie Gebrauch des Eignes* [sic]] is the most difficult thing'. (*UB* 88)

We can now see, with some clarity, how Hölderlin accompanies and traverses all of the phases of Agamben's *oeuvre*. It is worth asking, however, having seen how intimately the name of Hölderlin is connected to the thought and memory of Heidegger (it is not for nothing that we find in *The Use of Bodies* an autobiographical anecdote about Heidegger which represents precisely a return to the scene of the first Le Thor seminar; cf. *UB* 242), whether there is not an element of divergence in Agamben's use of Hölderlin, despite this demonstratively epigonal stance.

An answer is perhaps provided in the other independent citation of Hölderlin's poetic works, from an essay in *The End of the Poem*. Here, Agamben comments on a change Hölderlin made to the final stanza of the ode '*Dichterberuf*' ('The Poet's Calling'), from

> *Und keiner Würde brauchts und keiner*
> *Waffen, so lange der Gott nicht fehlet.*
> (And there is no need for worth and for
> arms, as long as the god is not absent)

to:

> *Und keiner Waffen brauchts und keiner*
> *Listen, so lange, bis Gottes Fehl hilft.*
> (And there is no need for arms and for
> cunning, as long as God's absence aids.)[13]

In the correction, which inverts the safe certainty of a god's non-absence into an actively aiding absence of God, Agamben claims to find the birth of what he calls 'poetic atheology': 'Hölderlin's correction marks the point at which the divine and the human alike are ruined, at which poetry opens onto a region that is uncertain and devoid of a subject, flattened on the transcendental, and which can be defined only by the Hölderlinian euphemism, "betrayal of the sacred"' (*EP* 90–1). Echoing the aesthetic ruin invoked in *The Man Without Content*, Agamben here places Hölderlin at the beginning of a history of mutual ruin of divine and human. At this point, we still remain firmly within the conjunction of poetry and the destiny of metaphysics as staked out in Heidegger. Immediately, however, a break appears in the lineage, and atheology's 'date of birth' is brought into question. Hölderlin, it turns out, was not the beginning of atheology at all: 'atheology had already begun when Provençal and Dolce Stil Novo lyric poetry transformed poetry into the chamber or *stanza* in which an absolute experience of desubjectification and deindividuation went hand in hand with the ceremonious invention of figures of delirium' (*EP* 91). Here, Agamben is merely restating the argument made at length in the third part of *Stanzas*, but with this in mind, the book dedicated to Heidegger and whose readings of Hölderlin were invoked as testament to its most urgent task now appears in a slightly different light. Agamben's seemingly epigonal stance with regard to Hölderlin, that is, his uncritical acceptance of Heidegger's conjunction of poetry and philosophy, it could be argued, in reality amounts to a critical reinterpretation of this conjunction so as to allow for the contribution of other poets and another tradition to the fundamental scission of poetry and philosophy. And not just any tradition: Agamben is in fact opening up this conjunction to the very tradition Heidegger explicitly excluded: Latin and its vulgar Romance successors. The third part of *Stanzas* is perhaps best understood as an attempt to bring the protagonists of the *dolce stil novo*, along with representatives of the Provençal troubadours, into the position of Hölderlin, from where Agamben himself can begin a different trajectory of reworking the scission between poetry and philosophy. This, in turn, can be suspected of being nothing but Agamben's exercise of a free use of *his* own: after all, the inclusion of Hölderlin in a 'Romance' lineage occurs in a book with the original title *Italian Categories*, a book Agamben himself describes as a torso of an earlier collective attempt (with Italo Calvino and Claudio Rugafiori) to identify the proper categorial structure of Italian culture. Thus, the greatest fidelity to Heidegger, expressed in the preface to *Stanzas*, is paired with the sharpest possible dissent: a Latinate-Romance subversion of the Greco-German (or, as Hölderlin called it, Greco-Hesperian) destiny of being. From this point of view, Agamben's perceived eclecticism – from the Justinian Institutes to Dante, the *stilnovisti* and the troubadours, from the Church Fathers to St Francis – assumes a programmatic form.

However, one can of course elect to read the presence of Heidegger in Le Thor as a moment when cracks began to appear in the exclusive Greco-German relation. Hölderlin's two letters to Böhlendorff are separated by an arduous return journey on foot across southern France.

And another of Hölderlin's fragments, given the tentative title '... the Vatican' by its editors, and one that Heidegger, perhaps for that reason, never attempted to read, conjures just such a phantasm of a superposition of Greece and Rome, not in a joyous coming together, but expressed as a mutual farewell:

> [. . .] wenn die Glocke lautet
> Des Kirchturms, und es nachhallt unten
> Im Eingeweid des Tempels und der Mönch
> Und Schäfer Abschied nehmet, vom Spaziergang
> Und Apollon, ebenfalls
> Aus Roma, derlei Palästen, sagt
> Ade! unreinlich bitter, darum!
> Dann kommt das Brautlied des Himmels.

> ([. . .] when the bell rings
> Down from the church tower and reverberates in
> The temple's entrails below and the monk
> And shepherd take leave, from the walk
> And Apollo, likewise
> From Rome, suchlike palaces, say
> Farewell! dirtily bitter, that's why!
> Then comes the nuptial song of Heaven.)[14]

NOTES

1. Lending further support to the thesis that his interest in Hölderlin always implies Heidegger is the fact that Agamben does not engage with Walter Benjamin's work on Hölderlin, neither the dense early essay 'Two Poems of Friedrich Hölderlin' nor the passages devoted to Hölderlin in the more famous later texts 'The Task of the Translator' and 'Goethe's Elective Affinities'. In other words, the association with Heidegger seems to be so strong that it cannot be disturbed even by Benjamin, the other great German-language source of Agamben's philosophical method.
2. In *Homo Sacer*, an 'aleph'-excursion cites, within the chapter on *nomos basileus*, Hölderlin's translation of and subsequent commentary on Pindar's fragment 'The Highest' (*Das Höchste*), where it serves to frame a critique of Carl Schmitt's equation of *nomos* with the sovereign principle. It is worth nothing that Agamben defends Hölderlin's adaptation against Schmitt's criticism (cf. HS 25). The other exception, from *The End of the Poem*, is discussed below.
3. Martin Heidegger, *Four Seminars*, trans. Andrew Mitchell and Nicholas Walker (Bloomington: Indiana University Press, 2004), p. 9.
4. As presented in the 1935 lecture *Introduction to Metaphysics* (*Einführung in die Metaphysik*, in *Gesamtausgabe*, vol. 40 [Frankfurt a.M.: Vittorio Klostermann, 1983], p. 113). The section on Sophocles is referred to by Agamben in the opening chapter of *The Man Without Content* (MC 120).

At the same time, Heidegger's use of Sophocles entertains a palimpsestic relation to Hölderlin's own Sophocles translation, a fact that would have been impossible for his audience to ignore. For Agamben even less so, given the prominence of Hölderlin's translation in Walter Benjamin's essay 'The Task of the Translator'.

5. In *The Use of Bodies*, Agamben draws a direct line between this uncanny site of the political in Sophocles' *Antigone* and a constitutive passage in Aristotle's *Politics* (cf. *UB* 236).
6. Friedrich Hölderlin, *Sämtliche Werke und Briefe in drei Bänden*, ed. Jochen Schmidt (Frankfurt a.M.: Deutscher Klassiker Verlag, 2008), vol. 1, p. 479.
7. Friedrich Hölderlin, *Poems and Fragments*, trans. Michael Hamburger (London: Anvil Press Poetry, 1994), p. 715.
8. It is, as we can see in this context, no coincidence that the guiding question of *Homo Sacer* is 'In what way does bare life dwell in the polis?' (*HS* 12).
9. Friedrich Hölderlin, *Essays and Letters on Theory*, ed. and trans. Thomas Pfau (Albany: SUNY Press, 1988), p. 151.
10. Hölderlin, *Essays and Letters on Theory*, p. 152.
11. Hölderlin, *Sämtliche Werke*, vol. 1, p. 399.
12. Hölderlin, *Essays and Letters on Theory*, pp. 149–50.
13. Hölderlin, *Sämtliche Werke*, vol. 1, p. 307.
14. Hölderlin, *Sämtliche Werke*, vol. 1, p. 418; Hölderlin, *Poems and Fragments*, p. 613.

15 *Franz Kafka*

ANKE SNOEK

HEARING KAFKA'S LAUGHTER

From his earliest book (*The Man Without Content*) to one of his latest (*The Use of Bodies*) Agamben's work is inhabited by Kafka's characters: messengers, assistants, land surveyors, students, courtroom clerks, the bobbin Odradek and the mythical horse Bucephalus which becomes an attorney.[1] The references to Kafka are often brief but in strategic places: Kafka frequently pops up in the title of a chapter, or at the end of one of Agamben's arguments to illustrate and further deepen the point he has just made. Agamben regularly states that Kafka is the author who has most coherently or profoundly addressed the issues that he is working on (*MC* 112);[2] however, the work of the Prague author has not only influenced the content of Agamben's philosophy, but also his style.[3]

Kafka has become most famous for describing the nightmarish bureaucracy that we are living in. There are many schools of interpretation of Kafka's work, but most focus on the political threats Kafka describes or on his tragic life. However, there is a small group of scholars who argue that Kafka not only describes the catastrophe in which we are living, but also shows a way out.[4] This school focuses on a messianic interpretation, and to this tradition Agamben belongs. As he states: 'It is a very poor reading of Kafka's works that sees in them only a summation of the anguish of a guilty man before the inscrutable power of a God become estranged and remote' (*IP* 85).

What supports a messianic reading of Kafka? Anyone reading his works must be familiar with the following experience: Kafka's stories often seem to head towards an unfavourable and inevitable end for the main character. However, just at the end of the story something happens that leaves the reader puzzled, and it remains unclear whether the main character is defeated or has escaped in a strange way. The endings to his books and stories often contain an inversion that casts an entirely new light on the plot and forces us to reread the story (*HS* 58). Often what initially felt like a defeat could instead be an unorthodox escape.[5] Kafka was known for laughing exuberantly when his stories were read aloud at reading evenings – and he was apparently the only one who did so. He had to laugh especially at those times when his main characters were suffering the most, and this laughter indicates that the moment of the ultimate catastrophe also offers an important inversion for the protagonist.

Although from a chronological viewpoint we should start with Agamben's first references to Kafka in his books of the 1970s and 1980s, his use of Kafka becomes most enigmatic and elaborate in his political work, which takes off with *Homo Sacer*. Understanding the role that Kafka performs in Agamben's political work, therefore, will give us more insight into his use of Kafka in general.

KAFKA'S ROLE IN AGAMBEN'S POLITICAL PHILOSOPHY

The Crisis of the Law and the Messianic Inversion

Agamben points out that Kafka's work presents us with a profound insight into the nature of the law (*RA* 18). Here the law is ominously present, but its content remains unknown. For example, in the short parable 'Before the Law', a man from the country tries to familiarise himself with the law, but he is prevented from entering the law by a doorkeeper. The door is open and the man looks inside, but what he sees does not seem worth mentioning in the story, as if, Agamben suggests, there is nothing behind the door, as if the law is empty. Agamben sees a parallel with a Kabbalistic story about the nature of the law. According to this story, the original Torah was not a fixed text, but merely the totality of possible combinations of the Hebrew alphabet. God arranged the letters into words, but their order depended on how the lower world took shape. The Torah took a certain form because of Adam's sin, but the same letters could just as easily have been arranged differently. That is why the Torah has no vowels, punctuation or accents; it is an allusion to the Torah being originally just a heap of unordered letters. Although the Kabbalists never stated it so crudely, the Torah, the Law, was actually put together via a 'medley of letters without order and articulation', that is, without significance (*PO* 165).

Many of Kafka's stories seem to hint at the emptiness of the law, a phenomenon which Scholem called 'the nothing of revelation'. Kafka's world is one of revelation, but what it reveals is 'the nothing', the lack of transcendent meaning.[6] However, this revelation of lack of content does not result in the law being abolished; on the contrary, it enhances the force of the law. If the law does not prescribe anything, it is impossible to distinguish between the law and its violation. Agamben calls this survival of the law beyond its meaning 'imperfect nihilism'. Kafka's most proper gesture, Agamben adds, consists of showing that such a law 'ceases to be law and blurs at all points with life' (*SE* 63), and that is why the courtroom in which Joseph K.'s trial takes place borders his bedroom (*ME* 121).

Benjamin was the first to describe a link between Kafka's image of the law and a 'state of exception', and Agamben further develops this thesis in *State of Exception* and *The Time that Remains*. What characterises the state of exception is the fact that the law is preserved in its suspension; its content has been removed but it is in force all the more, just like the law Kafka describes. The state of exception is often seen as an emergency measure, but Agamben argues that it reflects the legal fundaments of the law. Herein lies Kafka's profound insight into the law, stressing that the force of the law seems to be more important than its content. Agamben even calls Kafka a prophet, stressing how the state of exception, or the law's being in force without content, has become increasingly dominant in our modern times.

Here Agamben closely follows Benjamin, who had already remarked that the state of exception has become the rule. However, when studying one of Kafka's aphorisms, Benjamin discovered a close connection between the state of exception and the messianic end of time. In one of his *Zürau Aphorisms* Kafka states: 'Only our concept of Time makes it possible for us to call the day of the Last Judgement by that name; in reality it is a summary court in perpetual session [*Standrecht*].'[7] *Standrecht*, summary judgement, is the law that is in force in the state of exception. Benjamin connects this aphorism with an apocryphal gospel: 'Where I meet someone, there will I judge him.'[8] According to this gospel, there is no difference between the Day of Judgement and other days: every day is a perpetual Day of Judgement (cf. also 'The Messiah and the Sovereign', *PO* 160). So the catastrophe that the state of exception brings is closely linked to, and almost indistinguishable from, its messianic redemption. Benjamin continues that we must arrive at a concept of history that corresponds to the fact that the state of exception has become the rule: 'Then we will clearly see that it is our task to bring about a real state of emergency.'[9] Our messianic task is, according to Agamben, to bring about a real state of exception, one that will not preserve the Nothing in an eternally and infinitely postponed state of being in force (*PO* 171), and he calls this a 'perfect nihilism'. He points out that the messiah was the figure *par excellence* through which the great monotheistic religions attempted to solve the problem of law, since his coming meant the fulfilment and complete consummation of the law (*HS* 56). But how can the messiah restore a law that has no significance, a law that is formed with random words (*PO* 163)? Here Kafka's work also offers us important insights.

Kafka's Messianic Creatures

Agamben sees a messianic gesture occurring in many of Kafka's parables, a gesture which inverts imperfect nihilism into perfect nihilism, or the virtual state of exception into a real state of exception: 'Kafka's characters – and this is why they interest us – have to do with this spectral figure of the law in the state of exception; they seek, each one following his or her own strategy, to "study" and deactivate it, to "play" with it' (*SE* 64).

So let us look more closely at a few of those strategies: the ruse of the man from the country, the self-slander of Joseph K., and Bucephalus's study. The man from the country spends his whole life in front of the door to the law; when he is dying, he asks the doorkeeper why no one has tried to enter this door except him, and the doorkeeper replies that this door was especially meant for him, so he will go now and shut it. Agamben wonders why most interpretations of this story read it as a defeat for the man from the country (*HS* 55). When in *The Trial* the prison chaplain tells Joseph K. this parable, Joseph K. exclaims that the doorkeeper has misled the man from the country, but the chaplain replies that 'it is the doorkeeper who is deceived'.[10] Agamben argues that by acting as if he wants to enter, while knowing that there is nothing to enter, the man from the country forces the doorkeeper to finally close the door, to cancel the law's being in force while having no significance (*HS* 58).

The parable 'Before the Law' is narrated in *The Trial* in order to give Joseph K. some advice as to how to relate to the law. This advice is sorely needed, since in Agamben's interpretation Joseph K.'s crafty strategy fails. Agamben focuses on the opening sentence of the book, which is often cited, but barely subjected to interpretation: 'Someone must have slandered Joseph K., for one morning, without having done anything wrong, he was arrested.'[11] Agamben argues that Joseph K. has slandered himself. When a law is in force without significance, guilt and innocence become indistinguishable, so Joseph K. tries to toy with this by self-slandering. Guilt does not exist in the case of self-slander or, better: the only guilt is that of self-slander, which consists in accusing oneself of a non-existent guilt or accusing oneself of one's own innocence – and that is the comic gesture *par excellence*. However, this strategy is insufficient, because by entering the law, Joseph K. already acknowledges its being in force without significance (*NU* 31).

Again, the parable 'Before the Law' offers a clue to a new strategy. While in his strategy of self-slander Joseph K. tries to enter the law to make it inoperative from within, what he really should have done was to try to stay out of the law, and not give in to its invitation of accusation, even in his crafty way. The man from the country manages to stay outside of the law all his life, and the way he does that, according to Agamben, is to devote himself unceasingly to study – not a study of the law, which in itself does not recognise guilt, but a 'long study' of the doorkeeper (*NU* 31).

Study is an important strategy in Agamben's work, and here, too, he follows Benjamin, who argued that study is the lens through which we should read Kafka. It is important to note that this study is not an action with a specific goal (gaining insight into the law), but rather it is a 'gesture'. The students who inhabit Kafka's works (for example in *Amerika*) are mostly useless creatures; their study seems endless. As Benjamin pointed out, the students have lost the *Schrift* (*HS* 51), the connection to a transcendent goal of study, and now nothing stops them on their 'untrammelled, happy journey'.[12] The most enigmatic example of the student in Kafka's work may be Alexander the Great's horse Bucephalus, which happens to become a lawyer. However, he does not practise law since this would only be a repetition of the mythical forces, given that law is in force without significance. Rather, Bucephalus does nothing more than study the law, leafing through the pages of old books in tranquil lamplight. Bucephalus is now free, the burden of Alexander the Great is removed from his back, and so Agamben argues (with Benjamin): 'That which opens the passage to justice is not the abolishment of the law but its deactivation and inactivity – that is, another use of the law' (*SE* 63). This is a law that is liberated from all discipline and all relation to sovereignty, and Bucephalus represents a figure of the law that is possible after its link with violence and power has been deposed, a law that is no longer in force and applied (*SE* 63–4). Agamben concludes: 'One day humanity will play with law just as children play with disused objects, not in order to restore them to their canonical use, but to free them from it for good' (*SE* 64).

This is just a selection of the strategies in response to the law and the bare life that law creates that Agamben derives from Kafka's work. There are many, many more in his books.[13] For example, Joseph K.'s shame (RA 104), Odradek's being without purpose (EP 64), or the challenging of the boundaries between the sacred and the profane of the land surveyor in 'K.' (NU 35).

Redemption for God and its Messengers

In one of his more recent books, Agamben takes an unexpected turn. Whereas in *Homo Sacer* and *State of Exception* sovereign power was the antagonist of bare life, in *The Kingdom and the Glory* Agamben suddenly shifts his attention from the sovereign power to the practice of governing. The actual problem is, according to Agamben, 'not sovereignty but government; it is not God but the angels; it is not the king but ministry; it is not the law but the police' (KG 276), that is, the state machine that they constitute and maintain. Although he does not mention Kafka explicitly in *The Kingdom and the Glory*, this move arguably grows out of his study of Kafka in his earlier work. In *Homo Sacer* Agamben states that we all risk taking the role of the doorkeeper, guarding a law that has no content and maintaining its being in force (HS 54). And in *Idea of Prose* he states that the only happy ending we can imagine for Kafka's novels 'is the redemption of Klamm, of the Count, of the anonymous, theological crowd of judges, lawyers, and guardians indiscriminately packed together in dusty corridors or stooped beneath oppressive ceilings' (IP 85). And it is striking that in Agamben's interpretation of 'In the Penal Colony', it is precisely the sovereign who takes the role of the messiah upon himself.[14] By taking the place of the condemned man in the machine and inserting the order 'be just', the officer intends to destroy the machine (IP 117), to destroy the Foucauldian *apparatus*[15] in a messianic gesture.

CONCLUSION

Once we understand Agamben's use of Kafka in his political philosophy, much also becomes clear about how he uses Kafka in his philosophy of language and history. When Agamben stages one of Kafka's creatures and their messianic gestures, it is often to reveal a 'nothing', to reveal that there is no transcendental meaning behind law, language, time, the work of man, or the impossibility of transmissibility. This 'nothing' is revealed by the gestures of Kafka's creatures, who irrevocably put their lives at stake to free us not so much from sovereignty, but from the doorkeepers of its meaningless power.

NOTES

1. Although Agamben mostly refers to Kafka briefly, he also devoted two longer essays to Kafka: 'K.' (in *Nudities*) and 'Quattro Glosse a Kafka'. The latter ('Four Commentaries on Kafka') has not yet been translated into English, but is partly re-published in *Idea of Prose*. Cf. Giorgio Agamben, 'Quattro Glosse a Kafka', *Rivista di estetica* 26 (1986): 37–44.
2. Cf. also Giorgio Agamben, 'Il pozzo di Babele', *Tempo presente* 11.11 (1966): 42–50.
3. Cf. Carlo Salzani, 'In a Messianic Gesture: Agamben's Kafka', in Brendan Moran and Carlo Salzani (eds), *Philosophy and Kafka* (Plymouth: Lexington Books, 2013), pp. 261–81.
4. See, for example, Walter Benjamin, 'Franz Kafka: On the Tenth Anniversary of His Death', in *Selected Writings*, ed. Michael W. Jennings et al. (Cambridge, MA: The Belknap Press of Harvard University Press, 1996), vol. 2, pp. 794–818; *The Correspondence of Walter Benjamin and Gershom Scholem, 1932–1940*, ed. Gershom Scholem (Cambridge, MA: Harvard University Press, 1980); Albert Camus, 'Hope and the Absurd in the World of Franz Kafka', in Ronald D. Gray (ed.), *Kafka: A Collection of Critical Essays* (Upper Saddle River, NJ: Prentice-Hall, 1962), pp. 147–56; Gilles Deleuze and Félix Guattari, *Kafka. Toward a Minor Literature* (Minneapolis: University of Minnesota Press, 1986); Peter Rehberg, *Lachen Lesen. Zur Komik Der Moderne Bei Kafka* (Bielefeld: transcript Verlag, 2007). Agamben especially engages with Benjamin's interpretation of Kafka.
5. Malynne Sternstein, 'Laughter, Gesture, and Flesh: Kafka's "In the Penal Colony"', *Modernism/Modernity* 8.2 (2001): 315.
6. *The Correspondence of Walter Benjamin and Gershom Scholem*, p. 142.
7. Franz Kafka, *Zürau Aphorisms* (New York: Schocken Books, 2006), p. 41. Translation adapted by Agamben, MC 113.
8. Walter Benjamin, 'Paralipomena to "On the Concept of History"', in *Selected Writings*, vol. 4, p. 407.
9. Walter Benjamin, 'On the Concept of History', in *Selected Writings*, vol. 4, p. 392.
10. Franz Kafka, *The Trial* (New York: Schocken Books, 2009), p. 157.
11. Kafka, *The Trial*, p. 5, cited in 'K.' (*NU* 13); translation adapted by Agamben.
12. Benjamin, 'Franz Kafka', p. 815.
13. See Anke Snoek, *Agamben's Joyful Kafka: Finding Freedom beyond Subordination* (New York: Bloomsbury, 2012).
14. Cf. Vivian Liska, 'The Messiah before the Law. Giorgio Agamben, Walter Benjamin and Kafka', in Claas Morgenroth, Vittoria Borsò, Karl Solibakke and Bernd Witte (eds), *Benjamin – Agamben. Politics,*

Messianism, Kabbalah (Würzburg: Königshausen and Neumann, 2010), pp. 159–75.
15. Cf. David Kishik, *The Power of Life: Agamben and the Coming Politics* (Stanford: Stanford University Press, 2011).

16 Immanuel Kant

SUSAN BROPHY

Agamben's complicated engagement with Immanuel Kant celebrates the brilliance of the German idealist's thought by disclosing its condemnatory weight in Western philosophy. Kant was writing in the midst of burgeoning industrial capitalism, when each new scientific discovery seemed to push back the fog of religion in favour of science and reason; meanwhile Agamben's work develops in concert with the crises of advanced capitalism and borrows significantly from those philosophers who endured the most demoralising upheavals of the first half of the twentieth century. Whatever *lanugo* Kant was eager for us to shed in the name of individual freedom,[1] Agamben sees in this crusade for civic maturity a surprising prescience: '[I]t is truly astounding how Kant, almost two centuries ago and under the heading of a sublime "moral feeling," was able to describe the very condition that was to become familiar to the mass societies and great totalitarian states of our time' (*HS* 52). To a remarkable extent, Agamben finds that Kant's transcendental idealist frame of thought lays the philosophical foundation for the state of exception.

As a response to this finding, Agamben offers three conceptual reversals that expose the fiction of the 'sublime "moral feeling"': infancy, remnant and destituent potential. After identifying the guiding logic that persists throughout Kant's thought, I examine the evocative ways in which Agamben references this logic in the development of his three conceptual reversals. Overall, this approach accentuates Agamben's effort to make Kant partially accountable for what befell Western philosophy after 'having substituted an ontology of command for an ontology of substance' (*OD* 122), and underscores the import of Agamben's own contributions to Western philosophy.

KANT'S GUIDING LOGIC

Across his works, Kant grapples with various sets of philosophical antinomies,[2] but it is in the *Critique of Pure Reason* that he inaugurates the logic that guides him throughout these encounters. Faced with the ontological antinomy between actuality and idealism, and the epistemological antinomy between empiricism and transcendentalism, he purports to clear a safe passage by adhering to a particular framework that is immune to the pitfalls of philosophical dogmatism.[3] This is the domain of his transcendental idealism, the attendant logic of which necessitates the seminal split between the 'empirical I' and the 'transcendental I' (*IH* 39). For Kant, it is imperative that the individual adopt a transcendental standpoint, that is, a 'pure' position of autonomy that facilitates the systematic unity of objective reason.[4] Individual autonomy must reign over the object 'as a thing-in-itself' (that is, *noumenon*),[5] or else '[n]ature will then be the complete and sufficient determining cause of every event'.[6] For Kant, only the appearance of that object as it is represented by intuition is knowable.[7]

The prevailing logic therefore operates as follows: the 'empirical I' encounters objects and internalises them, which sets in motion their transposition from intuition to appearance, and operates as the first line of protection against the subsumption of experience by the empirical realm; simultaneously, the self-consciousness of the 'transcendental I' remains pure because it 'precedes all data of intuitions',[8] which sanctions the individual's prescriptive agency. By relegating the empirical and the actual, the individual wilfully surrenders to the ruling limits of reason and adopts an idealist position of transcendental subjectivity. In this paradigm of 'perfect circularity' (*OD* xii), autonomy requires submission, while submission is an expression of autonomy; in effect, the two are indistinguishable.

When Kant turns his attention to morality, autonomy thus conceived becomes self-referentially conscripted as an inalienable duty.[9] He insists that the morality of dutiful action dwells not in the outcome of the act, but in the '*principle of volition*' apart from interest or desire.[10] To substantiate this proposition, he dissects the process of will-formation as a way of explaining the necessity of autonomy in relation to duty.[11] Reason demands dutiful action, the respected moral principles of which are predicated on the individual's autonomous stance per his guiding logic in the First Critique. Alien from interests, desires and concern about consequences, pure process presumes pure intent, which supplies the individual with all of her or his moral authority. In the *Critique of Practical Reason*, Kant further suggests that the individual's respect for moral law produces the 'moral feeling' that inclines '*free* submission'.[12] 'Sublime' is how he describes this duty – an inner calling to obedience in which free will is indistinguishable from submission.[13] In the *Critique of Judgment*, he adds that this moral feeling is 'sublime' because it shows that reason 'transcends the domain of nature', providing further evidence of the mind's 'superiority to sensibility'.[14]

In sum, the catalytic element that renders authority and submission indistinguishable is the transcendental idealist bias which animates his guiding logic as a whole. We encounter this again when Agamben describes the 'relation of abandonment' (*HS* 60, 83 and 109); but even at this early stage, we can discern the fertile but perilous effects of Kant's thought on Western philosophy.

THE REVERSALS: INFANCY, REMNANT AND DESTITUENT POTENTIAL

Agamben's opening lines in *The Man Without Content* include a quote from Nietzsche, who scoffs at the pretensions of Kant's 'disinterested' judgement of beauty (*MC* 1–2). Subsequently, however, Agamben refers to the Third Critique as 'the most coherent meditation on aesthetic judgment that the Western world has', while also recognising in it Kant's adherence to the 'transcendental analytic' (*MC* 41). He observes that the ontological displacement of substance that Kant's approach to beauty necessitates leaves us with 'non-art', a 'shadow', or 'nothingness' (*MC* 42), and he casts Kant's original negation of art as a 'blemish' and a 'burden' (*MC* 44) on modern philosophy. The introduction of *Stanzas* similarly calls forth Kant's legacy, as Agamben references the imagery of the 'island of truth' from the First Critique and reads it as part of Kant's prescription for rational maturity.[15] In doing so, Agamben identifies the island enclosure as an 'ironic self-negation' that transpires when the 'scission [. . .] between the poetic word and the word of thought' is most pronounced in Western culture (*S* xvi). Opposed to the self-defeating sublimity of Kant's logic, Agamben seeks a return to the 'original experience' as a means of circumventing the imperative to transcend the experience as such (*S* 156).

In *Infancy and History*, Agamben explains that as a corollary to the Kantian campaign for the self-legislating transcendental subject, the object of experience was relegated to the realm of the unknowable in order to make knowledge possible (*IH* 26). 'Thus anyone proposing to recover traditional experience today would encounter a paradoxical situation', says Agamben; 'they would have to begin first of all with a cessation of experience, a suspension of knowledge' (*IH* 26). While he recognises Kant's First Critique as Western philosophy's final source on 'pure' experience (*IH* 38), Agamben also discloses the totalising appetite of Kant's guiding logic. Because of these strict a priori rules that delineate knowledge, Agamben reckons that the individual 'cannot even know itself as a substantial reality' (*IH* 35), and, following Benjamin,[16] he turns to the notion of 'pure language' to orchestrate the conceptual reversal of Kant's vision of political maturity: infancy. Infancy resides in the paradigm of 'pure language', where it is possible to approximate original experience (*IH* 60) as a tonic against the 'nullified present of the metaphysical tradition' (*IH* 112) inherited from Kant.

Up to this point, Agamben discloses the architecture of the 'nullified present' from an individual standpoint, revealing along the way the absolutism of Kant's transcendental subjectivity. This turns into an expression of astonishment in *Homo Sacer* when he discovers that this guiding logic can also explain the totalising paradigm of the state of exception – in fact, it is the flipside of the same coin (*HS* 84). Kant's logic and the accompanying 'sublime "moral feeling"' amount to a compulsion towards nothingness in order to produce the transcendental subject. With the vanishing ground of being as the becoming of 'political existence', we have the conceptual template for bare life (*HS* 8) as well as a way of analysing the type of sovereign power that likewise exercises authority on the basis of absolute but 'empty principle[s]' (*HS* 52). Where Kant harnesses the force of respectability that accompanies content-free law in order to secure the autonomy of the transcendental subject, Agamben asserts that 'law is all the more pervasive for its total lack of content' (*HS* 53). The compulsive life of Kant's self-negating subject is thus indistinguishable from law in the state of exception.

Kant's suspension of the ontological being divulges the roots of the relation of abandonment that operates as the nexus between sovereign power and the subject in the state of exception (*HS* 109) – even more so in the site of normalised exception: the camp (*HS* 170). Under the weighty inheritance of an elaborate philosophical structure that champions submission to content-free rules, what accounts for Agamben's expression of astonishment is the realisation that authority becomes absolute in its deontological self-referentiality; in other words, 'political disorder and undecidability' result when 'the opposition between liberal democracy and absolutism' is erased.[17] Kant's guiding logic reasserts itself when Agamben elaborates on this in *Remnants of Auschwitz*. Humanity is the first casualty of the camp that is inhabited by the *Muselmann*, who represents the negation of life its most extreme (*RA* 64). Referencing Kant, Agamben explains that while the *Muselmann* experiences pure passive subjectivity and the witness occupies the realm of the 'actively passive', the two factions 'are both distinct and inseparable' (RA 109–11). Instead, Agamben offers a conceptual reversal of the Kantian subject – indeed, he states that the very way that we think about subjectivity 'must be wholly called into question' (CC 58–9). The witness is a subject whose authority derives from 'an incapacity to speak'; as such the *Muselmann* represents 'the complete witness' (RA 158), a claim he advances by sourcing those unscientific theological tomes that Kant was keen to abandon (RA 164). Against the absolutist posturing of Kant's transcendental subject, the 'remnant is a theologico-messianic concept' (RA 162) – the witness is what 'remains' between the 'dead' and the 'survivors' (RA 164).

In *The Time that Remains*, the remnant is the doubly negated 'impossibility' (TR 50). In this book, Agamben also holds Kant's guiding logic up as the source of the malignant 'fiction' in modern ethics, wherein reason proceeds 'as if' there is a substantive connection to *noumenon*, despite this connection being precluded from the outset (TR 35). This relation of deactivation becomes the definitive ingredient in *State of Exception*, but here we get a preliminary assessment of its mechanics. The validity of a norm stems from its separation from the empirical realm of fact, yet at the same time the validity of the norm is taken as a fact; the norm can then only apply through a relation of suspension – that is, by producing an exception (TR 104). In the praxis of suspension, therefore, sovereign power validates its authority in a self-referential manner.

In *State of Exception*, Agamben likens this 'fiction' to a 'mistake' (SE 39), arguing that when it comes to the law, the act of application cannot be assessed in terms of the logical processes of individual reason. When framed instead as a practical action – one of public 'enunciation', not private cognition – we see that the institutions of juridical power function as a factual referent that prefigures the force of the enunciation, as opposed to the transcendental or universal referent of the logical process (SE 39) wherein 'existence is not a real predicate' (ST 66). This fiction-mistake sheds light on the depth of the problem as it pertains to the law, namely that these 'operative' institutional referents do not necessarily derive from the norm itself. Agamben goes so far as to suggest that if they did, the 'grand edifice of trial law' would be unnecessary (SE 40); as it stands, however, the edifice proves that the realisation of a norm is not a predetermined outcome. The enunciation of a juridical norm, as praxis, therefore occurs in a field of prefigurative referents that further distort the *logos* of the norm; such is the violent paradigm that is the state of exception, which results from the need to suspend the norm in order for it to apply (SE 58).

According to the fiction-mistake of Kant's logic, we (self-)govern 'as if' there is a formative connection to *noumenon* despite the fact that the application of the rule negates this possibility. In the state of exception, the prevailing fiction-mistake does not disappear; rather, it is aggravated in the state's attempts to domesticate the anomie between norm and fact. However, if we halt processes of command, application or realisation, we expose the fiction and reveal the 'remnant', which in this instance is the law that 'is studied but no longer practiced' (*SE* 63). This is what Agamben calls for, that point at which the violence of the juridical order is revealed because we relegate the 'ontology of command' instead of the 'ontology of substance'; the self-negating subject is then just a subject, a 'complete witness' (*RA* 158).

Agamben revisits the relation between being and praxis from a different angle in *The Kingdom and the Glory* (*KG* 54), casting it as the relation between 'theologia *and* oikonomia, *between the being of God and his activity*' (*KG* 5, original italics).[18] At this juncture the distinction between the 'empirical I' and the 'transcendental I' reasserts itself on the plane of God and the economy, wherein the economy does not have an immediate foundation in ontology and the praxis of God's authority becomes a 'mystery' (*KG* 54). The mystery is strikingly familiar. In theology, praxis relies on the possibility of 'free will', but the concept of will itself presupposes 'the groundlessness of praxis' (*KG* 55). Praxis is thus inseparable from its aporetic foundation (*KG* 83): since human praxis becomes the means by which divine law can apply, the authority of the individual corresponds to their submission to empty laws (*KG* 211). As a rejoinder to the 'sublime "moral feeling"', 'the life of creatures culminates in obedience', which ensures the circularity of this administrative process (*KG* 215). This study occasions Agamben's conclusion that we should focus on the administrative praxis that sustains the sovereign (*KG* 276), and hints at two questions that become paramount in his later work: How is this obedience constructed? And what of life prior to law?

Agamben addresses the first question in *Opus Dei*, a text laden with references to Kantian moral philosophy. As he elucidates how Kant's prescriptive autonomy becomes self-referentially constructed as an absolute duty, he asserts that '[i]t is obvious that the paradigm of duty of office finds its most extreme and aporetic formulation in Kantian ethics' (*OD* 111). After his expression of astonishment in *Homo Sacer*, he becomes more pointed with regard to Kant's place in Western philosophy, charging that Kant's logic is the modern locus of the 'ontology of operativity' (*OD* 118), and later, that 'Kant's thought represents the secularized reappropriation of the ontology of *estō* [*having-to-be*] in the bosom of the ontology of *esti* [*being*], the catastrophic re-emergence of law and religion in the bosom of philosophy' (OD 122). In the wake of these declarations, Agamben indicts Kant for failing to realise what would befall humanity once the indistinguishability between submission and authority became a moral imperative (OD 123): the camp in particular, and the state of exception in general. This concern saturates *The Highest Poverty*, where in attempting to address the second question, Agamben looks to Franciscan monasticism for an 'extreme reversal', one that absolves us from the preoccupation with the application of the norm in relation to life and focuses instead on how life is applied to the norm (HP 61). On such an occasion, when life and 'form (or norm)' are in complete correspondence (HP 99), administrative praxis and its corresponding aporia disappear. This reversal signals a move away from the 'ontology of command' – that 'fictitious' (HP 140) and 'inessential' realm of the 'purely operative and effectual' (HP 136) – in favour of the real of inoperativity, the terrain of destituent potential.

In the epilogue to *The Use of Bodies*, Kant's philosophy is once again the site of 'a decisive crisis', where 'philosophy loses its relation with Being' (UB 271). To 'settle accounts' with this burdensome inheritance (UB 112), Agamben argues that we must undertake a reversal of the 'constituent power' of Kant's transcendental subject in favour of 'destituent potential' (UB 266). As with infancy and remnant, that which was relegated by Kant, in Agamben's reversal becomes the basis for a regenerative type of 'human praxis' (UB 30). The 'new creature' makes use of the 'old inoperative' in a manner that does not merely reify the longstanding paradigm of administrative praxis, but takes what was already there – the 'factical condition' – and on that plane creates anew (UB 56). The 'new creature' is the old 'empirical I' first relegated by Kant, who, in Agamben's vision, lives in a contemplative, inoperative relation to the command (UB 63). This negation of the 'ironic self-negation' (S xvi) – which allows the Kantian subject to find 'refuge in the stronghold of the transcendental' (UB 113) or on the 'island of truth'[19] – supplants the sovereign ban that is integral to 'constituted power' (UB 268). This deactivation of self-negation, its inoperativity, is not a destruction but a liberation of potentiality (UB 273). Whereas in Kant's thought the individual is compelled to be through internalised content-free commands, destituent potential is the separation of being and praxis that exposes the possibility of 'properly human life' (UB 277–8).[20]

CONCLUSION

Agamben, like many before him, situates his own work in philosophical opposition to Kant, and in doing so, undertakes three conceptual reversals that uncover the fiction of Kant's notion of the 'sublime "moral feeling"'. Infancy, remnant and destituent potential are defining features of Agamben's thought, and when taken together, advance his claim that despite the totalising reach of Kant's logic, there is always something that remains – a realm that can be neither rarefied nor sublimated by the constituted power of the transcendental subject. Evidently, therefore, it is in sloughing the fetters of Kant's legacy that the distinctive facets of Agamben's philosophical contributions take shape.

NOTES

1. Immanuel Kant, 'An Answer to the Question: What Is Enlightenment?', in *Kant: Political Writings*, trans. H. B. Nisbet (Cambridge: Cambridge University Press, 1991), p. 54.
2. For example, in *Critique of Practical Reason*, trans. Mary Gregor (Cambridge: Cambridge University Press, 1997), p. 95, 5:113–5:114, Kant identifies the conflict between natural necessity and freedom as the core antinomy; in *Critique of Judgment*, trans. Werner S. Pluhar (Indianapolis: Hackett Publishing, 1987), p. 211, 5:338–5:339, he addresses the 'antinomy of taste'.
3. Immanuel Kant, *Critique of Pure Reason*, trans. Norman Kemp Smith (New York: Palgrave Macmillan, 2nd edn, 2003), pp. 350, A377, and 427, A471/B499.
4. Kant, *Critique of Pure Reason*, p. 569, A702/B730.
5. Kant, *Critique of Pure Reason*, p. 268, B307.
6. Kant, *Critique of Pure Reason*, p. 466, A536/B564.
7. Kant, *Critique of Pure Reason*, p. 219, A190/B234–5.
8. Kant, *Critique of Pure Reason*, p. 136, A107.
9. Jerome B. Schneewind, *The Invention of Autonomy: A History of Modern Moral Philosophy* (Cambridge: Cambridge University Press, 1998), p. 483.
10. Immanuel Kant, *Groundwork of the Metaphysics of Morals*, trans. Mary Gregor and Jens Timmermann (Cambridge: Cambridge University Press, 1998), p. 13, 4:399–400.
11. Kant, *Groundwork of the Metaphysics of Morals*, p. 16, 4:403.
12. Kant, *Critique of Practical Reason*, p. 68, 5:80 (original italics).
13. Kant, *Critique of Practical Reason*, p. 71, 5:86.
14. Kant, *Critique of Judgment*, pp. 128, 5:268, and 127, 5:267.
15. Kant, *Critique of Pure Reason*, p. 257, B294/A235; see Alex Murray, 'Expropriated Experience: Agamben Reading Benjamin, Reading Kant',

in Brendan Moran and Carlo Salzani (eds), *Towards the Critique of Violence: Walter Benjamin and Giorgio Agamben* (London: Bloomsbury Academic, 2015), pp. 217–18.
16. Walter Benjamin, 'On the Program of the Coming Philosophy', in *Benjamin: Philosophy, History, Aesthetics*, ed. Gary Smith (Chicago: University of Chicago Press, 1989), p. 9.
17. Daniel McLoughlin, 'In Force Without Significance: Kantian Nihilism and Agamben's Critique of Law', *Law and Critique* 20.3 (2009): 253.
18. Arguably, *The Kingdom and the Glory* is one of the most lucid genealogical assessments of Hans Kelsen's 'pure theory of law', which was not only thoroughly Kantian, but was also a key target in Carl Schmitt's critique of liberalism which produced his notion of the state of exception. See Hans Kelsen, *General Theory of Law and State*, trans. Anders Wedberg (New York: Russell & Russell, 1961), and *Pure Theory of Law*, trans. Max Knight (Berkeley: University of California Press, 1967); Carl Schmitt, *Legality and Legitimacy*, trans. Jeffrey Seitzer (Durham, NC: Duke University Press, 2004), and *Political Theology: Four Chapters on the Concept of Sovereignty*, trans. George Schwab (Chicago: University of Chicago Press, 2005).
19. Kant, *Critique of Pure Reason*, p. 257, B294/A235.
20. Thanos Zartaloudis, 'Violence Without Law? On Pure Violence as a Destituent Power', in Moran and Salzani (eds), *Towards the Critique of Violence*, p. 179.

17 Friedrich Nietzsche

VANESSA LEMM

THE ETERNAL RECURRENCE OF THE SAME

Readers of Giorgio Agamben would agree that the German philosopher Friedrich Nietzsche (1844–1900) is not one of his primary interlocutors. As such, Agamben's engagement with Nietzsche is different from the French reception of Nietzsche's philosophy in Michel Foucault, Gilles Deleuze and Georges Bataille, as well as in his contemporary Italian colleague Roberto Esposito, for whom Nietzsche's philosophy is a key point of reference in their thinking of politics beyond sovereignty. Agamben's stance towards the thought of Nietzsche may seem ambiguous to some readers, in particular with regard to his shifting position on Nietzsche's much-debated vision of the eternal recurrence of the same.[1]

Nietzsche's eternal recurrence finds mention in a great number of Agamben's books, including *Idea of Prose* (IP 56), *The Coming Community* (CC 103), *Means Without End* (ME 53, 79),[2] 'Bartleby, or On Contingency' (PO 267–8), *Homo Sacer* (HS 48) and *Remnants of Auschwitz* (RA 99); furthermore, Agamben dedicated an entire essay, written in 1986, to Nietzsche's thought experiment.[3] Whereas Agamben fully endorses Nietzsche's vision of the eternal recurrence as a way of conceiving artistic activity beyond nihilism (MC), as a way of overcoming transcendence (IP), as a redeeming affirmation (CC 103), as a great thinking of repetition,[4] as illuminating Guy Debord's idea of a 'constructed situation' (ME 79), and as an example of the idea of potentiality ('a gesture in which potentiality and act, natural and mannered, contingency and necessity become indistinguishable' [ME 53]), according to de la Durantaye, with 'Bartleby, or On Contingency', 'the dynamic oscillation that Agamben found in his earlier explorations of the idea come to a grinding halt'.[5]

In 'Bartleby, or On Contingency', Agamben's critique of Nietzsche concerns his reading of the past as deprived of its potentiality, as foreclosing contingency: 'Nietzsche completely forgets the laments of what was not or could have been otherwise' (PO 267). Agamben's assessment culminates in *Remnants of Auschwitz*, with the view that the event of Auschwitz 'refutes it beyond all doubt, excluding the possibility of its even being proposed' (RA 99). De la Durantaye argues that this is due to Agamben siding with Walter Benjamin contra Nietzsche on eternal recurrence.[6] An interview with Agamben seems to confirm this hypothesis: 'like Benjamin I see eternal recurrence as like having to stay after school, when you have to write the same sentence a thousand times'.[7] What does Agamben's change of position vis-à-vis Nietzsche's eternal recurrence mean? Is it just a matter of a shifting between his interlocutors from Heidegger to Benjamin? De la Durantaye speculates that Agamben's changing views on eternal recurrence may not be about Nietzsche but about his singular ambivalence and difficulty in 'developing a philosophy of potentiality able to come to terms with the past'.[8]

In her lucid reading of Agamben and Nietzsche, Paula Fleisner comes to a different answer on the question of the changing identity of Agamben's readings. Relying on *Means Without End*, she suggests that the idea of the eternal recurrence is like a phantasm that traverses Agamben's work: it functions like a messianic shift that *integrally* changes his philosophy, leaving it, at the same time, *almost* intact (ME 79).[9] But in *Means Without End* Agamben adds: 'Everything stayed the same but lost its identity' (ME 79). In my view, the point of Agamben's readings is not to take sides for or against Nietzsche; rather, when one reads Nietzsche as 'a work of art without the artist', identity is lost.[10] In the preface to *The Signature of All Things*, Agamben writes: 'Only a thought that does not conceal its own unsaid – but constantly takes it up and elaborates it – may eventually lay claim to originality' (ST 8). Nietzsche's vision of eternal recurrence may be one of those unsaids in Agamben's thought that keep returning to him until he can (eventually) lay claim to an original reading of it.

In response to de la Durantaye, the difficulty of developing a philosophy of potentialities that comes to terms with the past may explain why Agamben, in one of his latest books, *Pulcinella* (2015), turns to comedy as a way of recovering from the seriousness of philosophy (PU 20), a lesson he learned from Nietzsche, whom Agamben appreciates as the only philosopher who truly embraced the irrational, extravagant and boundless potential of laughter.[11] Agamben even goes so far as to speculate whether Nietzsche might have escaped madness if only he had opted for Pulcinella instead of Zarathustra, and Naples instead of Turin (*PU* 21).

A WORK OF ART WITHOUT THE ARTIST

Agamben's engagement with Nietzsche's philosophy is continuous and ongoing throughout his *oeuvre*. In a 2004 interview, Agamben confirmed that 'Nietzsche was important for me also', and when asked about his vision of the philosophical life, he answered: 'Nietzsche's idea of a work of art without the artist'.[12] Interestingly, Agamben's first intervention on Nietzsche concludes on the same note with a citation from Nietzsche's posthumous work: 'The work of art, where it appears without an artist, e.g., as body, as organism [. . .]. To what extent the artist is only a preliminary stage. The world as a work of art that gives birth to itself' (*MC* 93).[13] Does this continuity indicate that, after all, the main inspiration that Agamben draws from Nietzsche is the idea of the work of art without the artist?

Agamben's first book, *The Man Without Content*, dedicated to a 'destruction of aesthetics', opens with a citation from the third essay of Nietzsche's *On the Genealogy of Morals* in which he rejects the Kantian idea of *aesthesis* which considers art from the viewpoint of the spectator (*MC* 1–2). Nietzsche's 'identification of art with the will to power in the idea of the universe "as work of art that gives birth to itself"' is 'tributary to a determination of the essence of human activity as will and vital impulse, and is therefore founded in the original forgetting of the original productive status of the work of art as foundation of the space of truth' (*MC* 71–2). In line with Heidegger's reading of Nietzsche, Agamben concludes that, with Nietzsche's 'artist's metaphysics', Western aesthetics arrives at a metaphysics of the will (*MC* 72). Nietzsche's idea of art as 'the highest task and truly metaphysical activity of man' (*MC* 85) culminates in the idea of the eternal recurrence of the same, which he identifies with will to power (*MC* 91), as the most extreme point of nihilism. Agamben approvingly cites Nietzsche: 'the nothing ("the meaninglessness") eternally' (*MC* 89).

But this end point of Western aesthetics in Nietzsche also announces a new beginning, the overcoming of nihilism in the name of Dionysus and *amor fati*, exemplified by the figure of the artist and the *Übermensch*, who both love and embrace the meaninglessness of the world. As such, the 'highest task' points towards a becoming nature of art that is at the same time a becoming art of nature (*MC* 93). This is also the reading of the eternal return given by Karl Löwith, who argues that the eternal recurrence of the same is the last step in Nietzsche's naturalisation

(*Vernatürlichung*) of morality, in which 'nature frees itself from the shadows of God and man naturalises himself' (*MC* 93).[14]

Whereas *The Man Without Content* opens with Nietzsche, *Language and Death* closes with Nietzsche. *Language and Death* presents a reading of an imaginary monologue by Oedipus from Nietzsche's early work which Agamben cites in full (*LD* 94–5). Agamben writes in the final chapter of the book that 'now having reached the end of our research [. . .] we can begin to read a text in which Nietzsche seems to want to stage the end of philosophy and the beginning of its "posterity" in a brief tragic monologue of Oedipus' (*LD* 94). In *Language and Death*, Agamben endorses Nietzsche as a philosopher who not only understood the relationship between philosophy, voice and death, but who put forward an experience of language that is not marked by negativity and death, an experience that leads beyond the end of philosophy understood as a taking place of voice within language.[15] As in *The Man Without Content*, in *Language and Death* Nietzsche's thought intervenes to initiate a new beginning, here the questioning of what language without voice is, what a word not grounded in meaning is (*LD* 95).

Nietzsche is mentioned several times in Agamben's *The Signature of All Things*, where his genealogical method is featured as a model for what Agamben refers to as 'Philosophical Archaeology'. This time Agamben does not read Nietzsche directly. In *The Signature of All Things*, Nietzsche appears three times through the readings of others: through Michel Foucault's 1971 essays on 'Nietzsche, Genealogy, History' (*ST* 82–4), Enzo Melandri's reading of 'critical history' in Nietzsche's second *Untimely Meditation* understood as a 'history that criticizes and destroys the past to make life possible' (*ST* 87), and through a reading by Nietzsche's friend, Franz Overbeck. Agamben points out that

> the idea that all historical inquiry involves the identification of a fringe or of a heterogeneous stratum that is not placed in the position of a chronological origin but is qualitatively other, derives not from Nietzsche but from Franz Overbeck, the theologian who was perhaps the most faithful and lucid of Nietzsche's friends. (*ST* 84)

In the context of Agamben's observations on method, the reference to Nietzsche's friendship with Overbeck is not accidental. Agamben points out in the preface of his book that anyone familiar with research in the human sciences knows that method is a matter to be discussed among friends and colleagues (*ST* 7). Nietzsche's exchange with his friend Overbeck exemplifies Agamben's insight into this characteristic of method in the humanities.

But method is not the only context in which Agamben refers to friendship in Nietzsche. In his text 'Friendship',[16] a work largely dedicated to Aristotle, Nietzsche is referred to three times. Agamben comments on Derrida's *Politics of Friendship* and claims that the book reflects a Nietzschean move: 'Derrida's gesture repeated that of Nietzsche' ('Friendship', p. 2). For both Nietzsche and Derrida, friends are at the same time the closest and the furthest away from each other: 'the necessity of friendship and, at the same time, a certain distrust towards friends were essential to Nietzsche's strategy' ('Friendship', p. 2). Agamben asks: 'What is friendship, in effect, if not a proximity such that it is impossible to make for oneself either a representation or a concept of it?' ('Friendship', p. 4). Nietzsche's vision of 'stellar friendship' may provide an answer to this question of Agamben and offers another point in common between the two.[17]

In his reading of Aristotle's treatise on friendship, Agamben also mentions that the text in question reveals an 'equivalence between being and living, between awareness of one's existing and awareness of one's living', and adds: 'This is decidedly an anticipation of the Nietzschean thesis according to which: "Being: we have no other experience of it than 'to live'"' ('Friendship', p. 5). Nietzsche's intuitions on 'the intimate interweaving of being and living' also traverses other texts of Agamben (*UB* xix). In particular, Nietzsche's reflections on how to give style to one's life and their reception through Foucault's idea of an 'aesthetics of existence' play a role in Agamben's thinking on the relationship between *zoè* and *bios* in form-of-life. In *The Use of Bodies*, Agamben is working towards an ontology of style which 'names the mode in which a singularity bears witness to itself in being and being expresses itself in the singular body' (*UB* 233). Readers of Nietzsche will recall the author's project in *Ecce Homo* where he tells his life to himself.[18] In this context, it is not surprising that we find another reference to Nietzsche in the chapter 'Towards an Ontology of Style' (*UB* 225). Agamben reflects on a mode of life in which *zoè* and *bios* coincide at every point: 'What can a mode of life be that has for its object only life, which our political tradition has always already separated into bare life?' (*UB* 225). According to Agamben, this same question must have motivated Nietzsche when he spoke of 'great politics' as physiology: 'Here one sees the limit and, at the same time, the abyss that Nietzsche had to have glimpsed when he speaks of "great politics" as physiology' (*UB* 225). There is no doubt that, for Agamben, Nietzsche is a thinker of biopolitics,[19] who grasps what Esposito referred to as 'the enigma of biopolitics':[20] 'Here the risk is the same one that the biopolitics of modernity has fallen into: to make bare life as such the preeminent object of politics' (*UB* 225). Against the background of Agamben's biopolitical thought, readers of Nietzsche may find it disappointing that Nietzsche as a philosopher of animality[21] does not find mention in Agamben's *The Open*, so as to compare the question of how to 'render inoperative' the anthropological machine (*O* 92) with the question of how to overcome the domination and exclusion of animality inherent to Nietzsche's politics of civilisation.[22]

Agamben's readings of Nietzsche are oscillating, multifaceted and inherently plural. They are traversed by the readings of others – Heidegger, Foucault, Benjamin, among others – to the point of indetermination. They are like 'an open, traversed and criss-crossed system of readings and ideas', resembling the one Ulrich Rauff ascribes to Nietzsche's philosophy.[23] When Agamben was questioned about his position on Nietzsche, his answer perhaps indicates how he read Nietzsche, namely, as 'a work of art without the author': 'If that is so, then we need to learn to forget the presence of the subject. We must protect the work against the author.'[24] Agamben's shifting positions and mediated readings of Nietzsche may be his singular way of forgetting the subject and protecting the work against the author (and her interpreters).

NOTES

1. On eternal recurrence in Nietzsche, see in particular two passages in his published works: aphorism 341, 'The Heaviest Weight', in *The Gay Science*, trans. Josefine Nauckhoff (Cambridge: Cambridge University Press, 2001), pp. 194–5, and the section 'The Convalescent' in the third book of *Thus Spoke Zarathustra*, trans. Walter Kaufman (New York: Modern Library, 1995), pp. 215–21. The aphorism in *The Gay Science* is cited in full in *MC* 90–1. For two extensive but different discussions of Agamben's readings of Nietzsche's vision of the eternal recurrence of the same, see Leland de la Durantaye, *Giorgio Agamben: A Critical Introduction* (Stanford: Stanford University Press, 2009), pp. 314–23; and Jenny Doussan, 'Writing Lines: Agamben Contra Nietzsche', *Cultural Critique* 92 (2016): 114–36.
2. In *Means Without End*, Nietzsche appears in the notes on gesture (*ME* 49–60) and in the marginal notes on Guy Debord (*ME* 73–89). See also Giorgio Agamben, 'Difference and Repetition: On Guy Debord's Films', in *Guy Debord and the Situationists International: Texts and Documents*, ed. Tom McDonough (Cambridge, MA: MIT Press, 2004), pp. 313–19, for another mention of Nietzsche on p. 315.
3. Giorgio Agamben, 'The Eternal Return and the Paradox of Passion', in *Nietzsche in Italy*, ed. Thomas Harrison (Saratoga, CA: Anima Libri, 1988), pp. 9–17.

4. See Agamben, 'Difference and Repetition', p. 315.
5. de la Durantaye, *Giorgio Agamben*, p. 319.
6. This is not the place to discuss Walter Benjamin's interpretation of eternal recurrence in Nietzsche. For a different reading of eternal recurrence in Benjamin and Nietzsche that relies on the importance of Karl Löwith's 'Nietzsche's Philosophy of the Eternal Recurrence of the Same' for Benjamin, see Miguel Vatter, *The Republic of the Living: Biopolitics and the Critique of Civil Society* (New York: Fordham University Press, 2014), pp. 290–325.
7. Ulrich Rauff, 'An Interview with Giorgio Agamben', *German Law Journal* 5 (2004): 609–14, here p. 614.
8. de la Durantaye, *Giorgio Agamben*, p. 323.
9. Paula Fleisner, 'La vida entre estética y política. En busca de las posibles herencias nietzscheanas en el pensameinto de Giorgio Agamben', *Pléyade: Revista de Humanidades y Ciencias Sociales* 17 (2016): 65–88, here p. 83.
10. Rauff, 'An Interview with Giorgio Agamben', pp. 612–13.
11. See also Fleisner, 'La vida entre estética y política', p. 83.
12. Rauff, 'An Interview with Giorgio Agamben', pp. 612–13.
13. Agamben cites the same passage in full also in *UB* 100.
14. Karl Löwith, *Nietzsche's Philosophy of the Eternal Recurrence of the Same*, trans. J. Harvey Lomax (Berkeley and Los Angeles: University of California Press, 1978).
15. Fleisner, 'La vida entre estética y política', p. 68.
16. Giorgio Agamben, 'Friendship', *Contretemps* 5 (December 2004): 1–6.
17. Nietzsche, *The Gay Science*, aphorism 279, p. 159.
18. Friedrich Nietzsche, *Ecce Homo*, trans. Walter Kaufman (New York: Vintage Books, 1967), p. 221.
19. Vanessa Lemm, 'Nietzsche and Biopolitics: Four Readings of Nietzsche as a Biopolitical Thinker', in *The Routledge Handbook of Biopolitics*, ed. Sergei Prozorov and Simona Rentea (London: Routledge, 2016), pp. 50–65.
20. Roberto Esposito, *Bios: Biopolitics and Philosophy* (Minneapolis: University of Minnesota Press, 2008), pp. 13–44 and 78–109.
21. On animality in Nietzsche, see Christa Davis Acampora and Ralph R. Acampora, *A Nietzschean Bestiary: Becoming Animal Beyond Docile and Brutal* (Lanham, MD: Rowman & Littlefield, 2004); Vanessa Lemm, *Nietzsche's Animal Philosophy: Culture, Politics and the Animality of the Human Being* (New York: Fordham University Press, 2009).
22. See, for example, Mathew Abbott, 'The Animal for which Animality is an Issue: Nietzsche, Agamben, and the Anthropological Machine', *Angelaki* 16.4 (2012): 87–99.
23. Rauff, 'An Interview with Giorgio Agamben', p. 614.
24. Rauff, 'An Interview with Giorgio Agamben', p. 614.

18 Plato

MIKA OJAKANGAS

I

There are not many books by Agamben in which Plato does not figure. In *The Man Without Content* (MC 52–64), Agamben discusses the Platonic discrepancy between politics and poetry; in *Stanzas*, he examines Plato's conceptions of love (S 115–21) and phantasm (S 73–5); in *Infancy and History* (IH 73), Agamben takes up Plato's concept of time (*aion* and *chronos*), while in *The End of the Poem* (EP 17) he examines Plato's criticism of tragedy. In *Language and Death* (LD 91–2), he gives an account of Socrates' 'demon' and Plato's Idea (*eidos*) – though he investigates the latter more thoroughly in *Potentialities* (PO 27–38), in which he also briefly touches upon Plato's doctrine of matter (*khôra*) (PO 218). In *Idea of Prose* (IP 120–3) and *The Coming Community* (CC 76–7), it is the Platonic Idea again that is under scrutiny, albeit more implicitly than in *Potentialities*. In *Homo Sacer* (HS 33–5), Agamben offers an interpretation of Plato's treatment of Pindar's *nomos basileus* fragment and the sophistic opposition between *nomos* and *physis*, whereas in *The Sacrament of Language* (SL 29) he touches on Plato's critique of oath. In *The Signature of All Things* (ST 22–6), Agamben gives an account of Plato's 'paradigmatic' method, while in *Stasis* (STA 5–12) we find an analysis of Plato's conception of civil war (*stasis*). In *The Use of Bodies*, finally, Agamben returns to many of the above-mentioned Platonic topics, to the idea of the Idea in particular and thereby to the presuppositional structure of language (UB 115–33), but he also adds new Platonic themes not discussed in his previous books, including an interpretation of the myth of Er (UB 249–62) narrated at the end of the *Republic* and of the Nocturnal Council (UB 279) introduced at the end of the *Laws*. This list is not exhaustive, but it illustrates well the extent to which Plato is present in Agamben's work from the very first to the latest book he has published.

Furthermore, the majority of these interpretations present Plato in a most positive light. In *Homo Sacer* (*HS* 30–8), Plato's concept of 'natural justice' is introduced, perhaps a bit unexpectedly, as an antidote to 'the sovereign confusion of violence and law' (*HS* 35) – despite the fact that violence in the mode of legal penalty, including expulsion and even the death penalty, is recommended in all of Plato's major political works from the *Republic* via *Statesman* to the *Laws*. In *The Signature of All Things* (*ST* 22–6), on the other hand, Agamben gives an account of Plato's concept of paradigm and his 'paradigmatic' method in a way that gives the impression that Agamben's own 'paradigmatic' method is a mere replica of Plato's. In *The Use of Bodies*, furthermore, in the context of his interpretation of the myth of Er (including the most extended citation of any author in Agamben's entire *oeuvre*), the Platonic soul (*psykhê*), arguably the most significant Platonic concept alongside the Idea, is unequivocally represented as an example of the Agambenian form-of-life:

> Form-of-life, the soul, is the infinite complement between life and mode of life, what appears when they mutually neutralize one another and show the void that united them. *Zoè* and *bios* – this is perhaps the lesson of the myth – are neither separate nor coincident: between them, as void of representation of which it is not possible to say anything except that it is 'immortal' and 'ungenerated' (*Phaedrus* 246), stands the soul, which holds them indissolubly in contact and testifies for them. (*UB* 262)

In *The Use of Bodies*, even the Nocturnal Council – the supreme political body whose task is to secure the salvation (*sôtêria*) of the city of Magnesia (*Laws* 968a) with unlimited (and one could also say dictatorial) authority (*Laws* 968c) – is exalted as an example, not of sovereignty, but of destituent potential that renders sovereign decisions inoperative:

> Plato had in mind something of the kind [destituent potential] when at the end of the *Laws* (968c), he mentions as 'protector' (*phylake*) of the city a 'Nocturnal Council' (*nykterinos syllogos*), which, however, is not an institution in a technical sense because, as Socrates [sic] specifies, 'it is impossible to lay down the council's activities until it has been established [*prin a kosmethe*] [...] through a long standing together [*metà synnousia pollen*]'. (*UB* 279)[1]

One could easily extend the list of sympathetic 'appropriations' of Plato's thought by Agamben (though we could as easily speak of 'expropriations', as Agamben's interpretations are not only very intriguing but sometimes also quite bewildering), but given the limited space of this chapter, I will restrict my analysis to the most pervasive Platonic theme in Agamben's work, that of the Idea.

II

In modern renditions, Plato's Ideas are usually understood as temporally and spatially transcendent and unchanging models of immanent beings existing in time and space, which are imperfect copies of the Ideas that constitute the essential foundation of reality. For example, there is a variety of beautiful objects in the world but in addition to these there exists 'beauty itself', the Idea of beauty. And in order to attain true knowledge, one must grasp the world of Ideas with one's mind, but in contrast to the modern concept of idea, the Platonic Ideas exist independently of minds. Sometimes Ideas are understood as perfect examples, sometimes as universals, but it is generally acknowledged that Plato himself in different dialogues offers several incompatible definitions and oscillates between different positions even in the course of individual dialogues.

What then is Agamben's interpretation of Plato's Idea? One finds the most thoroughgoing accounts of the Idea in his article 'The Thing Itself' published in 1984, and in *The Use of Bodies* published thirty years later. These slightly different constructions, based mainly on Agamben's reading of the philosophical digression in Plato's Seventh Letter and section 511b of the *Republic*, show that his interpretation of the Idea is – to put it mildly – quite different from other modern interpretations. It is true that there is nothing extraordinary in Agamben's identification of 'the thing itself' (*to pragma auto*) discussed in the Seventh Letter with the Idea (*auto* is generally recognised as a technical expression of the Idea: circle *itself*, beauty *itself*, and so on). However, by relocating the discourse on Ideas from the sphere of ontology into that of linguistic signification, he takes a step that is not very often taken in Plato scholarship:

> One could say, with an apparent paradox, that the thing itself, while in some way transcending language, is nevertheless possible only in language and by virtue of language: precisely the thing of language. (*PO* 31)

In order to grasp what kind of a thing the thing of language is, we must reconstruct the philosophical context of Plato's theory of Ideas as Agamben understands it.

As already noted, Agamben relocates the ontological question of Ideas into the sphere of language, arguing that the Greeks – Plato and Aristotle in particular – were well aware of the complex relation between language and the world. They were aware of the fact that, by speaking of beings, beings are presupposed by language in language. Plato, Agamben writes, was 'perhaps the first to thematize the presuppositional power [*il potere presupponente*] of language' (*UB* 119). Similarly, 'Aristotle frequently expresses with perfect awareness the onto-logical interweaving of being and saying' (*UB* 120). Thus ontology has been onto-*logy* from the very outset of Western philosophy. According to Agamben, however, there is a decisive difference between Plato and Aristotle as to how they deal with the fact – in Agamben's estimation what is at issue is precisely a fact – that beings are presupposed by language, decomposing the thing itself into a being (*on*) about which something is said and a quality (*poion*) that is said of it (*PO* 106).

In Aristotle's ontology, Agamben holds, the presuppositional structure of language is affirmed: being is divided into an 'existentive being' (*un essere esistentivo*) and a 'predicative being' (*un essere predicativo*), that is, into a presupposed subject (existence) on the basis of which something is said and a predication that is said of it (essence) in which the named existing being is presupposed (hypothesised) as non-linguistic (and therefore ineffable) (*UB* 115–18, 125; *PO* 36–7) – analogous to the way natural life (*zoè*), in the political thought of Aristotle, is included in the political form of life (*bios*) in the mode of its exclusion (*HS* 7–9). In contrast to this Aristotelian approach, Plato's ontological paradigm is 'completely different' (*UB* 130). While Aristotle affirms the presuppositional power of language – though in a sense, he also tries to surpass it (the separation of existence and essence) by *temporalising* being, but without success (*PO* 36–7; *UB* 115–29) – Plato overcomes it, freeing human speech from presuppositions: 'The Platonic constitution of truth, unlike the Aristotelian, never comes to a halt at a presupposition' (*PO* 109; see also *UB* 130). Both Aristotle and Plato were aware of the presuppositional power of language, but while Aristotle located this power at the basis of his philosophy (*UB* 131), Plato, with his 'non-presupposed principle' (*arkhê anypthetos*), rendered it inoperative, effacing the ineffable from philosophical discourse (*PO* 35, 77, 107; *UB* 130). Let us quote section 511b of the *Republic*, cited in 'The Thing Itself' (*PO* 35) and *The Use of Bodies* (*UB* 130), on which Agamben's interpretation is based and which he unconventionally translates (in this context *logos* is seldom translated as 'language' but usually as 'reason') as follows:

> Then also understand the other subjection of the intelligible, I mean that which language itself [*autos ho logos*] touches on [*haptetai*] with the

potential of dialoguing [*tei tou dialegesthai dynamei*]. It does not consider these presuppositions [*hypotheseis*, etymologically, 'that which is placed under, at the foundation'] as first principles [*arkhai*] but truly as presuppositions – as stepping-stones to take off from, enabling it to reach the non-presupposed [*anypotheton*] toward the principle of everything and, having touched on it [*hapsamenos autes*], it reverses itself and, keeping hold of what follows from it, comes down to a conclusion without making use of anything visible at all but only ideas themselves, moving from ideas to ideas and ending in ideas. (UB 130; see also PO 35)

The thing itself, the Idea, is this non-presupposed principle, a word freed from its shadow (a word in which *on* and *poion* have become indistinguishable):

> The philosopher frees language from its shadow and, instead of taking hypotheses for granted, seeks to ascend from these latter – namely, from denotative words – toward the non-presupposed principle. The Idea is this word freed from its shadow, which does not presuppose the *arkhe* as given but seeks to reach it as what is not a presupposition to name and discourse. (UB 130–1)

For Agamben, in other words, Plato's theory of Ideas is an attempt to philosophise without supposing and hypothesising, without subjectifying that about which one speaks – an attempt to speak *absolutely* (PO 33). This also means that Agamben rejects the esoteric and mystical readings of Plato inspired by the Seventh Letter (341c–d), in which it is said that the thing itself 'does not at all admit of verbal expression'. Drawing attention to the immediately following phrase 'like other disciplines', Agamben argues that the thing itself, although it cannot be expressed in the same way as in other 'disciplines' (meaning name [*onoma*], definition [*logos*], image [*eidôlon*] and knowledge [*epistêmê*]), it is not for that reason simply unsayable (PO 31). It is, as Plato continues further on (344b–c), in a passage quoted by Agamben (PO 30), only when the names, definitions and sense-perceptions are 'rubbed against each other [. . .] that wisdom [*phronêsis*] along with insight [*nous*] will commence to cast its light in an effort at the very limits of human possibility'. Similarly, when Plato in this same Letter (342e) speaks about the 'weakness of language' (in asserting something of something else, a *logos* can only qualify this something else, not express its inherent being), Agamben argues that it is precisely the recognition of this weakness that paves the way, not for the rejection of language, but for the need to *help* speech so that in speech, 'speech itself does not remain presupposed but instead comes to speech' (PO 35). The weakness of *logos* does not consist in its inability to represent beings adequately but in the fact that – without help – it can *only* represent them without being able to bring 'sayability' (*dicibilità*) to expression.² The Platonic theory of the Ideas is not a theory against *logos* but a theory the aim of which is to help speech, so that the sayability of the said does not remain presupposed (ineffable) but is expressed in full:

> The thing itself is not a *quid* that might be sought as an extreme hypothesis beyond all hypotheses, as a final and absolute subject beyond all subjects, horribly or beautifully unreachable in its obscurity. We can, in truth, conceive of such a nonlinguistic thing only in language, through the idea of a language without relation to things [. . .]. Thing itself is not a thing; it is the very sayability, the very openness at issue in language, which, in language, we [but not Plato!] always presuppose and forget. (*PO* 35)

The question of language has been at the heart of Agamben's philosophy from the outset: the human being is a being whose proper dwelling-place is in language (for us, there is no object outside language), but insofar as we remain caught by language without seeing language itself (without being able to say sayability), we remain alien to our authentic nature – separated from what is constitutive of us. Therefore, the task of the coming philosophy, according to Agamben, is to bring language, which mediates all things and all knowledge, into language, to mediate the immediate: 'To restore the thing itself to its place in language [. . .] is the task of the coming philosophy' (*PO* 38).

Yet as the choice of the word 'restore' indicates, philosophy has always already succeeded in bringing language into language, in mediating the immediate. The Platonic Idea, which in Agamben's estimation remained undefined by Plato (*WA* 1), is the taking place of this immediacy, constitutive of 'authentic human community and communication' (*PO* 35). In Agamben's view, however, the Western philosophical tradition from Aristotle onwards has either ignored the Idea, replacing it with the first substance (the presupposition of all presuppositions) (Aristotle), or misunderstood it, identifying the Idea with the ineffable and incomprehensible One (Neoplatonism).³ Therefore, we need to return to Plato, the first to discover the presuppositional power of language and, with the help of the theory of Ideas, to render this power inoperative and to efface the ineffable from philosophical discourse. The coming philosophy is thus also the come-back of a philosophy, the philosophy of Plato.

III

As already noted, Agamben's interpretations of Plato's Idea are not absolutely identical. In 'The Thing Itself' and in *Idea of Prose* (1985), Agamben underlines the coincidence of the sensible and the Idea in the immediacy of language. In *Idea of Prose* he formulates the thought as follows:

> What is reached here [in the Idea], that is, is something still sensible (from this comes the term idea, which indicates a vision, an *idein*). But not some sensible thing presupposed by language and knowledge, but rather, exposed in them, absolutely. Appearance which is no longer based on a hypothesis, but on itself, the thing no longer separated from its intelligibility, but in the midst of it, is the Idea, is the thing itself. (IP 122–3)

In *The Use of Bodies*, Agamben recapitulates what he had written earlier, but at one point the emphasis is a bit different inasmuch as he also pays attention to the verb 'to touch' (*toccare / haptetai*), which occurs twice in the passage from the *Republic* (511b) I quoted above. While in his previous interpretation Agamben had stressed that in the Idea the sensible is not represented but *exposed* in language without sensible referent, now, in *The Use of Bodies*, the Idea is defined as a (self-signifying) word in which the thing itself and language itself are *in contact* with each other (just like the soul between *zoè* and *bios* in Agamben's interpretation of the myth of Er) – united only by a void of signification and representation: 'The idea is a word that does not denote but "touches". That is to say, as happens in contact, it manifests the thing and at the same time also itself' (UB 131). The idea of 'contact' may appear enigmatic in this context, but anyone familiar with Jean-Luc Nancy's 'haptology' recognises a homology. Touch entails neither fusion nor representation: it exposes the thing ('body') to the exteriority of the touched, but in this exposing the thing ('body') is also exposed to itself.[4] We may still wonder how a word can touch itself, but perhaps it is not only Agamben's genius but also his ability to philosophise at the limits of understandability that has made him one of the leading intellectuals in the contemporary tradition of continental philosophy.

NOTES

1. Interestingly, Agamben omits the part in which Plato asserts that the members of the Council 'must themselves ordain what authority they should possess' from the sentence he quotes above. Socrates does not feature in the *Laws*.
2. In *Language and Death* (LD 91), Agamben identifies Socrates' daimon (*daimonion*) with the unsayable, that is, with the mute voice of conscience that has haunted Western metaphysics as that which is inclusively excluded from speech (*logos*) so that speech can emerge. From this perspective, Agamben's interpretation of Plato's theory of Ideas depicts Plato as essentially anti-Socratic: the Idea is the revocation of the demonic.

3. In 'The Passion of Facticity' (*PO* 194), Agamben points out that in the Heideggerian *Dasein*, existence and essence are as inseparable as *on* and *poion* are in Plato's 'soul'. In *The Use of Bodies* (*UB* 144–5), however, Agamben asserts that even Heidegger remained bound up with the aporias of the Aristotelian–Neoplatonic tradition.
4. See Jean-Luc Nancy, *Corpus*, trans. Richard A. Rand (New York: Fordham University Press, 2008).

19 *Plotinus*

MÅRTEN BJÖRK

I

The philosophy of Plotinus plays a contradictory role in Giorgio Agamben's *corpus*. He comments on Plotinus in a lapidary fashion in several articles and essays before commencing the *Homo Sacer* series, where he undertakes a longer and more ambiguous analysis of Plotinus in *Opus Dei* and *The Use of Bodies*. In *Opus Dei*, Agamben develops the brief criticism of Plotinus he proposed in *The Kingdom and the Glory* in order to describe the crucial instance when Western metaphysics starts to designate being as operativity: 'The place and moment when classical ontology begins that process of transformation that will lead to the Christian and modern ontology is the theory of the hypostases in Plotinus' (*OD* 58). Agamben is referring to the development in the *Enneads* of the idea of the three hypostases of being – the One, the Soul and the Intellect – from which the whole complex of reality emanates.[1]

Just as in *The Kingdom and the Glory*, Agamben draws here on Heinrich Dörrie's reading of the Neoplatonist master in order to argue that Plotinus develops the term *hypostasis* beyond its original meaning as sediment or deposit into a concept that signifies a process 'of putting-to-work, in which the categories of classical ontology (being and praxis, potential and act) tend to be indeterminated and the concept of will [. . .] develops a central function' (*OD* 58).[2] This indetermination of being and action is parallel to the configuration of human practice as an office or a duty where 'being and praxis, what a human does and what a human is, enter into a zone of indistinction, in which being dissolves into its practical effects and, with a perfect circularity, it is what it has to be and has to be what it is' (*OD* xii). The development of the idea of the *officium*, which Agamben identifies with the rise of duty in the form of rules that ecclesial and political apparatuses require in order to reproduce themselves, is exemplified in *Opus Dei* by the sacramental office of the Catholic clergy.

The minister is only a vessel for his office whose being is determined, as Augustine put it, *ex opere operato*, from the works worked, that is, not from the activity of the priest, such as the individual actions of the priest who baptises a child, but from Christ's work itself; according to Augustine: 'they whom a drunkard baptized, those whom a murderer baptized, those whom an adulterer baptized, if it was the baptism of Christ, were baptized by Christ' (qtd. in *OD* 21). The logic of *ex opere operato* is the instigation of a sacramental bureaucracy, where the clergy implements a work that does not belong to them as moral and ethical subjects but to their office. Agamben scrutinises the role of the Catholic Church as an institutional apparatus which separated the life of the minister from the efficacious work of the ministry as a consequence of schisms and struggles between rival Christian factions. The defeat of the Donatists and other movements paved the way for an ontology where being is put to work by will, and where the category of duty becomes hegemonic for political and ethical thought as Christian eschatology is turned into a sacramental office (*OD* 21).

But, as we have already noted, Agamben does not argue that orthodox Western Catholicism is the instigator of the cleavage between action and being. He traces this separation to Plotinus' use of the Greek term *hoion* – 'as if, so to speak' – 'whose strategic meaning clearly appears in the passage of the *Enneads* in which the will to overcome the duality of being and acting, potential and acts, goes together with the impossibility of dropping it altogether' (*OD* 58). Referring to Ernst Benz's *Marius Victorinus und die Entwicklung der abendländischen Willensmetaphysik*, Agamben argues that the development of office and Plotinus' metaphysics of will have to be read together. In the treatise of the sixth *Ennead* bearing the title 'Free Will and the Will of One', Agamben notices that will, for Plotinus, is 'will of self; [it] names the intradivine movement through which the One [...] is constituted as intellect (*nous*) and gives itself reality and existence in three primary hypostases' (*OD* 126). The One wills itself into existence in hypostatic union with the soul and the intellect and this, which Benz calls *Voluntarisierung* of being, is parallel to what Agamben sees as the indetermination of potentiality and actuality, being and act, in Plotinus' philosophy.[3]

Will, from this perspective, is a form of efficiency posited by the split between life and form, function and action, but also an instrument to overcome it. If being is produced by will, then being is something which is put to work by a willing subject. This is the paradigm of operativity:

being is seen as action caused by will. Yet here we reach a contradiction, or at least an ambiguity, in Agamben's reading of Plotinus.

II

In *Opus Dei*, Agamben writes that what is decisive in Plotinus' treatise 'On Free Will and the Will of the One' is 'that the movement of being is here not produced in itself and by nature but implies [...] an incessant "putting-to-work," [...] that refers to the effectuation on the part of a subject [...] identified with the will' (*OD* 128). But in *The Use of Bodies*, Agamben returns to his brief but more positive evaluation of Plotinus in his earlier work, and this affirmation is continued in his latest book, *Che cos'é la filosofia?* (*PO* 120, 217; *CF* 102–4).

In *The Use of Bodies*, Agamben even examines Plotinus' treatise in order to develop a counter-ontology to the paradigm of operativity by identifying being with use. In this treatise Plotinus not only develops a notion of the hypostasis of being as an action implementing the will of a subject. Agamben argues that Plotinus also differentiates use, *chrestai*, from substance, *ousia*, as Plotinus – and here I use Stephen MacKenna's perhaps more poetic than philologically correct translation – thinks that

> never having come to be but being as He is, [the One] is still not master of his own essence but being as He is, not self-originating but acting out his nature as He finds it, must He not be of necessity what He is, inhibited from being otherwise?[4]

Agamben translates *on tes autou ousias kyrios*, which MacKenna renders as 'not master of his essence', as 'not master of his own substance' and differentiates it from the sentence *ouk hypostesas heaouton, chromenos de heautoi hoios estin* which he translates as 'not hypostatizing himself but using-himself as what he is' in order to reveal that Plotinus differentiates substance from use (*UB* 55). Even if, as Agamben says, Plotinus does not develop this idea of a use-of-oneself, Agamben still bases his ontology of use on Plotinus' idea of the One (*UB* 55). He returns to Dörrie's discussion of the concept of hypostasis and Plotinus' indeterminacy of being and action, but now exemplified by the use of the term *hoion* – of what kind, such as – in the *Enneads*, rather than *hoios* as in *Opus Dei*:

> Dörrie has shown that beginning with Neoplatonism the term *hypostais* acquires the meaning of 'realization': *hyphistamai* thus means 'to be realized in an existence' [...] Using-oneself means not pre-supposing oneself, not appropriating being to oneself in order to subjectivate oneself in a separate substance.

And, he continues, the 'self of which use makes use is expressed, for this reason, only by the anaphora *hoios*, "some such," which always recovers being from its hypostatization into a subject' (*UB* 55).

In contrast to *Opus Dei*, in *The Use of Bodies* Plotinus is singled out as one of the few thinkers in the history of Western metaphysics who tries to grasp the One as a use-of-itself, in other words as a modality which comes before being: 'Use-of-oneself, [...] precedes being [...] [and] is "a primary *energeia* without being," in which the self itself takes the place of hypostasis ("it itself is, as it were, its hypostasis" [...])' (*UB* 55–6). The ontology of the One as a modality of use which, in MacKenna's translation, is what it is 'not because He could not be otherwise but because so is best',[5] becomes, in Agamben's reading, the truth of subjectivity itself. The One as a use of life reveals that the modality of use is what makes 'a subject – a hypostasis – [which] can say: I am, I can, I cannot, I must' possible (*UB* 56).

III

In *The Use of Bodies* it becomes evident that Plotinus is not a mere instigator of operativity for Agamben, but also a thinker of modality and use, which, as something that 'has a constitutively *adverbial* nature ... expresses not "what" but "how" being is' (*UB* 164). But if it is the modality of use that turns the hypostatic efficiency of the will into a subject which can posit itself as an ego with the capacity to articulate its being (I am), its potentiality (I can), its impotentiality (I cannot) and its obligations (I must), then we have to ask if Plotinus does not reveal that all imperatives border on the subjunctive.

The subjunctive mood articulates states of unreality such as wishes, emotions, possibilities, but also judgements, obligations and actions that have not yet occurred. The will of the subject therefore not only implies the efficacy of imperatives and commands, but also the mode of the *irrealis*, used for counterfactual and hypothetical situations. The indeterminacy of being and action in Plotinus' work is not necessarily the cancellation of the modality of use, but the truth of use itself; a truth that is perhaps best expressed in the *Enneads* when Plotinus urges his students to 'break away towards the High' and transcend, in other words surpass or flee, their contemporary existence.[6]

Agamben comments on Plotinus' concept of flight in *The Highest Poverty*, noting that his proposed exile from the world is a political gesture that binds Plotinus to Philo's and Ambrose of Milan's identification of flight with community (*HP* 51). Agamben had already called attention to Plotinus' notion of community as a modality, a manner of being, in *Infancy and History* and *The Coming Community* (*IH* 9; *CC* 27), but it is in *The Highest Poverty* and *The Use of Bodies* that Plotinus' exhortation to flee the world is analysed as an explicit political gesture related to the communal life of our species. The High, and hence the One, is the pure potentiality of what Plotinus terms life and is what subjectivises (in other words hypostatises) itself in different forms of life. It is to this source of life, a use beyond being, that mankind must flee and seek its exile if it desires to dwell in the pure potentiality of an existence free from any boundaries. But can finite life exist without boundaries? In the *Enneads* Plotinus states that '[w]e cannot break Life into parts, if the total was Life, the fragment is not. But do we not thus sunder Intelligence, one Intelligence in this man, another in that? No; such a fragment would not be Intelligence.'[7] Life and intelligence are common to all living beings as they are hypostatised as a multiplicity of forms. This notion of a common life, and a shared intellect, is in Agamben's perspective perhaps the most compelling idea in Plotinus' philosophy.

Plotinus, Agamben writes, transforms Aristotelian ontology in the sense that the unique substance of being 'is not a subject that remains behind or beneath its qualities but is always already homonymically shared in a plurality of forms of life, in which life is never separable from its form and, quite to the contrary, is always its mode of being, without for that reason ceasing to be one' (*UB* 218). Agamben's famous but contested division of *bios* and *zoè*, as the political life of mankind and the life common to all living beings, contracts in the *Enneads* 'to one another in a peremptory gesture that, while irrevocably taking leave of classical politics, points toward an unheard-of politicization of life as such' (*UB* 219).[8] The flight from the world, so important for later Christian philosophers and theologians, becomes the flight into the eternal life, which for Agamben is 'the name of [the] inoperative center of the human' (*KG* 251). The contradiction between Agamben's reading of Plotinus as a thinker legitimising the paradigm of operativity, and as a privileged interlocutor of being as a modality of use, can therefore be transposed on to Agamben's ambivalence towards the Christian tradition. This is evident in *The Kingdom and the Glory*, where Agamben comments on Augustine's supposed inability to think an inoperative God as he answers what Agamben calls 'the blasphemous question par excellence: "What was God doing before He made heaven and earth?"', by mentioning 'the ironic reply, which in truth betrays incredible embarrassment: He was getting hell ready for people who pry too deep' (*KG* 162). But this must be said to be a deliberate misquotation. The Church Father, influenced by Plotinus, mentions this ironic reply only to reject it and then bluntly states: 'I boldly declare: Before God made heaven and earth, he was not making anything.'[9] God dwelled in the rest of his own eternal life, which Augustine sees as the origin and goal for every creature and which Agamben describes, in relation to Plotinus' philosophy, as living contemplation (UB 214–19).

IV

We can now turn to the chapter 'Exile of Alone with One Alone' in *The Use of Bodies*, which to an extent reproduces Agamben's earlier article 'Politica dell'esilio', because here the Plotinian concept of *phygé*, flight, which is also the technical Greek term for exile, reveals itself as the ground of politics (UB 235). Basing his reading of Plotinus on the Catholic theologian Erik Peterson's discussion of the concept of flight in Plotinus' philosophy as both a bond and a separation, Agamben writes that 'Plotinus' "most proper and original contribution consists", then, in having united a juridico-political term that means exclusion and exile to a syntagma that expresses intimacy and being together' (UB 235).[10] What Peterson describes as the bond of flight – in other words flight as an attempt to connect with life as such, that is, to survive, and flight as a separation of the living from the apparatuses that bind the living to a definite life form, such as being pauperised or persecuted – reveals itself in what Agamben calls the 'superpolitical and apolitical' existence of the human organism (UB 236). For Agamben, the truth of Plotinus' philosophy is the truth of the biological order of mankind, namely, that the life of the species does not belong to any *polis* but rather to the apolitical form of the exiled and the stranger. These figures are posited as examples of abjected forms of life, which from Agamben's perspective cannot ground their political being in the actuality of the state as they dwell in the forces of destitution which both produce and undo the apparatuses and paradigms of operativity constituting the biopolitical order of the West.

The theory of exile from the world as a form of life, a theory which Plotinus developed in his school and laid the basis for in the *Enneads*, becomes, in Agamben's hands, the secession of the human species' organic life from a world in which no legitimate power is to be found (CR 40). But this secession can only become a political act if the exiled, such as the gigantic informal proletariat in the slums of the world or the migrants from today's wars, develop their capacity to survive beyond the apparatuses that reproduce the ontological division of what one is from what one does to a process that destitutes the paradigm of operativity itself. Plotinus' indetermination of being and action thereby becomes a sign for a new use of life outside the apparatuses of the economy and the state, which the growing masses of unemployed, migrants and pauperised, in other words the wageless and stateless surplus populations of the world, reveal the necessity of: 'To use – hence the semantic breadth of the term, which indicates both use in the strict sense and habitual praxis – means to oscillate unceasingly between a homeland and an exile: to inhabit' (UB 87). The indetermination of being and action which in *Opus Dei* lays the ground for the paradigm of operativity inverses itself as the redemptive oscillation of homeland and exile in *The Use of Bodies*. This is perhaps not primarily an ambiguity in Agamben's reading of Plotinus. It could in fact be seen as a real contradiction of the civilisation whose theological and philosophical sources Agamben criticises. The question of how the human species could inhabit the world beyond the civilisation that upholds the paradigm of operativity, and at the same time through its decline makes another use of its apparatuses possible, can only be answered by the appropriation of life by those sectors of the human species who are attempting, as Plotinus urged them, to leave this world.

NOTES

1. For an introduction to Plotinus' theory of the three hypostases, see, for example, Kevin Corrigan, *Reading Plotinus: A Practical Introduction to Neoplatonism* (West Lafayette: Purdue University Press, 2005), pp. 23–6.
2. Cf. Heinrich Dörrie, *Hypostasis: Wort- und Bedeutungsgeschichte* (Göttingen: Vandenhoeck & Ruprecht, 1955).
3. Ernst Benz, *Marius Victorinus und die Entwicklung der abendländischen Willensmetaphysik* (Stuttgart: W. Kohlhammer, 1932), p. 414.
4. Plotinus, *The Enneads*, trans. Stephen MacKenna (London: Penguin, 1991), p. 322.
5. Plotinus, *The Enneads*, p. 523.
6. Plotinus, *The Enneads*, p. 167.
7. Plotinus, *The Enneads*, pp. 442–3.
8. A critique of Agamben's distinction between *zoè* and *bios* can be found in Fabián Ludueña Romandini, *La comunidad de los espectros. I. Antropotecnia* (Buenos Aires: Miño y Dávila 2010), pp. 28–40.
9. Augustine, *Confessions*, trans. Henry Chadwick (Oxford: Oxford University Press, 1991), p. 579.
10. Cf. Erik Peterson, 'Herkunft und Bedeutung der Monos pro monon-Formel bei Plotin', *Philologus* 88 (1933): 30–41.

20 Marquis de Sade

CHRISTIAN GRÜNNAGEL

Donatien Alphonse François, Marquis de Sade (1740–1814), appears in European literature and culture like a ghostly figure whose prolific and monstrous works haunt not only nineteenth-century French novels and the surrealist artists (Magritte, Man Ray), but also thinkers, essayists and philosophers of the twentieth (and twenty-first) century.[1] After the Second World War and the devastation that it caused worldwide, some influential thinkers – such as Klossowski, de Beauvoir, Horkheimer and Adorno[2] – reread the *oeuvre* of the divine marquis, long decried as the product of a troubled, ill and wicked mind. Lacan and Adorno and Horkheimer even proposed structural parallels between Sade's *libertinage* and Kant's philosophy.[3] Keeping this history of reception in mind, it is not completely surprising that Agamben includes commentaries on Sade's political and philosophical writing in one of his own central projects, *Homo Sacer*, and comes back occasionally to Sade in other works.[4]

THE DIVINE MARQUIS AND AGAMBEN'S *HOMO SACER* PROJECT

The Sadeian *oeuvre* resurfaces in other Agambenian texts,[5] but the cornerstone of this reception is undoubtedly Agamben's reading of 'Français, encore un effort si vous voulez être républicains' ('Make More of an Effort, Frenchmen, if You Want to Be Republicans'; the translation is borrowed from *HS* 134), a fictionalised pamphlet included in Sade's *Philosophie dans le boudoir*, published in 1795, six years after the outbreak of the French Revolution. This 'Philosophy', situated in a *chambre séparée* of an aristocratic manor, assembles various members of Sade's own class, the French nobility, in dangerous times after 1789, introducing a young female novice (Eugénie) to unrestricted sexuality and the philosophy of radical, atheistic Enlightenment,[6] combined with practical 'exercises' in both fields. The protagonists of Sade's dialogically and theatrically constructed work are Dolmancé, an ageing libertine, the Marquise de Saint-Ange[7] and her brother, the Chevalier de Mirval, all of them willing to 'enlighten' a girl in full puberty – Eugénie.

In a brief digression, Agamben integrates this (rather long) fictional-political pamphlet into his own *Homo Sacer*, giving us the sketch of an interpretation of the Sadeian text:

> The pamphlet *Make More of an Effort, Frenchmen, if You Want to Be Republicans*, read by the libertine Dolmancé in the Marquis de Sade's *Philosophy in the Boudoir*, is the first and perhaps most radical biopolitical manifesto of modernity. (*HS* 134)

One could point out that there is a misunderstanding here right from the beginning, since it is *not* Dolmancé who reads the pamphlet to the assembled audience, but the Chevalier, brother to the Marquise de Saint-Ange,[8] because he has 'a beautiful voice': 'Chevalier, you possess a fine organ, read it to us.'[9] Agamben's slip is, however, not completely trivial, because it does make a difference whether Dolmancé's authoritative voice reads the pamphlet or that of the Chevalier, portrayed as 'libertine and young', that is, inexperienced and still clinging to 'old' notions of pity and love, as Dolmancé does not fail to point out.[10] At least two interpretations of Sade's choice are possible: either the Chevalier is singled out as a reader in order to teach him the 'right' and central principles of radical politics and ethics, or his 'beautiful', but problematic, unauthoritative voice hints at argumentative problems intrinsic to the pamphlet itself.

Agamben passes over this complex framing and concentrates deliberately on the text of the pamphlet. As we have seen, his reading situates this text in his own, vast project on the evolution of European biopolitics, and he conceives the fictional pamphlet as 'the first and perhaps most radical biopolitical manifesto of modernity' (*HS* 134). As becomes clear in *Philosophy in the Boudoir*, the establishment of the Republic, based on the murder of the old sovereign (the monarch by divine right), leads consequently, in Sade's thought, to a permanent state of exception and the suspension of all laws, making even murder 'perfectly' licit. The consequence is a paradoxical political order that turns all citizens into individual sovereigns and *homines sacri* at the same time, a structure that Agamben re-encounters in sadomasochism as a 'political' or 'politicised' form of sexuality:

> [I]n Dolmancé's project, the boudoir fully takes the place of the *cité*, in a dimension in which the public and the private, political existence and bare

life change places. The growing importance of sadomasochism in modernity has its root in this exchange. Sadomasochism is precisely the technique of sexuality by which the bare life of a sexual partner is brought to light. Not only does Sade consciously invoke the analogy with sovereign power [. . .], but we also find here the symmetry between *homo sacer* and sovereign, in the complicity that ties the masochist to the sadist, the victim to the executioner. (*HS* 134–5)

Further on, Agamben gives a brief account of the presence of 'bare life' in Sade's political philosophy and inscribes his own reading of the divine marquis in the problematic tendency to parallel Sadeian fantasy and the horrors of Nazi concentration camps:

Sade is as contemporary as he is because of his incomparable presentation of the absolutely political (that is, 'biopolitical') meaning of sexuality and physiological life itself. Like the concentration camps of our century, the totalitarian character of the organization of life in Silling's castle [. . .] has its root in the fact that what is proposed here for the first time is a normal [!] and collective (and hence political) organization of human life founded solely on bare life. (*HS* 135)[11]

Absent (as an explicitly cited source) from *State of Exception*, *Stasis*, *The Sacrament of Language*, *The Kingdom and the Glory* and *Remnants of Auschwitz*, Sade resurfaces briefly in *Opus Dei* (*OD* 117), and is discussed in a little more detail in the two final volumes of Agamben's project on 'bare life': *The Highest Poverty* and *The Use of Bodies*. In the latter, a long dissertation given by one of the protagonists of Sade's novel *Histoire de Juliette* (1796) is cited – again as a digression, this time inserted in Agamben's discussion of the Aristotelian conception of slavery – to show that Sadeian thought perceives the difference between master and servant as something based on 'physical' evidence that differentiates human beings 'naturally' (cf. *UB* 9). In the chapter 'The Inappropriable', Agamben comes back to Sade's *Philosophy in the Boudoir*, alongside the (fragmentary) Sadeian novel *120 Days of Sodom* (cf. *UB* 92–3), reusing most of the arguments, interpretations and even literal phrases already present in *Homo Sacer* (*HS* 134–5).[12] Again, the similarities that tie Sadeian fiction to the 'atrocities of the *Lager*', established by the Third Reich, are underlined (cf. *UB* 93), but this time Agamben's reflections on Sade form an integral part of the main textual body and are not relegated to a mere digression, as seems to be Agamben's preference when dealing with Sade elsewhere. A third and final hint on the *120 Days of Sodom* eventually parallels the novel's Castle of Silling and Foucault's 'California bathhouses', since both are examples of a 'form-of-life' that is incapable of becoming a 'principle of community', creating instead 'a special community of its own' (*UB* 232).

While *The Use of Bodies* reformulates some of the key notions that Agamben has already discussed in *Homo Sacer*, the function of mentioning Sade is somehow different in *The Highest Poverty*, for here Agamben concentrates to a much greater extent on Sade's novel *120 Days of Sodom*, written secretly in a prison cell, with its plot uniting four powerful libertines of the Ancien Régime in a hidden castle to celebrate 'an orgy that would be without limits and yet perfectly and obsessively regulated' (*HP* 7). Agamben interprets this text as a narrative structure whose 'model' is still to be found in 'the monastic rule', already parodied in Rabelais's satirical novel *Gargantua* (1534), a Renaissance text that Agamben discusses just before turning to Sade and his own 'perversion' of monastic life. Agamben points out the differences between Rabelais's curious (anti-)rule '*Fay ce que vouldras*' ('Do what you will', *HP* 6) and the meticulously regulated orgy that Sade gives his readers in *120 Days of Sodom*, culminating in the regulation of 'even the boys' and the girls' defecation' (*HP* 7) and the severe punishment for all violations of the 'rule'. As Agamben underlines, Sade's pseudo-monastic community follows exactly the patterns that usually regulate a monk's life. Even the *lectio* (lecture) with all community members assembled can be easily found in Sade's novel, where 'the ritual narration that the four *historiennes*, la Duclos, La Champville, la Martaine and la Desgranges, make of their depraved life' supplants the monks' reading of sacred texts (*HP* 8).

It has to be pointed out eventually that the position of these various and scattered readings of Sade's thought in the overall architecture of Agamben's *Homo Sacer* project does not attain the importance accorded to other dialogue partners who are discussed at much greater length by the Italian philosopher, since most interpretations, as with Agamben's reading of *Philosophy in the Boudoir*, are separated from the main textual body as digressions, introduced by Agamben's favourite digression marker, the first letter of the Hebrew alphabet, 'Aleph' (א). This could indicate that Sade is not deemed appropriate to be discussed on the same philosophical level as other thinkers.

OCCASIONAL ENCOUNTERS

Even if the short passages on Sade's political philosophy to be found in the *Homo Sacer* project are the central locus of Agamben's reception of the divine marquis, it might be useful to have a brief look at other places in Agamben's prolific writings where we meet Sade again. In this context, it is necessary to underline that Sade is somewhat like an old travel companion of Agamben's, not always present on the surface of a text and never analysed in detail, but alluded to here and there or briefly mentioned across Agamben's work from its very beginning. One of the Italian philosopher's first publications, 'La 121a giornata di Sodoma e Gomorra', dealt with the 'Theatre of Cruelty' created by another *enfant terrible* of French culture, Antonin Artaud, and he chose as the essay's title an obvious allusion to Sade's own 'theatre of cruel libertinage'.[13] More hints and brief commentaries on Sade are present throughout the article's eleven pages: a sketched-out comparison between Sade and Kleist (who shocked the eighteenth-century public with *Penthesilea*, a sort of 'Theatre of Cruelty' *avant la lettre*), the interpretation of Sade's *120 Days of Sodom* as an 'immense black theatre' to be understood as 'a metaphysics of the body', the vision of Sade as late Enlightenment's 'sinister doppelgänger', and an appreciation of Sade's thought, based on Blanchot.[14] The final reference comes back to the title chosen by Agamben for his essay: according to him, Artaud's theatre surpasses even Sade by becoming the '121st Day of Sodom and Gomorrah'.[15]

As we can observe, Sade stands at the very beginning of Agamben's philosophical (published) thought, not as a central interlocutor, but as an occasional acquaintance to be summoned now and then. So Sade's genealogy is recalled to Agamben's reader in *Profanations* in order to highlight what Agamben calls the '[r]epressed' or 'the eschatological form of parody' (*PR* 47) whose emblematic form he encounters in pornography. While Sade's ancestor, Petrarch's muse Laura (de Sade!), represents 'fiction' as opposed to parody (cf. *PR* 49), the *oeuvre* conceived by Sade embodies 'the most implacable revocation of the *Canzioniere*' (*PR* 47).[16]

Relatively more space is reserved for a structural interpretation of Sadeian 'perversion' in the 'glosses' of *Infancy and History* ('Cavalcanti and Sade [need and desire]', *IH* 25–8). What becomes clear in Sadeian writing is, according to Agamben, that the function of 'perversion', its 'necessity', resides in its capacity to conjoin 'need and desire, convert[ing] the essential frustration of desire into pleasure' (*IH* 27). Agamben sees a structural parallel between 'the Sadeian Eros', its 'perversion' and the rules of courtly love, where 'the same function [is] entrusted to the phantasm and the woman-angel' (*IH* 27). Thus, 'perversion' is poetically exalted as 'the redeeming archangel which rises in flight over the bloody theatre of Eros to raise the Sadeian man to heaven' (*IH* 27). The gloss culminates in a brief discussion of the consequences for 'political practice' by offering a last parallel reading of Sadeian thought and Hegel's *Phenomenology of the Spirit*, namely the well-known dialectics of 'lord' and 'bondsman' (cf. *IH* 27–8).

WHY SADE?

I am not sure that there is any way of 'really' knowing the exact function of the occasional summoning of the Marquis de Sade as a dialogue partner for Agamben. What is evident, however, is the potential for provocation inherent in overtly citing a writer whose work seems still to be 'impossible' to discuss in an academic context, for example with students, due to its 'monstrous' passages on sexuality and violence, on lust and murder. So it remains an open question why Agamben tends to read Sade's *oeuvre* next to Nazi thinkers such as Carl Schmitt, and Christian apostles, philosophers and theologians like St Paul or St Augustine. Perhaps a general tendency in Agamben's reading should be pointed out: he seems (almost always) to prefer an open dialogue with all these thinkers, underlining more the strength of their thought rather than pointing out flaws or at least problematic passages in their works. What Agamben frequently does is a 'synthetic' reading, incorporating 'the best' that his interlocutors from antiquity to postmodernism have to offer, the divine marquis and his troubling contribution to radical Enlightenment being one minor member of this illustrious circle.

NOTES

1. Sade's influence on European literature is usually hidden and undeclared. Surrealism, by contrast, as an avant-garde movement, tends to expose overtly its fascination with the divine marquis; see, for instance, André Breton, *Manifestes du surréalisme* (Paris: Pauvert, 1962), p. 41; Man Ray's reception of Sade and sadomasochistic practices is discussed in Amy Lyford's study *Surrealist Masculinities: Gender Anxiety and the Aesthetics of Post-World War I Reconstruction in France* (Berkeley: University of California Press,. 2007), pp. 149–64; for the case of Belgian surrealism (Magritte, Nougé) and Sade, see Christian Grünnagel, 'Bruxelles, boudoir sadien. Le divin marquis et le surréalisme belge', in Thomas Amos and Christian Grünnagel (eds), *Bruxelles surréaliste. Positionen und Perspektiven amimetischer Literatur* (Tübingen: Narr, 2013), pp. 84–105.
2. See Pierre Klossowski, *Sade mon prochain* (Paris: Seuil, 1947); Simone de Beauvoir, *Faut-il brûler Sade?* (Paris: Gallimard, 1955); Theodor W. Adorno and Max Horkheimer, *Dialectic of Enlightenment* (1944) (London: Verso, 1997), pp. 81–119 ('Juliette or Enlightenment and Morality').
3. See Adorno and Horkheimer, *Dialectic of Enlightenment*, pp. 81–6, especially p. 86: '[t]he work of the Marquis de Sade portrays "understanding without the guidance of another person": that is, the bourgeois individual freed from tutelage'. See also Jacques Lacan, 'Kant avec Sade', in *Écrits*

(Paris: Seuil, 1966), pp. 765–90 (alluded to by Agamben himself in OD 117).
4. As a general introduction to Sade's philosophical thought, Timo Airaksinen, *The Philosophy of the Marquis de Sade* (London: Routledge, 1995) is still recommendable.
5. There is also a passage in *Remnants of Auschwitz* (*RA* 107–9) that discusses sadomasochism, but without a direct hint at Sade's *oeuvre*; other examples of Sade's (explicit) presence in Agamben's work will be addressed at the end of this chapter.
6. On radical Enlightenment and atheism, see Philipp Blom, *A Wicked Company. The Forgotten Radicalism of the European Enlightenment* (New York: Basic Books, 2010).
7. An (ironically) telling name ('Holy Angel'): this young noblewoman has nothing of an angel, nor of sanctity.
8. See Christian Grünnagel, 'Sade mit Agamben gelesen. Das Paradox der Souveränität in der *Philosophie dans le boudoir*', *Diskurs. Politikwissenschaftliche und geschichts-philosophische Interventionen* 2 (2006): 6–7, n. 10.
9. Sade, *Philosophy in the Bedroom*, in *Justine, Philosophy in the Bedroom, and Other Writings*, ed. and trans. Richard Seaver and Austryn Wainhouse (New York: Grove Press, 1990), p. 295.
10. See Sade, *Philosophy in the Bedroom*, p. 341.
11. Even given the list of 'authoritative' voices on this subject (Adorno and Horkheimer in the *Dialectic of Enlightenment*, Agamben himself, et al.), it should be noted that the parallel between Sade and the Nazi extermination camps tends to lose its persuasiveness on at least two (central) points: Sade's Château de Silling is based on lust, the concentration camp as a bureaucratic whole was not (it was a machine to eradicate people for a [certainly perverse] 'higher goal', that is, national socialism, racism, antisemitism, etc.); as for sadomasochism, the link is even less convincing, since the great majority of sadomasochistic encounters or relations seem to be based on free negotiation and tend to acknowledge overtly their own theatrical and fictional framing. As Pat Califia has pointed out, the fact that oppressive societies tend to demonise sadomasochistic sexualities indicates that sadomasochism's theatrical 'nature' seems to pose more of a threat to 'the system', rather than being some kind of 'collaborator and supporter' in its (sexist) political and social ideology; see Pat Califia, *Public Sex: The Culture of Radical Sex* (San Francisco: Cleis Press, 2000), pp. 168–80. This is even more evident in totalitarian regimes that suppress all sexual 'perversions'. One might also doubt whether the Sadeian Castle of Silling, a fictional creation, is adequately understood as a 'normal [. . .] organization of human life' (*HS* 135), since both the place (an impregnable fortress, completely cut off from 'normal' human life) and the *dramatis personae* (four extremely rich libertines) are conceived as staging a state of exception.

12. The misunderstanding that Dolmancé reads the pamphlet (see *UB* 92) is also copied from *Homo Sacer* (*HS* 134).
13. As far as I know, there is no English translation of this early article: Giorgio Agamben, 'La 121a giornata di Sodoma e Gomorra', *Tempo presente* 11.3 (1966): 59–70; the title translates as 'The 121st Day of Sodom and Gomorrah'; all subsequent translations are mine.
14. See Agamben, 'La 121a giornata di Sodoma e Gomorra', pp. 66–7.
15. Agamben, 'La 121a giornata di Sodoma e Gomorra', p. 70.
16. Agamben reused this whole chapter ('Parody') in 2010 as the tenth chapter of the second, expanded edition of *Categorie italiane* (the passage on Sade can be found on p. 127). The existing English translation (*The End of the Poem*) translates the first edition (1996) and does not include this chapter.

21 *Baruch Spinoza*

JEFFREY A. BERNSTEIN

There is currently a paucity of literature relating to Agamben's philosophical treatment of Spinoza (Julie Klein, Dimitris Vardoulakis and Miguel Vatter being notable exceptions).[1] There has certainly been no attempt to show how Agamben's manifold references to the seventeenth-century Dutch-Jewish philosopher form a constellation in his thought. In this chapter, I will attempt to bring those references together under the categorial headings of (1) 'Living in the Middle Voice' and (2) 'The Contemplative Life as Inoperativity'. I choose these categories because Agamben's key concern (as I read him) involves radically rethinking the figures of 'life' and 'living' as well as providing a new *apologia* for contemplation. First, however, a few methodological remarks.

Agamben often comes under scrutiny for making use of philosophical ideas and figures for his own project. This is, of course, not a practice exclusive to Agamben. Moreover, it is arguably essential to the practice of philosophy – at least if one characterises this discipline as an interpretative enterprise. Agamben is, in fact, quite open about his approach: 'Our goal here is not the elaboration of Spinoza['s] [. . .] thought but the elaboration of categories' (*UB* 168). If Agamben seeks to find a way of thinking that is not simply reducible to the current actual politics or to its ontological grounding, it only makes sense that his approach, to that end, would be to read thinkers and texts against the grain. Agamben's treatment of philosophy is, thus, 'strategic' – that is, his readings open up avenues for potentially new ways of thinking. Coincidentally, this is exactly the import he attributes to Spinoza's major posthumous work: 'not only Machiavelli's *The Prince* but also Spinoza's *Ethics* are treatises on strategy: operations *de potentia intellectus, sive de libertate*' (*ME* 73; see also *ME* 115). Spinoza's *Ethics* thus helps readers to explore the possibilities inherent in thinking or (rather) freedom. For Agamben, this holds for the *Hebrew Grammar* and the *Metaphysical Cogitations* as well.

LIVING IN THE MIDDLE VOICE

Discussions of the middle voice (i.e., verbs that are bound by no distinctions between active/passive, agent/patient or subject/object) have come to the fore in contemporary philosophy ever since Heidegger's well-known etymological account of 'phenomena' (in *Being and Time*) – *to phainesthai* – as that which shows itself from itself. Interestingly, Agamben steers clear of that account and instead finds an analogue in Spinoza's thought. Focusing on the *Hebrew Grammar*, Agamben notes that certain Hebrew verbs (active reflexive) and nouns (infinitive) express this important linguistic figure:

> because it frequently happens that one and the same person is both the actor and the person acted upon, it was necessary for the Hebrews to form a new [. . .] infinitive which should express an action recorded simultaneously in the active and passive, that is, which should have the form of active and passive at the same time.[2]

These middle-voice linguistic creations express

> what an object experiences from its own self; or rather, because the accusative is not a different thing from the nominative, like when a *man visits himself, is refreshed*, when *he entreats himself*, when *he guards himself*, etc. Or when *a man causes himself to visit another, applies himself toward walking, toward knowing*, etc.[3]

For Agamben, this linguistic figure – expressing as it does the *immanence* of subject, activity and object to one another – does not simply refer to a logical character of language. Rather, it makes visible an ontological feature of reality:

> [T]he coincidence of agent and patient in one subject has the form not of an inert identity, but of a complex movement of auto-affection in which the subject constitutes – or shows – itself as passive (or active), such that activity and passivity can never be separated, revealing themselves to be distinct in their impossible coincidence in a *self*. The *self* is what is produced as a remainder in the double-movement – active and passive – of auto-affection. (RA 111–12; see also UB 29–30)

As this auto-affection characterises not simply individuals, but the entirety of existence, Agamben holds that '[t]he vertigo of immanence is that it describes the infinite movement of the self-constitution and self-manifestation of Being' (PO 235).

Sans Heidegger, how does Agamben move from taking the middle voice as a linguistic operator to an ontological one? Here again, Spinoza provides valuable resources. Agamben rightly construes Spinoza's statement (E1P15D) 'nothing exists except substances and modes'[4] as a key to Spinoza's radical revision of ontology – albeit in traditional language (*UB* 159–60). To say that substance and modes are immanent to one another – to say that 'God is the immanent, not transitive, cause of all things', as Spinoza does at E1P18[5] (*UB* 165) – is to say that God/nature/substance are not distinct from modes; that God is the immanent cause of modes is to posit a realm of indistinction between God and modes – that is, the very distinction between them becomes 'modaliz[ed]' (*UB* 164). The radical immanence expressed in the middle-voice verbs and nouns is given its proper ontological reference in Spinoza's *Ethics*:

> in order to think the substance/modes relationship, it is necessary to have at our disposal an ontology in the middle voice, in which the agent (God, or substance) in effectuating the modes in reality affects and modifies only itself [. . .] Spinozan pantheism [is] [. . .] a process in which God affects, modifies, and expresses Godself. (*UB* 165)

Spinoza's oft-quoted phrase to the effect that God is *causa sui* must be understood in just this sense (*PO* 120). As discussed above, Agamben has little desire to present Spinoza's thought as a finished product; rather, he seeks to extend it in the direction of his own project:

> it is necessary [. . .] to radicalize the Spinozan thesis according to which there is only being (substance) and its modes or modifications. Substance is not something that precedes the modes and exists independently from them. Being is not other than its modes, substance is only its modifications, its own 'how' (its own *quomodo*).[6]

Whether or not Agamben actually radicalises Spinoza's thesis – as opposed to simply getting it right – is a discussion that exceeds the purviews of the present treatment. At any rate, readers should note that, in Agamben's estimation, Spinoza was not in fact able to fully reconcile the logical and ontological registers (bequeathed to Western philosophy by Aristotle) (*UB* 160–1).

The significance of Spinoza's emphasis on modes and modalisation (for Agamben) can be seen through a number of discussions. The immanence of substance and modes, according to Agamben, registers (in a particular manner) a more general emphasis on corporeality unknown to the political world prior to the seventeenth century: 'This new centrality of the "body" in the sphere of politico-juridical terminology thus coincides with the more general process by which *corpus* is given such a privileged position in the philosophy and science of the Baroque age, from Descartes to Newton, from Leibniz to Spinoza'

(*HS* 125). Similarly, the modal immanence between affect and intellect (explored by Spinoza in Books 3 and 4 of *Ethics)* allows Spinoza (and Agamben) to critique those social and political actions that stem from sadness (such as repentance) in favour of those that stem from joy (*ME* 128; see also *CC* 90 for a qualification of this). Finally, the modalisation of substance and modes leads to the interesting consequence (in Agamben's consideration of Elsa Morante's discomfort over the question of Spinoza's lack of concern for animals) that the modalisation between substance and modes also operates between the ontological and ethical realms:

> th[e] absolute ontological proximity, not only between men and animals but also between all individuals of every species, is confirmed by their divergence on the plane of ethics. Precisely because they are all modes of a single substance, they can gather together or not gather together according to the diversity of their natures. The great right of man over animals does not, therefore, express a hierarchical or ontological supremacy; instead it corresponds to the general diversity of living beings. (*EP* 105)

Differently stated, the 'production of the common' (to use Negri's expression) is in no way *guaranteed* by Spinozan immanence. Rather, it turns on the actualisation of joyous or sad affects: 'The knowledge of good and evil [. . .] finally shows itself, in Spinoza's sober words, nothing but the knowledge of sadness and delight' (*EP* 108). It is for this reason that Spinozan understanding or 'comprehension' is 'far more despairing than every tragedy and far more festive than every comedy' (*EP* 107).

The Spinozan term, for Agamben, that yokes together all of the issues I have discussed thus far is *conatus*: the striving 'with which each thing endeavors to persist in its own being' (E3P7).[7] If substance and modes are immanent to each other, and if modes are themselves immanent to one another, then conative striving is simply the (middle-voice) movement of living. *Conatus* names the immanent movement of modalisation that expresses the quality and intensity of living (together). Does Spinozan *conatus* carry a prescriptive dimension with it? According to Agamben's above account, it could not do so, because good and evil simply amount to joy and sadness. However, in *The Use of Bodies*, Agamben comes close to reversing his earlier view: 'When Spinoza defines essence as *conatus*, as "the force by which it endeavors to persist in its own being" [. . .] he thinks something like a demand [*esigenza*]' (*UB* 171). Agamben proposes to translate *conatus* by 'demand' 'on the condition of not forgetting the medial nature of the process that is here in question: the being that desires and demands, in demanding, modifies, desires and constitutes itself. "To preserve in its being" means this and nothing else' (*UB* 171). Thus, if *conatus* cannot contain a 'moralising' prescription, it can indeed contain an *ethical* one (in the Greek sense of *ethos* as character or disposition). Humanity needs to be (or become) disposed towards that which allows its being to flourish rather than decline. The more people who are involved in this disposition, the more will substance persevere in joy: '*In* conatus, *desire and Being thus coincide without residue*' (*PO* 236).

THE CONTEMPLATIVE LIFE AS INOPERATIVITY

If Agamben is attempting to find a new use for Spinoza – if he is trying to effect a difference in relation to the thought of Spinoza as it might possibly inform human life – what is it about life as presently constituted from which Spinoza's thought offers us a possible egress? A full treatment of biopolitics in Agamben's thought would take us far afield from the present chapter (it might, in fact, be coextensive with the entire *Homo Sacer* series). However, for the present purposes, this much can be said: from near its inception, Western thought – and the institutions that emerged from it – has been hamstrung around the distinction between essence and existence (to use the terminology of *The Use of Bodies*). It is this distinction that informs the aforementioned distinctions against which Agamben's employment of the middle voice pushes. The thought of Spinoza (as with many other thinkers) furnishes Agamben with the conceptual tools to begin to articulate what a different way of living might look like. It would surely be one where human life was not sutured to the categories of public/private, theory/practice, active/passive, lawful/unlawful, authentic/inauthentic and work/rest (to name only a few). For Agamben, the thinkers worthy of consideration all give articulation to a moment of indistinction where these categories are (as it were) put out of play. This is what Agamben means by the category of 'inoperativity'. Agamben is not interested in destroying what exists; rather, he seeks to highlight the fact that actual, conventional existence is (or can become) un-employed, put out of 'work'. By recasting all of life in terms of *conatus* – which *conatus* is simultaneously the entirety of life, each individual life, and the immanent modalisation of the two – Agamben's project concerns the rearticulation of what it means to be a human animal amid the entirety of nature.

If *conatus* is the immanent and modalised movement of desire and being, in their simultaneity and coincidence, what human disposition corresponds to this? For Agamben, the answer (paradoxically, the most traditional of answers) is the contemplative life. In contemplation of one's desire, one's need, one's acts and one's *potential* acts, contemplation is the (conative) disposition that illuminates *conatus*. As Agamben notes,

> [i]n Spinoza, the idea of beatitude coincides with the experience of the self as an immanent cause, which he calls *acquiescentia in se ipso*, 'being at rest in oneself', and defines precisely as [. . .] 'rejoicing accompanied by the idea of the self as a cause'. [. . .] [T]he expression *acquienscentia in se ipso* is an invention of Spinoza's, which is not registered in any Latin lexicon. Spinoza must have had in mind a concept that, as an expression of an immanent cause, corresponded to the Hebrew reflexive verb [. . .] formed to express the apex of the movement of an immanent cause. (*PO* 237–8)

The experience of coming to rest in the awareness of oneself as an immanent cause is the apex of the human conative activity. Elsewhere, Agamben notes that this 'self-acquiescence' or 'self-contentment' (E4P52D),[8] this contemplation of one's own power (the telos of which coincides completely with the contemplative activity), constitutes a hallmark of inoperativity:

> Spinoza describes as 'contemplation of [. . .] power' what one might describe as an inoperativity within the operation itself, that is, a sui generis 'praxis' that consists in rendering all specific powers of acting or doing inoperative. The life which contemplates its (own) power to act, renders itself inoperative in all its operations, and lives only (its) livability [. . .] In this inoperativity, the life that we live is only the life through which we live; only our power of acting and living, our act-*ability* and our live-*ability*. (*KG* 250–1)

Contemplation thus amounts to the immanent operation of gaining the distance on one's life to be able to envision it otherwise; in so doing, the actual configuration of one's life is rendered inoperative (i.e., not inevitable).

It is the ability to access the potential, the non-inevitable, that Agamben seeks to offer as a countermeasure to a life based on actually existing circumstances – that is, 'a new and coherent ontology of potentiality (beyond the steps that have been made in this direction by Spinoza, Schelling, Nietzsche, and Heidegger) [which will replace] the ontology founded on the primacy of actuality and its relation to potentiality' (*HS* 44). Only after this new ontology is created will humanity be able to render inoperative political (i.e., sovereign), legal (i.e., judgemental) and social (i.e., conventional and occupational) forms of violence. As Agamben claims:

> Contemplation and inoperativity are in this sense the metaphysical operators of anthropogenesis, which, in liberating living human beings from every biological and social destiny and every predetermined task, render them available for that peculiar absence of work that we are accustomed to calling 'politics' and 'art'. Politics and art are not tasks nor simply 'works';

rather, they name the dimension in which works – linguistic and bodily, material and immaterial, biological and social – are deactivated and contemplated as such in order to liberate the inoperativity that has remained imprisoned in them. And in this consists the greatest good that, according to the philosopher, the human being can hope for: 'a joy born from this, that human beings contemplate themselves and their own potential for acting'. (*UB* 278)[9]

Politics and art, therefore, are immanently related to contemplation and inoperativity. By contemplating politics and art in a new manner – by rendering them inoperative through thinking the potentiality in them – they are freed (in turn) to be contemplative and inoperative.

One surely understands that the inoperativising of language in poetry (and in art more generally) to free language for a new manner of presentation is one of the crucial features of poetry. How do things stand with respect to politics? If politics is to be thought along the lines of an ontology of potentiality rather than one of actuality, Agamben's near-complete silence about Spinoza's *Theological-Political Treatise* and *Political Treatise* becomes intelligible. The question remains whether politics can indeed be re-grounded in this manner. But readers should also bear in mind that Agamben *promises* nothing of the sort. As immanent to the very activity upon which it reflects, the search for an ontology of potentiality (in the manner of Spinoza) can only ever be on the way.

NOTES

1. Cf. Julie R. Klein, 'Nature's Metabolism: On Eating in Derrida, Agamben, and Spinoza', *Research in Phenomenology* 33 (2003): 186–217; Dimitris Vardoulakis, 'The Ends of Stasis: Spinoza as a Reader of Agamben', *Culture, Theory and Critique* 51.2 (2010): 145–56; Miguel Vatter, 'Eternal Life and Biopower', *The New Centennial Review* 10.3 (2011): 217–50.
2. Benedict de Spinoza, *Hebrew Grammar*, in *Complete Works*, trans. Samuel Shirley, ed. Michael L. Morgan (Indianapolis: Hackett, 2002), p. 629.
3. Spinoza, *Hebrew Grammar*, p. 645.
4. Benedict de Spinoza, *Ethics*, in *Complete Works*, p. 224.
5. Spinoza, *Ethics*, p. 229.
6. Giorgio Agamben, 'What is a Destituent Power?', trans. Stephanie Wakefield, *Environment and Planning D: Society and Space* 32 (2014): 73; see also *UB* 164.
7. Spinoza, *Ethics*, p. 283.
8. Spinoza, *Ethics*, p. 347.
9. The last quotation is from Spinoza, *Ethics*, p. 347 (E3P53).

22 Aby Warburg

ADI EFAL-LAUTENSCHLÄGER

IMAGISM AND ART HISTORY

One preliminary point which must be stated regarding Agamben's relation to the art historian Abraham ('Aby') Moritz Warburg (1866–1929) is that this line of questioning is *not* reducible to problems regarding imagery or 'visual' art. Agamben says explicitly that 'only the myopia of a psychologizing history of Art could have defined [Warburg's art history] as a "science of the image"' (*ME* 53). Although most scholarship on Warburg has indeed viewed the latter's work as laying the foundations for image and visual studies, in Agamben's account Warburg ushers the humanities towards another kind of inquiry, one having more to do with the concept of *time* than with any sort of imagery or visual phenomena. In this, Agamben's reading of Warburg differs substantially from those of major art historians influenced by Warburg, such as Horst Bredekamp (*Bildakt*)[1] or Georges Didi-Huberman (*images malgré tout*).[2] In fact, Agamben's reading of Warburg's art historical inquiries can be elaborated as a fruitful critique of the recent 'imagist' turn in the history of art, viewing visual artworks as being primary and essentially 'images'. The Warburgian project was 'conducted through the medium of images' and therefore 'it was believed that the image was also its object. Warburg instead transformed the image into a decisively historical and dynamic element' (*ME* 53). Therefore, for Agamben, Warburg's science is first of all a science of history and of time, and what is superficially recognised in his art history as an image is in fact a reservoir of intensified and contracted historical material.

THE *PATHOSFORMELN* BETWEEN WARBURG AND AGAMBEN

An important term which stands at the binding line between Warburg and Agamben is Warburg's so-called 'pathos formula', for which Agamben uses in most if not at all instances the German, *Pathosformel*.[3] The term pathos formula, constructed from its two parts, summarises well what interests Agamben in Warburg's project. On the one hand, one is reminded by this term that at the *archē* of any inquiry lies the substance of *pathos*. Pathos here should not be understood simply as psychological (or physical) suffering, but rather as a substantial character of life as such. Pathos is a fundamentally passive gesture of being affected, burdened, laid upon, subjugated of the living, that is to say, un-dead, being.[4] Any *Pathosformel*, according to Warburg, is an encrustation of some movement, some power affecting, moving, pressing and pushing some other corporeal reality. This is why the 'pictures' carrying a *Pathosformel* will always have something to do with movement: hair blowing in the wind, garments in motion, a gesture of walking. We will immediately see that the *Pathosformel* combines in Agamben's thought with his theory of signatures, and this, I think, goes back in fact to the concept of pathos. *Pathos*, or passivity, is a continual theme in Agamben's writings.[5] Pathos is the condition of suffering, carrying, receiving and absorbing, a surrender to potentiality while paying the price of losing actuality on the way and living at the mercy of the past. Agamben understands the human, and the human sciences studying it, as having to do with the possibility of being gestured, that is to say, the ability to receive and to *endure*.[6] And the *Pathosformel*, as conceived by Warburg, represents exactly that state of affairs.

The other part of the phrase 'pathos formula' is of course the *formula* itself. A formula is not identical with a Form, but is much more like a figure,[7] or indeed, as we shall see just below, a signature.[8] A formula is also like a recipe for cooking, medicine or magic. It is a 'gathering' or a 'sucking' of matter within the borders of an outline, a silhouette continuing and containing the movement, the *dynamis* that produced it in the first place. The formula is literally a cloth impregnated with potentiality (*PO* 177–84). In other, simpler words, the pathos formula is in fact a body (being exactly that lump of matter gathered and contoured by some borderline). In this sense, a pathos formula, which can be epitomised in a work of art but also in texts, rituals, or emphatically any human production, takes an energetic state of work, an *energeia*, and condenses and intensifies it into a state of *potentiality*. It is a turning over of a work into its own latency, its own infancy (*IH* 89–106), gathering and condensing together power and intensity. In *Nymphs* (2007) Agamben concentrates on one of Warburg's most important texts regarding a fresco by Domenico Ghirlandaio in the Tornabuoni Chapel in Santa Maria Novella in Florence.[9] Warburg speaks in this case of a figure of a servant girl, in Warburg's words a 'nymph', who 'appeared to be the embodiment of movement'.[10] Indeed, as Gombrich notes, the Nymph appeared to the young Warburg as the embodiment of passion.[11] The Nymph, says Agamben, 'is the image of the image, the cipher of the *Pathosformeln* which is passed down from generation to generation and to which generations entrust the possibility of finding or losing themselves, of thinking or of not thinking' (*NI* 57).

THE *ATLAS MNEMOSYNE* AS AN ALBUM OF SIGNATURES

The 'signature' of the Nymph also appears as the subject of Plate 46 of the *Atlas Mnemosyne*, which was Warburg's most monumental art historical apparatus (c. 1923–29; see *PO* 95–6). Aided by the staff of the Kulturwissenschaftliche Bibliothek Warburg in Hamburg, directed by Fritz Saxl, Warburg collected and mounted a vast collection of pictures, drawn from the history of art as well as from contemporary newspapers and advertisements.[12] These printed pictures, which were processed, developed and printed in the photographic laboratory of the Warburg Haus and reproduced in the 79 plates of the atlas,

> should not be seen [. . .] as photographic reproductions of works or objects to which we should ultimately be referring. On the contrary, they have value in themselves, since they themselves are *ymagines* [. . .], in which the signature of the objects they appear to reproduce has been affixed. In other words, the *Pathosformeln* are not found in works of art or in the mind of the artist or of the historian: they coincide with the images precisely recorded in the atlas. [. . .] *Mnemosyne* is the atlas of signatures that the artist – or the scholar – must learn to know and handle if he or she wishes to understand and perform the risky operation that is at issue in the tradition of the historical memory of the West. (*ST* 56–7)

Therefore, Warburg's *Mnemosyne* is conceived by Agamben as a reservoir of signatures that in themselves are to be handled as an essential instrument enabling access to the history of civilisation.

Warburg is one of the authors who allow Agamben to turn to the vocabulary and structure of liturgy and magic, which are found throughout his corpus (most notably in *Opus Dei*). Warburg considered art as originating in primitive sympathetic magic, taming the powers of nature and invigorating human capacities. This is most evident in Warburg's well-known '*Schlangenritual*' lecture, given at the Binswanger Senatorium in 1923, which refers to an experience Warburg had in 1896, when he was travelling in America. In the ritual that Warburg describes, a tribal dance was performed with a snake, symbolising the overcoming of the raw and threatening world of nature.[13] For Warburg, all art behaves as this kind of ritual, where the dynamics of nature are tamed and captured by the artistic dispositive (see *PO* 90–2). Agamben insists that Warburg's scientific considerations function literally (and not metaphorically) as magical instruments, making their possessor able to master a certain natural energetic force:

> Warburg, with para-scientific terminology that is, in truth, closer to that of magic than of science, can refer to the *Pathosformeln* as 'disconnected dynamograms' (*abgeschnürte Dynamogramme*) that reaquire their efficacy every time they encounter the artist (or the scholar). [. . .] The 'engrams' and the *Bilder* Warburg seeks to grasp are neither signs nor symbols but signatures; and the 'nameless science' he was unable to found is something like an overcoming, an *Aufhebung* of magic by means of its own instruments, an archaeology of signatures. (*ST* 57)

But beside all these specific themes, Warburg also takes up a methodological place in Agamben's work.[14] This regards the search for a science which exists but which nevertheless has 'no name', a placeless science in search of the shapes and means of its own territories (*PO* 89–103). Already in the 1975 text 'Aby Warburg and the Nameless Science', written after a research period spent at the Warburg Institute in London, Agamben presents Warburg's art history as carrying an epistemological potential that exceeds the borders of the history of art: 'What is unique and significant about Warburg's method as a scholar is not so much that he adopts a new way of writing art history as that he always directs his research towards overcoming the borders of art history' (*PO* 90). Turning to an epistemology which is nameless and borderless, posited on the borderline *between* established and well-defined domains of knowledge, brings to mind Agamben's central concepts of *bare life* and *homo sacer*. Though Agamben himself does not say so explicitly, a curious connection can be delineated between Agamben's politico-theological inquiries regarding the *homo sacer*, and a nameless method, a praxis whose function is to disturb, question, contaminate and be expulsed, but which subsumes localised domains of inquiry of thought under its magic-like spell.

WARBURG, FOUCAULT AND THE NAMELESS SCIENCE

Notably again in *The Signature of All Things*, Agamben makes an original connection between Foucault's archaeology and Warburg's 'nameless science', defining his own position between the two thinkers. Indeed Foucault and Warburg also have in their background the influence of Friedrich Nietzsche, and Nietzsche's reference to tradition, to philosophy and to pre-history is a possible link between Agamben, Warburg and Foucault.[15] Foucault's and Warburg's endeavours suggest to Agamben an approach that Agamben himself names *philosophical archaeology*: 'Provisionally, we may call "archaeology" that practice which in any historical investigation has to do not with origins but with the moment of a phenomenon arising and must therefore engage anew the sources and tradition' (*ST* 89). Agamben is again correct on this point: in his investigations Warburg was interested in showing what makes an image appear in the first place, not as its origin but as its soil, as Warburg himself says in the fragment on the Nymph mentioned above: 'turning the philological gaze to the ground' (*den philologischen Blick auf den Boden zu richten*).[16] Agamben indeed would like the human sciences to be interested in 'the very idea of an ontological anchoring' (*ST* 111), and for that end Warburg's nameless science serves as a prototype.

Therefore, we have both the formula and the nameless science functioning as a median, an 'open', a neuter, a domain between (similar) domains, enduring between consciousness and the unconscious: 'The gesture is the exhibition of *mediality*: it is the process of making a means visible as such' (*ME* 57). The gesture, or the signature, is what can replace the philosophical 'idea'. The *Mnemosyne Atlas*, according to Agamben's interpretation, is an apparatus aimed at making images move, loaded with gestural tenor:

> It is as if a silent invocation calling for the liberation of the image into gesture arose from the entire history of Art. This is what in ancient Greece was expressed by the legends in which statues break the ties holding them and begin to move. But that is also the intention that philosophy entrusts to the idea, which is not at all an immobile archetype as common interpretations would have it, but rather a constellation in which phenomena arrange themselves in a gesture. (*ME* 56)

Warburg's nameless science is one based not merely on logic *tout court*, but on ana-logy (*ST* 19–20), on a *cohesion of logics* (in the plural). It is the science of the paradigm, a logic moving 'from singularity to singularity': 'In the paradigm, there is no original or arche; every phenomenon is the origin, every image archaic' (*ST* 31). For example, the paradigm of the Nymph mentioned above is an *Urphänomen* (*ST* 29), neither archaic nor contemporary, archaic but totally present.

MEDIALITY AND ITS CARRIERS: *PATHOSFORMELN*, IMAGES, GESTURES, SIGNATURES

In concluding this route between Warburg and Agamben, let us return to (what is left of) the image: an image, in Agamben's critique, is not a representation but rather a meeting point of spirits; it is a movement in which consciousness is entangled, wrapped, as in a swirl: 'The image is called image because the forces of the spirits are conjoined here: the operation of the imagination [*cogitacio*] is included in the thing that contains the virtue of the planet' (*ST* 56). Consciousness does not therefore direct the swirl of signatures but rather betrays, in a moment of negligence, the ontological anchoring: 'Morelli's principle according to which the personality of the author must be found where the effort is less intense, recalls that of modern psychology, according to which it is our small unconscious gestures that betray the secret of our character' (*ST* 69). Gestures, as well as signatures, are conceptual figures in Agamben's vocabulary of the Warburgian *Pathosformeln*: 'What characterizes gesture is that in it nothing is being produced or acted, but rather something is being endured and supported. The gesture, in other words, opens the sphere of *ethos* as the more proper sphere of that which is human' (*ME* 56–7). Both *Pathosformeln* and gestures are proper to that which is human. They are incorporations of the original subjugated, arrested and affected state of human life. In the theory of signatures, the function of *transference* is again accentuated: 'A signature does not merely express a semiotic relation between a *signans* and a *signatum*; rather, it is what [. . .] displaces and moves it into another domain, thus positioning it in a new network of pragmatic and hermeneutic relations' (*ST* 40).

Pathosformeln, signatures, gestures, images: all these are understood by Agamben as carriers of *mediality*. In other words, Warburg is a philosopher neither of the subject nor of images, but of mediality, a philosopher of the *metaxu*, a philosopher of transference which is neither 'social' nor 'individual', as Agamben says explicitly:

> For Warburg, the significance of images [. . .] lay in the fact that, being strictly speaking neither conscious nor unconscious, they constituted the ideal terrain for a unitary approach to culture, one capable of overcoming the opposition between history, as the study of 'conscious expressions', and anthropology, as the study of 'unconscious conditions'. (*PO* 99)

In the end, the meaning that one draws from Agamben's Warburgian critique of the science of history leads to the viewing of the humanities as *mnemotechnique*. Agamben explicitly refers to the *Mnemosyne* as a 'mnemotechnical initiatory atlas of Western culture' (*PO* 96). This aspect of Agamben's work was obviously energised by his correspondence with the great iconologist Frances Yates, who brought him to the Warburg Institute in London, where she worked.[17] Remarkably, it was Ernst Gombrich who summarised this most poignantly:

> The Mneme carries with it the relics of a mental state in which the ego was not yet master, a state of immediate reflex movements resulting in the abandonment to maenadic frenzy and barbarous struggles – a state, also, in which the difference between the self and the outer world was not yet perceived and in which the magic attitude to image and symbol held undisputed sway.[18]

NOTES

1. Horst Bredekamp, *Theorie des Bildakts* (Frankfurt a.M.: Suhrkamp, 2010).
2. Georges Didi-Huberman, *Images malgré tout* (Paris: Seuil, 2003).
3. On the pathos formula, see Colleen Becker, 'Aby Warburg's *Pathosformel* as methodological paradigm', *Journal of Art Historiography* 9 (December 2013), https://arthistoriography.files.wordpress.com/2013/12/becker.pdf (accessed 15 September 2016). See also my early 'Warburg's "Pathos Formula" in Psychoanalytic and Benjaminian Context', *Assaph: Studies in the History of Art* 5 (2001), shttp://www5.tau.ac.il/arts/departments/images/stories/journals/arthistory/Assaph5/13adiefal.pdf (accessed 15 September 2016).
4. For an elaboration on the pathetic character of Warburg's *Pathosformeln*, see Georges Didi-Huberman, *L'image survivante: Histoire de l'art et temps des fantomes selon Aby Warburg* (Paris: Minuit, 2002), pp. 115–270.
5. On this, see Thomas C. Wall, *Radical Passivity: Levinas, Blanchot and Agamben* (New York: SUNY Press, 1999), pp. 115–62.
6. This understanding puts Agamben's philosophy in line with Henri Bergson's philosophy of duration, a correspondence that has not been noted up until now and that requires further research.
7. On figuration in the methodology of the humanities, see my *Figural Philology: Panofsky and the Science of Things* (London: Bloomsbury Academic, 2016).
8. For a telling comparison between Warburg and the art historian Heinrich Wölfflin regarding the subject of form, see Philipp Ekardt, 'Maß und Umriss. Bilder als Regulative bei Winckelmann und Warburg', in Ingeborg Reichle and Steffen Siegel (eds), *Maßlose Bilder* (Munich: Fink, 2009), pp. 85–98.

9. See Aby Warburg, 'Nimfa Fiorentina: Fragmente zum Nymphenprojekt', in *Werke in einem Band*, ed. Martin Treml, Sigrid Weigel and Perdita Ladwig (Frankfurt a.M.: Suhrkamp, 2010), pp. 198–210.
10. '*Ja sie schien die verkörperte Bewegung*', qtd. and translated in Ernst Gombrich, *Aby Warburg: An Intellectual Biography* (Oxford: Phaidon, 1986), p. 108. Warburg's Nympha is discussed extensively in Barbara Baert, *Nymph: Motif, Phantom, Affect: A Contribution to the Study of Aby Warburg* (Leuven: Peeters, 2014), especially pp. 21–5. This book refers to Agamben several times, but not to *Nymphs*.
11. Gombrich, *Aby Warburg*, p. 109.
12. On the Atlas, see the book by Roland Recht, *L'atlas Mnémosyne* (Paris: L'Ecarquillé, 2012).
13. Aby Warburg, *Schlangenritual: Ein Reisebericht* (Berlin: Wagenbach, 2011). For an English version, see Aby Warburg, *Images from the Region of the Pueblo Indians of North America*, trans. M. P. Steinberg (Ithaca, NY: Cornell University Press, 1997).
14. Well summarised by Alex Murray, 'Aby Warburg', in Alex Murray and Jessica Whyte (eds), *The Agamben Dictionary* (Edinburgh: Edinburgh University Press, 2011), pp. 199–200.
15. See Robert Sinnerbrink, 'Friedrich Nietzsche', in Murray and Whyte, *The Agamben Dictionary*, p. 137.
16. Qtd. in Gombrich, *Aby Warburg*, p. 113.
17. See Frances Yates, *The Art of Memory* (1966) (London: Pimlico, 2014).
18. Gombrich, *Aby Warburg*, p. 254.

PART III
Submerged Dialogues

23 Theodor W. Adorno
COLBY DICKINSON

I

In his somewhat controversial book *Remnants of Auschwitz*, Agamben makes brief reference to Theodor Adorno's apparently contradictory remarks on perceptions of death post-Auschwitz, positions that Adorno had taken concerning Nazi genocidal actions that had seemed also to reflect something horribly errant in the history of thought itself. There was within such murderous acts, he had claimed, a particular degradation of death itself, a perpetration of our humanity bound in some way to affect our perception of reason itself. The contradictions regarding Auschwitz that Agamben senses to be latent within Adorno's remarks involve the intuition 'on the one hand, of having realized the unconditional triumph of death against life; on the other, of having degraded and debased death. Neither of these charges – perhaps like every charge, which is always a genuinely legal gesture – succeed in exhausting Auschwitz's offense, in defining its case in point' (*RA* 81). And this is the stance that Agamben wishes to hammer home quite emphatically vis-à-vis Adorno's limitations, ones that, I would only add, seem to linger within Agamben's own formulations in ways that he has still not come to reckon with entirely: 'This oscillation', he affirms, 'betrays reason's incapacity to identify the specific crime of Auschwitz with certainty' (*RA* 81).

There is a trespass of reason, of the bounds of intelligibility, that Auschwitz represents, and it is one that cannot be understood, in the strict sense of the word, for Auschwitz represents the unrepresentable, or what will come to be in Agamben's thought elsewhere, the 'unthought'. For Agamben, the only way to locate and understand this oscillation is through a figure who stands on the threshold between the two positions and is rendered unthought by the established social order:

the *Muselmann* of the camps. His recourse to a sketch of this figure, much like the figure of the *homo sacer*, establishes his attempt to go beyond the dichotomous tension of the representable/unrepresentable, or the thought/unthought, and towards a space where the dichotomy itself might be undone. This move will in fact become the cornerstone elsewhere of his quest for a 'pure potentiality' beyond the split between actuality and potentiality (cf. the essays collected in *Potentialities*).

What Agamben does not draw our attention to in this context is the fact that such an oscillation was present not only in Adorno's views on death, but on the im/possibility of poetry after the horrors of Auschwitz. To be precise, though Adorno had initially speculated that the making of poetry after Auschwitz was impossible, he later relented and spoke out for the creation of meaning in poetic terms, despite what appeared to be poetry's untimely end.[1] In other words, this oscillation or apparent contradiction seems to be part and parcel of Adorno's thought, and, as I will claim in what follows, it plays much the same role in Agamben's work.

What we see unfold in this single commentary by Agamben on Adorno's thought would seem to capture the essential elements of Agamben's interactions with Adorno: there is often a critique of the latter's work, at times perhaps precipitated by their rivalry as major interpreters of Walter Benjamin's *oeuvre*, as well as a stress placed emphatically upon the vital differences between them. In what follows, however, I want to take inventory of these interactions, as Agamben stages them, in order to show how these alleged differences, which are based almost entirely on the work of the early Adorno, might be exaggerated to some extent, a point that becomes clearer when we stop to contemplate developments in the later Adorno's writings.

II

In his *Infancy and History*, written twenty years before *Remnants of Auschwitz*, Agamben cites an epistolary exchange between Adorno and Benjamin from late 1938 wherein Adorno offers a critique of Benjamin's thought in such a way as to provide, for Agamben, an 'unassailable guarantee of Marxist orthodoxy' in Adorno's work (*IH* 128). The appearance of this citation, and its consequent connection to his later infrequent comments on Adorno, is particularly illuminating in that it both confirms Agamben's reluctance to peer more deeply into Adorno's philosophy than the latter's frequent, but early, engagements with Benjamin – the major source for much of Agamben's reflections – while also perhaps revealing a potential blind spot in Agamben's analysis that actually might reveal a unique mechanism of blindness operative within his work.

The juxtaposition of their epistolary exchange towards the end of Agamben's book serves mainly to highlight Adorno's commitment at the time to a 'total social process' that would see the separation between structure and superstructure, as between form and content or nature and culture, resolved in the Hegelian-Marxist unity ('mediation') of material praxis. Agamben's commentary on this commitment is therefore fitting: 'There is but a short step from this to declaring that every moment in history is merely a means to an end' (*IH* 130). In sharp contrast to this rebuke of Adorno's Marxist grasping for a dialectic totality, Benjamin's search for a dialectic outside of linear time becomes, for Agamben, a quest to link a sort of 'negative dialectic' with a messianic time – also inspired by Benjamin's 'weak messianic force' moving through history – which typifies 'dialectics at a standstill' (*IH* 137).[2] There is no need at this point to indicate how indebted Agamben's work is to the development of such a messianic concept, and his ability to link it to other concepts within his philosophical toolkit, but there is still a need, I would argue, to discover just how indebted Agamben may also be to a blindness within his point of view on Adorno's later thought – a voluminous corpus with which Agamben rarely engages.

To assume that Adorno's embrace of the 'total social process' remains unaffected by the development of a negative dialectics in his work would seem to overlook a major, promising point of connection between their respective outlooks. And yet, despite this promise, Agamben deftly avoids any such engagement. If all learning after Auschwitz should be a form of 'critical self-reflection' according to Adorno, then it is with this mandate squarely in mind that I turn to investigate what exactly is at stake in this particular blindness to Adorno's subsequent work for Agamben.[3]

III

Agamben only invokes Adorno's later philosophy briefly in his writings, most significantly as a point of contrast with Pauline thought in *The Time that Remains*, published originally in 2000. What we see in this case, however, is not only the same critique of Adorno's penchant for the 'total social process' as had been present in *Infancy and History*, but also a declaration that such a position inevitably leads to 'an absolutely non-messianic form of thought', the view Agamben clearly opposes in his reformulation of a Pauline-Benjaminian messianic suspension of dialectics. In this particular text, Agamben cites Jacob

Taubes's critique of Adorno's alleged 'aestheticization of the messianic in the form of the *as if*', which, Taubes had argued, prevented Adorno from contemplating any concrete state of actual redemption. In *Minima Moralia*, Adorno had claimed that '[t]he only philosophy which can be responsibly practiced in face of despair is the attempt to contemplate all things as they would present themselves from the standpoint of redemption'.[4] To consider an altered form of philosophy simply because it is viewed from a different perspective is what had prompted Taubes to consider it an *as if* philosophy and not as an endeavour that sought the *as suchness* of reality (TR 35).[5]

Agamben, however, referring to Adorno's harsh words concerning the definition of aesthetics in general as 'the spell over spells' in his *Aesthetic Theory*, wonders aloud if this *as if* nature of philosophy is truly the case for Adorno, as Taubes had claimed, or whether something else might be at work. The stakes in detecting a conditional, perhaps even *spectral*, nature of representation within Adorno's philosophy are high, for, if true, it would be essentially the same charge levied against Adorno as Agamben would bring again and again against Jacques Derrida, whose deconstructionist commitment to the *as if* was enough to possibly deter him away from the concrete political and social change that Agamben is after.

This looming charge against Adorno should give us pause to consider what exactly is at stake in Agamben's critique, as the feud against Derrida, which I am here claiming runs parallel to his remarks concerning Adorno, was a complex but ultimately highly revealing affair. As I have argued elsewhere, the debate between Agamben and Derrida was perhaps the most significant moment of both overlap in terms of their respective philosophical projects and yet blindness to the true aims of both thinkers. It was very much the case, in my opinion, that both thinkers were unable to escape the spectral nature of the messianic critique – its perpetual aloofness from direct political praxis – though they both sought to do so in multiple ways.[6] In this sense, perhaps Agamben's critique of Adorno, much as with Derrida, conceals a good deal of similarity between their thought that Agamben wants to overcome, but perhaps may not be able to in the end.

Agamben's proposal to deal with Taubes's critique of Adorno – that the latter basically suspends any concrete material reality in his speculative thought – is to read Adorno's line from *Minima Moralia* alongside another from his *Negative Dialectics*: 'philosophy lives on because the moment to realize it was missed'.[7] His commentary on this single line from Adorno's later work is a reductive one in that Adorno's entire philosophy can be read through it. As Agamben puts it,

> The fact of having missed the moment of its realization is what obliges philosophy to indefinitely contemplate the appearance of redemption. Aesthetic beauty is the chastisement, so to speak, of philosophy's having missed its moment. Only in this vein may we truly speak of an *als ob* [*as if*] in Adorno. This is why aesthetic beauty cannot be anything more than the spell over spells. There is no satisfaction in it, for the *as if* is the condemnation that the philosopher has already inflicted on himself. (*TR* 37)

Beyond this charge that the *as if* seems to be the punishment that Adorno is forced to bear because he had believed all of philosophy as having had to bear it post-Auschwitz, Agamben relegates Adorno's entire philosophical project to the dustbin of history in that he had succumbed, as had many others (Derrida included), to engaging in the consideration of a 'point of view' rather than, and here following Pauline thought, 'actualising' power in weakness. Hence Adorno bears the brunt of one of Agamben's harshest critiques of any philosopher, with the possible exception, as already noted, of Derrida:

> The whole of Adorno's philosophy is written according to impotential meaning that the *as if* can only be taken as a warning signal at the heart of this intimate modality of his thought. Philosophy had been realizing itself, but the moment of its realization was missed. This omission is at one and the same time absolutely contingent and absolutely irreparable, thus impotential. Redemption is, consequently, only a 'point of view'. Adorno could never even conceive of restoring possibility to the fallen, unlike Paul, for whom 'power [*potenza*] is actualized in weakness' (2 Cor. 12:9). Despite appearances, negative dialectics is an absolutely non-messianic form of thought, closer to the emotional tonality of Jean Améry than that of Benjamin. (*TR* 38)

As in *Infancy and History*, here it is the thought of Benjamin that allows us to see that which Adorno missed, that philosophy is not to be contemplated from the perspective of redemption – a notion that was connected, in Agamben's eyes, to Adorno's orthodox Marxist view on the dialectical outcomes of the 'total social process'[8] – but rather that it can only be thought from the standpoint of what cannot be saved. The loss of our identities, through a messianic suspension or deactivation of them, is the only location from which to contemplate the subject anew. This is the messianic vocation that has no room for the *as if*, according to Agamben, but which offers us a possible presentation of the thing itself, *as such*, beyond all forms of representation (*TR* 42).

The question that must continually be put to Agamben, however, is whether his own philosophy, despite his insistence that we must find a way to go beyond the spectral-speculative position and actually change the concrete reality before us, actually succeeds in doing so, or whether, rather, he falls prey to the exact same theoretical-spectral edifice to which Adorno, and Derrida too for that matter, had fallen victim. It is clear, of course, that Agamben frames his entire *oeuvre* towards instantiating such changes in concrete, historical terms; this is what his yearning for the 'coming community', the 'coming politics', the 'coming ethics' and so forth, would seem to be centred on. Whether he actually manages to escape from simply repeating Derrida's insistence that a call for such structures was only ever 'to come' is less clear, though I do find Agamben's possible description of human nudity as a form of the *as such* constantly covered by our representations (i.e., clothing) to be somewhat convincing.[9] Undoubtedly, however, one could mount a certain critique of Agamben that would indict each emphatic effort as wanting 'to be immediately concrete without sliding into mere facticity', the very thing that had rendered Heidegger susceptible to 'the jargon of authenticity', as Adorno called it.[10] Much more could be said here too in the same vein, for example, about Agamben's enthusiasm for a Levinasian encounter with the face of the other as a 'permanent metaphysical subvention'.[11]

To put the question in those terms through which he criticised Adorno: Is Agamben's rejection of redemption as the perspective from which to take on history in favour of seeing history as catastrophe really something that precludes redemption in other, previously unheard of forms, or is it the basis through which we might learn to re-conceive of something like redemption anew?[12] Agamben's dismissal of the *as if* would certainly explain to some extent his relegation of narrative and fiction to the margins of his own work. In this sense, an attempt to live out the *as if* could be seen as a perhaps nihilistic effort to negate reality, an ontologisation of an aesthetic preference that Agamben would prefer not to entertain.[13] Agamben's own choice is rather for the *as such* as perceived through the *as not*, understood in its Pauline register as the negation of negation itself.

IV

This messianic logic of the *as not*, for Agamben, returns again and again as the major impetus behind his philosophy. In the context of Pauline thought, which he returns to as well at the end of his summation of the *Homo Sacer* project, *The Use of Bodies*, he lingers upon the Pauline 'division of division itself' as his response to the wayward efforts of traditional forms of dialectic. Agamben's self-described task is to render the polarised dichotomy between *bios* and *zoè* inoperative rather than attempting to dialectically, permanently hold them in tension or produce a third term. It is only through their deactivation that something like a 'form of life' can be said to exist beyond them (*UB* 225).

The immediate contrast of Agamben and Adorno on this score would seem to be that, if Agamben's negation of negation functions in such a way as to open up new, previously unthought historical possibilities, Adorno's negative dialectics would seem to be much more focused on 'the cracks and fissures of damaged life itself' and the ways such problematic spots can be transformed.[14] Whereas Agamben's reading of the messianic, following Benjamin's 'weak messianic force' moving through history, appears to call for an upending of all representations *tout court*, Adorno's vision would seem rather to promote a messianic force that 'serves as a negative interruption of history, which illuminates the incompleteness and injustice of damaged life'.[15] From this angle, Agamben's focus presents us with the seemingly perennial problem his work runs up against: what historical subjects are we presented with? What concrete, political alternatives does Agamben propose instead of the laws, institutions, structures and identities we currently utilise? Is his project not merely some vague utopian dream that may in fact conceal a deeper, ambivalent desire, one that could eventually be harnessed for totalitarian goals?

These questions are not easy ones to answer, and they seem to plague Agamben as much as they have plagued those others who have been confronted with similar questions, and who likewise appear to offer little in terms of practical political direction. One might think here of Derrida, whom I have already mentioned, as well as Slavoj Žižek.[16] Each of these three, Agamben, Derrida and Žižek, have offered their own answers, all of which converge upon possible aporias of human existence, and each, in a certain sense, provides somewhat unsatisfying, but also perhaps equally realistic, responses.

To address only Agamben's perspective, there has been a certain oscillation within his own work between stressing the importance of a deactivation of social apparatuses and identities and the more prosaic recommendation of a hermeneutical tension between opposing forces, such as when he suggested in his brief Paris talk, published as *The Church and the Kingdom*, that, in order for a community to form, there must be a prevailing dialectical tension between law (or state) and the messianic (or Church) (*CR* 35). This is an unresolved issue within Agamben's work that would seem to push his position far closer to Adorno's in some respects than he has been willing to admit thus far.

V

But does not Adorno's critique of the 'negation of negation' as utilised to provide some form of positivity in the end, when he embraces a form of the 'negation of negation' that yields a permanently negative dialectics, not run parallel to Agamben's own endorsement of the Pauline 'division of division' which likewise remains wholly negative in its revocation of all identity?[17] Despite his seeming to cling to the 'total social process', as Agamben had critiqued him for, Adorno was resolutely focused on a form of negative dialectics that does 'not come to rest in itself, as if it were total'.[18] As with Agamben's many speculations concerning the nature of the absolute within a wholly negative movement, Adorno expresses how 'the absolute, as it hovers before metaphysics, would be the nonidentical that refuses to emerge until the compulsion of identity has dissolved'.[19]

Negative dialectics, in Adorno's formulations, proceeds always from an 'identitarian logic' which it then seeks to negate precisely so that it might oppose any aspirations to totality through recourse to a non-identity already lodged within identity.[20] A negative dialectics born from the human experience of suffering and the lack of respect that is shown to those forms of human life that are living out differences cannot simply be subsumed under a given, accepted rubric for political, social and religious representations. Identity is formed upon a variety of social divisions that are concealed through the establishment of identity itself. In this fashion, negative dialectics provides an immanent break within the framework of identity, one that negates any established identity that is, for its part, established only insofar as it rests upon a previous cultural representation (or 'division', in Agamben's parlance).

What remains then is the hope for an almost utopian state wherein the dialectic between identity and non-identity dissolves, leaving us with only a sort of non-identity that might just be capable of providing an alternative sort of identity, yet *as not* an identity. In Adorno's words, '[u]topia would be above identity and above contradiction; it would be a togetherness of diversity'.[21] Philosophy, at least in Adorno's estimation, and especially as we move deeper into these reflections, does remove us from existing reality in some measure – a point that would square quite well with Agamben's attempts to do the same, which subject him to a seemingly endless barrage of criticisms that he has left behind the pragmatic, actual domain of political action.[22] Such sentiments, however, yet appear to underpin Adorno's utopian hopes for a negative dialectics that seeks to do away with the dialectical antagonisms that ground human representational claims.[23] They also resonate a good deal with Agamben's fairly utopian expression of 'whatever being', a formulation allowing for a diversity that, if embraced, could provide a sense of being-together in diversity that mirrors Adorno's own conjecture.

VI

> There are few thinkers whose concerns coincide with Agamben's so often as Adorno's. Given this fact, it is surprising how rarely Agamben refers to Adorno.[24]

As Leland de la Durantaye has already astutely remarked, the unstated relationship between Agamben and Adorno runs deeper than surface readings of Agamben's work might otherwise indicate. Noting in particular their proximity in terms of their respective interpretations of Auschwitz, concentration camps in general and the concept of profanation, de la Durantaye draws attention to the overlap in their work, while also pointing out potential, though I would add, somewhat minimal divergences.[25] There is so much resonance between their theoretical speculations that it is difficult in fact to separate the general direction in which their works point, a notion I am trying here merely to underscore.

In all of these considerations we return to the relationship between thought and the unthought, in Agamben's work, or identity and non-identity, in Adorno's. In Agamben's *Idea of Prose*, the book that I would claim most originally expresses the almost near entirety of Agamben's project, from his earliest works to the end of the *Homo Sacer* series, the 'unthought' or 'unknowable' that must somehow be thought or known comes to express the core of his philosophical task (IP 31–4). My claim here has been simply that Agamben's quest for the unthought at the heart of thought does more than simply resemble Adorno's 'unthought' within the history of philosophy, expressed in his *Negative Dialectics* as the search for a non-identity at the heart of identity. There is a resonance between them that is unmistakable, providing a good deal of instruction for what exactly Agamben's philosophical method may be about. In both thinkers, the relationship of the negative element – the unthought or non-identity, respectively – to the positive construction of thought or identity is only accessible through the negation of the dialectic that sustains a political order that we cannot yet do away with entirely. The fact that both thinkers wavered between the two, and offer a variety of competing claims or contradictions in order to deal with such a reality, is not a condemnation of their methods; it is rather a reflection of the inherent ambiguity within human existence that both thinkers were repeatedly unafraid to face.

NOTES

1. Theodor W. Adorno, *Negative Dialectics*, trans. E. B. Ashton (London: Continuum, 1973), p. 362.
2. See also Walter Benjamin, 'On the Concept of History', in *Selected Writings*, ed. Howard Eiland and Michael W. Jennings, vol. 4, trans. Edmund Jephcott et al. (Cambridge, MA: The Belknap Press of Harvard University Press, 2003).
3. See Theodor W. Adorno, 'Education After Auschwitz', in *Critical Models: Interventions and Catchwords*, trans. Henry W. Pickford (New York: Columbia University Press, 1998), p. 193.
4. Theodor W. Adorno, *Minima Moralia: Reflections on a Damaged Life*, trans. E. F. N. Jephcott (London: Verso, 2005), p. 247.
5. See Jacob Taubes, *The Political Theology of Paul*, trans. Dana Hollander (Stanford: Stanford University Press, 2003), p. 74.
6. I say more about this tension between Agamben and Derrida in *Between the Canon and the Messiah: The Structure of Faith in Contemporary Continental Thought* (London: Bloomsbury Academic, 2013).
7. Adorno, *Negative Dialectics*, p. 3.
8. See the commentary on Adorno and Agamben on the dialectic in Leland de la Durantaye, *Giorgio Agamben: A Critical Introduction* (Stanford: Stanford University Press, 2009), pp. 104–10.
9. See Agamben's *Nudities*. See also chapter 10 in Colby Dickinson and Adam Kotsko, *Agamben's Coming Philosophy: Finding a New Use for Theology* (Lanham, MD: Rowman and Littlefield, 2015).
10. Theodor W. Adorno, *The Jargon of Authenticity*, trans. Knut Tarnowski and Frederic Will (London: Routledge, 2003), p. 75.
11. Adorno, *The Jargon of Authenticity*, p. 62.
12. I am thinking here of the way in which Jessica Whyte frames her discussion of just such a possibility in her *Catastrophe and Redemption: The Political Thought of Giorgio Agamben* (Albany: SUNY Press, 2013). This suggestion runs parallel to Slavoj Žižek's comment on Agamben's work that the latter's quest for an absolute form of profanation might actually yield us new forms of the sacred, is in fact the bare minimum of what sacrality is considered to be. Slavoj Žižek, *Less Than Nothing: Hegel and the Shadow of Dialectical Materialism* (London: Verso, 2012), p. 987.
13. William Watkin explicitly links this insight in Agamben's work to the latter's critique of Adorno in *The Literary Agamben: Adventures in Logopoiesis* (London: Continuum, 2010), pp. 89–91.
14. Christopher Craig Brittain, *Adorno and Theology* (London: T&T Clark, 2010), p. 135.
15. Brittain, *Adorno and Theology*, p. 138.

16. I have spoken at length of Derrida and Žižek on the political in my 'Slavoj Žižek on Jacques Derrida, or On Derrida's Search for a Middle Ground Between Marx and Benjamin, and his Finding Žižek Instead', *Philosophy Today* 59.2 (2015): 291–304.
17. Adorno, *Negative Dialectics*, pp. 158–61.
18. Adorno, *Negative Dialectics*, p. 406.
19. Adorno, *Negative Dialectics*, p. 406.
20. Adorno, *Negative Dialectics*, pp. 147, 150.
21. Adorno, *Negative Dialectics*, p. 150.
22. Adorno, *Negative Dialectics*, p. 364.
23. Adorno, *Negative Dialectics*, p. 11.
24. de la Durantaye, *Giorgio Agamben*, p. 360.
25. One could also note here the way in which both authors maintain a certain critical distance from phenomenology. See, in particular, Theodor W. Adorno, *Against Epistemology: A Metacritique*, trans. Willis Domingo (Cambridge: Polity, 1982).

24 Jacques Derrida

VIRGIL W. BROWER

There is no auto-analysis[1]

INITIAL AFFECTIONS

There's kinship, no doubt. Traces of Derrida ever haunt Agamben, brilliantly, even in the dark. He is expressly ingratiated by *'Derrida's critique of the metaphysical tradition'* (LD 39, original italics). Amid the myriad of his coeval influences, it is certainly worth considering that Derrida is Agamben's 'primary contemporary interlocutor'. His 'critical engagement with deconstruction can indeed be identified as the context out of which emerge almost all of his key concepts'.[2] Attell offers compelling discussions of this polemical relationship with regard to voicing language, sovereignty and animality. The former accounts for Agamben's direct textual engagements with Derrida which, for the most part, address his earlier works, specifically *Of Grammatology*, *Voice and Phenomena* and *Margins of Philosophy*. To address his contemporary intellectual situation, Agamben roots himself in that one he finds most rooted, dedicating an early essay, *'Pardes'*, to Derrida, which hails him as 'the philosopher who has perhaps most radically taken account' of the 'crisis [...] of terminology [that] is the proper situation of thought today ...' (PO 208). Here, Agamben mounts a deferential defence against caricaturisations of deconstruction (oft heard to this day) as a hermeneutical relativism of infinite deferral: '[I]t would be the worst misunderstanding of Derrida's gesture to think that it could be exhausted in a deconstructive use of philosophical terms that would simply consign them to an infinite wandering or interpretation' (PO 209).

Donee honors donor. An early imperative driving the budding dreamer of anomie is: *'we must certainly honor Derrida as the thinker who has identified with the greatest rigor [. . .] the original status of* gramma *and of meaning in our culture'*. One 'must' do so even though Derrida '*merely brought the problem of metaphysics to light*', rather than opening a genuine '*way to surpassing*' it (*LD* 39, original italics). Agamben desires to surpass. He has – or had, at one time (perhaps in 'infancy') – a kind of *telos*. This '*surpassing*' drive is symptomatic of a 'common temptation of both Agamben and Foucault', suggested by Derrida, based on their adoption of 'linear history' in which '*epistémés* that follow on from each other [. . .] render each other obsolete'.³ The trace 'would unbind the [. . .] dialectical pact' of 'the insistent authority [or sovereignty] of [. . .] the third [. . .] this double motif' of oppositional dialectics. Deconstruction is 'not only counter-archaeological but counter-genealogical'. 'What is put in question by its work is not only the possibility of recapturing the originary but also the desire to do so.'⁴

Almost as a rule, Derrida employs refreshing fallibility and admits, early on, that 'the enterprise of deconstruction always in a certain way falls prey to its own work'.⁵ Already there is humble self-reference of deconstruction with itself ('its own') that forfeits any desire of 'surpassing' which would imply a sovereign authority on the part of deconstruction itself. A *sovereignty of surpassing* is perhaps detectable in the 'essential claim of sovereignty' that Derrida discerns in Agamben's style: that 'most irrepressible gesture' repeated throughout *Homo Sacer* (and not only there) to be 'the first to say who *will have been first*'.⁶ Worse, he 'wants to be first twice, the first to see and announce [. . .] and also the first to recall that [. . .] it's always been like that'.⁷

Honouring Derrida as the thinker who brings such problems to light *without* addressing that light itself (e.g., photology or heliocentrism)⁸ is one of the problems that needs be brought along, while doing so, perhaps, reveals much about Agamben's selective reading of Derrida. The insurpassability might be attributed to Agamben's Heideggerian reading of Hegel that thereby authorises a tweaked Hegelian (or is it Aristotelian?) reading of Derrida.⁹ More often than not, it insists on thinking *gramma* as a mode of *voice* and *negativity* rather than *writing* and *trace*.¹⁰ But trace leaves the heaviest impression. '*The concept "trace" is not a concept* [. . .]: this is the paradoxical thesis that defines the proper status of Derrida's terminology' (*PO* 213, original italics). As such, 'the notion of trace constitutes the specific achievement of Derrida's thought' (*PO* 214).

Yet, for Derrida, trace would be 'neither negative nor positive';¹¹ '[I]t is not negative'.¹² It's resistant to – and misbegotten for – any binary opposition structurally conceptualised as positivity and/or negativity.¹³ Nevertheless, Agamben conceives *gramma* to have 'the structure of a *purely negative* self-affection' (*LD* 39, emphasis added). The alleged proper status of Derrida's terminology does not deter him from translating trace into a function of negativity. This is something Derrida goes to great lengths to discourage.[14]

... UNOPPOSED

On these points, a criticism that Derrida makes of Husserl can be redirected – almost seamlessly – at Agamben: 'the *negativity of the crisis is not a mere accident*. But it is then the concept of crisis that should be suspect, by virtue of what ties it to a dialectical and teleological determination of negativity.'[15] It is as if ideality is to Husserl as purity is to early Agamben. Something similar can be said for some of Derrida's later criticisms of Schmitt, who, he believes, 'goes to great lengths [. . .] to exclude from *all other* purity [. . .] the purity of the political, the *proper and pure impurity* of the concept or meaning of the "political"'.[16] Schmitt allows himself 'to decide for the *presence* of the political [. . . which . . .] potentializes a logic of negativity [. . .] only to expand the control of the political [. . .] in its most pristine philosophical purity'.[17] Further – between Husserl and Schmitt – Heidegger is suspect along similar lines. All three would 'have in common [. . .] not only oppositional logic (dialectical or not) [. . .] not only pure distinctions [. . .] but oppositionality itself, ontological adversity'.[18] It is as if Agamben never escapes the oppositional shortcomings and crypto-teleologies that Derrida forewarns to be the very legacies of Foucault, Husserl, Heidegger and Schmitt from out of which he develops, inheriting their congenital perjuries (not to mention those of Hegel[19] and Aristotle).

Despite his thresholds and zones of indifferences, Agamben remains an oppositional thinker; as if never 'truly'[20] testing (or losing) that 'fundamental belief of metaphysicians' vilified by Nietzsche as 'the *belief in oppositions of values*'.[21] The oppositional ideality on which his project grounds itself seems automatically, even unconsciously, determined by compulsive repetition to develop only ever within the binary confines of one canonical opposition after another, ever doubling-down on a dialectics. Even in his more mature breakthrough text, Derrida finds him 'putting his money on the concept of "bare life," which he identifies with *zoè*, in opposition to *bios*'.[22] The decisive and foundational event of modernity that Agamben desires to announce to the world – auto-constituting himself in Foucault's footsteps, to surpass, 'correct' and 'complete' him (*HS* 9) – is made to live and let to die only by insisting on a dull 'distinction [. . . that is . . .] never so clear and secure'[23] between Greek forms of life in opposition. Such a task, after deconstruction, 'isn't easy [...] even impossible'.[24]

Trace is no longer simply a negativity in *The Time that Remains*. Hegel returns as the reference point. Purely negative self-affection develops into a state of dialectical suspension (which may well be what 'negativity' was all along. Very little, if anything, has changed.) 'In this instance, the arche-trace simultaneously shows its link to – and difference from – the Hegelian *Aufhebung* [... the movement of which ...] becomes a principle of infinite deferral' (*TR* 103). Here one might 'smile'.[25] It almost seems that Agamben sanctions himself to enframe Derrida in the very way that he, himself, discourages in '*Pardes*' (*PO* 209). 'In this way, the trace is a suspended *Aufhebung* [...] deconstruction is a thwarted messianism, a suspension of the messianic' (*PO* 209).

If 'thwarted messianism' is 'a suspension of the messianic', then would not the 'suspended *Aufhebung*' of trace be, at the same time, a thwarted opposition? It is as if messianism, alone, must be thwarted in order to secure oppositionality itself. Perhaps nothing less than a messiah could possibly thwart dialectics. Could an unthwarted messianism ever become messianic, anyway? Especially in any Pauline valence? (At times, Derrida seems to play a role in Agamben's works much like Paul does in those of Nietzsche.) If thwarting the messianic entails opening it to a future coming of justice (or finding it opening itself, as such), yet doing so 'without horizon of expectation [... nor ...] prophetic prefiguration', then Derrida perhaps thwarts it into a 'messianicity without messianism'[26] ... but a messianicity, nonetheless.

Note that the very notion of suspension – exceptional as it is, in Agamben – is a practice he finds at the feet of Derrida,[27] for better or worse; even if it must undergo Schmittianisation (almost sovereignly so). Such 'suspension' barely evades Derrida's own suggestions on how trace or deconstruction relate to speculative philosophy. If an unopposed alliance between them is not apparent in *Glas*, it is glossed again – with refreshing directness – in a later interview:

> If we take [...] that which makes a dialectical process possible – namely, an element foreign to the system [...] – this foreign element, more originary than the dialectic, is precisely that which the dialectic is to dialectize, [...] *there* is a non-oppositional difference that transcends the dialectic, which is itself always oppositional. There is a supplement [...] that does not let itself be dialectized [... As such,] the dialectic consists in dialectizing the non-dialectizable. [...] I have never *opposed* the dialectic [... but rather tried to think] the dialecticity of dialectics that is itself fundamentally not dialectical.[28]

After deconstruction, readers might encounter Agamben's method much as Derrida does Hegel's: 'It wants to keep what it wants to lose.

Desire is *of/for the Aufhebung*.'[29] 'Speculative philosophy removes every difficulty, and then leaves me the difficulty of trying to determine what it really accomplishes by this so-called removal (*aufheben*).'[30] The sovereign state of exception seems ever to suspend innumerable zones of indistinction, leaving Agamben – barely alive – to determine what it accomplishes by its so-called suspension ... so that he may solve, resolve and surpass it.

INITIATED AUTO-AFFECTIONS

For Agamben, such suspension is not so simple, for it is, simultaneously, an 'autosuspension' (*TR* 105). This is but one autographed neologism among 'a whole series of other *auto*-prefixed words'[31] resembling those also found in Derrida. It uncannily auto-becomes difficult to auto-distinguish the deconstructive Coppola from the biopolitical and theo-economic Coppelius.

If the most important aspect of Agamben's reading of Derrida is 'trace', then the most significant facet of 'trace' is its *self-referentiality*. Trace is exceptional self-reference. This will develop throughout Agamben's works into a form of auto-affection that is perhaps his most primal – even inventive – lesson learned from Derrida. It sets the stage for later investigations: mode, modification and self-modification; affect, affection and auto-affection; suspense, suspension, 'autosuspension'; constituency, constitution and 'autoconstitution'. One might track the course of this auto-affective development from Excursus 3 of *Language and Death*, to '*Pardes*', to §3.12 and §3.18 of *Remnants of Auschwitz*,[32] to its most striking articulations in §2.4, §5 and §8.3 of *The Use of Bodies*. Here, early Derridean traces iterate themselves within later readings of the Stoa, specifically Lucretius, followed by a somewhat surprising gesture to Husserl with regard to the *Leib* (one's proper living body) as self-modifying/auto-affective use of one's own body.

The 'negative self-affection' quickly mentioned in *Language and Death* (*LD* 39) receives fuller treatment in '*Pardes*', in which trace or *différance* '*in some manner* signifies itself; it is self-referential [...] inscribed in the domain of paradoxes of self-reference' (*PO* 211, original italics). Such self-reference cannot function by the colloquial standards of referentiality, by which it properly achieves 'no self-reference' at all: 'Only if one *abandons* this first level of self-referentiality does one reach the heart of the problem' (*PO* 212, emphasis added).

A *ban* is required. Or, so it seems. Must '*Pardes*' be abandoned by the author of *Homo Sacer* on this point? Is the philosopheme '*autos*' applicable to trace, at all? If ever there were a thing without or beyond *autos*, would it not be trace? Is a sovereign decision required by such a 'self' (if it is that) in order to abandon, deactivate or render inoperative its own capacity for denotation (and even connotation) from the place of reference – as if they were werewolves threatening the very survival of itself-reference – to secure this strange capacity to reference itself? If so, is this pure, negative, self-reference thereby already political (decisively sovereign)? Is it perhaps yet another articulation of a political element ever unfit for the *polis* (indecisively *sacer*)? If the ban is a sovereign apparatus of what Agamben 'so calmly call[s]'[33] modern politics and if the 'totalitarian politics of the modern [. . .] is the will to total self-possession' (*ME* 97), then perhaps any possible will beyond politics might only affect itself as erasure of its own self-possession. Agamben might call this use. Derrida might call it ex-appropriation.

Unabandoned, *différance* (or trace) may 'signify itself, but signify itself only insofar as it signifies'; 'refer to itself' and '*exhaust itself* neither in the pure presence of an [intention] nor in its absence' (*PO* 212, emphasis added). Agamben has just cited *Margins*: the trace 'must be described as an erasure of the trace itself [. . .] produced as its own erasure. And it belongs to the trace to erase itself' (*PO* 210–11, citing Derrida; repeated in *TR* 103). Here, in '*Pardes*', this experience is described as one that 'exhausts itself' and 'refer[s] to itself' (with neither the presence or absence of intention), with no mention of its self-erasure other than the quotation of Derrida. But it is this singular experience of self-erasure that Agamben shall continue to reference.

Agamben on his tracks, Derrida traces a trail to ethics. Self-tracing (or trace-selving) – the self-erasure of trace – radicalises self-affection and discovers a path to a form-of-life beyond political life (cf. *OD* 98, 129, *passim*). The most precious gift Derrida might give 'is not a theory of polysemy or a doctrine of the transcendence of meaning [. . .] but a radicalization of the problem of self-reference' (*PO* 213). Self-referentiality is, for Agamben, 'the decisive event of matter [. . . that . . .] opens onto an ethics. Whoever experiences this ethics [. . .] can then dwell in the paradoxes of self-reference' (*PO* 213).

This inspires nothing less than Agamben's signature reading of Aristotle. After '*Pardes*', it is difficult to imagine that the potency of his understanding of potentiality or capacity – perhaps his most significant contribution to the philosophical tradition – would have come about without Derrida. From this fodder, alone, does *dynamis* seem to bloom; revealing itself as 'the potentiality of a potentiality', 'a potentiality that is capable and that experiences itself [. . .] that suffers not the impression of form but the imprint of its own passivity', 'a *tabula rasa* that suffers its own receptivity', 'to experience a passivity' (*PO* 216–17; q.v. *OD* 94–5). That previously conceived in terms of negativity and purity (*LD* 39), now seems more about passivity and receptivity. With the help of Plotinus (though using an example just as easily taken from Husserl), Agamben explains it as an eye in the dark 'affected by its own incapacity to see'; an 'experience of one's own passivity' (*PO* 217): 'Trace [. . .] is from the beginning the name of this self-affection' (*PO* 217). It transgresses territory canonically marked by the *cogito*, but accompanies its own deactivation: the 'potential to think, experiencing itself and being capable of itself as potential not to think, makes itself into the trace' (*PO* 218).

The trace of this experience returns in *Remnants of Auschwitz*. The quick flirtation with the passive experience of one's potential to think in '*Pardes*' provides the bridge between the two discussions. Agamben suggests that the experience of shame in Levinas finds a 'perfect equivalence' in 'the structure of subjectivity that modern philosophy calls *auto-affection*' (*RA* 109), that is, the inner sense of Kantian time, which Kant claims acts 'upon a passive subject'. Time is auto-affection but requires that one 'behave toward oneself as passive' (*RA* 109, citing Kant). The lesson (already hinted in '*Pardes*') is this: 'As auto-affection, passivity is thus a receptivity [. . .] a receptivity that experiences itself, that is moved by its own passivity' (*RA* 110).

The fracture of this experience would account for the impossible simultaneity of Levi's *Muselmann* and the witness. The former is 'a purely receptive pole', the latter is 'an actively passive pole' (*RA* 111). Regardless of the veracity of such a conclusion (and putting aside the insistence that passivity – specifically sexual – must be shameful [*RA* 110]), alongside this continuation of receptive 'purity' already developed as an amalgamation of '*Pardes*' and *Language and Death*, here the possibility of an *active passivity* is introduced.

Several pages later (§3.18) this subjectification process of passive auto-affection twice returns to Derrida (only once by name and, even then, without citation). Subjectification can be traumatic precisely because of 'the event of discourse'. Agamben then gestures to the phrase from *Margins* that he has cited repeatedly in previous works. Traumatic or not, 'the fragile text of consciousness incessantly crumbles and *erases itself*' (*RA* 123, emphasis added). It is because auto-affection is receptive that the subjectification of any alleged subjectivity may incessantly auto-erase itself. This discloses a *constitutive* prior to anything constituted. It reveals

> the disjunction on which [consciousness (perhaps subjectivity)] is erected: the constitutive desubjectification in every subjectification. (It is hardly astonishing that it was precisely from an analysis of the pronoun 'I' in

Husserl that Derrida was able to draw his idea of infinite deferral, an originary disjunction – writing – inscribed in the pure self-presence of consciousness.) (*RA* 123)

Is it hardly astonishing that Agamben fails 'precisely' to mention that Derrida draws this idea as much from an analysis of Aristotle as from Husserl?[34] The self-erasure of the trace as receptive self-reference now coincides with the passive auto-affection of subjectivity. A receptive *constitutive* auto-affection (self-erasure) is indissociable from an actively *constituted* result from that (yet still passive) auto-affection. The former is the desubjectificating *dynamis* at the very inception or 'origin' of the subjectification of the subjective consciousness of the latter.

AUTO-ERASURE OF SELF-AFFECTION

This theoretical advance from self-erasure to *receptively passive self-affection* marks the most lasting Derridean impression to persist throughout Agamben's works. These two uses of it – first (in *Language and Death* and '*Pardes*') in terms of voicing language; second (in *Remnants of Auschwitz*) in terms of subjectivity or selfhood – are restated in *The Use of Bodies*. The former finds expression through Benveniste (§2.4); the latter through the Stoa (§1.5). No longer is any overt gesture to Derrida to be found.

In the discussion of *chresis*, Benveniste's explanation of middle voice (or diathesis) is 'situated in a zone of indetermination between subject and object (the agent is in some way also object and place of action) and between active and passive (the agent receives an affection from his own action)' (*UB* 28).[35] This 'process does not pass from an active subject toward the object separated from his action but involves in itself the subject [... which ...] "gives himself" to it' (*UB* 28). *Chresthai*, therefore, '*expresses the relation that one has with oneself, the affection that one receives insofar as one is in relation with a determinate being*' (*UB* 28, original italics). Applied to the use of the body – *somatos chresthai* – it becomes '*the affection that one receives insofar as one is in relation with one or more bodies*' (*UB* 29, original italics).

The 'constitutive' element of self-erasure in *Remnants of Auschwitz* here discloses itself through the terminology of 'constitution', through which it is brought to life and enters the land of the living. By way of Diogenes Laertius and Chrysippus, synaesthesia uncovers an auto-affective experience that, 'from the very beginning familiar to each living thing, is *its own constitution* and the sensation it has of it' (emphasis added); a 'sensation of itself and familiarity of itself' (*UB* 50, citing Hierocles). As the discussion moves on to Lucretius, the earlier language of erasure is replaced (probably under the influence of Hobbes and *stasis*) with that of dissolution (and *hypostasis*): 'The familiarity [...] of the living being with itself is *dissolved without remainder* into its self-perception' (*UB* 51, emphasis added). This is how a 'living being uses-itself, in the sense that in its life and in its entering into relationship with what is other than the self, it has to do each time with its very self, feels the self and familiarizes itself with itself' (*UB* 54). The auto-affective feeling-oneself at the heart of use-of-oneself reaches its apex in a turn to phenomenology and Husserl (§1.8.3), which seems to offer a 'correct posing of the problem of the body [... but which was, unfortunately ...] put durably off course' by 'the problem of empathy' (*UB* 82).

Empathy is phenomenology's white whale. It dogged Husserl all his life. The problem is the other,[36] the impossible incorporation of an improper hetero-affection into the proper auto-affective experience of one's lived body. Agamben's emendation of Husserl – which is one of the most startling developments of the painstaking time and space of the *Homo Sacer* project – is an application of self-erasure (now, 'dissolving without remainder') (in)to the proper phenomenological auto-affection of one's lived body that, upon application, may yet somehow take account (if such a thing is possible) of the passive, receptive and hetero-affective trace from which it is ever indissociable. What the disruption of empathy

> shows is that however much one affirms the originary character of the 'propriety' of the body and of lived experience, the intrusiveness of an 'impropriety' shows itself to be all the more originary [...] as if the body proper always casts a shadow, which can in no case be separated from it. (*UB* 84)

These theoretical threads that weave from the self-reference of trace in earlier works, through the constitutive self-erasing element haunting subjectification, to the shadowed impropriety of auto-affection in/as the use of one's body, all tie themselves off into a magnificent bow. Its knot is nothing less than an embodied, psycho-subjective iteration of political sovereignty and the state of exception at the core of constitutional law. It is even one of biopolitics, since it is the traumatic or shameful process of desubjectification that bans a *Muselmann* – avatar of bare life – from humanity, political life and the capacity to witness. From the first texts to the latest, all these signature motifs have tangled tendrils stretching roots back to Derrida, even while his very name disappears from the discussions ... ever faithful to its vocation.

IMMUNODEFICIENCY OF ONE'S INFIRM CONSTITUTION

Given (a) Agamben's overt affection for Derrida's early works, and appreciating that (b_1) the element of death that haunts the colloquial living presence of speech or the physical act of writing – that is 'trace' – in those works continues to develop throughout Derrida's later ones (e.g., 'lifedeath', *survivance, hauntologie* and, ultimately, autoimmunity) and (b_2) Agamben's textual indifference to these later Derrida texts in which they show themselves, then (c) it is worth considering that Agamben's zones of 'autosuspension', 'autoconstitution', auto-affection, etc., are para-deconstructive endeavours to resolve and surpass what an ignored Derrida comes later to call auto-immunity (rooted in the very aporia of trace, upon which all these discussions of Agamben are arguably borne). 'Autoconstitution'[37] is an articulation – an impressive one at that – of an ineradicable auto-immunity more 'originary' to constitutionality (as are the states of exception themselves). After *The Use of Bodies*, it is perhaps only thinkable as a mode of auto-affection and self-use. It is a way (of which there are several) by which 'constituent power' constitutes itself while attempting to capture (and, thereby, indemnify itself from) any 'distituent potential' (*UB* 266–8) resistant to it. The prosthesis of exception to this performative capture is, for example, 'the task of modifying the text of the constitution' (*UB* 267), after the fact, mystical foundation and inception of law.

Autoconstitution is not auto-immunity. The former interrupts the (para-legal) activity to defend, secure or indemnify itself (as legal) from any passive distituents within its very constituency, while receptively constituting itself from them, nonetheless. It is, rather, a *fatale* epiphenomenon of auto-immune processes that accompanies any exercise of *autos*. It is the shadow compromising the very autonomy by which one allows oneself to dream of anomie.

NOTES

1. Jacques Lacan, *The Seminar of Jacques Lacan*, Book X, *Anxiety*, trans. A. R. Price (Cambridge: Polity, 2014), p. 23.
2. Kevin Attell, *Giorgio Agamben: Beyond the Threshold of Deconstruction* (New York: Fordham University Press, 2015), p. 3.
3. Jacques Derrida, *The Beast and the Sovereign*, trans. Geoffrey Bennington (Chicago: University of Chicago Press, 2009), vol. 1, p. 333. Agamben suggests that Foucault's adoption of the term 'historical *a priori*' (indicative

of a 'linear history') probably stems 'from Husserl's *Origin of Geometry*, which Derrida had translated into French in 1962' (*UB* 112).
4. Jacques Derrida, *Resistances of Psychoanalysis*, trans. Peggy Kamuf, Pascale-Anne Brault and Michael Naas (Stanford: Stanford University Press, 1998), p. 27.
5. Jacques Derrida, *Of Grammatology*, trans. Gayatri Chakravorty Spivak (Baltimore: Johns Hopkins University Press, 1974), p. 24.
6. Derrida, *Beast and the Sovereign*, p. 92.
7. Derrida, *Beast and the Sovereign*, p. 330.
8. See *Of Grammatology*, 91–2; Jacques Derrida, *Writing and Difference*, trans. Alan Bass (Chicago: University of Chicago Press, 1978), p. 27; *Margins of Philosophy*, trans. Alan Bass (Chicago: University of Chicago Press, 1982), pp. xxvii–xxviii, 91–2.
9. Not surprisingly, Agamben finds 'the thought of Derrida to have its basis [. . .] in that of Heidegger' (*S* 158 n. 15). This linear intellectual trajectory found to 'originate' in Heidegger alone seems to disqualify – *avant la lettre* – any due diligence of Derridean readings of Hegel, which may account for the over-negativising character of Agamben's earlier writings.
10. This is less the case in the quick gesture to *Of Grammatology* in *Stanzas* (*S* 155–6) than it is in '*Pardes*'.
11. Derrida, *Of Grammatology*, p. 167.
12. Jacques Derrida, *Limited Inc*, trans. Samuel Weber (Evanston: Northwestern University Press, 1988), p. 53.
13. Although simple synonymy between 'negativity' and 'negative' (or 'negation') must not be presumed.
14. See, for example, Jacques Derrida, 'How to Avoid Speaking: Denials', trans. Ken Frieden, in *Derrida and Negative Theology*, ed. Harold Coward and Toby Foshay (Albany: SUNY Press, 1992), pp. 73–142 (whose title alone almost performs a perfect Derridean response to *Language and Death*).
15. Derrida, *Of Grammatology*, p. 40 (emphasis added).
16. Derrida, *The Politics of Friendship*, trans. George Collins (New York: Verso, 1997), p. 116 (emphasis added). It is noteworthy that in this text – which devotes half of itself to critiques of Schmitt – Derrida is already citing Nicole Loraux (p. 75). It is possible, despite these criticisms, that Derrida 'generally accepts Schmitt's diagnoses'; Michael Naas, *Derrida From Now On* (New York: Fordham University Press, 2008), p. 65.
17. Derrida, *Politics of Friendship*, p. 133 (emphasis added).
18. Derrida, *Politics of Friendship*, p. 249.
19. Compare Derrida's readings of 'Hegelian philosophy – through and through a philosophy *of* religion' (*Glas*, trans. John P. Leavey, Jr, and Richard Rand [Lincoln, NE: University of Nebraska Press, 1986], p. 32), in which the 'truth of Christianity is philosophy' (p. 62, q.v. p. 70), with *The Sacrament of Language* (in which Hegel makes virtually no appearance): 'philosophy [. . .] must necessarily put itself forward as *vera religio* [true religion]' (*SL* 66).

20. Cf. Derrida's comments on Agamben's tactical use of 'truly' in the brackets of his block quotation of *Homo Sacer* (*Beast and the Sovereign*, pp. 92–3; as well as 'true', *Beast and the Sovereign*, p. 328).
21. Friedrich Nietzsche, *Beyond Good and Evil*, trans. Judith Norman (Cambridge: Cambridge University Press, 2002), p. 6 [§2] original italics).
22. Derrida, *Beast and the Sovereign*, p. 325.
23. Derrida, *Beast and the Sovereign*, p. 316.
24. Derrida, *Beast and the Sovereign*, p. 327.
25. Twice Derrida smiles while reading *Homo Sacer* (*Beast and the Sovereign*, pp. 92, 94).
26. Jacques Derrida, 'Faith and Knowledge', trans. Samuel Weber, in *Acts of Religion*, ed. Gil Anidjar (New York: Routledge, 2002), pp. 56 and passim. Cf. Jacques Derrida, *Rogues: Two Essays on Reason*, trans. Pascale-Anne Brault and Michael Naas (Stanford: Stanford University Press, 2005), pp. 110, 153.
27. 'Deconstruction suspends the terminological character of philosophical vocabulary' (*PO* 208).
28. Jacques Derrida and Maurizio Ferraris, *A Taste for the Secret*, trans. Giacomo Donis (Cambridge: Polity, 2001), pp. 32–3. Cf. *Glas*, p. 162: 'Isn't there always an element excluded from the system that assures the system's space of possibility'? Cf. the 'nondialectizable antinomy' 'common' to an '*autoimmune process*' in Derrida, *Rogues*, p. 35.
29. Derrida, *Glas*, p. 120.
30. Derrida, *Glas*, p. 200.
31. Naas, *Derrida From Now On*, p. 125.
32. Which could also include Part I, §1.10 of *The Highest Poverty*.
33. Derrida, *Beast and the Sovereign*, p. 326.
34. In 'Ousia and Grammé', it is an analysis of Aristotle's *Physics* from which is drawn 'thinking time and movement [. . .] that keeps its *tracing* close to itself, that is, *erases its tracing*' (Derrida, *Margins*, p. 60; Derrida's italics of 'tracing'; other italics mine).
35. Once again, the lesson is one just as easily lifted from Husserl's description of *Leib* in *Cartesian Meditations*.
36. And though he dares not utter 'other' – as if shibbolethed or shamefaced – it is no accident that Agamben mentions Levinas in all three of the steps to which I am drawing attention. He is quickly identified as one of Derrida's inspirations in the first (*LD* 39), introduces the problem of desubjectification by way of shame in *Remnants* (*RA* 104–6), and immediately follows the return to Husserl's proper body in the end (*UB* 84–5).
37. E.g., 'the sovereign autoconstitution of Being' (*UB* 147).

25 Sigmund Freud

VIRGIL W. BROWER

> ... *invidiosa feri radiabant atria regis*
> *unaque iam tota stabat in urbe domus.*[1]

Can Freud be abandoned? Interrelations between *sacer*, ambivalence, exception, suspension, property, use and civil war around the origin of law are traces of Freud that manifest themselves throughout the development of Agamben's thought. Most direct engagements are found in early texts,[2] best articulated in *Stanzas*. Here is incipient indication of (a) Freud's guilt by association with shortcomings of the sociology of religion (*S* 137).[3] Agamben displays (b) lessons learned from Freud in terms of phantasm, fetishism and the unconscious (*S* 22–3, 31–3, 145–7; *IH* 48), but overall performs (c) critical discouragement of an alleged Freudian delimitation (under the influence of Schelling) of the *Unheimlich* in terms of repression (*S* 144).[4] Damage done by repressions return in a later text, *The Signature of All Things*, specifically Chapter 3, burrowed within its summary of (d) Foucault's critique of Freud as justification for Agamben's own idiomatic adoption of the archaeological method (*ST* 96–107). In essence,

> archaeological regression is elusive: it does not seek, as in Freud, to restore a previous stage, but to decompose, displace, and ultimately bypass it in order to go back not to its content, but to the modalities, circumstances, and moments in which the split, by means of repression, constituted it as an origin. (*ST* 102–3)

Two laudatory supplements to these include (e) a quick deferential comment with regard to Freud's study of the sacred[5] (which seems to be more about ambivalence) and (f) an evocative association – distanced by two degrees of citation[6] – of exceptionality with festival and *mourning*, both of which supplements disclose an understated indebtedness to *Totem and Taboo*, in which Freud equates (perhaps flippantly) the word *taboo* with the Latin *sacer* as it may relate to exception and sovereignty: 'It is difficult for us to find a translation for [taboo] [...] It was still current among the ancient Romans, whose "*sacer*" was the same as the Polynesian "taboo".'[7] It is on these latencies, kept in the shadows, that my essay wishes to impress.

Reactionary rebuttal against these comparisons (and those to follow) might insist – evidenced by his tactical preferences for Schelling, Hegel, Nietzsche or Heidegger – that Agamben is *not* an oedipal or psychoanalytic thinker; that the sovereign, king, chief or ruler (and, indeed, god) are merely iterated avatars of the father for Freud, but not so simply for Agamben. But a far from subtle paternalism is primal in Agamben's explanation of *homo sacer*'s capacity to be killed but not sacrificed. The 'crimes that [...] merit *sacratio*' are, at one time, expressed as '*verberatio parentis*, the violence of the son against the parent [which] constitute[s] the originary exception in which human life is included in the political order' (*HS* 85). Sovereign law is based on a parental (specifically *paternal*) relation. The violence of the child to the parent is exceptional to the power of the parent over the child. This piecemeal argument might be read as one that begins in Part II, §4 of *Homo Sacer*, continues through §§3, 5–6 of *State of Exception*, and culminates in Part 1 (§§1.3–1.10, 1.13) of *Stasis*. (This discussion sets the stage for the role of economy and *oikos* in *The Kingdom and the Glory*, for which it serves an indispensable introduction.)

It begins with 'Numa's homicide law (*parricidas esto*) [which] forms a system with *homo sacer*'s capacity to be killed (*parricidi non damnatur*) and cannot be separated from it' (*HS* 85).[8] More importantly, Agamben continues, the 'first time we encounter the expression "right over life and death" in the history of law is in the formula *vitae necisque potestas*, which designates not sovereign power but rather the unconditional authority [*potestas*] of the *pater* over his sons' (*HS* 87). Each Roman is, thereby, born into sacerhood by way of Roman paternity. There, 'every male citizen [...] is in some way *sacer* with respect to his father' (*HS* 89). The *potestas* of progenitor over progeny determines the very understanding of life (and death) in the land of *lex*. It is not based on a mythic father of a primal horde but rather on the crucial difference Agamben discerns between (1) the power of the father over the son *as opposed to* (2) the power of the husband over the wife or servants. The latter is conditional, while

> the *vitae necisque potestas* attaches itself to every free male citizen from birth and thus seems to define the very model of political power in general [...] *life exposed to death* [...] *is the originary political element*. (*HS* 87–8, emphasis added)

Paternity is becoming to polity. Like *zoè*, an alleged 'originary' political element here has an origin outside the *polis*. Agamben explicitly states as much in *Stasis*: '*zoè*, natural life, is included in the juridical-political order through its exclusion, so analogously the *oikos* is politicized and included in the polis through the *stasis*' (*STA* 22). Even though the domination of the *pater* over the *dominus* is distinct from the power of *potestas* over the son, the latter would yet be borne upon domestic elements of power privileged to the father (that are, in turn, transferred to that one *identified* as the ruling sovereign over time).

In Freud's mythopoetic musings on the emergence of law, taboo prohibitions 'grew into a conscious *law*: "No sexual relations between those who share a common *home*"'.[9] Agamben insists that *sacer esto* 'is not the formula of a religious curse sanctioning the *unheimlich*' (*HS* 85).[10] He relies on his earlier critiques and sidesteps Freud's theorisations of *Unheimlich* in later works, opting instead for its Heideggerian conceptions (e.g., *UB* 43). Something similar could be said for Agamben's interest in Oedipus, which prefers its Hegelian or Nietzschean conceptions, in his earlier work (e.g., *S* 137–9; *LD* 94–5), since '[i]n the psychoanalytic interpretation of the myth of Oedipus, the episode of the Sphinx [. . .] remains obstinately in the shadows' (*S* 137).[11]

Yet an uncanny paternalism sanctions the state of exception and sovereign law. This 'originary'[12] structure of sovereign law is not simply the capacity to be killed but rather *vitae necisque potestas*, that is, the potent power of the *pater* out of which homicide law, as such, burgeons. This is perhaps *a kind of inverted oedipality*, no less uncanny by way of its inversion. In *Homo Sacer*, the problem is less about the son's parricidal proclivities towards the father than the *pater*'s power over the life and death of the son, which discourages any Roman from killing another. This hardly escapes the mythologic of *Totem and Taboo*. The sons' parricidal penchant is not simply desire for the mother (or women of the horde), so often dismissed as/with Freudian pansexualism. It is also rebellion against unconditional *potestas* or authority exercised by the *pater*, 'the *tyrannical* father', 'the *father's supreme power* [. . .] *unlimited power*'.[13]

Colloquial caricatures of Freud overemphasise primal parricide. The radical hypothesis of *Totem and Taboo* is not simply the child's pre-genital libidinal desire to fuck/kill parents, but rather the primal impotence of parricidal aggression. The grand reveal is that parricide fails. '[V]ictory lay' *not* with the deed, but rather with the drives towards the deed; 'the impulses that led to parricide'.[14] Agamben's understanding of *vitae necisque potestas* would already be an expression of what

Freud considers to be the 'climax' of these drives' gradual development through group psychology, society, religion, morality and legislation. This climax is *'the dominance of authority'* or 'revived paternal authority';[15] a hair's breadth away from Agamben's understanding of *verberatio parentis*, which may be but a reaction to it. This develops into sovereign power, for Freud, as the ruler becomes surrogate of the *pater*.

Politicisation of paternal power develops further throughout *State of Exception*. Agamben casts it as more complicated than anything resembling taboo: 'It is certainly possible to see the *iustitium* (in the sense of public mourning) as nothing other than the sovereign's attempt to appropriate the state of exception by transforming it into a family affair. But the connection is even more intimate and complex' (*SE* 68). This intimate complexity never frees Agamben from the powers of the father:

> In the sphere of private law, *auctoritas* is the property of the *auctor*, that is, the person of the *sui iuris* (the *pater familias*) who intervenes [. . .] in order to confer legal validity on the act of a subject who cannot independently bring a legally valid act into being. Thus, the *auctoritas* of the tutor makes valid the act of one who lacks this capacity, and the *auctoritas* of the father 'authorizes' – that is, makes valid – the marriage of the son *in potestate*. (*SE* 76)

The senate is not simply magistrate, just as *auctoritas* is not *potestas*. But it still acts as father: 'with a strong analogy to the figure of the *auctor* in private law, the *auctoritas patrum* intervenes to ratify the decisions of the popular *comitia* and make them fully valid' (*SE* 78). The powers of the father may well dissipate into a complex more complicated than any oedipality, but the revenges of the latter seem inescapable:

> As we have seen, in public law *auctoritas* designates the most proper prerogative of the Senate. The active subjects of this prerogative are therefore *patres: auctoritas patrum* and *patres auctores fiunt* [the fathers are made *auctors*] are common formulas for expressing the constitutional function of the Senate. (*SE* 77)

Transference of paternal power to sovereign power is not absent in Agamben, even as it complicates nuclear familial simplicity: 'For whoever may have been the person technically qualified to proclaim a *iustitium* [court holiday or suspension of law], it is certain that it was always and only declared *ex auctoritate patrum* [on the authority of the fathers]' (*SE* 47).

Agamben's focus (or that of any anti-oedipal project)[16] on synechdocal politics *ex auctoritate patrum* beyond any insinuated simplicity of the Freudian family is as necessary or required as it is heuristic or corrective. Forfeiting oedipality as a concept prone to *ignoratio elenchi* is understandable,[17] but Freud, himself, less so. *Totem and Taboo* itself suggests thinking 'more correctly, [a] parental complex [*Elternkomplex*]'.[18] If the problem is unilateral movement solely from the child's psyche to the parent, it must be remembered that infantile unconscious is not apostate to Agamben's project. 'The search for a *polis* and an *oikìa* [. . . that . . .] is the infantile task of future generations' (*IH* 10) is one that can 'of course [. . .] correspond to Freud's unconscious' (*IH* 48).

At times, Agamben reads as hard-earned resistance against a unilateral understanding of the authority of the father as presented in *Totem and Taboo*. But if this is anti-oedipal thinking, it is as well-born as it is grandfathered. Freud would hardly disagree and is well aware of the boundless projections of the authority of *the fathers*. By the time of *Massenpsychologie* (1921), Freud's most overtly political text, it is ethnographic and socio-economic in scope and any exclusive unilateralism of it is compromised:

> If we survey the life of an individual man of to-day [. . .] he is bound by ties of identification in *many directions*, and he has built up his ego-ideal [internalised paternal authority] upon the most various models [. . .] those of his race, of his *class*, of his creed, of his *nationality*.[19]

This socio-political development of *identification* is the most important advance made in Freud's thought as *Totem and Taboo* matures into *Group Psychology*.

Agamben's paternal complex culminates in *Stasis* through the course of his disagreement with Nicole Loraux, for whom 'the original place of the *stasis* is the *oikos*; civil war is a "war within the family", an *oikeios polemos*' (*STA* 13). He, instead, hypothesises that *stasis*

> takes place neither in the *oikos* nor in the *polis*, neither in the family nor in the city; rather, it constitutes a zone of indifference between the unpolitical space of the family and the political space of the city. In transgressing this threshold, the *oikos* is politicized; conversely, the *polis* is 'economized', that is, it is reduced to an *oikos*. (*STA* 16)

Stasis 'forms part of a device that functions in a manner similar to the state of exception' (*STA* 22). In/as a state of exception, 'politics is a field incessantly traversed by the tensional currents of politicization and depoliticization, the family and the city' (*STA* 23). Lessons learned from ambivalence succour Agamben's conclusion that 'so long as the words "family" and "city", "private" and "public", "economy" and "politics" maintain an albeit tenuous meaning, it is unlikely that [*stasis* or civil war] can ever be eliminated from the political scene of the West' (*STA* 23–4).

The eventual identification of the state of exception as an aggressive *stasis* at the threshold of the family and politics invites (at least) three return visits to Freud. First, Agamben refrains from reconsidering that, like Loraux, *Totem and Taboo* also suggests civil war emergent within the family. Further, it evokes Hobbes while doing so. Parricidal failure and its resultant 'new organization would have collapsed in *a struggle of all against all*'.[20] Secondly, what Agamben calls the 'archetype of the modern *Ausnahmezustand*' (SE 41), rooted in Schmitt's dictum 'Sovereign is he who decides on the *exception*' (emphasis added), need not be exclusively delimited to Schmitt alone. If it has a type of *archē*, it is perhaps discernible a decade earlier. Before the 'essential contiguity between the state of exception and sovereignty was established by Carl Schmitt in his book *Politische Theologie*' (SE 1), Freud had attempted in 1912 to articulate a plurality of states of exceptions in an *Imago* article that came to be published as Part II of *Totem and Taboo* in the following year. The same word (in the singular) that Schmitt uses to define sovereignty is that which Freud makes use of (in the plural) to describe uncanny taboo powers. Taboo is a 'power [that] is attached to all *special* individuals, such as kings [. . .] to all *exceptional states* [*Ausnahmszuständen*] [. . .] and to all uncanny [*unheimlich*] things'.[21]

A series of nodal points emerge throughout the *Homo Sacer* project at which Schmitt and Freud (or *Political Theology* and *Totem and Taboo*) commingle. These proto-Schmittian *Ausnahmszuständen* have sovereign expressions. They specifically (though not exclusively) apply to the king, chief or ruler. The kind of power attached to the sovereign is akin to that which attaches itself to Freud's *states of exception* or 'exceptional states' (examples of which include 'the physical states of menstruation, puberty or birth').[22] Their legal or juridical expressions soon follow. For 'the earliest human penal systems may be traced back to taboo', because 'taboo has become the ordinary method of *legislation*'.[23]

The state of exception at the core of law, ever complicit in its own transgression – the illegality or criminality upon which law, as such, is grounded – further discloses possible reasons for a people's ambivalence towards the sovereign. At the heart of Freudian taboo is indistinction between law and crime, sovereign and criminal:

> [E]arly kingdoms are despotisms in which people exist only for *the sovereign* [. . .] *the sovereign* in them exists only for his subjects; his life is valuable so long as he discharges the *duties* of his position by *ordering the course of nature* for his people's benefit. So soon as he fails to do so [. . .] he is dismissed ignominiously [. . .] Worshipped as *a god one day*, he is killed as *a criminal the next*.[24]

In *Group Psychology*, exception becomes the rule: '[A] periodical *infringement of the prohibition is the rule*'; the psychic interiorisation of parental authority, that is, 'the ego-ideal[,] is inclined to display a peculiar strictness, which then results in its *temporary suspension*'.²⁵

Identification may function for Freud much as *stasis* does for Agamben. Should Freud be granted entrance, his ban lifted, and be allowed to participate alongside the schema Agamben offers near the end of Part 1 of *Stasis* (22):

depoliticisation / economisation → politicisation / an-economisation
←
oikos————| stasis |————*polis*

it might, perhaps, be supplemented:

Ausnahmnszuständen————| identification |————*Ausnahmezustand*
    (Freud)   (Schmitt)
Primal horde————| 'all against all' |————Leviathan
    (Freud)   (Hobbes)

Identification is a way by which the family is politicised and the political is economised. It is the mode through which the parental complex becomes political in public life and, simultaneously, by which political powers of the sovereign leader come to function in private life (*especially* if it is 'wildly useful to have an id agitating amid the superegos').²⁶

Finally, if the paternal complex in the earlier volumes of the *Sacer* project sows seeds of possible resistance to, or deactivation of, nomie and law crafted by exception that develops – in the later volumes (specifically, *The Highest Poverty* and *The Use of Bodies*) – as a mode, way or form of *use*, then it might also benefit from reconsideration of *Totem and Taboo*. Freud's investigations into the dark origin of the law already consider a possible converse of taboo related to a kind of *common use*: 'The converse of "taboo" [. . .] is *noa*, which means "common" or "generally accessible".'²⁷ Sovereigns are not tabooed, alone (nor are the enemy and the dead). Taboo attaches itself to things and objects.

There follows a prohibition not only 'against touching' the taboo object, but also 'against [. . .] making *use* of it for one's own purposes'.²⁸ While mourning, the tabooed 'are secluded and forbidden to touch their own head or body; the cups and cooking *vessels which they use may be used by no one else*'.²⁹ Use of bodies – even use of one's own body[30] – goes hand in hand with the peculiar practice. Anything used by a tabooed person becomes prohibited to be used by another.

Taboo, as such, applies not only to objects but also the bodies of persons. 'Touching is the first step towards [...] attempting *to make use of, a person or object.*'[31] Such high use is indissociable from certain revaluations of *property*, for example, in 'taboos imposed by chiefs and priests for the protection of their own property',[32] that is, property owned (and determined by) the sovereign and law. Use is the secret core of taboo and, given time and gods, the unconscious itself. Perhaps this is the great testament of the *Sacer* project.

NOTES

1. Evoking Nero, 'once gleamed the odious halls of a *cruel monarch*, and in all Rome there *stood* a single *house*'; Martial, *Epigrams*, vol. 1, trans. D. R. Shackleton Bailey (Cambridge, MA: Harvard University Press, 1993), pp. 12–13 (emphasis added).
2. Agamben employs the trope of Medusa's head in his inaugural book (*MC* 7), a vestige perhaps of Celan (e.g., *The Meridian*), but no less Freudian on that account, since Celan was a great reader of Freud. Cf. also *IP* 47–9; *EP* 126–9. Cf. the role of the Gorgon in *RA* 33, 52–3, 81.
3. Such as, 'Freudian interpretation has left [the mythologeme] in the dark' (*S* 137). This is perhaps the caricature of Freud that remains throughout Agamben's later writings.
4. Despite these critiques (c and d), Agamben yet indulges in use of the Freudian syntagma (perhaps revaluated), *the return of the repressed* (e.g., *UB* 21).
5. 'When Freud set out to write *Totem and Taboo* [...] the field had therefore already been prepared for him. Yet *only with this book does a genuine general theory of the ambivalence of the sacred come to light* on the basis not only of anthropology and psychology but also of linguistics' (*HS* 78, emphasis added).
6. Agamben cites 'an extensive study published in 1980' by H. S. Versnel, who – 'by proposing an analogy between the phenomenology of mourning [...] and periods of political crises, in which social institutions and rules seems suddenly to dissolve' – further cites Victor Turner with regard to liminality: 'perhaps Freud and Jung, in their different ways, have much to contribute to the understanding of these [...] aspects of liminal situations' (*SE* 66).
7. Sigmund Freud, *The Standard Edition of the Complete Psychological Works of Sigmund Freud*, trans. and ed. James Strachey et al. (London: Hogarth Press and the Institute of Psycho-analysis, 1953–74), vol. 13, p. 18. Freud continues this reductive equivocating to include the Greek word ἄγος and the Hebrew word *kadesh*. Agamben makes mention of this

gesture to *sacer* by Freud in a short essay on Karl Abel written a couple years prior to this one in *Totem and Taboo* (*HS* 78).
8. *Parricido* is not exclusively patri- or parricidal here, and can play in the field of a false cognate. It is about *cido* – killing (or slaughter) – of, perhaps, a *pars* or part, specifically a fellow Roman, tantamount to treason. But recall that Numa himself is paternally authorised by 'Father Jupiter [*Iuppiter Pater*]'; Livy, *The Early History of Rome*, trans. Aubrey De Sélincourt (New York: Penguin, 1960), p. 52; and *History of Rome*, vol. 1, *Books 1–2*, trans. B.O. Foster (Cambridge, MA: Harvard University Press, 1919), p. 66 (emphasis added).
9. *Standard Edition*, vol. 13, p. 126 (emphasis added).
10. It is difficult to imagine that Agamben is not thinking *unheimlich* (here, in *Homo Sacer*) in a Freudian valence rather than the Heideggerian one (on which he focuses in *The Use of Bodies*).
11. Yet, for Freud, it represents the first intellectual exercise of one's mental life. Cf. 'The Riddle of the Sphinx' section of *Three Essays on Sexuality* (*Standard Edition*, vol. 7, pp. 194-5).
12. Or, perhaps, *co-originary*, since: 'Every creation is always a cocreation, just as every author is always coauthor' (*SE* 76). See Laclau's criticism of the archaeological preoccupation with 'the *origin* [that] has a secret determining priority over what follows from it'; Ernesto Laclau, 'Bare Life or Social Indeterminacy', in Matthew Calarco and Steven DeCaroli (eds), *Giorgio Agamben: Sovereignty and Life* (Stanford: Stanford University Press, 2007), p. 11.
13. *Standard Edition*, vol. 13, pp. 142 n. 1, 148 (emphasis added).
14. *Standard Edition*, vol. 13, p. 146.
15. *Standard Edition*, vol. 13, pp. 150, 151.
16. Deleuze and Guattari correctly formulate a 'rule [. . .] applicable in all cases: the father and the mother exist only in fragments [. . .] directly coupled to [. . .] the elements of the political and historical situation – the soldier, the cop, the occupier, the collaborator, the radical, the resister, the boss, the boss' wife – which constantly break all triangulations [. . .] the family is never a microcosm in the sense of an autonomous figure'; *Anti-Oedipus*, trans. Robert Hurley, Mark Seem and Helen R. Lane (Minneapolis: University of Minnesota Press, 1983), p. 97. This is 'the double bind [. . .] between the family and the State – the Oedipus of familial authority and the Oedipus of social authority' (p. 81). Agamben's piecemeal paternal complex (*HS*, *SE*, *STA*) allies itself with the anti-oedipality of Deleuze and Guattari, who yet acquiesce: 'We are not saying that Oedipus [amounts] to nothing. *We are oedipalized* [. . .]. [P]sychoanalysis didn't invent [this] operation'; 'And to be sure, it is not a question of knowing whether or not the familial determinations or indeterminations play a role. *It is obvious that they do*' (pp. 67, 90, emphasis added). Deleuze and Guattari also understand that 'it is the problem of identifications' (p. 91).
17. 'This term [. . .] seems the most unsuitable one possible'; Carl Jung, *Freud*

and Psychoanalysis, trans. R. F. C. Hull (Princeton: Princeton University Press, 1961), p. 152.
18. *Standard Edition*, vol. 13, p. 157 n. 1.
19. *Standard Edition*, vol. 18, p. 129 (emphasis added).
20. *Standard Edition*, vol. 13, p. 144 (emphasis added).
21. *Standard Edition*, vol. 13, p. 22 (emphasis added).
22. Sovereign speciality functions like exceptional physiology. It is as if puberty or menstruation are sovereign expressions of one's living body; perhaps as *modes* of auto-affective self-modifications. (Cf. physiology vs. anatomy in *HS*.)
23. *Standard Edition*, vol. 13, pp. 20, 36 (emphasis added).
24. *Standard Edition*, vol. 13, p. 44, citing Frazer (emphasis added). Sovereignty is as much about nature or *phusis* as it is about duty or office.
25. *Standard Edition*, vol. 18, pp. 131, 133 (emphasis added).
26. This prescient phrase is Maureen Dowd's, referring to Donald Trump among his rivals for leadership during the Republican primaries leading up to the 2016 US presidential election (*New York Times*, 8 August 2015). The unconscious does not lie.
27. *Standard Edition*, vol. 13, p. 18 (emphasis added).
28. *Standard Edition*, vol. 13, p. 23, citing Wundt.
29. *Standard Edition*, vol. 13, p. 53, citing Frazer (emphasis added).
30. Cf. the body's accompanying auto-affection in *US* 28–9, 50–4.
31. *Standard Edition*, vol. 13, pp. 33–4 (emphasis added).
32. *Standard Edition*, vol. 13, p. 36. Cf. 'Taboos are imposed in order to secure against thieves the property of an individual' (pp. 19–20, citing Thomas).

26 Jacques Lacan

FRANCES L. RESTUCCIA

> The being of the subject [is] that which is there beneath the meaning. If we choose being, the subject disappears, it eludes us, it falls into non-meaning. If we choose meaning, the meaning survives only deprived of that part of non-meaning that is, strictly speaking, that which constitutes [. . .] the unconscious.
>
> Jacques Lacan, *Seminar XI*

> To bring to light – beyond every vitalism – the intimate interweaving of being and living: this is today certainly the task of thought (and politics).
>
> Giorgio Agamben, *The Use of Bodies*

Agamben only sporadically alludes to psychoanalysis and invokes psychoanalytic concepts. He does so most prominently in *Stanzas*, where he dedicates Part III to '*geniisque Henry Corbin et Jacques Lacan*' (S 61); refers to 'the Lacanian thesis according to which [. . .] the phantasm makes the pleasure suited to the desire', in order to elaborate a point in Plato about desire and pleasure relying on images in the soul (S 74); and takes up melancholia and fetishism – both of which, it is important to note, circumvent lack. But Agamben is by no means 'psychoanalytic'. He presents and employs melancholia and fetishism as paradigms for accessing the inaccessible (perhaps we can say that he plays with them). Melancholia, in Agamben, becomes an 'imaginative capacity to make an unobtainable object appear as if lost' so that it 'may be appropriated insofar as it is lost' (S 20), a strategy for saving the unsavable that evolves into his conception of the messianic. And, although Agamben is preoccupied with 'a zone of non-consciousness', he underscores that it is 'not the fruit of a removal, like the unconscious of psychoanalysis' (UB 64).[1] I will here indicate the crux of the distinction between Lacanian theory and Agamben's messianic vision, by showing that lack, intrinsic to psychoanalysis, is very deliberately elided in Agamben's way of thinking, as it is replaced by his emphasis on happening and falling, potentiality/impotentiality, for a serious political reason: to render inoperative the structure of the ban.

While this chapter is certainly meant to be a cross-reading of Lacanian theory and Agambenian messianism, it also aspires to expose a broad contemporary theoretical bifurcation to which critics who wander back and forth between the two paths seem oblivious. Here we have two irreconcilable philosophical lines of force – one privileging lack and the other non-lack – whose conflictuality for the most part has gone unnoticed as they have been blurred together. The project encapsulated in these few pages might be seen, then, as an extension of Agamben's own distinction in *Potentialities* between philosophers of 'transcendence' – Kant, Husserl, Levinas and Derrida – and philosophers of 'immanence' – Spinoza, Nietzsche, Foucault and Deleuze – with Heidegger dangling in the middle (*PO* 239).

I shall briefly explore the myriad ways in which Lacan and Agamben disagree – on the law, including the theological apparatus that undergirds it; ethics; death; language; antagonism or violence; eroticism and the sexual relation/fulfilment or love; and redemption – again, to illuminate and confront an aporia in contemporary theory between an emphasis on lack/negativity/Nothingness (installed by the law) and an antinomian opposition to all such negative conceptions.

THE LAW

Lacan understands the law in terms of the incest taboo that places a wedge between the budding subject and the mOther, what he calls the Name-of-the-Father or the paternal metaphor, a law akin to the Symbolic Order that effects a double relation to *das Ding*. In a more social vein, Agamben defines the law or sovereignty (*à la* Carl Schmitt) according to its ability to suspend law so that it may operate beyond its usual parameters, that is, to determine the exception to the rule (an exception that to Agamben has now become the rule). Whereas Lacan concentrates on the enabling of desiring subjectivity through the subject's transgressive encounter with *das Ding*, Agamben cares about power, its violence and its production as well as control of bare life. Apples and oranges?

Not quite. For, given that Lacanian law, or the paternal metaphor, generates not only desire but also *jouissance* that is situated both outside the law and included in it, just as the Symbolic Order is predicated on the excluded/included Real, one is led to wonder if the extimate structures of sovereignty/bare life and Lacanian law/its excess are commensurable. Such commensurability would enable us, paradoxically, to pose the question of whether these colliding positions on the law (Lacan upholds the law, while Agamben seeks to render it inoperative) provide the core of two radically different philosophies that produce a significant divide in contemporary theory.

But, first, I need to clarify desire's relation to *jouissance* in Lacanian theory. For true or 'radical desire' to occur, an experience of *jouissance*, an encounter with the Real, even with death in some form, is required. 'Realizing one's desire is necessarily always raised from the point of view of an absolute condition. [. . .] It is this trespassing of death on life that gives its dynamism to any question that attempts to find a formulation for the subject of the realization of desire.'[2] Organising *jouissance*, Lacanian law galvanises the subject's necessary relation to a lost/impossible object, an 'object' in the Real. Lacan upholds the law in order to facilitate an almost painfully blissful experience beyond it. Strutting through Kafka's door of the law, a door Agamben seeks to close, Lacan leaves behind what becomes fascinating. He in fact ends *The Four Fundamental Concepts* with a description of love as 'outside the limits of the law'.[3] An outside, almost always, requires a boundary that can be surpassed.[4]

By way of the barrier that Lacanian law constructs which results in a lure beckoning the subject into the Real, such law, then, we might propose, produces its own state of exception, the locus of an unspeakable, ineffable *jouissance*. Here, too, in Lacanian theory, as in Agamben's theory of sovereignty, everything outside the law – in depending on the limit of the law and insofar as the law depends on what it excludes – also exists within the domain of the law. We would seem, therefore, to have a valid parallel between sovereignty/bare life and the Symbolic Order/its excess, insofar as both sovereignty and the Symbolic turn out extimately to include their exclusions. In both cases, law might appear to be in force (most insidiously) especially when it is surpassed – pleasing Lacan but very much displeasing Agamben.

VEILING

But to tighten the juxtaposition of Lacan with Agamben, I want to refresh the terms of the relation of Lacanian law and desire, as it is 'agitated in the drive'[5] and so always involves some sort of positive run-in with *jouissance*, by conceiving of such law as a kind of veil or at least as what erects a veil-structure, which posits something hidden that serves as a (negative) foundation. While it might be (naively) assumed that Lacanian law is meant to preclude transgression, even desire, and certainly *jouissance*, it turns out to provoke transgression, incite desire and catalyse the quest for *jouissance*, just as a literal veil may be meant to deflect attention away from an erotic object underneath but has the inverse effect of producing that very attention and perhaps even the erotic object itself. In his *Écrits*, Lacan describes the always enigmatic phallus as in the place of the Other only insofar as it is veiled. In *Seminar V*, he explains the hysteric's provocation as what constitutes desire insofar as she flaunts a veil covering over the phallus. And this early notion of the veiled phallus evolves into Lacan's later conception of the (also covered) *objet a*. In *The Four Fundamental Concepts*, Lacan uses the metaphor of a veil in painting to convey his idea of desire in relation to its object cause, by referring to the classical tale of Zeuxis and Parrhasios. Parrhasios is victorious over Zeuxis in their art competition by painting on the wall a veil that is 'so lifelike' that Zeuxis asks him to unveil what has been painted behind it.[6] This is, for Lacan, a triumph (not of the eye but) of the gaze. 'Legal', linguistic and artistic formations conceal, or perhaps I should say produce, for Lacan, something beyond appearance – the gaze, the *objet a*, a symbol of the lack, a missing structural piece.

In stark contrast, Agamben privileges non-unveilability and a 'nudity without veils' (*NU* 88). And he urges us to 'liberate nudity from the patterns of thought that permit us to conceive of it solely in a privative [. . .] manner'. Striptease, for Agamben, ironically epitomises 'the impossibility of nakedness'; he designates it as 'the paradigm for our [unsatisfying] relationship with nudity', in that it is 'an event that never reaches its completed form' (*NU* 65). While Lacan's law stages a provisional and insatiable encounter with the gaze (defined as the subject's constitutive lack), Agamben's antinomian position, a stance against exclusions, assumes that the eye *can* be satiated by the naked object. Nothing is mysteriously hidden or missing, whereas in Lacan what is mysteriously missing is Nothing. And, while Lacan emphasises the impossibility of lasting satisfaction – in *Encore*, he writes that 'love is impossible and the sexual relationship drops into the abyss of nonsense'[7] – Agamben insists on our not missing the ongoing experience of the fulfilment of nudity. The 'matheme of nudity' is, Agamben states, 'simply this: *haecce!* there is nothing other than this' (*NU* 90), whereas the Lacanian approach is not to experience a revelation but to confront a remainder that gives the subject a sense of what does *not* appear. Lacanian theory describes and prioritises the pursuit of an 'object' that is unattainable – a process that is, I think, appropriately metaphorised by the striptease Agamben condemns.

THE THEOLOGICAL APPARATUS

Agamben blames our obsession with unveiling on the theological apparatus that presupposes 'the [corrupt] naked corporeality of human nature' (*NU* 64). He presents his 'ontology of nudity', as I call it, in order to defuse this apparatus by exposing 'the prestige of grace' and 'the chimeras of corrupt nature' as mechanisms of control. Nudity and clothing, in Agamben's view, must shake themselves free of their 'theological signature', to open up the possibility of a certain invaluable *dwelling*, through a messianic folding of apocalyptic time into *chronos* manifested in a 'special trembling' (*NU* 90) – a condition of nude (not bare) life that precludes the abandonment of *zoè* that turns it into bare life.

In contrast, in promulgating the 'law of the veil', Lacan may seem to perpetuate the theological apparatus that Agamben exposes as depriving us of an experience of simple nudity. Just as, for the Church, grace brings into being corrupt nature so that such nature may serve as grace's negative basis, in Lacanian theory the Law-of-the-Father gives rise to an ineffable, unspeakable, ungraspable Real foundation that houses an unobtainable 'object', the *objet a*, all of which leads us to sacrifice a *jouissance* considered to be dangerous, if not deadly, and thus blocks us from experiencing 'joy that never ends',[8] whereas in Agamben's messianic kingdom enjoyment of the object of desire may be sustained. The question posed here, then, is whether any structure that insists that one cannot perceive or experience things in all their 'opaque splendor' (*NU* 8) – nudity – is complicit with sovereignty's projection of a state of exception. I raise this question especially since Agamben regards ontological paradigms that set up a tension between the veil and what is veiled (as in Heidegger) as political paradigms. To Agamben, it is because of notions such as that man is open to a closedness that something like a *polis* in opposition to *zoè* is, unfortunately, possible. Likewise, a definition of 'man' as he who recognises himself as a non-man reinforces this same pernicious political paradigm that generates states of exception and bare life.

And although Lacan is an atheist, he admits in *Seminar VII* that we 'still cannot help hearing' the commandments, for 'in their indestructible character they prove to be the very laws of speech'.[9] His translation of the Fourth Commandment especially, 'On the Seventh Day, You Shall Rest', makes for an illuminating contrast with Agamben. Lacan reads the suspension and emptiness implied by the Sabbath as 'the sign of a gap, a beyond relative to every law of utility [. . .] that [. . .] has the most intimate relationship to something that', he adds, 'we are on the track of here'.[10] Kenneth Reinhard and Julia Lupton fill in the blank by understanding this Fourth Commandment as suggesting that the subject is created 'out of the *nihil* that interrupts the symbolic circuit of alienation'.[11] A linear trajectory crowned by a set-aside day of rest or arrest, however, is exactly the kind of temporal model that Agamben's messianic time – the holding of apocalyptic time within chronological time – is meant to correct. For, to Agamben, 'the messianic event has already happened, but its presence contains within itself another time, which stretches its *parousia*, not in order to defer it, but, on the contrary, to make it graspable' (*TR* 71). Agamben reads the Sabbath as 'not simply a day of repose that is added to the workweek (as our calendars would have it)' but as signifying 'a special time and a special activity' that italicises the '*continuity* [. . .] *between work and repose*' (*NU* 109, emphasis added). Agamben's move here is, as always, to void voids and eliminate spaces of Nothingness and lack, to fill in, to fulfil.

The redemption of the subject of religion, like that of the Lacanian subject, however, is always deferred – perhaps indefinitely in the case of the Lacanian subject. Žižek claims in *The Fragile Absolute* that psychoanalysis indicates that 'our lives involve a traumatic kernel beyond redemption' – 'there is a dimension of our being which forever resists redemption–deliverance'.[12] In contrast, Agamben theorises the redemption of every moment, insofar as the unsavable is what is saved: 'the ultimate figure of human and divine action appears where creation and salvation coincide in the unsavable' (*NU* 8).

And yet it is nothing less than Lacanian *ethics* that centres on insatiable desire. Lacan defines ethics as not ceding, or compromising on, one's desire – which, let us keep in mind, requires exceeding the law in a way that upholds it, engaging one's lack of being, experiencing a radical limit at the boundary of a certain lethal abyss, and hence establishing a relation to death/Nothing as well as to the register of the Real, all of which produces an extimate structure like that of sovereignty/bare life. Lacanian ethics enjoins us to participate in the leftover, in what is excluded from the Symbolic Order, to enter into/encounter (one might say) the exception or the ban. It may seem, therefore, that the very structure of the veil that Agamben is dedicated to rendering inoperative allows for the ethics of psychoanalysis. Agamben's 'ethics – understood as a proper dwelling place' – not only appears to clash with the Lacanian ethical injunction not to cede one's desire (lack), but situates Lacan at the end of a problematic metaphysical line that rests on negative ground, within a 'tradition of thought that conceives of the self-grounding of being as a negative foundation' (*LD* xiii).

EXPUNGING NEGATIVITY

Agamben condemns 'the ontological tradition in Western philosophy' that rests on 'negative ground' – from Aristotle, through Hegel, up to and including Heidegger – that has arrived finally and devastatingly at 'its final negative ground' of nihilism (*LD* xiii), beyond which Agamben clearly wishes to venture. He especially targets Heidegger, who conceptualises 'man' as 'the placeholder (*platzhalter*) of nothingness' (*LD* xii). Agamben challenges the importance of the Heideggerian 'being-toward-death', suggesting that instead 'simply to die [...] is precisely, for man, [...] his most *habitual* experience, his *ethos*'. He points out that a 'negativity [...] thoroughly intersects and dominates Dasein' (*LD* 2) – '[N]othingness is [...] the "veil" of being' (*LD* 60) – and he exposes the fallacy of the idea that 'the human being is truly such only when, in becoming Dasein, it is opened to Being', since 'this means that there is before or beneath it a non-human human being that can or must be transformed into Dasein' (*UB* 181).[13] Pushing back against all this, Agamben advocates an *ethos* that is no longer simply a *sigetics* (an evocation via the privative). Lacan's indebtedness especially to Heidegger would certainly support Lacan's placement on such a trajectory, which is, to Agamben, implicated in the sovereignty/bare life structure.

Agamben clearly prefers to think beyond a metaphysics that bases its speakability on the unspeakable (*LD* 88) – exactly the arrangement in Lacanian theory, which gives us a 'choice' between fullness of being (a phantasmatic image of wholeness implied by a bodily imago) and entry into the Symbolic or the flow of signifiers predicated on the sacrifice of that full being. Agamben favours instead an experience of language that is not based on a presupposed unattainable foundation. He looks to the poetic tradition for language that 'does not rest on the negative foundation of its own place' (*LD* 66). To reach such a dwelling place, we need to traverse 'negativity and scission' (*LD* 92) by embracing 'simply the *trite* words that we have' (*LD* 94).

Lacanian theory, in contrast, is riddled with separations, splits, lacks and ruptures – all of which Agamben's philosophy seeks to 'heal'. There is an antagonism at the core of things for Lacan, whereas Agamben attributes violence to the *construction* of a false foundation (especially of negativity/Nothing/lack) that hides the truth of our ungroundedness and uses that base for the sake of control. Consistent with the fracturing Agamben complains about, from a Lacanian standpoint we are alienated in language; the subject needs to separate from the Other or mOther; the subject is 'not'; two lacks must overlap for the subject to experience desire; there is no such thing as a sexual relation; and love is impossible – whereas for Agamben love is the not-to-be-missed 'experience of taking-place in a whatever singularity' (CC 25). Prizing the intimacy of a sexual relation that happens within strangeness, Agamben describes love profoundly and beautifully as living 'in intimacy with a stranger, not in order to draw him closer, or to make him known, but rather to keep him strange, remote: unapparent – so unapparent that his name contains him entirely. And, even in discomfort, to be nothing else, day after day, than the ever open place' (IP 61). In sum, Lacanian castration entails a sacrifice of *jouissance*, which, although it may be harnessed, remains forever ineffable and unspeakable. All such Lacanian concepts, from an Agambenian vantage point, sustain the mystical foundation of unspeakableness on which the logic and ethics of Western culture are, unfortunately, supposedly based, concealing and luring us away from the true *ethos* of dwelling and the use of language unmarked by negativity and death.

ETHICS

Having juxtaposed Lacanian theory with Agamben's philosophy, we are faced with two distinctive ethical outlooks: an ethics of not ceding desire supported by the law and an ethics of dwelling that neutralises the law. Agamben makes it possible to wriggle free of the limited Lacanian 'choice' of 'your money or your life' by showing a way to have both 'money' – or being – and 'life' – or living: living being. Avoiding the pitfall of lack (perversely?), he advocates such a 'form-of-life' – one in which *bios* or political life is poured fully into *zoè* or natural life, precluding their division.[14] Agamben wants the 'biopolitical body that is bare life [. . .] transformed into [. . .] a form of life that is wholly exhausted in bare life and a *bios* that is only its own *zoè*'. He uses the term 'form-of-life' to capture nude existence, life that, 'being its own form, remains inseparable from it' (HS 88).

Agamben's attack on formations that depend on fabricated negative undersides leads him to celebrate the power of potentiality that happens through fulfilling, without exhausting, impotentiality (Glenn Gould plays 'with his potential to not-play' [CC 36]). Agamben's vision incorporates the collapse of what is actualised, and even what never achieves actualisation, and in this way bypasses negativity or anything like the register of an extimately excluded Real. For there 'the metaphysical aporia shows its political nature' (HS 48). No traumatic kernel, no *das Ding*, no remainder or leftover, or anything outside the Open – therefore no state of exception or bare life – exists in Agamben's messianic kingdom. Instead, we have nudity, a messianic conjoining of *kairos* and *chronos*, excluding and therefore abandoning nothing. A blessed 'letting be', rejoicing 'in itself', Agamben's simple, non-unveilable nudity (*NU* 85) razes the sovereignty/bare life hierarchy.

NOTES

1. In *Stanzas*, Agamben charges psychoanalysis with 'a complete translation of unconscious symbolic language into conscious sign' (*S* 145).
2. Jacques Lacan, *The Ethics of Psychoanalysis 1959–1960*, ed. Jacques-Alain Miller, trans. Dennis Porter (New York: W. W. Norton, 1992), p. 294.
3. Jacques Lacan, *The Four Fundamental Concepts of Psycho-Analysis*, ed. Jacques Alain-Miller, trans. Alan Sheridan (New York: W. W. Norton, 1981), p. 276.
4. Agamben's Open, however, is an openness without a closedness.
5. Lacan, *Four Fundamental Concepts*, p. 243.
6. Lacan, *Four Fundamental Concepts*, p. 103.
7. Jacques Lacan, *Encore: On Feminine Sexuality/The Limits of Love and Knowledge 1972–1973*, ed. Jacques-Alain Miller, trans. Bruce Fink (New York: W. W. Norton, 1998), p. 87.
8. Agamben concludes his chapter 'The Joy That Never Ends' in *Stanzas* with the idea that 'in the poetry of (in)spiring love [as in Dante's *Vita Nuova*] [. . .] desire, supported by a conception that constitutes the sole coherent attempt in Western thought to overcome the metaphysical fracture of presence, celebrates, for perhaps the last time in the history of Western poetry, its joyful and inexhaustible "spiritual union" with its own object of love, with that "joy that never ends"' – as though offering a theory of *jouissance* (*S* 130).
9. Lacan, *Ethics of Psychoanalysis*, p. 174.
10. Lacan, *Ethics of Psychoanalysis*, p. 81.
11. Kenneth Reinhard and Julia Lupton, 'The Subject of Religion: Lacan and the Ten Commandments', *Diacritics* 33.2 (2003): 85.
12. Slavoj Žižek, *The Fragile Absolute – or, Why is the Christian Legacy Worth Fighting For?* (London: Verso, 2000), p. 98.
13. In *Agamben and Indifference* (London: Rowman & Littlefield International, 2013), William Watkin acknowledges the divide between Agamben and Heidegger in describing Agamben's sense of 'being's full communicability as the indifference between the ontico and the ontological'. Watkin deduces from this that Agamben is making a 'radical critique of Heidegger' (p. 102). In *Homo Sacer*, Agamben, however, entertains the possibility that the Heideggerian concept of *Ereignis* might divest being of 'all sovereignty'. But he quickly decides that, while it may 'push the aporia of sovereignty to the limit', the *Ereignis* (like Melville's Bartleby) is not completely free 'from its ban' (*HS* 48).
14. Avoiding (disavowing) lack or castration is a perverse move in

psychoanalysis, as is playing with the law. Agamben hopes that 'One day humanity will play with law just as children play with disused objects, not in order to restore them to their canonical use but to free them from it for good' (*SE* 64). Agamben unequivocally advocates perversion. In 'The Glorious Body' he explains that an organ of the body 'whose organicity has been suspended' can take on a new use through 'so-called perversion', since such novelty is what such activity achieves each time it uses 'the organs of the nutritive and reproductive functions and turn[s] them – in the very act of using them – away from their physiological meaning, toward a new and more human operation' (*NU* 102). Even sexually perverse play would seem to be a beneficial way of circumventing the law, allowing the body to exhibit its 'potentiality' in a way that 'removes the spell from it and opens it up to a new possible common use' (*NU* 103). As Kevin Attell points out in *Giorgio Agamben: Beyond the Threshold of Deconstruction* (New York: Fordham University Press, 2014), 'For Agamben, beginning with the 1978 essay "In Playland," the experience of play – in the sense of a child absorbed in play – is an index or a prefiguration of what he calls a "truly political action," a praxis that has liberated itself from the metaphysical powers of law and sovereignty, a praxis which in its immediacy becomes a "means without end"' (p. 9).

27 Karl Marx

JESSICA WHYTE

In the concluding volume of his *Homo Sacer* project, *The Use of Bodies*, Giorgio Agamben briefly turns to Marx to distinguish his own account of what he terms 'inoperativity' from a Marxist account of production. Accepting Marx's account of the decisive relationship between production, social relationships and culture, he nonetheless suggests that Marx neglected the forms of *inoperativity* that exist within every mode of production, opening it to a new use. 'One-sidedly focused on the analysis of forms of production, Marx neglected the analysis of the forms of inoperativity', he writes, 'and this lack is certainly at the bottom of some of the aporias of his thought, in particularly as concerns the definition of human activity in the classless society' (*UB* 94). Agamben's reference to Marx is typically brief and enigmatic, and he neither expands on the claim that Marx, the thinker of the classless society, neglected inoperativity, nor identifies the aporias to which he refers. Nonetheless, in these brief and enigmatic remarks we find the crystallisation of a position developed in works stretching back to Agamben's first book, *The Man Without Content*. Marx remains a subterranean influence on Agamben's thought, and the diverse accounts of his work throughout Agamben's *oeuvre* oscillate between critiques of his supposed productivism and praise for his thematisation of a non-substantive, self-negating subject.[1] It is in the course of this oscillation that Agamben has clarified his own accounts of both political subjectivity and inoperativity.

'Marx', Agamben charges in *The Man Without Content*, 'thinks of man's being as production' (*MC* 49). This early claim that Marx remains trapped within a metaphysical account of human praxis is taken up forcefully more than thirty years later, in the 2005 essay 'The Work of Man', where Agamben examines Aristotle's attempt to determine whether the human *qua* human has a work (*ergon*). In raising the possibility that 'man' – in contrast to the flute player, the carpenter or the shoemaker – may lack a specific work, or vocation, Aristotle, in Agamben's view, signals the possibility of breaking with the privileging of work and production – only to abandon it. The question of whether the human has a work is of decisive importance for Agamben, as it also determines whether we can be assigned a proper nature or essence.[2] Ultimately, Agamben argues, Aristotle identifies the work of man in a particular form of life – the life according to *logos*.[3] The work of man depends on the 'actualization of the vital rational potentiality', and both politics and ethics will thus be defined through the participation in this function.[4] Consequently, politics is transformed into a work, which coincides with a metaphysical task: 'the realization of man as a rational living being'.[5]

It is within this legacy that Agamben positions Marx's thought. Referring to the 1844 *Economic and Philosophical Manuscripts*, he writes: 'the thought of Marx, which seeks the realization of man as a generic being (*Gattungswesen*), represents a renewal and radicalization of the Aristotelian project'.[6] This renewal, he suggests, implies two aporias: first, the subject of the work of man is an 'unassignable class', a class without a specific vocation, which negates itself insofar as it represents a specific activity; second, 'the activity of man in the classless society is impossible or, in any case, extremely difficult to define'.[7] Here, we find an earlier iteration of the claim that is made in passing in *The Use of Bodies*. In what follows, I situate this enigmatic account of the aporias of Marx's thought in the context of Agamben's broader engagements with Marx and Marxism. In doing so, I aim to excavate the extent of Agamben's proximity, as well as his divergence from, the 'father of communism'.

THE UNASSIGNABLE CLASS

Most socialists who believed themselves to have been Marxists, the Hungarian intellectual G. M. Tamás provocatively claims, have in fact been Rousseauists. Singling out E. P. Thompson, Tamás argues that, rather than seeing the 'Faustian-demonic' expropriative power of capital as the condition of possibility of a class 'with nothing to lose but its chains', these socialists have instead valorised the 'actually existing' working class and its culture, habits and social values. A central feature of this Rousseauian socialism, as Tamas frames it, is its affirmation of the auto-poetic quality of the working class, which, as Thompson famously put it, 'did not rise like the sun at an appointed time [but] was present at its own making'.[8] Framing this opposition in the starkest of terms, Tamás writes: '[w]hereas Karl Marx and Marxism aim at the *abolition* of the proletariat, Thompson aims at the *apotheosis* and triumphant survival of the proletariat'.⁹ If we accept Tamás's dichotomy, Agamben is firmly on its Marxist, rather than Rousseauist, side.

Agamben's concern with a redemption that would also be a self-negation is present as early as his 1970 essay 'Sui limiti della violenza' ('On the Limits of Violence'). There, Agamben finds in the work of Marx and Engels the single criterion by which violence could be called revolutionary: 'Only those who consciously confront their own negation through violence may shake of "all the muck of ages" and begin the world anew', he writes, citing *The German Ideology*.¹⁰ Echoing Marx and Engels' argument that only through revolution will the proletariat become fit to found a new society, Agamben argues that only a class which experiences its own negation in the negation of the ruling class is capable of opening a new historical age.

Agamben returns to this theme in *The Time that Remains*, where he identifies a shared self-negating impetus in the Pauline messianic subject and the Marxian proletariat. The proletariat, like the 'new creature' who must die to the old world to be granted a new life, is a self-negating subject, Agamben argues, which must realise itself by suppressing itself. Agamben relies on the Apostle Paul, for whom social conditions and identities are nullified by the messianic vocation, which strips them of meaning while leaving them factually unchanged. It is this account of the hollowing out of juridically constituted identities and social positions by the messianic event that Agamben sees as analogous to the 'great transformation introduced into the political fabric by the domination of the bourgeoisie' (*TR* 29). The bourgeoisie, he suggested, dissolves all the fixed privileges of particular estates, and, in so doing, reveals the *contingency* of social positions and the split between individuals and their social existences.

As long as estate persisted, and social positions were inherited and grounded in a natural or theological order, the individual was entirely defined by his conditions of existence; 'for instance', as Marx and Engels put it, 'a nobleman always remains a nobleman, a commoner always a commoner, apart from his other relationships, a quality inseparable from his individuality'.¹¹ It is only with the emergence of the proletariat that 'the accidental nature of the conditions of life for the individual' become starkly apparent.¹² The revolutionary vocation of the proletariat, Agamben argues, is therefore not a new factical vocation but the nullification, or hollowing out, of every vocation. Thus, 'the fact that the proletariat ends up over time being identified with a determinate social class – the working class that claims prerogatives and rights for itself – is', he argues, 'the worst misunderstanding of Marxian thought' (*TR* 31).

OFFICE

I have written elsewhere about the way in which Agamben's earlier accounts of the hollowing out of vocations tends to conflate the demise of class identities and cultures with the end of class itself, and thus to obscure the nullifying power of capitalist abstraction.[13] From this perspective, Agamben's more recent work on office, which is motivated by a concern with the putting to work of abstract human capacities rather than with substantive identities, appears more fruitful for thinking through a reality in which, as Tamás notes, '[c]lass as an economic reality exists, and it is as fundamental as ever, although it is culturally and politically almost extinct'.[14]

In *Opus Dei*, Agamben defines *office* as a zone of indistinction between being and acting – a *functional being*. Using the priest as an exemplary figure of an office holder, Agamben points to what he sees as the strange circularity of inhabiting an office: 'The priest must carry out his office insofar as he is a priest and he is a priest insofar as he carries out his office' (*OD* 87). What is significant about this account of office is that the *being* of the one who inhabits an office is insignificant from the point of view of the effectiveness of the tasks he carries out. Drawing on debates about whether the sacraments were effective if delivered by a sinful priest, Agamben notes that (insofar as the effectiveness of the sacraments is concerned) the priest himself is insubstantial, and his character a matter of indifference, as he is merely the instrument of God's will. The priest is what Thomas Aquinas termed an 'instrumental cause', which 'acts according to its nature only in so far as it is moved by a principle agent who uses it as an instrument' (*OD* 52). Being merely an instrument, his own qualities become a matter of indifference. The problem with inhabiting an office is therefore not the problem of substantive identities but an altogether different problem of how an abstract potentiality is instrumentalised or put to work. Office is defined not by substance but by command.

It was Hegel who developed an account of office according to which office holders sacrifice their own particular interests and subjective ends in order to 'find their satisfaction in the performance of their duties, and that alone'.[15] Hegel depicts the civil service as the universal class, which is defined by the mutual relation of an office and an individual – a relation that is established only by the decision of the sovereign. In contrast to the naturalised vocations of the feudal order, the relation of an individual to the office he inhabits is not intrinsic but contingent. Nonetheless, the civil servant makes of his relationship to his work a duty and the 'main interest of his spiritual and particular existence'.[16] In his own critique of the *Philosophy of Right*, which focuses on refuting this account of the bureaucracy as the universal class, Marx casts the bureaucratic spirit as a thoroughly theological and Jesuit spirit. 'The bureaucracy', he writes, 'is the republic as priest.'[17]

Agamben's own account of the priest as the exemplary office holder has wider political significance. The spectre of Eichmann hovers over his account of office, yet his critique is not simply of a model of the state functionary whose paradigmatic status is increasingly being eclipsed by the entrepreneur, the precarious worker and the unemployed. Rather, through the figure of the office holder, Agamben is attempting to theorise a form of praxis through which human capacities are instrumentalised and put to work. To the extent that his key concern in his more recent works is with praxis that is transformed into being, he is closer than ever to Marx, for whom the 'substance of value is not at all the particular natural substance, but rather objectified labour'.[18]

Just as Agamben stresses that the potentiality of the one who inhabits an office must be made effective by an external will, the central feature of capitalist wage labour, as Marx defines it, is that the individual worker cannot put her potential to work, cannot actualise it, because she is separated from the means of production. 'The worker's labour is the mere *possibility* or potentiality of value-positing activity which exists only as a capacity, as a resource in the bodilyness of the worker', Marx writes.[19] In order to realise her potential, the worker must therefore serve as an instrument, subjected to the will of the capitalist. When it enters into a relation of command with capital, this potentiality is objectified; 'it modifies its own form', as Marx puts it, 'and changes from activity into being'.[20]

Significantly, for Marx, neither 'capitalist' nor 'worker' is a substantive identity. Rather, they are personifications of social relations. In Agamben's terms, the proletarian's 'very being is factical and functional', referring to 'a praxis that defines and actualizes it' (*OD* 54). Thus, Marx notes that a capitalist who loses his capital ceases to be a capitalist, and a worker who ceases to work loses the quality of being a worker.[21] At first, this would appear to be an account of the proletariat that defines it *through the act of working* itself. Yet Marx's examples of a worker who ceases to be a worker, by *stealing* or *inheriting* money, suggest a new freedom not merely from labour itself, but from the *compulsion to sell one's labour power* in order to put it to work. That the worker is faced with such compulsion is no guarantee that she will find a buyer. The unemployed worker may be free of work, but she is nonetheless faced with perpetual insecurity and the compulsion to sell her labour power in order to survive.

For Agamben too, inoperativity cannot simply be equated with the absence of work. In modernity, he notes, it has not been possible to think inoperativity except in the form of the suspension of labour. The feast, for instance, is viewed as a temporary suspension of productive activity, yet Agamben stresses that it is also a state in which what *is* done 'becomes undone, rendered inoperative, liberated and suspended from its "economy", from the reasons and purposes that define it during the weekdays'.[22] Thus, inoperativity is not simple inactivity. Rather, in it the activities may continue but they are freed from the instrumentality that usually defines them. While Agamben announces that inoperativity has replaced work as the fundamental ontological question of the present, he also stresses that 'this inoperativity can, however, be deployed only through a work'.[23] This definition of an activity that is no longer subjected to the duty, or the compulsion, to work would seem to bring us close to the account that Marx and Engels provide of activity in the classless society. To understand Agamben's break with Marx, we must now return to those 'aporias' that Agamben identifies with regard to this activity.

THE APORIAS OF ACTIVITY IN THE CLASSLESS SOCIETY

In the early 1950s Hannah Arendt prepared manuscripts on Marx's thought, which exerted a strong influence on Agamben. Arendt identifies Marx's unprecedented innovation as the 'glorification of labor'.[24] Marx, she suggests, was the first thinker able to philosophically grasp the central event of modernity: the political emancipation of the working classes. Yet, she argues, Marx's thought is animated by a fundamental contradiction: on the one hand, he overturns the traditional definition of the human as *animal rationale* in order to make labour the 'most human and productive of man's activities'.[25] On the other, he is convinced that the revolution will abolish labour. Marx, she writes, 'defines man as the *animal laborans* then leads him into a society in which this greatest and most human power is no longer necessary'.[26]

For Arendt, this seeming aporia is connected to what she depicts as the one truly utopian aspect of Marx's thought: his account of the abolition of labour. And yet, she writes, 'if utopia means that this society has no *topos*, no geographical and historical place on earth, it is simply not utopian: its geographical *topos* is Athens and its place in history is the fifth century before Christ'.²⁷ This may seem a peculiar claim, given, as Arendt is only too aware, that the freedom of those citizens who devoted their lives to 'walking and talking in the market-place [. . .] going to the gymnasium [. . .] attending meetings of the theatre, or [. . .] judging conflicts between citizens' was premised on their rule over slaves.²⁸ In contrast to Greek citizens – for whom the freedom from labour 'was based on rulership of slaves as its pre-political condition' – the distinguishing character of Marx's 'utopia', as Arendt defines it, is that he thought both freedom and the abolition of labour under the condition of universal equality.²⁹

On this point, Agamben is closer to Marx than to Arendt. The exclusion of 'necessity', or the maintenance of biological life, from the *polis* is, in his view, the abandonment that structures all subsequent Western politics, rendering it biopolitical from its inception. And like Marx, Agamben envisages a world, which he tends to locate at the end of history, in which humanity will be freed from the compulsion to labour. Despite this proximity to Marx's thought, Agamben appears to accept Arendt's argument that this thought is marked by a basic contradiction, or aporia: Marx elevates the activity of labour and therefore makes necessity, rather than freedom, central to human nature, meaning that 'the free, laborless man who is supposed to emerge after the end of history would simply have lost his most essentially human capacity'.³⁰

But how does Arendt understand Marx's abolition of labour? Marx, she argues, seeks the abolition of humanity's metabolism with nature, and of the work of craftsmanship. 'Hardly anything could be more revealing of Marx's original impulse', she writes, citing *The German Ideology*, 'than the fact that he banishes from his future society not only the labor that was executed by slaves in antiquity, but also the activities of the *banausoi*, the craftsmen and artists: "In a communist society there are no painters, only men who, among other things, paint".'³¹ Here, the citation that Arendt takes from *The German Ideology* to illustrate her point in fact contradicts her claim that Marx banishes the *activities* of the craftsman from his future society. Rather, Marx and Engels stress here that what is banished in a communist society is not the *activity* of painting but the division of labour that makes this activity the specific vocation of 'the painter', of whom, Marx and Engels stress, 'the very name amply expresses the narrowness of his professional development and his dependence on the division of labor'.³²

What will be abolished under communism, Marx and Engels suggest, is not the activity of painting, but the 'exclusive concentration of artistic talent in particular individuals, and its suppression in the broad mass [which] is a consequence of the division of labor'.³³ In a situation marked by the division of labour, individuals are subordinate to distinctive modes of activity; the painter, for instance, is always a painter, defined by a fixed vocation, and his capacity to paint is premised on the manual work of others, just as much as the freedom of the Greek citizen was premised on the labour of the slave.

This understanding of communism as a state in which forms of activity persist but are stripped of their obligatory form, and their place in the division of labour, is clearest in another, more famous, passage of *The German Ideology*, which reads:

> as soon as the division of labour comes into being, each man has a particular, exclusive sphere of activity which is forced upon him and from which he cannot escape. He is a hunter, a fisherman, a shepherd, or a critical critic, and must remain so if he does not want to lose his means of livelihood.[34]

In communism, as Marx and Engels describe it, things are quite otherwise. It is not, as Arendt suggests, that the activities of hunting, fishing, herding sheep or criticising would be entirely abolished. What would be abolished, rather, is the division of labour and the assignment of individuals to fixed vocations. It is this freedom from the division of labour that would make it possible, as Marx and Engels famously write, 'for me to do one thing today and another tomorrow, to hunt in the morning, fish in the afternoon, rear cattle in the evening, criticize after dinner, just as I have a mind, without ever becoming hunter, fisherman, shepherd or critic'.[35] While fishing is an activity chosen from a number of potential ones, to be a fisherman is to be a 'functional being' whose life is determined by a position in the division of labour. Although the activities may be the same in both cases, one is a free expression of human potentiality, which exposes potentiality in the act, in Agamben's terms; the other is human activity subjected to the compulsion of an external will (*UB* 94).

What, then, of Arendt's claim that this '"utopian" side of Marx's teachings constitutes a basic self-contradiction'?[36] Marx saw the tendency to reduce socially necessary labour time as the historical justification of capitalism, but he did not believe either that the human metabolism with nature would come to an end, or that the activities of the craftsman would cease. In their critique of the division of labour, Marx and Engels prefigure important aspects of Agamben's account of the 'essential inoperativity of man', which he stresses 'is not to be understood as the cessation of all activity, but as an activity that consists in making human works and productions inoperative, opening them to a new possible use'.[37] Just like the abolition of labour that Marx and Engels wrote of, Agamben's inoperativity is not simply an idleness but a human activity freed of instrumentality and a necessary relation to an end. What would such an activity look like? Perhaps, if we were to envisage it in a bucolic key, we would 'hunt in the morning, fish in the afternoon, rear cattle in the evening, criticize after dinner' – all 'without ever becoming hunter, fisherman, shepherd or critic'.[38]

NOTES

1. See Jessica Whyte, '"Man Produces Universally": Praxis and Production in Agamben and Marx', in Jernej Habjan and Jessica Whyte (eds), *(Mis)readings of Marx in Continental Philosophy* (Basingstoke: Palgrave Macmillan, 2014), pp. 178–94.
2. Giorgio Agamben, 'The Work of Man', in Matthew Calarco and Steven DeCaroli (eds), *Giorgio Agamben: Sovereignty and Life* (Stanford: Stanford University Press, 2007), p. 2.
3. Agamben, 'The Work of Man', p. 5.
4. Agamben, 'The Work of Man', p. 5.
5. Agamben, 'The Work of Man', p. 6.
6. Agamben, 'The Work of Man', p. 6.
7. Agamben, 'The Work of Man', p. 6.
8. E. P. Thompson, *The Making of the English Working Class* (New York: Pantheon Books, 1963), p. 9.
9. G. M. Tamás, 'Telling the Truth about Class', in *Socialist Register 2006: Telling the Truth* (London: Merlin Press, 2005), p. 229.
10. Giorgio Agamben, 'On the Limits of Violence', ed. Lorenzo Fabbri, trans. Elisabeth Fay, *Diacritics* 39.4 (2009): 108–9.
11. Karl Marx and Friedrich Engels, *The German Ideology* (Moscow: Progress Publishers, 3rd edn, 1976), p. 87.
12. Marx and Engels, *The German Ideology*, p. 87.
13. Jessica Whyte, *Catastrophe and Redemption: The Political Thought of Giorgio Agamben* (Albany: SUNY Press, 2013); Whyte, 'Man Produces Universally'.
14. Tamás, 'Telling the Truth about Class', p. 255.
15. Georg Wilhelm Friedrich Hegel, *Elements of the Philosophy of Right*, ed. Allen W. Wood, trans. H. B. Nisbet (Cambridge: Cambridge University Press, 8th edn, 1991), p. 333.
16. Hegel, *Elements of the Philosophy of Right*, p. 333.
17. Karl Marx, *Critique of Hegel's Philosophy of Right*, in *Selected Writings*, ed. David McLellan (Oxford: Oxford University Press, 2000), p. 37.
18. Karl Marx, *Grundrisse: Foundations of the Critique of Political Economy*, trans. Martin Nicolaus (London: Penguin, 1993), p. 299.
19. Marx, *Grundrisse*, p. 298.
20. Marx, *Grundrisse*, p. 300.
21. Marx, *Grundrisse*, p. 300.

22. Giorgio Agamben, 'Elements for a Theory of Destituent Power', trans. Stephanie Wakefield (2013), https://livingtogetherintheheartofthedesert.files.wordpress.com/2014/02/agamben-elements-for-a-theory-of-destituent-power-1.pdf (accessed 24 April 2017).
23. Agamben, 'Elements for a Theory of Destituent Power'.
24. Hannah Arendt, 'Karl Marx and the Tradition of Western Thought', *Social Research* 69.2 (2002): 283.
25. Hannah Arendt, *The Human Condition*, ed. Margaret Canovan (Chicago: University of Chicago Press, 2nd edn, 1999), p. 105.
26. Arendt, *The Human Condition*, p. 105.
27. Arendt, 'Karl Marx and the Tradition of Western Thought', p. 292.
28. Arendt, 'Karl Marx and the Tradition of Western Thought', p. 293.
29. Arendt, 'Karl Marx and the Tradition of Western Thought', p. 292.
30. Arendt, 'Karl Marx and the Tradition of Western Thought', p. 295.
31. Arendt, 'Karl Marx and the Tradition of Western Thought', p. 293.
32. Marx and Engels, *The German Ideology*, p. 418.
33. Marx and Engels, *The German Ideology*, p. 417.
34. Marx and Engels, *The German Ideology*, p. 53. For a brilliant reading of this passage, see Charles Barbour, *The Marx Machine: Politics, Polemics, Ideology* (Lanham, MD: Rowman & Littlefield, 2012).
35. Marx and Engels, *The German Ideology*, p. 53.
36. Arendt, 'Karl Marx and the Tradition of Western Thought', p. 294.
37. Agamben, 'Elements for a Theory of Destituent Power'.
38. Marx and Engels, *The German Ideology*, p. 53.

28 Antonio Negri

INGRID DIRAN

READING AS USE

Agamben describes his posture as a reader as one of seeking a text's *Entwicklungsfähigkeit*, or capacity for elaboration.[1] In examining Agamben's practices of reading, we can attend to the opposite phenomenon: the counter-elaboration that a text, in having being read by the philosopher, performs upon Agamben's own thought. This reciprocal elaboration might constitute a paradigm for Agamben's *use* of reading, according to his own idiosyncratic definition of use as an event in the middle voice, in which (according to a definition of Benveniste) the subject '*effects* an action only in *affecting itself* (*il effectue en s'affectant*)' (*UB* 28). With this definition in mind, we could say that Agamben *effects* a text (he writes) only to the extent that he is also *affected* by another text (he reads). This is why Agamben's position as a reader proves particularly important to any assessment of his work, quite aside from the problem of influence or intellectual genealogy.

For this same reason, however, assessing Agamben's relation to Antonio Negri – a figure with whom, by most measures, he is at odds – poses an unexpected challenge: how can Agamben's thought be a *use* of Negri? Answering this question means not only assessing the critical distance between the two thinkers, but also taking this distance as a measure, in the Spinozan sense, of *mutual affection*.

Indeed, Spinoza's relevance here is far from incidental, not only because Negri and Agamben both avow his centrality to their respective projects, but also because their divergent readings of Spinoza correspond to, and reverberate in, their differences across a number of theoretical domains. For Negri, whose *The Savage Anomaly* (1991) offers a virtuosic reading of Spinoza's metaphysics and political (a)theology, Spinoza's most lasting innovation consists in distinguishing between potentiality (*potentia*) and power (*potestas*), which Negri famously reimagines as an asymmetrical struggle between constituent and constituted power. For Agamben, by contrast, Spinoza offers a paradigm of life as absolute immanence in the form of *conatus*, a striving to persevere in one's being that becomes a paradigm, later, for Agamben's theorisation of the use of self and of the body. Moreover, it is precisely Spinoza's philosophical and philological[2] attention to the ways in which 'potentiality coincides with actuality and inoperativeness with work' (*PO* 235) that prompts Agamben to invoke Spinoza against Negri.

As Kevin Attell notes, Negri and Agamben travelled a largely parallel philosophical course throughout the 1980s and 1990s,[3] before reaching a turning (or breaking) point with their synchronous rereading of Foucault's late work on biopolitics. Furthermore, Negri's hostility towards Agamben's idiosyncratic reading of Aristotle's *dynamis* (potentiality) and especially *adynamia* (impotentiality) is symmetrically inverted in Agamben's privileging of use over productivity and destituent potential over constituent power. Let us turn, then, to Negri's strategic inter-articulation of constituent potential and production before considering Agamben's displacement of these terms.

CONSTITUENT POWER

Negri begins his seminal 1992 work *Il Potere Costituente* (translated into English as *Insurgencies: Constituent Power and the Modern State* in 1999) with the legal biography of a limit-concept: constituent power. One need not venture too far into this story before certain complications arise, antinomies and anomalies which, for Negri, mark nothing less than the crisis of juridical thought. From the perspective of the law, he explains, constituent power appears as 'the power to establish a new juridical arrangement, to regulate juridical relationships within a new community'.[4] But this, Negri asserts, 'is an extremely paradoxical definition: a power rising from nowhere organizes law'.[5]

Of signal importance here are the logical games that the law plays to remediate constituent power as a crisis of its own legitimacy. As Negri puts it,

> constituent power must itself be reduced to the norm of the production of law; it must be incorporated into the established power. Its expansiveness is only shown as an interpretative norm, as a form of control of the State's constitutionality, as an activity of constitutional revision. Eventually, a pale reproduction of constituent power can be seen at work in referendums, regulatory activities, and so on, operating intermittently within well-defined limits and procedures.[6]

In other words, the relation of sovereign power to constituent power is primarily *reductive*. Ironically, however, this same reduction enables constituent power to distinguish itself from the law by virtue of two qualities: expansiveness and intensity.

How, then, does sovereignty perform its 'sovereign reduction'? Negri answers by citing three opposed but complicit schools of legal thought. First, there are jurists such as Georg Jellinek and Hans Kelsen, who see constituent power as *transcendent*; this strategy, while acknowledging the magnitude of the constituent, nevertheless negates its persistence *within* the state. Conversely, jurists such as John Rawls imagine constituent power as an *immanent* proto-legality which can be easily reabsorbed within existing structures. Finally, there are jurists such as Hermann Heller and Ferdinand Lassalle, who imagine constituent power neither as immanent, nor as transcendent, but as fully coextensive with the state. What a survey of such contradictory legal theories makes clear is that whatever the strategy in play, its aim is to *neutralise* any force that remains heterogeneous to, and in excess of, itself.

By the time Negri turns to Carl Schmitt, it is to situate Schmitt's concept of the exception within the larger context of the neutralisation of constituent power. Thus the sovereign 'decision' forms only one variation on the same legal theme: in Schmitt's work, says Negri, constituent power's 'immanence [in the juridical system] is so profound that at first sight the distinction between constituent and constituted power fades, so that constituent power appears according to its nature as originary power or counterpower, as historically determined strength, as a set of needs, desires, and singular determinations'.[7] This tightened linkage of constituent and sovereign power is only the most extreme strategy for enacting the sovereign reduction. Schmitt's concept of the exception is, in this way, less a paradigm than a declension of a single sovereign verb: to neutralise.

Having laid bare the law's aporetic strategies, Negri now presents his counter-image of constituent power. Importantly, this counter-image is not merely juxtaposed to the legal theories, but gleaned from the shadows cast by their logic. Constituent power, a legal opacity, is 'the mark of a radical expression of democratic will'. In perhaps his most resonant formulation, Negri writes: 'the praxis of constituent power has been the door through which the multitude's democratic will (and consequently the social question) has entered the political system – destroying constitutionalism or in any case significantly weakening it'.[8] At this point, the tables begin to turn as constituent power weakens constituted power to the point of destruction. Far from being neutralised upon the plane of juridical representation, constituent power proves both its expansiveness and its intensity in a manner that sovereignty cannot but look upon as savage. Breaking definitively with law and speaking for what he will later call the 'political monster',[9] or *multitude*, Negri defines constituent power in a way that not only resonates far beyond his critique of legal theory, but also offers in miniature both a refutation of extant legal theories of constituent power and a mode of theorising a savage legal anomaly by affirming its enigma. In a string of explosive verbs – 'burst apart, breaks, interrupts, unhinges'[10] – Negri characterises the transcendence of constituent power in a way that cannot be reduced to an exception and that, instead, turns the thesis of sovereign exceptionality against itself. Furthermore, the 'preformative and imaginative' dimensions of constituent power no longer prefigure the state, but anticipate 'the democratic totality' whose order is that of an emergent and productive temporality. This pregnant moment – this democratic *kairos* – is one whose full legitimation arrives only in a time still to come.[11] Finally, in obvious distinction from the time of the law which everywhere seeks precedence (past explains present), the anteriority of constituent power *awaits* legibility. It is best grasped in the tense which forms the name of the important journal that Negri published around the same time as *Il Potere Costituente*: the 'future anterior'.

If we note, in turn, that Negri describes this future anteriority as a 'constitutive temporality' (one that power wishes to 'block'), we also see that constituent power not only preforms democracy, but also partakes of the power and time of production. Indeed, democracy will, for this reason, be tightly bound up with production: it is that which 'produces and reproduces itself everywhere and continually', even while remaining heterogeneous to its representation within the time of bourgeois history. This productive telos, ultimately, enables Negri to define constituent power without reference to the law. For constituent power is, quite simply, power which *constitutes*. Herein consists both its absoluteness and its inexhaustibility. Constituent power is, for Negri, a power of the common that constitutes (or produces) not order, but power.

At this point, in anticipation of a turn to Agamben, we might reassess the significance of Negri's remark that 'the praxis of constituent power has been the door through which the multitude's democratic will (and consequently the social question) has entered the political system'. For it is now legible, especially given the temporal turn his argument takes, as a modification of Walter Benjamin's dictum that each moment is 'the small door through which the Messiah can enter' (qtd. in *TR* 71). Here, having transposed this statement into the terms of constituent power, Negri draws the following analogy: constituent power is to the existing legal system and its temporality what the messiah is to linear time and the historical continuum. In this way, Negri translates the messiah's ability to redeem the present as constituent power's ceaseless disruption of systemic 'equilibrium'. That such a notion remains operative in Negri's philosophy of history is confirmed as soon as a few lines later when he states: 'power becomes an immanent dimension of history, an actual temporal horizon'; and, on the following page: 'the crisis of the concept of constituent power will not reside only in its relationship to constituted power [...] [but] will also concern the concept of representation'.[12]

Beginning with a paraphrase of a legal logic that it subsequently destroys and displaces, the opening chapter of *Insurgencies* might be said to contain in microcosm the fundamental lineaments not only of Negri's politics, but also of his ontology and philosophy of history. We can summarise his claims as theses: (1) constituent power is generative of both a politics and a temporality – indeed, of a political temporality; (2) constituent power bursts open the representation of politics and time as instituted government and continuous history; (3) constituent power is the very 'motor of the politicodemocratic dynamic as such', though it appears to law only as 'absence, void, and desire';[13] and (4) constituent power, to the extent that it reconstitutes itself, is not only productive in nature but also continually *operative*.

In Negri's later thought, and in collaborations with Michael Hardt, constituent power will take on a number of aliases, the most significant of which are 'multitude', 'the biopolitical', 'democracy' and the 'common', just as constituted power will operate as 'sovereignty', 'biopower' and, most famously, 'Empire'. Whatever the terminology Negri puts into play, however, one thing remains certain: since the inception of 'eugenic' Western thought, a war has been raging between the productive forces of the democratic multitude and the imperial and limited power that seeks, through a strategy that never ceases to betray its own limits, to reduce and neutralise them.

Agamben's distance from these positions (which even results in his aligning Negri's antithesis of Empire and multitude with Christian political theology [KG 11]) hinges in large part upon what might be considered a contradictory element in Negri's praise of constituent power's actuality and operativity: namely, that while he frames constituent power as fundamentally disruptive of every continuity (in time, law, or representation), he also claims, in the same breath, that it 'produces and reproduces itself everywhere and *continually*' (my emphasis). The question thus arises: why must a power that bursts apart every continuous order of power be one whose own production never ceases?

CONSTITUENT EXCLUSION

In the first volume of *Homo Sacer*, Agamben seeks out the most basic and ineliminable dimension of the law: not (like Negri) what force constitutes, resists or surpasses it, but how *there is law* at all. Recapitulating and transposing a problem he had treated earlier – *that there is language* – during a period that Negri somewhat dismissively refers to as his philological and 'literary apprenticeship',[14] Agamben now asks: what are the conditions under which something like law or rule becomes applicable?

In response, Agamben turns with renewed interest to Carl Schmitt, glimpsing in Schmitt's concept of sovereignty the basis for any and all law: the exception. 'The most proper characteristic of the exception', Agamben writes, 'is that what is excluded in it is not, on account of being excluded, absolutely without relation to the rule. On the contrary, what is excluded in the exception maintains itself in relation to the rule in the form of the rule's suspension' (*HS* 18). Thus the answer to the question 'whence law?' is precisely the exception since it alone establishes a *juridical relation* to that which is excluded from law and from which it withdraws. Furthermore, the very withdrawal of law appears as 'the very space in which the juridico-political order can have validity' (*HS* 19).

In *State of Exception*, Agamben refers to this space as a *fictio legis* (*SE* 26). And yet what is made to abide in this empty zone of law is, on the one hand, *fact* (since the rule can apply to the singular case only by not being one itself) and, on the other, *bare life* (since the law can qualify life only by disqualifying the naked fact of living).[15] Notably, then, bare life remains as distinct from natural life as facts are from experience, and bare life, like the singular case, refers to nothing but the realm of the living *inasmuch as it is abandoned* – and thereby captured – by the law. The mechanism of this abandonment – the exception – is that which, while never appearing within the bounds of legal representation, continually founds and produces the legal order.

Precisely here a crucial, if surprising, proximity emerges between Schmitt and Negri: for what, in the end, distinguishes the exception (and the sovereignty it founds) from constituent power? While praising Negri's assertion of an incommensurability between constituted and constituent power, Agamben asserts that his compatriot 'cannot find any criterion, in his wide analysis of the historical phenomenology of constituting power, by which to isolate constituting power from sovereign power' (*HS* 43). The latter are, in fact, characterised by what Agamben calls a 'symmetry of [. . .] excess' with regard to the law that 'attests to a proximity that fades away into indistinction' (*HS* 43). This, despite its subtlety, is a damning critique of constituent power, for it asserts that Negri's free, productive and continuous praxis turns out to inform not the 'democratic totality' but, rather, the very sovereignty of law it had hoped to resist.

Still, Negri's aporia is, for Agamben, a crucial provocation to investigate 'an entirely new conjunction of possibility and reality [that would] make it possible to cut the knot that binds sovereignty to constituting power'; for 'only if it is possible', he continues, 'to think the relation between potentiality and actuality differently – and even to think beyond this relation – will it be possible to think a constituting power wholly released from the sovereign ban' (*HS* 44). In the opacity of this thinking beyond relation, a new constellation of terms – impotentiality, inoperativity and destituent potential – presents itself.

DESTITUENT POTENTIAL

Agamben's recent work has broached a notion of *destituent potential* (*potenza destituente*), which he defines explicitly as a counter-concept to constituent power. Far from simply a polemical gesture, however, this turn to the destituent – as well as to figures of destitution, as in his work on the Franciscan order, *The Highest Poverty* – tries to think a type of power that shatters the dialectic between constituent power and constituted power, exception and law, potential and act.

That Agamben would emphasise the limitations of thinking these terms under the aspect of *relation* is, given his elucidation of the structure of both sovereignty and constituent power, unsurprising: the law in the state of exception (or as constituent power) proves most violent when it presents itself as capable of applying and also of not applying – or of applying precisely insofar as it does not apply (when it is 'in force without significance' [*HS* 51]). Describing this dimension further, he explains: 'this potentiality [of law] maintains itself in relation to actuality in the form of its suspension; it *is capable* of the act in not realizing it, it is sovereignly capable of its own im-potentiality [*impotenza*]' (*HS* 45).

What becomes problematic, in this regard, is how this sovereign potential – or constituent power – passes into actuality: 'If every potentiality (to be or do) is also originally the potentiality not to (be or do), how will it be possible for an act to be realized?' (*HS* 45). Agamben's full answer to this question involves nothing less than his entire rethinking of Aristotelian *dynamis/adynamia*, but for our purposes it can be addressed by distinguishing the *existence* of potentiality from any notion of actuality as operativity or *energeia*. For if actuality is understood not as the realisation of a potentiality to (do or be), but, rather, as the *privation* of a potentiality not-to (do or be), then the realm of actuality will not only coincide completely with that of potentiality, it will also be the equivalent, according to Benjamin's phrase, to an *integral* actuality, one in which 'there will be nothing impotential (that is, there will be nothing able not to be)' (*HS* 45). And if this integral actuality is the realm in which 'nothing is able not to be', this means that, far from abolishing the possibility not-to, actuality is the realm in which impotentiality itself *is*.

But if impotentiality exists, how? Precisely in order to delineate the terms of impotentiality's existence – which is not merely an anticipation of existing, but itself a *mode* of being – Agamben takes up a hypothesis that Aristotle (and, we might imagine, Negri too) would dismiss: that man, unlike the carpenter or the tanner, is a creature without a specific *ergon* or work, a creature of (im)potentiality rather than one destined to act or produce.

Aristotle (like Negri, centuries later) embraces the opposite notion, that there is a 'work of man': 'the being-at-work of the soul according to the logos'. Yet, for Agamben, this is a choice with a lasting 'aporetic legacy' both because it 'binds the destiny of politics to a kind of work' even though the kind of work 'remains unassignable', and because it extracts 'the work of man as man [. . .] out of the living being through the exclusion – as unpolitical – of a part of its vital activity'.[16] Not only, then, is the thesis of man's constitutive operativity – or in Negri's terms, productivity – predicated upon the logic of the exception glossed above; it also requires that potentiality, in order to exist, be *made* actual.

When Agamben, by contrast, elaborates his counter-thesis (of man as *argos*, essentially inoperative, unproductive), it is in order to imagine forms of activity, *including* acts of production, that, precisely by operating, *deactivate* and *render inoperative*. In other words, he wishes to define a realm of praxis – which he will also call *use* – which fully exhibits the *actuality* of impotentiality, the *existence* of a potential not-to, detached from a productive telos. Agamben lists among the examples of such a deactivating operation (or destituent potential): the activities undertaken on a holiday during which one eats but not so as to be nourished, dresses but not so as to be kept warm, and exchanges goods (gifts) not as commodities; the poem as an operation in language that deactivates its communicative function; and, even, the very act of speech itself, which 'diverts the mouth from its [digestive] function to make it the site of language'.[17] One imagines that, to this list, Agamben could also have added the deactivation and revocation of constituted meaning, better known as reading.

ACTS OF INOPERATIVITY

In *The Use of Bodies*, Agamben identifies a figure who is in every way the antagonist not only to the earlier 'protagonist' of bare life (*HS* 8) but also to the productivity Negri associates with constituent power. This figure, drawn not from Roman law but from Greek antiquity, is the slave, whose *ergon*, according to Aristotle, is 'the use of the body' (*ergon doulou he tou somatos chresis*). Hardly lost on Agamben is the significance of this counter-elaboration of a work of man. For 'unlike the cobbler, the carpenter, the flute player, or the sculptor', Agamben writes (recalling the language of the *Nicomachean Ethics*), 'the slave, even if he carries out these activities – and Aristotle knows perfectly well that this can happen in the *oikonomia* of the household – is and remains essentially without work, in the sense that, in contrast to what happens with an artisan, his praxis is not defined by the work that he produces but only the use of the body' (*UB* 15).

What flashes up here, more than a reading of Aristotle, is an alternative archaeology – indeed an entirely new ontology – of labour not as poiesis or production, but as use. For just as Agamben disputes any relation by which potentiality is said to pass into act (or require actualisation in order to exist), so too does he reject the notion that human potential is, as Negri maintains, continually operative, or that production itself is the true vocation of the common. Such a poietic vocation is one that Agamben does not reject but deactivates. For like any good reader, he wishes to open poiesis – including Negri's own – to a new use.

NOTES

1. This is a concept that Agamben takes from Ludwig Feuerbach (*ST* 8).
2. Agamben draws both on Spinoza's discussion in the *Ethics* and upon his philological explanations in *Compendium grammatices linguae hebraeae*. See, for example, the essay 'Absolute Immanence' (*PO* 234–7).
3. For an in-depth reading of potentiality vs. constituent power, see Kevin Attell, 'Potentiality, Actuality, Constituent Power', *diacritics* 39.3 (2009): 35–53. For a discussion of Negri's relation to Italian Marxism of the 1960s and 1970s, see 'A Class Struggle Propadeutics 1950s–1970s', in Cesare Casarino and Antonio Negri, *In Praise of the Common: A Conversation on Philosophy and Politics* (Minneapolis: University of Minnesota Press,

2008), pp. 41–63; and Timothy C. Campbell, 'Introduction', in Roberto Esposito, *Bios: Biopolitics and Philosophy*, trans. Timothy Campbell (Minneapolis: University of Minnesota Press, 2008), pp. xix–xxvi.
4. Antonio Negri, *Insurgencies: Constituent Power and the Modern State*, trans. Maurizia Boscagli (Minneapolis: University of Minnesota Press, 1999), p. 3.
5. Negri, *Insurgencies*, p. 3.
6. Negri, *Insurgencies*, p. 4.
7. Negri, *Insurgencies*, p. 8.
8. Negri, *Insurgencies*, p. 10.
9. See Casarino and Negri, *In Praise of the Common*, pp. 193ff.
10. Negri, *Insurgencies*, p. 10.
11. For more on Negri's concept of *kairos* as a revolutionary temporality, see his *Time for Revolution,* trans. Matteo Mandarini (London: Bloomsbury Academic, 2003).
12. Negri, *Insurgencies*, p. 11.
13. Negri, *Insurgencies*, p. 4.
14. See 'Experimentum Linguae' (*IH* 1–12); and Antonio Negri, 'Giorgio Agamben: The Discreet Taste of the Dialectic', in Matthew Calarco and Steven DeCaroli (eds), *Giorgio Agamben: Sovereignty and Life* (Stanford: Stanford University Press, 2007), p. 110.
15. Negri will read the term very differently – as a fatalistic passivity: '*Naked life is the opposite of any Spinozian power and joy of the body*' (Casarino and Negri, *In Praise of the Common*, p. 210, original italics).
16. Giorgio Agamben, 'The Work of Man', trans. Kevin Attell, in Calarco and DeCaroli (eds), *Giorgio Agamben: Sovereignty and Life*, pp. 5, 6.
17. Giorgio Agamben, 'Vers une théorie de la puissance destituante', *lundimatin* 45 (25 January 2016), https://lundi.am/vers-une-theorie-de-la-puissance-destituante-Par-Giorgio-Agamben#identifier, translation mine (accessed 19 June 2016).

29 Gershom Scholem

JULIA NG

I

Giorgio Agamben's earliest encounter with Gershom Scholem concerns an essay from 1972 entitled 'Walter Benjamin and his Angel',[1] Scholem's first attempt to provide a definitive account of Benjamin's legacy. At its centre was a short text entitled 'Agesilaus Santander', which Benjamin composed on 12 and 13 August 1933 as a gift for the Dutch painter Anna Maria Blaupot ten Cate. In the text, the narrator is first given a 'secret' Jewish name, which is then revealed to contain an image of the 'New Angel' as well as a 'female' and 'male' form. Before naming himself as such, the 'new angel' presents himself as one of a host of angels that God creates at every given moment, whose only task, according to the Kabbalah, is to sing God's praises at His throne before returning to the void. By sending his 'feminine aspect' to the masculine one, however, the angel has only strengthened the narrator's 'ability to wait'; even when face to face with the woman he awaits he does not fall upon her *because* 'he wants happiness: [...] the conflict in which the rapture of that which happens just once [*des Einmaligen*], the new, the as-yet-unlived is combined with the bliss of experiencing something once more [*des Nocheinmal*], of possessing once again, of having lived'. Thus, the narrator continues, 'he has nothing new to hope for on any road other than the road home' to the future whence he came, where the as-yet-unlived will have been lived.[2]

In his reading, Scholem makes much of a letter from 1933[3] in which Benjamin describes Blaupot ten Cate as the 'female counterpart' of Paul Klee's drawing *Angelus Novus*. The figure it depicts, an 'angel' with claws and wings much like the 'razor-sharp pinions' of the 'new angel' in 'Agesilaus Santander', makes another, significant appearance in the Ninth Thesis on the Concept of History as the angel of history that is blown forward by the storm of progress while turned towards the ruins of the past.[4] To explain these associations, Scholem insists that *Agesilaus Santander* is an anagram of *Der Angelus Satanas* – the satanic angel who, adorned with claws and sharp wings,[5] sends his 'female form' to 'destroy' the narrator, a reading that Scholem corroborates with Benjamin's history of unrequited love and eluded happiness.[6] Moreover, as its Hebrew name suggests, the satanic angel is an 'accuser' who sings songs of lament, not praise.[7] Thus, Scholem concludes, the paradoxical formula that Benjamin gives for 'happiness' is an index of the dialectician's despondency at a historical process in which 'happiness' is situated at the origin and utopian future of man's redemption, never its present. Correspondingly, the angel of the Ninth Thesis is a fundamentally melancholic figure turned towards the unredeemed world whose pieces he is prevented from ever putting back together by the 'storm' of progress. Only a leap into transcendence, a messianic 'now-time' (*Jetztzeit*), can overcome history; imagining the melancholic *Angelus Satanas* allows Scholem to argue that Benjamin splits the messianic function of historical time between that of the angel who necessarily fails in his task *in* history, and the messiah who alone can fulfil it *as* the completion of history.[8]

Or, as Agamben writes, 'this unexpected metamorphosis casts a melancholic light on the entire horizon of Benjamin's reflections on the philosophy of history', obfuscating the 'properly redemptive role' that the angel plays in it (*PO* 138). His essay 'Walter Benjamin and the Demonic' thus sets out to complicate Scholem's account in order to trace 'the fundamental [. . .] lines of Benjamin's ethics', inasmuch as an ethics is impossible to establish without also adopting the context from which ethics first emerged as a doctrine: the alignment of the *daimonion* (the demonic) with *eudaimonia* (happiness). Agamben's first disagreement with Scholem, which sets the stage for many subsequent encounters up to and including the completion of the *Homo Sacer* project, thus seeks to establish the primacy of Benjamin's theory of happiness for his concept of redemption, such that the 'historical order' might be allowed to 'reach its own fulfilment' and transformation might be imaginable as a category of history and of 'world politics' (*PO* 154). In order to grasp what Scholem *per se* has to do with Agamben's recovery of redemption as *immanent* to history, however, it is helpful to revisit Scholem's role in a singular struggle over the interpretation of Benjamin's legacy.

II

Agamben's essay originally appeared in 1982, the same year as Jacob Taubes published a paper he had first submitted to the 1979 World Congress of Jewish Studies in Jerusalem, which was accepted only after a 'neutralisation' of its title.[9] The paper, 'The Price of Messianism', was considered 'the most radical critique' that Scholem encountered in his lifetime.[10] Although Agamben never discusses Taubes extensively, he dedicated *The Time that Remains* to him and is evidently indebted to Taubes's final lectures on Paul for his own discussion of the Letter to the Romans (*TR* 3). Indeed, Agamben's entire encounter with Scholem is tempered by Taubes's disagreement with Scholem, the crux of which was a letter that Walter Benjamin wrote to Carl Schmitt on 9 December 1930. In this letter, Benjamin announced that he was sending Schmitt a copy of his 1925 *Origin of German Tragic Drama*, and remarked on its indebtedness to Schmitt's presentation of sovereignty in the seventeenth century.[11] Gradually making itself known after Schmitt referred to it in *Hamlet or Hecuba* in 1956,[12] though controversially omitted from the 1966 edition of Benjamin's correspondence,[13] the letter's impact on German-Jewish intellectual history gained traction largely due to Taubes.

In fact, it was soon after meeting Scholem in Jerusalem in 1949 that Taubes became convinced of Schmitt's importance for understanding the apocalyptic character of juridical forms. For Taubes, Schmitt's anti-liberalism enabled him to see the world as a state of international civil war, which, far from being the end of constitutional law (as liberalism argued), revealed that even dictatorship can be a form of law. In Schmitt's view, juridical forms are created to hold back the chaos that threatens the continuation of the present age; Christian Rome's enforcement of orthodoxy by police and military means was legitimated by the idea that it, like the *katechon*, was a historical power capable of 'restraining' the coming of the antichrist.[14] By a similar logic, the Catholic Church was premised on a 'constitutive anti-Judaism', the idea that the Jews are God's chosen people who nevertheless do not believe in God. In a 1978 letter to Schmitt, Taubes refers to this friend–enemy status of the Jewish people, the 'Mysterium Judaicum', as a '"katechontic" form of existence' proper to the 'kairotic' time of emergency between the death of Christ and the end of time, which Romans 11 presents as the transformation of the chosen people into the people of the exception.[15] Like its Christian counterpart, Jewish messianism was therefore inseparable from the political forces that shape history. Moreover, Benjamin's letter to Schmitt proves that Benjamin was in agreement with these historico-philosophical consequences of Schmitt's anti-liberalism.

Initially personal in nature – in a letter of 7 October 1951[16] Scholem refers to an act of indiscretion that he still regarded as unforgivable twenty-five years later[17] – Taubes's break with Scholem developed into a disagreement over messianism's *historical* force and, by extension, Scholem's interpretation of Benjamin. Scholem's position, in 'Towards an Understanding of the Messianic Idea in Judaism', derived from his dichotomisation of Christian *interiorised* messianism and Jewish *history-oriented* messianism. Christianity, he argued, 'conceives of redemption as an event in the spiritual and unseen realm' that can operate as 'the true center of the historical process' because it need not correspond to anything in the external world. Judaism, by contrast, conceives of redemption as 'an event that takes place publicly, on the stage of history', which, being indissociable from an external event, remains strictly *anticipated*; Judaism flees from any 'illegitimate' attempt to verify the messianic claim on the historical stage.[18] Indeed, Scholem argued, it is the 'lack of transition between history and the redemption' that apocalypticists stress when imagining messianism as 'transcendence' that 'break[s] in' to 'transform' and 'liberate' history 'in its ruin'.[19] Associated with messianism is therefore a 'price' that corresponds to 'the endless powerlessness in Jewish history during all the centuries of exile, when it was unprepared to come forward onto the plane of world history'. This 'price' is a 'life lived in deferment, in which nothing can be done definitively, nothing can be irrevocably accomplished' by the unredeemed, and which makes for messianism's 'constitutional weakness'.[20]

For Taubes, Scholem's 'dividing the Messianic cake' entirely ignored the internal dynamics of messianism in its historical efficacy.[21] In fact, as Romans shows, Paul's interiorisation of the messianic idea was a response to the failure of prophecy, of the messianic mission of God's servant. Thus, whereas Scholem saw (Pauline) Christianity as a crisis *for* the Jewish people, Taubes saw in Paulinism a crisis within Jewish eschatology itself, a turning point at which the failure of the messiah to redeem the external world that nonetheless continues to exist provokes an 'interiorisation' *qua* intensification of the messianic idea in protest against the failure of politics to bring about redemption. If ever Jewish life took the form of a 'life lived in deferment', this was attributable to the branding of all manner of messianic movements as 'pseudo-messianic' by the rabbinic tradition, which used its 'katechontic form of existence' to consolidate its own political power. Paul's antinomianism is thus not an index of despondency at the non-fulfilment of the messianic promise on the historical-political plane (a 'lack of transition between history and the redemption', as Scholem says), but a strategy that calls all established law into question without attempting to realise another historical order. Crucially, for Taubes, Paul's concept of the insuperable nullity of worldly institutions in proximity to redemption (Romans 13) finds a parallel in another of Benjamin's writings, the 'Theologico-Political Fragment',[22] in which the concept of creation's suffering is coupled with the proposal that nihilism be the 'method' of 'world politics'.

Insofar as, like Taubes, he insists on the messianic idea's *historical operativity*, Agamben positions himself in *palintropos harmoniê* (counter-striving jointure) with Scholem. In 'Walter Benjamin and the Demonic', Agamben points out that according to Scholem's own description, Benjamin's clawed and sharp-winged angel iconographically aligns not with Satan but with Eros, a *daimon* in the Greek sense. Moreover, Benjamin likened the claws of Klee's *Angelus Novus* to those of 'the angel-thief who would rather free humans by taking from them than make them happy by giving to them' – whose destructive power is 'simultaneously liberating' and *overcomes* the demon 'at the point where origin and destruction meet' (PO 141–2). What Scholem should have exploited, Agamben argues, is the mystical source of the angel's double figure: the concept of the *Shekhinah*, which Agamben glosses as the 'feminine moment of divinity and of divine presence' that relates to the world 'in its judging role' (PO 143). As judgement, the feminine presence of the divine designates the 'sphere of redemption', which in the Kabbalah, however, *coincides* with the 'proper dimension of happiness' represented by the angel's masculine aspect (PO 143).[23] Furthermore, the angel of history is modelled after the personal angel, the *Tselem* or astral body, which denotes a 'celestial double and originary image' that links the prehistory of man with his salvation (PO 146). Derived from Jewish (onanistic) demonology, the astral body is a figure of indistinction between pleasure and spirit, where the very legal order by which distinctions are drawn and sentences passed is put into question by the ambiguous solidarity of origin and destruction (PO 150).

Finally, Agamben, like Taubes, draws on the 'Theologico-Political Fragment' to argue that it is 'the idea of happiness [that] allows the historical order to reach its own fulfilment'; unlike melancholy, whose gaze transfixes upon historical works too horrific to bring to completion, happiness is the rhythm of worldly restitution and the eternity of its downfall, which constitutes *historical* redemption proper and the task of world politics. Whereas Scholem sees in Benjamin's paradoxical formulation of happiness the coincidence of the 'as-yet-unlived' and 'having lived' deferred to the coming messianic age,[24] Agamben, following Taubes and Schmitt, intensifies the messianism in the 'now-time' of the paradox itself, magnifying the 'conflict' that alone remains as the historical force that brings history to an end.

III

What relation, if any, the law of the unredeemed world has to law at the time of redemption is the question Agamben poses in 'The Messiah and the Sovereign' (1992). Scholem had posed a similar question in 'The Meaning of the Torah in Jewish Mysticism': in fact, the authors of the *Zohar* drew a distinction between the law of the unredeemed world (Torah of Beriah), and the law in its original fullness (Torah of Aziluth). Each corresponds to one of the two trees of Paradise, each of which rules the world before and after the Fall, respectively, thus dividing the world into sacred and profane. What purpose will the law of the world that contains both good and evil have once the world is again subject to the law of the tree of life?[25] In 'Towards an Understanding', Scholem answers that the messianic age will imply profound changes in the very nature of commandments and prohibitions, since they were first called into existence by the division between good and evil. The new source of the law in the messianic age would instead be the spontaneity of human freedom. At this point, it would be possible to turn from the restorative conception of a re-establishment of the rule of law to a utopian view 'in which restrictive traits will no longer be determinative' and will instead be replaced by as yet 'totally unpredictable traits' that 'reveal entirely new aspects of free fulfilment'. Thus, says Scholem, 'an anarchic element enters Messianic utopianism'.[26]

For Agamben, however, the notion of a law of 'free fulfilment' merely perpetuates the 'Nothing of revelation', that is, the continued, yet empty, validity of the law. Revisiting the same medieval Kabbalists who Scholem discusses in 'The Meaning of the Torah', Agamben argues that Scholem depicts the original Torah as an *ars combinatoria* of the letters of the Hebrew alphabet, thus taking 'a decisive step in [the] progressive desemanticization of the law' that envisioned profane law as a jumble of letters awaiting a messianic event to assemble them into meaningful words (*PO* 164). This view engenders the surprising insight that 'the original form of the law is not a signifying proposition, but [. . .] a commandment that commands nothing' (*PO* 166). Scholem, however, was unable to grasp its significance, instead maintaining that messianism 'possesses a tension that never finds true release',[27] as though it nullified the law but maintained it as a perpetual state of exception (*PO* 171). Even when remarking to Benjamin that the law in Kafka's novels has 'validity without significance' (*Geltung ohne Bedeutung*) (a phrase that three years later would gain traction in the first of the *Homo Sacer* volumes), Scholem believed a secret key was needed for its actualisation. By contrast, Agamben finds 'validity without significance' in the Kabbalah's conception of the original Torah as a medley of letters without order or meaning *and* in Benjamin's 'absolutisation' of the (Schmittian) 'state of exception' in the Eighth Thesis on the Concept of History, in the hope of retrieving, *contra* Scholem, a *strategy* against the law *per se*.

It is in *The Time that Remains*, finally, that Agamben's search for a paradigm with which to conceive of the *eschaton* as belonging to historical time and existing law, and at the same time putting an end to both, comes to a head. Following Taubes, Agamben locates the time in which salvation is fulfilled in the 'now'; this 'now-time' of fulfilment, however, must be supplementary to the messianic event (of the resurrection) that has already happened according to believers. Scholem's notion of a 'life lived in deferment [. . .] in which nothing can be achieved'[28] captures this antinomy, but risks delaying fulfilment until the point of unreachability (*TR* 70). Instead, Agamben proposes, the Jewish exilic condition should be considered from within chronological time, as providing the opportunity to decouple messianism from eschatology in order to rethink messianic time as 'operational time': the supplementary 'time that is left us' to bring (historical) time to an end in the kairotic 'now-time', in which resurrection and full messianic presence are 'contracted' and the Jewish people's state of exception to the time of salvation's 'having been fulfilled' is uniquely absolutisable as a revolutionary force directed against the law that failed to be the site of redemption. To illustrate this, Agamben turns to Benjamin's description of each instant as 'the small door through which the Messiah enters' (*TR* 71).

Here, too, Agamben suggests that Scholem might have grasped the political significance of Jewish messianism – and of Benjamin's concept of the messianic instant – had he exploited the right resources in the mystical tradition: in this case, the 83rd of the theses that Scholem presented to Benjamin on his birthday in 1918, in which he wrote that 'messianic time is the time of inversive *waw*'.[29] The *waw* is a Hebrew letter which, when added to a verb, 'inverts' it from future to past and vice versa. According to Scholem, messianic time is thus neither complete nor incomplete in itself, but the time of inversion of *both*, and as such, an 'area of tension' in which the past can regain an 'unfulfilled' character *as* actuality. From this Agamben extracts an analogy to the inversion Paul enacts on the Greek opposition between potentiality and act, and to the conception of messianic time as the time of *de*-activation – in line with the notion, in 2 Cor. 12:9, that 'power realizes itself in weakness', which Taubes had previously connected to Benjamin's idea of 'weak messianism' in his Second Thesis on the Concept of History. Similarly, Agamben interprets 2 Cor. 12:9 as indicating a *strategic* consequence to the messianic 'inversion' of the potentiality–act relation: the rendering inoperative of the law *per se*, into whose 'unworking' the law itself had transposed the promise of redemption (*TR* 97).

IV

Agamben's *palintropos harmoniê* with Scholem thus comes full circle in *The Time that Remains*, where he suggests that *der Angelus Satanas* refers to the 'thorn in the flesh' in 2 Corinthians, which Paul describes as *aggelos satana* – and that, in spite of himself, Scholem establishes a proximity between Benjamin and Paul and therefore a 'messianic' theory of the undoing of power (*TR* 141). It is worth noting, however, that Scholem did in fact 'apply' his idea of the inversive *waw* to the realm of 'ethics' in an essay from 1918, which sheds light on some difficulties in Agamben's argument. In Scholem's account, the name of God, 'I will be who I will become', signifies 'eternal presence' that unfolds as temporal modulation in the '*waw-hippukh* of narration'. To illustrate, Scholem uses the 'inversive' story of Jonah, in which God's judgement transforms from being unheeded by Jonah to being commuted by God into 'justice' after the city of Nineveh repents. The story, says Scholem, was only ever about teaching Jonah about the nature of prophecy and its incommensurability with justice – and opens up the potential for the law to be overcome and justice to prevail in the name of God. Referring to the 'deferment on the part of the executive power' that results in the arrival of justice, the *waw-hippukh* of narration thus gives unique shape to the 'ethics' that give shape to the 'spiritual continuum of Judaism': infinite 'inversions' holding judgement and execution at a distance from one another in order to make space for the transformability of executive power, and hence for justice. As Scholem writes, justice is 'the idea of the historical annihilation of divine judgment', brought about by the deferral of one executive power by another.[30]

Absent the event of the resurrection, and therefore the exigency to produce a theory of the 'now' bookended by origin and destruction, the 'now' is at leisure to undergo continuous 'deferrals' and transformations. For Agamben, who invests everything in the 'katechontic form of existence' of this world, such a possibility of a non-emergent theory of action, or indeed any action other than wholesale annihilation of 'the

Law', is impermissible. For Scholem, however, justice is the present tense of transformation of past and future into one another, resulting from holding apart history and redemption by the (multiple) act of 'deferral'; only as such is it possible to imagine ethics as consisting in 'ethically different actions', multiple ethical actions, or even 'a steady stream of transformations' to existing executive power. By holding apart history and redemption, Scholem's text on Jonah suggests a way to imagine ethical or political action divested from the deed of the 'singular' and 'unsteady' actor. Finally, Scholem's text also recalls that the realm of the active life is still one of a differential relation, however small, between transformation and the self-same. As one footnote suggests, the active life – in the Torah, in politics – requires an examination of the relation between a hidden essence of power and the forms of its presence in the world: for instance the *Shekhinah*, the presence of the divine in the world, which as the other name for 'transformation' suggests that an ontology of transformation might yet be worked out.[31]

NOTES

1. Gershom Scholem, 'Walter Benjamin und sein Engel' (1972), in Scholem, *Walter Benjamin und sein Engel*, ed. Rolf Tiedemann (Frankfurt a.M.: Suhrkamp, 1983), pp. 35–72.
2. Walter Benjamin, 'Agesilaus Santander (First and Second Versions)', trans. Rodney Livingstone, in *Selected Writings*, ed. Howard Eiland and Michael W. Jennings (Cambridge, MA: The Belknap Press of Harvard University Press, 1999), vol. 2, pp. 712–16, here p. 715 (translation modified).
3. Walter Benjamin, letter to Scholem of 1 September 1933, in *Gesammelte Briefe*, ed. Christoph Gödde and Henri Lonitz (Frankfurt a.M.: Suhrkamp, 1998), vol. 4, p. 287.
4. Walter Benjamin, 'On the Concept of History', trans. Harry Zohn, in *Selected Writings*, vol. 4, p. 392.
5. Scholem, 'Walter Benjamin und sein Engel', p. 50.
6. Scholem, 'Walter Benjamin und sein Engel', p. 55.
7. Scholem, 'Walter Benjamin und sein Engel', p. 63.
8. Scholem, 'Walter Benjamin und sein Engel', pp. 66–7.
9. Jacob Taubes, 'The Price of Messianism', *Journal of Jewish Studies* 33.1–2 (1982): 595–600.
10. Thomas Macho, 'On the Price of Messianism: The Intellectual Rift between Gershom Scholem and Jacob Taubes', in Anna Glazova and Paul North (eds), *Messianic Thought Outside Theology* (New York: Fordham University Press, 2014), p. 29.
11. Walter Benjamin, letter to Carl Schmitt of 9 December 1930, in *Gesammelte Briefe*, vol. 3, p. 558.

12. Carl Schmitt, *Hamlet oder Hekuba* (Düsseldorf/Cologne: Eugen Diederichs Verlag, 1985 [1956]), p. 64.
13. Walter Benjamin, *Briefe*, 2 vols, ed. Theodor W. Adorno and Gershom Scholem (Frankfurt a.M.: Suhrkamp, 1966).
14. Jacob Taubes, *Ad Carl Schmitt: Gegenstrebige Fügung* (Berlin: Merve, 1987), pp. 18–19, 67, 73, 76.
15. Bruce Rosenstock, 'Palintropos Harmoniê: Jacob Taubes and Carl Schmitt "*im liebenden Streit*"', *New German Critique* 121.41 (2014): 55–92, esp. pp. 56–9.
16. Gershom Scholem, letter to Taubes of 7 October 1951, in *Briefe*, ed. Itta Shedletzky (Munich: Beck, 1995), vol. 2, pp. 25–8.
17. Gershom Scholem, letter to Taubes of 24 March 1977, in *Briefe*, vol. 3, p. 154.
18. Gershom Scholem, 'Towards an Understanding of the Messianic Idea in Judaism', in *The Messianic Idea in Judaism* (New York: Schocken Books, 1971), pp. 1–2.
19. Scholem, 'Towards an Understanding of the Messianic Idea in Judaism', p. 10.
20. Scholem, 'Towards an Understanding of the Messianic Idea in Judaism', p. 35.
21. Jacob Taubes, 'Der Preis des Messianismus', in Elettra Stimilli (ed.), *Der Preis des Messianismus. Briefe von Jacob Taubes an Gershom Scholem und andere Materialien* (Würzburg: Königshausen & Neumann, 2006), pp. 33–40.
22. Walter Benjamin, 'Theologico-Political Fragment', trans. Harry Zohn, in *Selected Writings*, vol. 3, pp. 305–6.
23. Agamben draws here on Scholem's 'Shekhinah: The Feminine Element in Divinity', in *On the Mystical Shape of the Godhead* (New York: Schocken Books, 1991), pp. 140–96, esp. p. 186.
24. Benjamin, 'Agesilaus Santander', p. 716.
25. Gershom Scholem, 'The Meaning of the Torah in Jewish Mysticism', in *On the Kabbalah and Its Symbolism*, trans. Ralph Manheim (New York: Schocken Books, 1965), pp. 32–86. Cf. *PO* 163.
26. Scholem, 'Towards an Understanding of the Messianic Idea in Judaism', p. 21.
27. Scholem, 'Towards an Understanding of the Messianic Idea in Judaism', p. 21.
28. Scholem, 'Towards an Understanding of the Messianic Idea in Judaism', p. 35.
29. Gershom Scholem, '95 Thesen über Judentum und Zionismus', in *Tagebücher* (Frankfurt a.M.: Jüdischer Verlag, 2000), vol. 2, pp. 300–6.
30. Gershom Scholem, 'On Jonah and the Concept of Justice', trans. Eric Schwab, *Critical Inquiry* 25.2 (1999): 353–61.
31. Scholem, 'On Jonah and the Concept of Justice', p. 359.

30 *Simone Weil*

BEATRICE MAROVICH

Few of Giorgio Agamben's works are as mysterious as his unpublished dissertation, reportedly on the political thought of the French philosopher Simone Weil. If Weil was an early subject of Agamben's intellectual curiosity, it would appear – judging from his published works – that her influence upon him has been neither central nor lasting.[1] Leland de la Durantaye argues that Weil's work has left a mark on Agamben's philosophy of potentiality, largely in his discussion of the concept of decreation; but de la Durantaye does not make much of Weil's influence here, determining that her theory of decreation is 'essentially dialectical' and still too bound up with creation theology.[2] Alessia Ricciardi, however, argues that de la Durantaye's dismissal of Weil's influence is hasty.[3] Ricciardi analyses deeper resonances between Weil's and Agamben's philosophies, ultimately claiming that Agamben 'seems to extend many of the implications and claims of Weil's idea of force',[4] arguably spreading Weil's influence into Agamben's reflections on sovereign power and bare life.

For Ricciardi, Weil's essay 'The *Iliad*, or the Poem of Force' presents a phenomenology that 'clearly prophesies' aspects of Agamben's work. In the opening passages of the essay Weil argues that 'the true hero, the true subject, the center of the *Iliad* is force. Force employed by man, force that enslaves man, force before which man's flesh shrinks away.'[5] In the wake of force, a human is stripped down and becomes a *thing*. Weil, notably, does not make a *protagonist* of this life laid bare by force.[6] Nonetheless, the thing-like body left behind in the wake of force – once the human flesh has shrunk away – bears an intriguing resemblance to the figure of bare life (*nuda vita*) in Agamben's work. I would extend Ricciardi's argument further, suggesting that Weil's figuration of creaturely life bears a resemblance to Agamben's figure of bare life – a semblance resonant enough that I believe Weil could be cited more frequently in genealogies of Agamben's bare life.

SIMONE WEIL AND CREATURELY LIFE

The figure of the creature is a subjective category that both includes the human and stretches beyond it. For this reason, creaturely life is often used in contemporary parlance to describe or illuminate a form of kinship or relatedness between mortal animals. But animality, for Weil, was problematic. She saw, in animal life, the possibility of uncontainable force and violence. And she was ultimately an ascetic who saw the animal body as something to be controlled and disciplined. Creatureliness, for Weil, had little to do with animals or animality. Instead, the figure of the creature was one that illuminated the strange contours of the human relationship with God.

Weil saw, in the creature–creator relationship, a radical form of difference that creatures experience as an isolation from God. She argued that the world of creatures exists infinitely far from God, who 'placed the greatest possible distance between the creation and Himself, who is pure good'.[7] The creature thus feels that God is distant and coldly unavailable. Weil argues, however, that this infinite distance is actually a sign of love. God imposed this great distance because if he did not hide, 'there would be only he'.[8] God kenotically emptied himself out in order to create space for existence. But creatures, with their sensing bodies, can perceive only the emptiness of a creation that reports God's absence.

It is perhaps because of this isolation from God that Weil believed affliction comes to have sovereign power over the living human creature. To speak about creaturely life in Weil's work, then, one must necessarily address the creature's afflicted state. Affliction conditions and animates the life of a living creature, in the perceived absence of God. Weil examines affliction at length in a little-discussed essay called 'The Love of God and Affliction', parts of which were published in her well-known *Waiting on God* (1951), but only published in full in *Pensées sans ordre concernant l'amour de Dieu* (1962) and later translated into English for the more obscure *On Science, Necessity, and the Love of God* (1968).[9]

In this essay Weil argued that suffering, like joy, was a 'precious gift': a transformative power that must be 'fully tasted' if we are to become sensitive to the material world around us.[10] Affliction, on the other hand, was different: more dramatic, violent and extreme. Affliction 'is an uprooting of life, a more or less attenuated equivalent of death', a kind of social death. But Weil was also clear that affliction is not merely social – to be affliction it must also affect the biological body, namely through pain so that it is 'made irresistibly present to the soul'.[11] Extreme affliction, then, is an amalgam of physical pain, spiritual distress and social debasement.[12] This predicament is essentially dehumanising, so perhaps this is why it reveals the contours of the stripped-down state of human creatureliness. Force is 'that x that turns anybody subjected to it into a *thing*';[13] force 'hangs, poised and ready, over the head of the creature it *can* kill at any moment'.[14] Affliction, on the other hand, is a kind of tool for the introduction of force into the life of a creature. It is 'a simple and ingenious device to introduce into the soul of a finite creature that immensity of force, blind, brutal, and cold'.[15] An afflicted person, says Weil, 'quivers like a butterfly pinned alive to a tray'.[16]

Affliction was also a political problem. Perhaps because affliction dehumanises us, Weil was unsurprised that it is often used as a method for political subjection. Affliction, as it dehumanises, leaves on us 'the mark of slavery'. The paradigmatic illustration of affliction was, for Weil, the institution of slavery in Ancient Rome.[17] Humans use affliction against one another as a political tool when we want to dehumanise and abuse, when 'the innocent are killed, tortured, driven from their country, made destitute or reduced to slavery, put in concentration camps or prison cells'.[18] The natural world, too, throws us into a state of affliction, and Weil was unsurprised by this.[19] What *is* surprising, to Weil, is the fact that 'God should have given affliction the power to seize the very souls of the innocent and to possess them as sovereign master'.[20] Weil seems to be suggesting that God allows something *other than God* to take sovereign power over creaturely life, indicating, perhaps, that God's power is not sovereign.

Weil's God leaves the creature to its own devices in the wake of pure force. Affliction 'causes God to be absent for a time, more absent than a dead man, more absent than light in the utter darkness of a cell' such that 'a kind of horror submerges the whole soul. During this absence there is nothing to love' because those struck down by affliction are 'at the greatest possible distance from God'.[21] Affliction, then, is a state or condition driven by a power other than God and made especially acute by a perceived isolation from God. Weil suggested that it was affliction's affective power that drove Jesus to lament, on the cross, that he had been forsaken by God.[22]

Weil argues that the only way out of the bind of affliction is to act in *imitatio Christi*: Christ models an escape from the power of affliction and an approximation of God's love. As earthbound beings

– creaturely, non-divine, mortal entities – we are destined to be infinitely far from God. Ironically, through a *coincidentia oppositorum* of sorts, Weil suggests that the closest a creature might ever get to God is when God is 'almost perfectly absent from us in extreme affliction'.[23] The afflicted creature is, without realising it, as close to the apparently absent God as a creature can be. To remain oriented towards God in affliction (at the greatest possible distance from God) is to be like 'the man whose soul remains oriented toward God while a nail is driven through it'. It is to find oneself 'nailed to the very center of the universe; the true center, which is not in the middle, which is not in space and time, which is God'.[24] It is to give in to our 'almost infinite fragility',[25] to find, in affliction, the 'fathomless eternal silence of the stars' which is 'the vibration of God's silence' that resonates and becomes attuned to a silence that is 'secretly' present within us.[26] The word of God, for Weil, 'is silence', and so 'God's secret word of love can be nothing else but silence'.[27] What is first perceived as God's abandonment of the creature, in a state of affliction, is more rightly perceived as the emergence of God's silence on the other side of affliction's sovereign power.

If the avenue out of affliction is to act in imitation of Jesus, then navigating around affliction's power – or accessing this fathomless silence of the stars – is ultimately a matter of decreation. Weil's decreation was a decimation of sorts and Jesus Christ was its paradigmatic model. If God created through a kenotic act of self-emptying, then Christ – through decreation – imitates God's act of withdrawal. Christ '*emptied* himself of his divine nature and took on that of a slave', thus decreating himself. To act in imitation of Christ, then, is to decreate.[28] Weil believed that we, unlike Christ, have no divine nature to empty ourselves of. For ordinary creatures to decreate, we must instead strip ourselves of ego: 'We possess nothing in the world, a mere chance can strip us of everything – except the power to say "I".' So there is 'no other free act which is given to us to accomplish – only the destruction of the "I"'.[29]

Weil called decreation the act of 'unmaking the creature in us'.[30] This is not the removal of our creaturely nature but, instead, an unmaking of ourselves such that we become nothing *but* a creature – undone into our bare creatureliness. 'We are nothing but creatures', says Weil, 'but that is like consenting to being nothing. Without knowing it, this being which God has given us is non-being.'[31] To consent to being a creature 'is like consenting to lose one's whole existence';[32] we are stripped of the identities that make us a person. The misery of affliction teaches us that 'as a human being as such' we are 'nothing', that is to say, 'a creature'.[33] To consent to be a creature is to consent to be nothing, the barest form of creation, without particular content. Affliction reduces us to this bare form, but it is also the only condition in which the silence of the absent God becomes comprehensible, through the channel of our own empty silence.

Creaturely life, for Weil, was not a figure that illuminated something about our animality, or expressed something about the divinely given nature of multi-species kinship relations. Rather, creaturely life was something more like a ground zero for human existence: a kind of positively charged negative at the base of our condition. It was a figure through which Weil could expose the dehumanisation of affliction – the extent to which the sovereign power of force makes us into a thing and leaves us afflicted physically, socially, spiritually and politically. The redemption of the creature's afflicted life called, Weil believed, for a decreation where we discover that as creatures we are without content.

SIMONE WEIL AND BARE LIFE

Weil never appears among the list of figures who have influenced the figuration of Agamben's *nuda vita*, usually translated as 'bare life'. Agamben is explicitly in conversation with Walter Benjamin's concept of *bloßes Leben* (translated most frequently as 'mere life') as the figure develops in *Homo Sacer*. In fact, de la Durantaye calls Agamben's figure a *translation* of Benjamin's term – 'a quotation without quotation marks from Benjamin'.[34] But Carlo Salzani urges caution in reading overly close parallels between Benjamin's and Agamben's forms of bare life. The Benjaminian influence here is, as Salzani puts it, 'explicit but problematic'.[35] Agamben's figure of bare life is also distinctly marked by Carl Schmitt's figure of the sovereign exception, so Salzani can argue that Agamben has 'developed, and not merely adopted' Benjamin's concept.[36] Bare life, then, is a complex and original figure with a genealogy that may be equally complex. Could Weil have been an unmarked influence? I have no evidence that Agamben has read any of the Weil texts that I have cited here, so there is no explicit philological relationship between Weil's figure of the creature and Agamben's figure of bare life. Any relationship is merely a matter of speculation, so I will speculate, here, that Weil's figure of the creature and Agamben's figure of bare life are *resonant* figures.

Bare life and Weil's creature are resonant, most obviously, in that they are both quasi-dehumanised figures: they each describe human figures that have somehow been rendered less than human. Weil, as I have already indicated, had little interest in the predicaments of animal life: her figuration of the creature was not a concept intended to illuminate something about human kinship connections with the non-human world. Instead, for her, creaturely life was a figure that expressed something about the human relationship to structures of power and divine life. In his discussion of bare life in *Homo Sacer*, Agamben does create parallels between bare life and the Greek concept of *zoè* – the form of life 'common to all living beings (animals, men, or gods)' (*HS* 1). But his concern in *Homo Sacer* is the politicisation of *zoè* (*HS* 4), or what happens to the *zoè* of bare life when it enters the sphere of human politics. Even in *The Open*, where he reflects on the relation between man and animal, Agamben is not interested in a positive revaluation of animality but instead in a better understanding of how the conceptualisation of specifically animal and human forms of life has resulted in a kind of political violence. The figure of creaturely life, however, is in most literary and philosophical contexts a description of a not-quite-human element within the human. So this parallel between Weil's figure of the creature and Agamben's bare life is rather obvious.

Perhaps a more particular resonance between Agamben's figure of bare life and Weil's creaturely life is the fact that both are rendered abject by a sovereign power that is not explicitly (or not exclusively) God. Weil, as I have already noted, suggests that affliction imposes itself on the life of a creature via a sovereign power that she does not explicitly connect to (and even dissociates from) the figure of God. This suggests that the sovereign power of force that leaves the creature abject and vulnerable to affliction is not God. It may even indicate that God is, in some way, non-sovereign. Agamben does not dissociate the figure of God from the abject bare life of the *homo sacer*; indeed, there are passages in which he directly addresses the connection between God and the *homo sacer*, as in his explanation that the structure of the exception applies to bare life in that 'the *homo sacer* belongs to God in the form of unsacrificability' (*HS* 82). But Agamben is interested in contemplating bare life as a figure located 'in a zone prior to the distinction between sacred and profane, religious and juridical' (*HS* 74), so God is relevant to his discussion to the extent that God is configured as the sovereign. But this might render a non-sovereign God external to this conversation in a manner not unlike the externality of God to the function of force in Weil's work.

Additionally, in the case of both Agamben's bare life and Weil's creature, the figure becomes a conceptual tool through which to consider forms of power over life itself. The power over life exhibited within the natural world is not exactly irrelevant to either thinker. But more important to both Agamben and Weil is that the figure represents a politically painful condition resulting from problematic applications or extensions of power. The figure illuminates, for both Weil and Agamben, the most abject conditions of human existence, such as slavery. Weil, as I mentioned earlier, uses slavery in Ancient Rome as the paradigmatic example of extreme affliction.[37] In Agamben's work, of course, the *homo sacer* – the 'obscure figure of archaic Roman law' in which human life is included in the political solely in its ability to be killed (*HS* 8) – also brings the modern relevance of Ancient Roman politics into his conversation. Weil references a laundry list of conditions that plague modernity and drive forces of affliction in creaturely life: when 'the innocent are killed, tortured, driven from their country, made destitute or reduced to slavery, put in concentration camps or prison cells'.[38] The paradigm of the concentration camp also becomes central to Agamben's illumination of bare life as 'the most absolute *conditio inhumana* that has ever existed on earth' (*HS* 166).

Finally, I see a resonance between Agamben's bare life and Weil's creaturely life in that – despite their abjected condition – the decreation of the figure provides an egress from the thrall of sovereign power, and a new site of possibility. For Weil, decreation offers a kind of exit from the state of affliction and the sovereign power that it holds over the creature. In stripping ourselves of the 'I', we act in imitation of Christ who, like God, decreated through a form of *kenosis* – stripping himself of divinity. We creatures strip ourselves not of divinity but of our markers of human identity and, in this unmaking, become decreated – we become nothing but a creature, or a kind of non-being.[39]

The connection between bare life and decreation, in Agamben's work, is more complicated. In his essay 'Form-of-Life' Agamben argues that the condition of bare, or naked, life prevents forms of life from cohering into what he calls a 'form-of-life' (*ME* 6): not bare life, but rather what results from the *désoeuvrement* of the sovereign ban. Life as form-of-life is only possible with the 'irrevocable exodus from any sovereignty' that drives and sustains the exclusion of bare life (*ME* 8). The condition he describes as form-of-life 'renders destitute and inoperative' all singular forms of life (*UB* 277) through which we are 'recodified' into particular identities: 'the voter, the worker, the journalist, the student, but also the HIV-positive, the transvestite, the porno star, the elderly, the parent, the woman' (*ME* 7). To be constituted as a form-of-life is to make destitute all social and biological conditions of life (*UB* 277) – to render these singular conditions inoperative. It is in the becoming inoperative of bare life that we see a link to decreation.

Inoperativity, in Agamben's philosophy, is not a negative condition (though the concept does appear to take direction from Bataille's *désoeuvrement*, or 'negativity without employ').[40] Rather, the inoperative marks 'the other side of potentiality: the possibility that a thing might not come to pass'.[41] The inoperativity of form-of-life is potentiality in its fullest sense – the potential both to be and not to be, or a potentiality that accommodates impotentiality. De la Durantye suggests that this is a decreated state of existence because, for Agamben, decreation refers not to creation but to 'God's second creation' wherein 'God summons all his potential not to be, creating on the basis of a point of indifference between potentiality and impotentiality'; thus 'the creation that is now fulfilled is neither a re-creation nor an eternal repetition; it is, rather, a decreation in which what happened and what did not happen are returned to their originary unity in the mind of God' (*PO* 270). This second creation that is *decreation*, then, is a state or condition in which potentiality exists in its richest instantiation: the potential to be, as well as the impotential not to be. Form-of-life, prior to the abandonment to sovereign power, renders inoperative the singular identities of bared lives and opens instead to a form-of-life that stirs in this decreated potentiality.

While, for de la Durantaye, Weil's decreation does not appear to prove deeply influential for Agamben, when we examine Weil's figuration of creaturely life – and its relationship to decreation – the resonances between Weil and Agamben's philosophies appear more profound. Decreation, for Weil, is the site of an almost negative potency. The redemption of creaturely life occurs in a space outside of affliction's sovereign power, in a condition marked with a kind of potent negativity. Decreation marks, for Agamben, another possible angle from which to contemplate the predicaments of bare life – one that envisions its disentanglement from sovereign power and the revelation of the impotential. The impotentiality of Agamben's decreation is not as explicitly negative as Weil's decreated state. But perhaps, as it does for Weil's creature, Agamben's decreation might also mark the end of bare life's affliction.

NOTES

1. Until November 2016 he appeared to mention her only once, and in passing, as one of the authors favoured by Elsa Morante (*EP* 102). At the end of 2016, however (long after the present chapter was written), Agamben published *Che cos'è il reale?*, which includes an eleven-page analysis of Weil's 1941 essay 'La science et nous' (*CRM* 19–30 and *passim*). While it was no longer possible to edit the chapter to take

this analysis into account, readers interested in Weil's relationship to Agamben's work will want to pursue this connection.
2. Leland de la Durantaye, *Giorgio Agamben: A Critical Introduction* (Stanford: Stanford University Press, 2009), p. 23.
3. Alessia Ricciardi, 'From Decreation to Bare Life: Weil, Agamben, and the Political', *Diacritics* 39.2 (2009), p. 75.
4. Ricciardi, 'Decreation to Bare Life', p. 89.
5. Weil, cited in Ricciardi, 'Decreation to Bare Life', p. 87.
6. As Agamben puts it in *Homo Sacer*, on the other hand, 'the protagonist of this book is bare life' (*HS* 8).
7. Simone Weil, *The Notebooks of Simone Weil*, trans. Arthur Wills (London: Routledge, 2004), p. 486.
8. Weil, *The Notebooks*, p. 230.
9. Simone Weil, 'The Love of God and Affliction', in *Science, Necessity, and the Love of God*, ed. and trans. Richard Rees (Oxford: Oxford University Press, 1968), p. 170.
10. Weil, 'The Love of God and Affliction', p. 180.
11. Weil, 'The Love of God and Affliction', p. 171.
12. Weil, 'The Love of God and Affliction', p. 182.
13. Simone Weil, 'The *Iliad* or the Poem of Force', in Siân Miles, *Simone Weil: An Anthology* (New York: Grove Press, 1986), p. 163.
14. Weil, 'The *Iliad* or the Poem of Force', p. 165.
15. Weil, 'The Love of God and Affliction', p. 182.
16. Weil, 'The Love of God and Affliction', p. 182.
17. Weil, 'The Love of God and Affliction', p. 170.
18. Weil, 'The Love of God and Affliction', p. 171.
19. Weil, 'The Love of God and Affliction', p. 172.
20. Weil, 'The Love of God and Affliction', p. 172.
21. Weil, 'The Love of God and Affliction', p. 175.
22. Weil, 'The Love of God and Affliction', p. 172.
23. Weil, 'The Love of God and Affliction', p. 177.
24. Weil, 'The Love of God and Affliction', p. 183.
25. Weil, 'The Love of God and Affliction', p. 185.
26. Weil, 'The Love of God and Affliction', p. 197.
27. Weil, 'The Love of God and Affliction', p. 197.
28. Weil, *The Notebooks*, p. 208.
29. Simone Weil, *Gravity and Grace*, trans. Emma Crawford and Mario von der Rurh (London: Routledge, 2002), p. 26.
30. Weil, *The Notebooks*, p. 241.
31. Simone Weil, *First and Last Notebooks*, trans. Richard Rees (Oxford: Oxford University Press, 1970), p. 217.
32. Weil, *First and Last Notebooks*, p. 217.
33. Weil, *The Notebooks*, p. 262.
34. de la Durantaye, *Giorgio Agamben*, p. 203.
35. Carlo Salzani, 'From Benjamin's *bloßes Leben* to Agamben's *Nuda Vita*:

A Genealogy', in Brendan Moran and Carlo Salzani (eds), *Toward the Critique of Violence: Walter Benjamin and Giorgio Agamben* (London: Bloomsbury Academic, 2015), p. 109.
36. Salzani, 'From Benjamin's *bloßes Leben* to Agamben's *Nuda Vita*', pp. 117–18.
37. Weil, 'The Love of God and Affliction', p. 170.
38. Weil, 'The Love of God and Affliction', p. 171.
39. Weil, *First and Last Notebooks*, p. 217.
40. de la Durantaye, *Giorgio Agamben*, p. 19.
41. de la Durantaye, *Giorgio Agamben*, p. 20.

Conclusion: Agamben as a Reader of Agamben

ADAM KOTSKO

Thus far, the contributors to this volume have considered the many and varied bodies of work that have left their mark on Agamben's project. In this concluding chapter, I would like to take up one final body of work that Agamben must somehow account for, if only implicitly – namely, his own.

The task is more difficult than it may sound, because Agamben is not nearly as self-referential as some major twentieth-century thinkers. Unless his habits change drastically, he will not leave behind a voluminous legacy of interviews on the stakes and intentions of his work, as Foucault did. His explicit cross-references between his own works are few and far between. Heidegger spent his entire career attempting to unpack the significance and shortcomings of *Being and Time*, while the later Derrida provided exhaustive footnotes demonstrating that the themes of his so-called 'ethical turn' were always already present in his earliest work. By contrast, Agamben rarely reflects directly on the relationship between any given text and the texts that preceded it. And within individual texts, the reader rarely finds the kinds of 'signposts' that explain why each book is structured in the way that it is.

In short, Agamben generally prefers for his authorial persona to remain immanent to the investigation itself, with very little room for explanation and reflection about how the investigation is proceeding. This approach helps to account for the immersive quality of his texts, but it also contributes to the challenge of interpreting them. Rarely has compulsive readability been so inextricably tied up with obscurity.

When Agamben does provide guidance to his readers, therefore, it is important to take heed. In what follows, I will organise my discussion around three forms of self-reference. First, I will bring together the passages in which Agamben reflects on the methodology that informs his work. Next, I will consider the places where he takes account of the overall shape of his intellectual project and the place of individual texts within it. Finally, I will turn to Agamben's declarations about what his work has actually achieved and what future tasks it points towards. In a sense, this arrangement is 'chronological', following the sequence of method, execution and result. Yet as we shall see, the temporality involved is, perhaps unsurprisingly, more complicated than it at first appears.

METHOD

In *The Signature of All Things*, Agamben claims that 'a reflection on method usually follows practical application, rather than preceding it'. Any explicit methodological claims are 'ultimate or penultimate thoughts, to be discussed among friends and colleagues, which can legitimately be articulated only after extensive research' (*ST* 7). It would appear that this particular methodological (or meta-methodological) reflection is among the conclusions that Agamben reached only late in life, because his early works make frequent methodological claims, which we have already discussed at length in our introduction to this volume.

In these works, Agamben also expresses his methodology by means of normative claims about the task of philosophy. Above all, philosophy is the discipline that draws attention to the fact that 'there is language' – a claim that echoes through *Infancy and History*, *Language and Death*, and essays such as 'The Idea of Language' and 'Philosophy and Linguistics' (later collected in *Potentialities*). He takes up this claim again in *The Sacrament of Language* and even more emphatically in *What is Philosophy?* (*Che cos'è la filosofia?*). In the latter work, he presents a revised version of an essay from the late 1980s, the period represented by the bulk of the essays in *Potentialities* (*CF* 7), along with more recent essays on the experience of the sheer fact of language as it is expressed in Plato's philosophy (and distorted by later interpreters). This conception of the task of philosophy therefore arguably counts as the most constant methodological commitment throughout Agamben's entire trajectory.

For Agamben, the fact of language is presupposed by all particular sciences, and as they begin to approach their limit point, they exceed themselves and enter into the territory of philosophy. This basic stance shapes Agamben's attitude towards the many scholarly sources he draws on without ever letting his investigations be determined by them. It helps make sense not only of his choice of scholarly interlocutors – namely, those who in his view are moving beyond the limits of their discipline and towards philosophy – but also of his claim to have access to a properly philosophical stance that allows him to complete the conceptual articulation that their particular disciplinary perspectives prevent them from achieving. This strain of his methodological reflections will culminate in *The Sacrament of Language*, where he begins by claiming that only a 'philosophical archeology of the oath' can break through the deadlocks of existing scholarly studies (*SL* 2) and concludes with the assertion that philosophy 'constitutively [. . .] puts in question the sacramental bond that links the human being to language, without for that reason simply speaking haphazardly, falling into the vanity of speech' (*SL* 72). As such, only philosophy can provide 'the indication of a line of resistance and of change' (*SL* 72).

Infancy and History concludes with a programmatic statement entitled 'Project for a Review', in which he calls for the journal to 'inhabit' a space that 'is neither a continuity nor a new beginning, but an interruption and a margin' corresponding to the gap 'produced early in modern Western culture between cultural patrimony and its transmission, between truth and its modes of transmission, between writing and authority' (*IH* 159). This gap has resulted in an ossified tradition and a decline in cultural legitimacy – themes that remain central to Agamben's reflections, for instance in *The Church and the Kingdom* and *The Mystery of Evil*.

The tool that he proposes to use to bridge that gap is 'philology', albeit a philology situated 'beyond the limits of any narrow academic conception' (*IH* 162), which will function as a kind of 'critical mythology' or 'new mythology' that brings together poetry and philosophy (*IH* 163). The importance of philology for his subsequent work is obvious, and indeed his works have increasingly taken the form of studies of the historical vicissitudes of particular words. As I have already noted, even when he explicitly takes up the question of 'What is Philosophy?' (*Che cos'è la filosofia?*), his investigation is primarily philological in character, attempting to clarify the stakes of the passage in Plato's Seventh Letter that had occupied his attention in 'The Thing Itself' (collected in *Potentialities*).

The other primary methodological principle that Agamben begins to develop in the pre-*Homo Sacer* period is the Benjaminian concept of messianism. The familiar connection between messianism and an interruption or halting of the law is clearly articulated in 'The Messiah and the Sovereign' (*P*). Previously Agamben had emphasised the messianic character of study in the segment of *Idea of Prose* entitled 'The Idea of Study', drawing an implicit connection between the themes of philosophy, philology and messianism and thereby laying the groundwork for the critical perspective on the Western tradition that informs the *Homo Sacer* project.

Even if Agamben was not as shy about making methodological claims as his comment in *The Signature of All Things* would suggest, the principle that method comes only after application is certainly true of the *Homo Sacer* project as such. Particularly in *Homo Sacer*, the methodological stakes are left unexplored as Agamben dives straight into a series of dense analyses. In 'What is a Paradigm?', Agamben notes that while 'certain figures such as *homo sacer*, the *Muselmann*, the state of exception, and the concentration camp [. . .] are all actual historical phenomena, I nonetheless treated them as paradigms whose role was to constitute and make intelligible a broader historical-problematic context' and he admits that 'this approach' – or, I would add, his lack of clarity about it – 'has generated a few misunderstandings' among readers expecting a more traditional scholarly treatment (*ST* 9). In light of his claim that method is always a *post hoc* affair, one would be justified in suspecting that it is precisely the objections of such readers that led Agamben to reflect on the exact status of these paradigmatic figures, which may not have been clear to him in advance.

Like all the methodological reflections in *The Signature of All Things*, 'What is a Paradigm?' takes the form of a reading of Foucault (in conjunction with other thinkers). In the preface to the book, Agamben explains this indirect approach by announcing that 'one of the methodological principles not discussed in the book – and which I owe to Walter Benjamin – is that doctrine may legitimately be exposed only in the form of interpretation' (*ST* 7). He supplements this with a second 'methodological principle – also not discussed in this book – which I often make use of', namely his view that

> the genuine philosophical element in every work [. . .] is its capacity to be developed. [. . .] It is precisely when one follows such a principle that the difference between what belongs to the author of a work and what is attributable to the interpreter becomes as essential as it is difficult to grasp. (*ST* 8)

With this in mind, we can say that Agamben's signature gesture is an interpretation that pushes through to the point where it is no longer mere interpretation and becomes truly creative philosophical work.

CONTINUITY

What is striking about 'What is an Apparatus?' and the studies in *The Signature of All Things* is how heavily Agamben's discussion overlaps with related passages in *The Kingdom and the Glory* and *The*

Sacrament of Language. That is to say, his explicit methodological reflections take their impetus from precisely the volumes that unexpectedly expanded the scope of the *Homo Sacer* project, which most readers expected to take the form of four short volumes: the three that had already appeared (*Homo Sacer*, *State of Exception* and *Remnants of Auschwitz*) and a concluding volume on the enigmatic concept of form-of-life. That expectation was upset by the publication of *The Kingdom and the Glory* (initially designated as volume 2.2 of the project) and *The Sacrament of Language* (volume 2.3), neither of which was anticipated in the original architectonic of the project and both of which contain significant methodological reflections.

In *The Kingdom and the Glory*, those reflections centre on the concept of the signature, which Agamben introduces in a dense and polemical ℵ-note on secularisation (*KG* 3–4). There he defines a signature as 'something that in a sign or concept marks and exceeds such a sign or concept referring it back to a determinate interpretation or field, without for this reason leaving the semiotic to constitute a new meaning or a new concept', and he claims that they are the object of 'Foucault's archeology and Nietzsche's genealogy (and, in a different sense, even Derrida's deconstruction and Benjamin's theory of dialectical images)' (*KG* 4). He later expands upon the concept of the signature significantly in *The Signature of All Things*, but it is telling that Agamben feels the need to make such an explicit – if extremely condensed – methodological claim in order to get his project in *The Kingdom and the Glory* off the ground. And this seemingly new methodological principle only highlights the disjunction between the subject matter and approach of *The Kingdom and the Glory* and the previous volumes of the series to which it is supposed to belong.

By contrast, *The Sacrament of Language* seems to unfold more clearly out of the previous volumes, even if the theme of the oath is unexpected. It explicitly expands upon the critique of conventional concepts of the sacred in *Homo Sacer*, and it adds greater rigour and clarity to the tightly intertwined relationship between politics, language and ontology that is often asserted but seldom explicitly justified in previous volumes. The primary means by which *The Sacrament of Language* achieves this is the concept of 'anthropogenesis', which had appeared for the first time in *The Open* (*O* 79–80), but which here takes on a central programmatic importance. The archaeological investigation of the oath that Agamben proposes to undertake is not merely the study of some particular phenomenon, but a path back to the moment of anthropogenesis – which also entails the possibility of a new and different anthropogenesis, a becoming-human in a new way. This is possible because anthropogenesis is not some determinate moment in the past, but 'just as the child in psychoanalysis expresses a force that continues to act in the psychic life of the adult; and just as the "big bang," which is supposed to have given rise to the universe, is something that never stops transmitting its background radiation to us', so too does the *arché* that is at stake in an archaeological investigation represent 'a field of historical currents stretched between anthropogenesis and the present' (*SL* 10–11).

The question that arises is whether the theory of signatures and the archaeological search for the experience of anthropogenesis are compatible, not only with each other, but with the actual procedure of the previous three volumes of the *Homo Sacer* project. A similar question could be asked about the concept of anthropogenesis and *The Kingdom and the Glory*'s concept of inoperativity. Are these more or less the same idea, viewed from a philosophical and a messianic perspective, respectively? Or are they unrelated concepts growing out of two books that are very different in scope and approach?

These questions converge in the question of what it actually means that all of these disparate studies are supposed to be part of a single overarching project. This question only became more urgent as the series expanded. When *The Highest Poverty*, the first part of the expected fourth volume on form-of-life, appeared, it was accompanied by an unanticipated *fifth* part of the second volume (skipping over 2.4), *Opus Dei*, whose investigation of liturgy Agamben deemed necessary for his study of monasticism. Agamben draws an explicit connection between *Opus Dei* and *The Kingdom and the Glory*, saying that in the latter volume 'we investigated the liturgical mystery above all in the face it turns toward God, in its objective or glorious aspect', whereas in *Opus Dei* 'our archeological study' – a designation that was not used for *The Kingdom and the Glory*, which was characterised as a genealogy – 'is oriented toward the aspect that above all concerns the priests' (*OD* xi). This connection is not elaborated, however, as the only explicit citation of *The Kingdom and the Glory* comes amid a review of Agamben's previous discussion of the concept of economy (*OD* 17). No similar reference to *The Sacrament of Language* appears in *The Highest Poverty*, however, even though it is clearly relevant to Agamben's extensive attempt to prove that monasticism does not require a binding oath. Indeed, assuming that the study of monasticism was always part of the plan, it helps to retroactively explain why Agamben thought a volume on the oath was necessary in the first place, making the lack of explicit reference all the more puzzling.

More broadly, it is difficult to tell why these particular works of

Agamben should be taken as more closely related than any others. As far as explicit references go, *Homo Sacer*, *State of Exception* and *The Kingdom and the Glory* all come in for discussion in *The Use of Bodies*, but *Remnants of Auschwitz*, *The Sacrament of Language* and *Opus Dei* are passed over in silence – making the latter three virtually orphan volumes in the series. If anything, the pattern of references suggests that *The Open*, which is discussed frequently in *The Use of Bodies*, has more right to be considered a part of the series than some of the official members of the set. And it is hard to account for the belated addition of *Stasis* (which represents two short seminars rather than a fully developed book) to the series as volume 2.2 *after* the publication of *The Use of Bodies* (4.2, the final volume), displacing *The Kingdom and the Glory* into the previously vacant 2.4 slot. This publication history is difficult to square with the idea that the series had a pre-established, systematic architectonic.

Nevertheless, *The Use of Bodies* takes great pains to present the series as in some way systematic (albeit necessarily incomplete). This is most clear in its concluding section, 'Toward a Theory of Destituent Potential', where Agamben gives an account of the series as a whole. There he argues that the structure of the exception is paradigmatic for all the volumes. No matter what sphere he is investigating, '[t]he strategy is always the same: something is divided, excluded, and pushed to the bottom, and precisely through this exclusion, it is included as *archè* and foundation' (UB 264). The same dynamic occurs in politics, language and ontology, and it also happens in *State of Exception*, *The Kingdom and the Glory* and, curiously, not one of the other official *Homo Sacer* volumes, but *The Open* (UB 264–5).

The remainder of the essay is an attempt to demonstrate that it is not sufficient to gain access to the submerged foundation, nor to destroy the parasitical dominating element. Rather, one must render the entire machine inoperative by unravelling the relationship of subordination between the two elements (UB 272). Throughout, Agamben is at great pains to demonstrate that exactly this is what is called for in *Homo Sacer*, and *The Use of Bodies* includes not only explicit references, but actual block quotations from that earlier work (UB 133, 263, 268) – something that is virtually unprecedented in Agamben's entire corpus.

These and other references throughout *The Use of Bodies* are often quite helpful for clarifying some of the most dense and obscure passages in *Homo Sacer* and demonstrating that, in some sense, the whole project was 'already there' in that pathbreaking first volume. Even so, *The Use of Bodies* appears to be imposing a retroactive continuity on the project. This is perhaps most clear in Agamben's list of 'concepts

[. . .] that have from the very beginning oriented' the entire project: 'use, demand, mode, form-of-life, inoperativity, destituent potential" (*UB* xiii). Aside from form-of-life, none of these concepts played a major role in the early volumes of the series. Demand came up briefly in *The Time that Remains* (where it is translated as 'exigency'), but *The Use of Bodies* is the first place where it is extensively discussed in the *Homo Sacer* series itself. The same is true of mode and destituent potential. Use and inoperativity are also relative latecomers, appearing first in *The Highest Poverty* and *The Kingdom and the Glory*, respectively. Are we to take literally his claim that these concepts provided orientation to the entire project, or does it amount to an indirect exhortation to read the earlier volumes with these concepts in mind?

In any case, whether or not the *Homo Sacer* series was prospectively systematic, it is clear that it is progressively *systematising* – a tendency that reaches its culmination in *The Use of Bodies*, but that can also be seen in the explicit methodological reflections in 'What is an Apparatus?' and *The Signature of All Things*. And indeed, if we look to the pattern of self-reference, it appears that *Homo Sacer* represents a turning point in Agamben's work, a shift away from occasional studies towards an overarching *project*. With the exception of a brief citation of *Language and Death* in *Remnants of Auschwitz*, no volume of the *Homo Sacer* series refers to any work of Agamben prior to *Homo Sacer* itself, even when such references would be obvious. For instance, even when he does refer to *Language and Death*, he does not mention the fact that the figure of the *homo sacer* appears in the conclusion of that very early work (*LD* 105), opting instead to refer to a small philological point on Greek tragedy. Nor, to take only one among many possible examples, does he refer back to his famous essay 'On Potentiality' (collected in *Potentialities*) when the topic comes up in *Homo Sacer*.

As much as Agamben wants to present the *Homo Sacer* series as systematic, then, he is much less concerned to do the same for his body of work as a whole. He makes frequent use of concepts and analyses from previous texts – indeed, for the reader well-versed in the texts of the *Homo Sacer* period, the temptation to read the earlier works as somehow 'already' containing the *Homo Sacer* project is intense. Only in a work published after the 'abandonment' of the *Homo Sacer* series, namely *What is Philosophy?*, does Agamben draw explicit attention to that book's connections with his earlier works (*Infancy and History*, along with several of the essays collected in *Potentialities*; *CF* 7), but in the main text itself, his only direct self-reference is, again, to a philological point in 'The Thing Itself' (*CF* 68).

Conclusion 311

While Agamben can sometimes refer back to detailed exegetical work for the sake of convenience, then, for the most part he seems to follow the same principle in reading his own texts that he describes in his reading of others. To the extent that he finds something capable of development in his own previous work, he must reach that point where 'he knows that it is now time to abandon the text that he is analyzing and to proceed on his own' (WA 13). The author's original intention is not finally binding on Agamben's creative appropriation of texts and concepts, even when that author is Agamben himself.

ACHIEVEMENT

The passage I have quoted from 'What is an Apparatus?' is not the only place where Agamben speaks of abandoning a text. In the prefatory note to *The Use of Bodies*, after clarifying that, as attentive readers should have predicted, one 'should not expect a new beginning, much less a conclusion', he characterises his project as 'an investigation that, like every work of poetry and of thought, cannot be concluded but only abandoned (and perhaps continued by others)' (UB xiii). On one level, this is a very humble admission that his work cannot in any sense claim to be the final word. To the extent that it has a future, it will only be because others take it up, presumably developing it in the same way that Agamben develops his own sources. In short, we are being invited to read Agamben as Agamben reads himself – meaning that he is also ultimately inviting us to abandon his work once we find the point where it can be developed.

Yet within this humble effacement there is a core claim that the *Homo Sacer* series does count as an authentic work of thought. Can we assume that it meets some of his early hopes for a radical 'destruction' of the Western tradition (*The Man Without Content*), for a truly critical work in the full Benjaminian sense (*Stanzas*), for a philological critical mythology that will revive a decaying cultural heritage (*Infancy and History*)? Has he finally fully elaborated what it means to practise a philosophy that relentlessly exposes the fact of language (*Language and Death*)? Given his lack of detailed references to these earlier works, we have no way of knowing for sure how he would respond to these questions – though we as readers can, of course, decide for ourselves.

To gauge what Agamben believes he has achieved in his work, and above all in the *Homo Sacer* series, we must look to his own explicit statements. Sometimes those statements come in the middle of a text, when Agamben lists a series of theses distilling the results of his investigations. It is worth noting that these sets of theses *never* conclude a work, but always lay the groundwork for further development. Every result is only a provisional stopping point.

There is another sense in which his investigations might provide a stopping point, however – namely, the messianic sense of bringing the Western machine to a halt, of rendering it inoperative. Here I believe we can detect a Pauline 'already/not yet' dynamic. On the one hand, it is obvious that Agamben's works, taken in themselves, have not produced the messianic kingdom. Yet there are hints that, in the very act of study, something of the kind is already going on. This claim echoes throughout his body of work, from the passage on the 'Idea of Study' in *Idea of Prose* up through *State of Exception*, where he memorably writes, 'One day humanity will play with law just as children play with disused objects, not in order to restore them to their canonical use but to free them from it for good. [. . .] This liberation is the task of study, or of play' (*SE* 64).

Here the reference to Agamben's own practice of 'study' is at best implicit. In *The Kingdom and the Glory*, by contrast, he is less circumspect. Dismissing the idea that the way forward is to 'oppose secularism and the general will to theology and its providential paradigm', he claims:

> what is needed is, rather, an archeological operation like the one that we have attempted here, one that, by moving upstream to a time before the separation that took place and that turned the two poles into rival but inseparable brothers, undoes the entire economic-theological apparatus and renders it inoperative. (*KG* 285)

Far from being a distant goal, the very act of study somehow renders the apparatus inoperative – here we seemingly have a return to the boldness of Agamben's earliest methodological claims. Even more striking is a passage in *The Signature of All Things* where Agamben will liken the work of archaeology to the theological concept of salvation. The latter 'acts as a kind of a priori that is immanent in the work of creation and makes it possible' (*ST* 108), much as anthropogenesis serves as the 'historical a priori' or 'fringe of ultrahistory' presupposed by our normal historical experience. As such,

> not only is archeology the immanent a priori of historiography, but the gesture of the archeologist constitutes the paradigm of every true human action. For it is not merely the work of an author's – or of anyone's – life that determines his or her rank, but the way in which he or she has been able to bring it back to the work of redemption, to mark it with the signature of salvation and to render it intelligible. Only for those who will have known how to save it, will creation be possible. (*ST* 108)

If this claim sounds grandiose, it is worth recalling that Agamben elsewhere characterises the work of the messiah as the smallest gesture of all. In *The Coming Community*, he quotes Benjamin's version of a rabbinic story according to which, in the messianic world, 'Everything will be as it is now, just a little different' (CC 53). As he clarifies,

> This cannot refer simply to real circumstance, in the sense that the nose of the blessed one will become a little shorter, or that the cup on the table will be displaced exactly one-half centimeter, or that the dog outside will stop barking. The tiny displacement does not refer to the state of things, but to their sense and their limits. (CC 54)

Grasping – or better, coming into contact with – this sense and this limit is the task of study. And it is here that we may be able to explicitly tie together the philosophical and messianic strains of Agamben's thought, if we read this 'tiny displacement' as the shift in our relationship to language that, in Agamben's view, it is the task of philosophy to make possible. No particular act of study necessarily achieves that tiny displacement in a global sense, and it may not even teach us how to achieve it in the sphere of action designated as play. Yet if Agamben is right, philosophical study does somehow anticipate and participate in the messianic movement, and in that sense it may equip us to recognise it when it comes.

Contributors

Mathew Abbott is Lecturer in Philosophy at Federation University, Australia. He is the author of *The Figure of This World: Agamben and the Question of Political Ontology*, published by Edinburgh University Press.

Jussi Backman is a senior research fellow in philosophy at the University of Jyväskylä, Finland. He specialises in phenomenology, philosophical hermeneutics, recent continental thought and ancient philosophy. He is the author of *Omaisuus ja elämä: Heidegger ja Aristoteles kreikkalaisen filosofian rajalla* (Eurooppalaisen filosofian seura, 2005) and *Complicated Presence: Heidegger and the Postmetaphysical Unity of Being* (SUNY Press, 2015), as well as being the Finnish translator of Heidegger's *Introduction to Metaphysics*.

Paolo Bartoloni is Established Professor of Italian at the National University of Ireland, Galway. He is the author of *Objects in Italian Life and Culture: Fiction, Migration, and Artificiality* (Palgrave, 2016), *Sapere di scrivere. Svevo e gli ordigni di* La coscienza di Zeno (Il Carrubo, 2015), *On the Cultures of Exile, Translation and Writing* (Purdue University Press, 2008) and *Interstitial Writing: Calvino, Caproni, Sereni and Svevo* (Troubador Publishing, 2003).

Jeffrey Bernstein is Associate Professor of Philosophy at the College of the Holy Cross. He works in the areas of Spinoza, German philosophy and Jewish thought.

Mårten Björk is a doctoral candidate at the University of Gothenburg, Sweden. His thesis is devoted to the discussion of eternal life and immortality in Germany between 1914 and 1945.

Susan Dianne Brophy is an Assistant Professor in the Department of Sociology and Legal Studies at St Jerome's University in the University of Waterloo, Canada. She has previously published articles on Agamben, anticolonialism and politico-legal theory. Her current research focuses on the history of legal and economic development.

Virgil Brower holds a PhD in Comparative Literary Studies from Northwestern University and another in Theology, Ethics and Culture from the Chicago Theological Seminary. His research focuses on the phenomenology of taste and its implications for both philosophy and theology.

Claire Colebrook is Edwin Erle Sparks Professor of English at Pennsylvania State University. She has published numerous works on Gilles Deleuze, visual art, poetry, queer theory, film studies, contemporary literature, theory, cultural studies and visual culture. She is the editor of the Critical Climate Change Book Series at Open Humanities Press.

Colby Dickinson is Assistant Professor of Theology at Loyola University, Chicago. He is the author of *Agamben and Theology* (Bloomsbury, 2011), *Between the Canon and the Messiah: The Structure of Faith in Contemporary Continental Thought* (Bloomsbury, 2013) and *Words Fail: Theology, Poetry, and the Challenge of Representation* (Fordham University Press, 2016).

Ingrid Diran is an instructor in liberal arts at Pacific Northwest College of Art. She is completing a book manuscript entitled *Mutinous Muteness: Radicalizing Illegibility in Twentieth-Century African American Literature*.

Adi Efal-Lautenschläger is a researcher at the University of Cologne. She has published *Figural Philology: Panofsky and the Science of Things* (Bloomsbury, 2016) and her *Habitus as Method: Revisiting a Scholastic Theory of Art* is forthcoming (Peeters, 2017).

Alysia Garrison is Assistant Professor of English at Dartmouth College. She specialises in eighteenth-century literature, Romanticism and critical theory. Her work on Agamben has appeared in *Law and Critique* and in *The Agamben Dictionary*.

John Grumley is the author of *History and Totality: From Hegel to Foucault* (Routledge, 2016) and *Agnes Heller: A Moralist in the Vortex of History* (Pluto Press, 2005), and many articles in international journals on critical theory. He is the Director of the Markus Archive.

Christian Grünnagel is Assistant Professor of Romance Literatures at the University of Gießen (Germany) and the author of articles dealing with European premodernity, the Marquis de Sade and literary/cultural theory, among others.

Nadine Hartmann is writing her doctoral thesis on epistemological challenges in Georges Bataille's *Summa Atheologica* at the Bauhaus-Universität Weimar and has published articles on Bataille, Freud and Lacan.

Ted Jennings is Professor of Biblical and Constructive Theology at the Chicago Theological Seminary and the author, most recently, of *Outlaw Justice: The Messianic Politics of Paul* (Stanford University Press, 2013).

Adam Kotsko is Assistant Professor of Humanities at Shimer College in Chicago, the author, most recently, of *The Prince of This World* (Stanford University Press, 2016), and the translator of many works by Giorgio Agamben.

Vanessa Lemm is a Professor of Philosophy and Head of School at the School of Humanities and Languages of the University of New South Wales, Australia. She is the author of *Nietzsche's Animal Philosophy* (Fordham University Press, 2009) and *Nietzsche y el pensamiento politico contemporáneo* (Fondo, 2013).

Dave Mesing is a PhD candidate in philosophy at Villanova University. He works primarily in political philosophy, and is preparing a dissertation on strategy informed by attempts to bring Spinoza and Marx together.

Beatrice Marovich is Assistant Professor of Theology at Hanover College. She is working on a book-length project with the working title, *Creature Feeling: Religion, Power, and Creaturely Life*.

Julia Ng is Lecturer in Critical Theory at Goldsmiths, University of London. She specialises in the intersection of mathematics, philosophy and political thought in the early work of Walter Benjamin.

Mika Ojakangas is Professor of Political Thought at the University of Jyväskylä, Finland. He is the author of seven monographs, most recently *On the Greek Origins of Biopolitics: A Reinterpretation of the History of Biopower* (Routledge, 2016).

Sergei Prozorov is Senior Lecturer in World Politics at the Department of Political and Economic Studies, University of Helsinki. He is the author of seven monographs, most recently *The Biopolitics of Stalinism* (Edinburgh University Press, 2016).

Frances Restuccia teaches contemporary theory and the world novel at Boston College. She is the author of *Amorous Acts: Lacanian Ethics in*

Modernism, Film, and Queer Theory (Stanford University Press, 2006) and is currently working on the relation of Agamben's philosophy to literature.

Carlo Salzani holds a PhD in Comparative Literature from Monash University. His latest publications include *Introduzione a Giorgio Agamben* (2013) and the collection of essays *Towards the Critique of Violence: Walter Benjamin and Giorgio Agamben* (2015).

Anke Snoek is a post-doctoral researcher at Maastricht University and has written a book on Kafka's influence on Agamben. Her main research interest concerns questions around the agency of marginalised people.

Henrik Sunde Wilberg is Assistant Professor of German at the University of Minnesota, Morris.

Jessica Whyte is Senior Lecturer and an Australian Research Council 'DECRA' Fellow at the University of Western Sydney. She is the author of *Catastrophe and Redemption: The Political Thought of Giorgio Agamben* (SUNY Press, 2013).

Index

a priori, 165, 312
  historical, 72, 239n, 312
abandonment, 61n, 164, 165, 256, 268, 277, 299; *see also* ban
Absolute, the, 67, 141, 142, 226
Acéphale, 111
action, 6, 19, 58, 71, 73, 102, 103, 105, 107, 128–9, 158, 163, 166, 186, 187–9, 192, 202, 237, 257, 289, 312
  ethical, 290
  historical, 30, 91, 110
  political, 78, 91, 103, 204, 226, 261n, 290
actualitas see actuality
actuality, 6, 18–21, 26n, 71, 96, 127, 142, 187, 191, 206, 207, 209, 220, 273, 276, 278–9, 288
  integral, 279
Adorno, Theodor W., 36, 147, 193, 198n, 199n, 219–29
adynamia, 19, 25n, 273, 278
aesthetics, 1, 2, 4, 29, 33, 39, 40, 125, 126, 127, 128, 129, 148, 173, 222
  of existence, 58, 175
aestheticisation
  of the messianic, 222
  of violence, 114
affection, auto-/self-, 202–4, 232–8, 239, 251n, 272
Agamben, Giorgio (works)
  'Absolute Immanence' ('L'immanenza assoluta'), 280n
  'Aby Warburg and the nameless science' ('Aby Warburg e la scienza senza nome'), 211
  'Author as Gesture, The' ('L'autore come gesto'), 35
  'Bartleby, or On Contingency'
  ('Bartleby o della contingenza'), 6, 171–2
  'Bataille e il paradosso della sovranità', 109, 111–12, 116n
  'Beyond Human Rights' ('Al di là dei diritti dell'uomo'), 31
  'Caro Giulio che tristezza questa Einaudi', 36n
  '121a giornata di Sodoma e Gomorra, La', 197, 200n
  Che cos'è il reale?, 299n
  Che cos'è la filosofia?, 188, 304, 305, 310
  Church and the Kingdom, The (*La Chiesa e il Regno*), 84, 191, 225, 305
  'Comedy' ('Commedia'), 127
  Coming Community, The (*La comunità che viene*), 19, 21, 31, 34, 41, 42, 43, 44–5, 47, 48, 49n, 60n, 68, 136, 144, 166, 171, 178, 190, 204, 259, 313
  'Difference and Repetition: On Guy Debord's Films', 48n, 176n, 177n
  'Dream of Language, The' ('Il sogno della lingua'), 127
  'Elements for a Theory of Destituent Power', 271n
  End of the Poem, The (*Categorie italiane*), 3, 83, 127, 150, 151, 152n, 159, 178, 200n, 204, 299n
  'Eternal Return and the Paradox of Passion, The', 176n
  'Experimentum linguae', 4, 118, 281n
  'Form-of-life' ('Forma-di-vita'), 115, 140, 298
  'Friendship' (*L'amico*), 175
  Fuoco e il racconto, Il, 40, 125, 127–8

'Glorious Body, The' ('Il corpo glorioso'), 261
Highest Poverty, The (*Altissima povertà*), 21, 41, 77, 81, 93, 108n, 168, 189, 190, 195, 196, 241n, 248, 278, 308, 310
Homo Sacer, 7, 15, 16, 18, 19, 20, 21, 31, 32, 33, 38n, 40, 51, 52, 53, 54, 56, 61n, 68, 69, 77, 87, 88, 89, 90, 92, 93, 95, 96, 101, 104, 105, 111, 113, 114, 116, 121, 122, 133, 139, 142, 148, 152n, 153n, 155, 157, 158, 159, 162, 164, 165, 167, 171, 178, 179, 181, 193, 194, 195, 196, 199n, 200n, 204, 206, 231, 232, 234, 241n, 243, 244, 249n, 250n, 251n, 259, 260n, 277, 278, 279, 280, 288, 296, 297, 298, 300n, 305, 306, 307, 309, 310
'Idea of Language, The' ('L'idea del linguaggio'), 304
Idea of Prose (*Idea della Prosa*), 3, 5, 8, 12n, 31, 55, 66, 154, 159, 160n, 171, 178, 183, 184, 227, 259, 305, 312
'Idea of Study, The' ('Idea dello studio'), 5, 12n, 305, 312
'Importante ritrovamento di manoscritti di Walter Benjamin, Un', 36n
'In Playland' ('Il paese dei balocchi'), 35, 261n
Infancy and History (*Infanzia e storia*), 3, 4, 30, 35, 37n, 82, 118–19, 126, 133, 138, 139, 163, 164–5, 178, 190, 197, 209, 220, 221, 223, 242, 246, 304, 305, 310, 311
'K.', 7, 159, 160n
Kingdom and the Glory, The (*Il Regno e la Gloria*), 20, 21, 40, 49n, 56–7, 61n, 69, 70–1, 73, 74, 77, 80, 84, 86, 93, 94, 125, 159, 167, 170n, 186, 190, 195, 206, 243, 276, 306, 307, 308, 309, 310, 312
'Kommerel, or On Gesture' ('Kommerel, o del gesto'), 35
Language and Death (*Il linguaggio e la morte*), 3, 30, 31, 65, 66, 67, 68, 69, 109, 110, 116, 117, 138, 139–40, 141–3, 174, 178, 184n, 230, 231, 232, 234, 236, 237, 240n, 241n, 257, 258, 304, 310, 311
'Language and History' ('Lingua e storia'), 30
Man Without Content, The (*L'uomo senza contenuto*), 2, 3, 7–8, 29, 33–4, 38n, 39, 40, 65, 139, 147, 148–9, 150, 152n, 154, 160n, 164, 171, 173–4, 176n, 178, 249n, 262, 311
'Marginal Notes on *Commentaries on the Society of the Spectacle*' ('Glosse in margine ai *Commentari sulla società dello spettacolo*'), 41–4, 45, 47, 49n, 176n
Means without End (*Mezzi senza fine*), 31, 35, 40, 41–4, 45, 47, 48n, 49n, 77, 79, 104–5, 109, 115, 140, 156, 171, 172, 176n, 201, 204, 208, 212, 213, 235, 298
'Messiah and the Sovereign, The' ('Il Messia e il sovrano'), 156, 287, 305
Mystery of Evil, The (*Il mistero del male*), 305
'Notes on Gesture' ('Note sul gesto'), 35, 176n
Nudities (*Nudità*), 7, 158, 159, 160n, 228n, 255, 256, 257, 260, 261n
Nymphs (*Ninfe*), 210, 215n
'On Potentiality' ('La potenza del pensiero'), 310
'On the Limits of Violence' ('Sui limiti della violenza'), 31, 264
Open, The (*L'aperto*), 34, 64, 85, 109, 142, 176, 297, 307, 309
Opus Dei, 21, 23, 25n, 71–2, 162, 163, 167–8, 186–7, 188, 189, 192, 195, 210, 265, 266, 308, 309
'*Pardes*: The Writing of Potentiality' ('*Pardes*: La scrittura della potenza'), 230, 233, 234, 235, 236, 237, 240n
'Passion of Facticity, The' ('La passione della fatticità'), 185n
'Philosophical Archaeology' ('Archeologia filosofica'), 174
'Philosophy and Linguistics' ('Filosofia e linguistica'), 304
'Politica dell'esilio', 191
Potentialities (*La potenza del pensiero*), 3, 6, 20, 30, 86, 119, 121, 134, 137, 141, 142, 145n,

Agamben, Giorgio (works) *(cont.)*
  Potentialities (cont.)
    155, 157, 171, 172, 178, 180,
    181, 182, 183, 185n, 188, 202,
    203, 205, 206, 209, 211, 213,
    214, 220, 230, 231, 233, 234,
    235–6, 241n, 253, 273, 280n,
    283, 286, 287, 288, 299, 304,
    305, 310
  'Pozzo di Babele, Il', 160n
  Profanations (Profanazioni), 86, 91,
    144, 197
  'Project for a Review' ('Programma
    per una rivista'), 3, 305
  *Pulcinella ovvero divertimento per li
    regazzi in quattro scene*, 172–3
  'Quattro Glosse a Kafka', 12n,
    160n
  *Remnants of Auschwitz (Quel che
    resta di Auschwitz)*, 17, 56, 79,
    85, 86, 105, 119, 120, 148, 155,
    159, 165–6, 167, 171, 172, 195,
    199n, 202, 219, 220, 234, 236–7,
    241n, 307, 309, 310
  *Sacrament of Language, The (Il
    sacramento del linguaggio)*, 41,
    79–80, 93, 123n, 178, 195, 240n,
    304, 305, 307, 308, 309
  *Signature of All Things, The
    (Signatura rerum)*, 4, 9–10, 35, 51,
    54–5, 87, 121–2, 140, 166, 172,
    174, 178, 179, 210, 211, 212–13,
    242, 280n, 304, 306, 307, 310,
    312
  Stanzas (Stanze), 2, 3, 8, 29, 109,
    110, 122, 124n, 125, 126, 128,
    130n, 146–7, 151, 164, 168, 178,
    240n, 242, 244, 249n, 252, 260n,
    311
  Stasis, 80, 84, 93, 178, 195, 243,
    244, 246, 248, 309
  *State of Exception (Stato di
    eccezione)*, 7, 28, 33, 35, 56, 73,
    78, 89, 90, 92, 93, 156, 157, 158,
    159, 166, 167, 195, 243, 245,
    247, 249n, 250n, 261, 277, 307,
    309, 312
  'Thing Itself, The' ('La cosa stessa'),
    180, 181, 183, 305, 310
  *Time that Remains, The (Il tempo
    che resta)*, 8–9, 28–9, 34, 78, 81,
    82–3, 85, 91, 92–3, 117, 143–4,
    156, 166, 221–2, 223, 233, 234,
    257, 264–5, 284, 288–9, 310

  'Toward a Theory of Destituent
    Potential' ('Per una teoria della
    potenza destituente'), 309
  Use of Bodies, The (L'uso dei corpi),
    10, 15, 16, 17, 20, 21–3, 34, 39,
    41, 42, 58–60, 72–3, 75n, 80, 81,
    87, 93, 94–6, 123, 125, 127, 128,
    129, 131, 135, 143, 144, 149–50,
    153n, 154, 168, 175–6, 178–9,
    180, 181–2, 184, 185n, 186,
    188–9, 190–1, 192, 195, 196,
    201, 203, 204–5, 206–7, 224–5,
    234, 237–8, 239, 240n, 241n,
    248, 250n, 252, 258, 262, 263,
    269, 272, 280, 298, 309, 310, 311
  'Violenza e speranza nell'ultimo
    spettacolo', 49n
  'Walter Benjamin and the Demonic'
    ('Walter Benjamin e il demonico'),
    30, 283, 286
  'What is an Apparatus?' (*Che cos'è
    un dispositivo?*), 306, 310, 311
  'What is a Paradigm?' ('Che cos'è un
    paradigma?'), 306
  'Work of Man, The' ('L'opera
    dell'uomo'), 262–3
Alexander the Great, 158
alienation, 8, 44, 47, 142, 267
Alighieri, Dante, 125–30, 151, 260n
Améry, Jean (Hanns Chaim Mayer),
  119, 223
Ammonius Grammaticus, 24n
angel, 94, 159, 197, 199n, 282–3, 286
  of history, 29, 282
Angelus Novus, 27, 282, 286
animal, 16, 17, 24n, 34, 53, 72, 85, 95,
  136, 140, 142, 176, 177n, 204,
  230, 293, 296–7
  human, 53, 123, 205
  laborans, 267
  rationale, 267
animality *see* animal
anomie, 88, 91, 92, 95, 167, 230, 239
  mystery of, 92
anthropogenesis, 72, 206, 307–8, 312
Antichrist, 84, 91–3, 284
anti-liberalism, 284–5
Apelles of Kos, 28–9
apocalyptic/apocalypticism, 82, 84,
  106, 256–7, 284, 285
apokatastasis, 55
apparatus, 4, 6, 8, 73, 86, 87, 88, 95,
  96, 97, 114, 129, 159, 186, 187,
  191, 192, 210, 212, 225, 235, 312

biopolitical, 69
  ontological, 73
  theological, 253, 256–7
Aquinas, Thomas, 80, 129, 265
Arab Spring, 103
Aragon, Louis, 27, 36n
archaeology, 2, 4, 10, 51, 54, 121, 211, 212, 280, 307, 312
  philosophical, 54, 121, 212, 305
arché, 18, 54, 121, 209, 212, 247, 308, 309
Arendt, Hannah, 15, 16, 33, 52, 101–8, 267–8, 269
argos, 279
Aristotle, 6, 11, 15–26, 33, 39, 53, 70, 75n, 123, 125–6, 129, 132, 134, 135, 140, 144, 153n, 175, 180, 181, 183, 203, 232, 235, 237, 241n, 258, 262–3, 273, 279, 280
art, 43, 59, 65, 128, 130n, 132, 139, 142, 149, 164, 173, 206–7, 208, 210, 211, 212, 255
  of existence, 58
  of government, 56–7, 61n
  of quoting without quotation marks, 1, 8, 29, 36n
  without the artist, 58–9, 172–3, 176
  work of, 33, 35, 58, 172–3, 176, 209, 210
Artaud, Antonin, 197
as if, 166–7, 187, 222–4
as (if) not, 80–2, 143, 224, 226
atheology, 113, 150, 151
auctoritas, 125, 245
Aufhebung, 3, 110, 138, 140, 143, 211, 233–4; *see also* sublation
Augustine of Hippo, 11, 187, 190, 191, 198
Auschwitz, 45, 57, 172, 219–20, 221, 223, 227
Ausnahmezustand, 247, 248; *see also* exception
authenticity, 63, 127, 224
authority, 8, 40, 89, 164, 165, 166, 167, 168, 179, 184n, 243, 244, 245, 246, 248, 250n, 305
  constituted, 91, 92, 93
  sovereign, 91, 231
  transcendent, 56, 167
autoconstitution, 20, 234, 239, 241n
Averroes (Ibn Rushd), 11, 126, 128, 129

ban, 89, 90, 105, 133, 234, 235, 253, 257, 260n
  sovereign, 32, 95, 168, 235, 278, 298
bare life *see* life: bare
Bartleby, 6, 21, 260n
Bataille, Georges, 27–8, 109–16, 140, 142, 171, 299
Baudelaire, Charles, 28, 30
Beauvoir, Simone de, 193
Beaufret, Jean, 147
Being, destiny of, 64, 147–8, 151
Benjamin, Walter, 1, 5, 7–8, 9, 10, 27–38, 40, 55, 63, 73, 76, 78, 79, 82, 84, 87, 92, 96, 97, 103, 106, 109, 111, 114, 118, 119, 123, 123n, 152n, 153n, 156, 158, 160n, 165, 172, 176, 177n, 220, 221, 223, 225, 275, 279, 282–3, 284–5, 286, 288, 289, 296, 305, 306, 307, 311, 313
Benveniste, Émile, 31, 117–24, 237, 272
Bergson, Henri, 214n
Berlusconi, Silvio, 28
bilingualism, 127
biopolitical, the *see* biopolitics
biopolitics, 33, 51–4, 56, 58, 60n, 63, 87, 88, 89, 90, 95, 104, 105, 175–6, 194, 205, 238, 273, 276
biopower, 52, 53, 276
bios, 15–18, 21, 22, 24, 24n, 53, 68, 70, 73, 75n, 95, 122, 127, 175, 179, 181, 184, 190, 192n, 224, 232, 259
Blanchot, Maurice, 11, 111, 197
Blaupot ten Cate, Anna Maria, 282
body, 80, 125, 126, 127, 128, 144, 173, 184, 203, 209, 234, 238, 241n, 248, 251n, 292
  animal, 293
  biological, 294
  biopolitical, 88, 89, 259
  glorious, 261n
  metaphysics of, 197
  political, 179
  singular, 58, 73, 95, 175
  use of, 22, 144, 234, 237, 238, 248–9, 273, 280
Boethius, Severinus, 126
Böhlendorff, Casimir Ulrich, 149, 150, 151
Brecht, Bertolt, 35
Bucephalus, 7, 154, 157, 158
bureaucracy, 46, 154, 187, 266

Calvino, Italo, 28, 151
camp, 148, 165, 168, 220
　concentration, 17, 52, 56, 195, 199n, 227, 294, 298, 306
　death, 101
　as paradigm, 53, 54, 55, 102, 104, 107
capital, 42–3, 112, 263, 266
capitalism, 46, 269
　advanced, 162
　industrial, 162
care, 22, 72
　of the self, 59
Casel, Odo, 11
catastrophe, 91, 154, 155, 156
　history as, 30, 224
Catholicism, 76, 187
cause, 66, 163
　causa sui, 203
　immanent, 203, 206
　instrumental, 265
　secondary, 57
Cavalcanti, Guido, 126–7, 197
Celan, Paul, 249n
Char, René, 147
chresis/chresthai, 18, 21–3, 143, 188, 237, 280
Chrysippus of Soli, 237
Christ, 113, 187, 284, 294, 295, 298; see also Jesus
Christianity, 56, 77, 78, 84, 91, 240n, 285
　Pauline, 77, 285
chronos, 25n, 82, 178, 256, 260
Church, 84, 187, 225, 256, 284
citation, 1, 40
　theory of, 7–9, 29
　without quotation marks, 1, 8, 29, 34, 296
class, 263–5
　ruling, 264
　struggle, 115
　universal, 265, 266
　working, 263, 264
command, 162, 167, 168, 189, 265, 266
commodification, 29, 104
commodity, 42, 43, 44, 45, 46, 50n
　fetishism, 30, 42
communism, 73, 263, 268–9
community, 4, 17, 22, 42, 44, 46, 68, 69, 112–13, 183, 189, 195, 196, 225, 273
　coming, 224

　of life, 144
　messianic, 82, 86
　negative, 111
conatus, 204–6, 273
constitutionalism, 106, 274
contemplation, 16, 113, 126, 130n, 191, 201, 205–7
corporeality, 126, 203
　naked, 256
creature, 32, 157–9, 167, 168, 264, 293–6, 297, 298
crisis, 2, 63, 69, 103, 105, 107, 168, 232, 273, 276, 285
　constitutional, 105
　of tradition, 2, 3, 29
culture, 8, 146, 151, 213, 221, 231, 262
　commodification of, 29
　museification of, 29
　Western, 5, 21, 164, 214, 259, 305
Cynics/Cynicism, 59

de Man, Paul, 147
deactivation, 4, 6, 7, 34, 78–80, 97, 158, 166, 168, 223, 225, 236, 248, 280
death, 3, 24n, 65–6, 90, 112, 139, 140, 141, 174, 219, 253, 254, 257, 258, 259
　penalty, 179
Debord, Guy, 33, 39–50, 171, 176n
decision, 23, 90, 96–7, 107
　sovereign, 53, 88, 96–7, 102, 105, 179, 235, 265, 274
deconstruction, 222, 230, 231, 233, 241n, 307
decreation, 292, 295, 296, 298–9
Deleuze, Gilles, 118, 131–7, 171, 250n, 253
democracy, 90, 104, 107, 275, 276
　liberal, 107, 165
　modern, 104
　parliamentary, 89
deposition, 32, 34, 78, 81
Derrida, Jacques, 32, 87, 110, 118, 122, 175, 222, 223, 224, 225, 228n, 229n, 230–41, 253, 303, 307
Descartes, René, 131, 203
désoeuvrement, 32, 34, 125, 142, 143, 298, 299
destiny, 63, 64, 66, 67, 68, 70, 71, 72, 74, 85, 147, 148
　of being, 64, 147, 148, 151

biological, 68, 206
historical, 64, 74n
social, 206
desubjectification, 151, 236, 238, 241n
dialectics, 110, 231, 232, 233
  lord-bondsman, 197
  master-slave, 144
  messianic suspension of, 221
  negative, 221, 223, 225, 226
  at a standstill, 221
diathesis, 23, 237; *see also* voice
différance, 234, 235
Diogenes Laertius, 237
dispositif see apparatus
division, 28, 85, 95, 138, 141, 191, 226
  of division, 224, 226
  of labour, 268–9
dolce stil novo, 126, 127, 151
Durkheim, Émile, 115
duty, 21, 71, 163, 164, 167, 186, 187, 251n, 266; *see also* office; *officium*
dynamis, 15, 18–21, 22, 25n, 209, 235, 237, 273, 278

economy, 29, 46, 47, 57, 69, 73, 84, 109, 167, 192, 243, 246, 267, 308
  divine, 20, 57
  political, 57
  of power, 57
  Trinitarian, 86
Eichmann, Adolf, 266
Einaudi, Giulio, 28
emergency *see* exception
Empire, 89, 149, 276
  Christian, 91
  Roman, 91, 92
energeia, 15, 18–21, 22, 71, 189, 209, 279
Enlightenment, 138, 194, 197, 198, 199n
Entwicklungsfähigkeit, 1, 9–11, 35, 272
Ereignis, 63, 67, 70, 72, 260n
ergon, 18, 21–2, 24n, 262, 279, 280; *see also* work
Eros, 126, 197, 286; *see also* love
eschatology, 28, 82, 84, 187, 285, 288
eschaton, 288
Esposito, Roberto, 171, 175
ethics, 1, 4, 58, 59, 68, 107, 128, 129, 166, 194, 204, 235, 253, 257, 259, 263, 283, 289, 290

coming, 224
Kantian, 167
ethos, 4, 18, 23, 68, 141, 144, 205, 213, 258, 259
eudaimonia, 17, 283
exception, 88–90, 91, 95, 96, 97, 111, 113, 166, 239, 242, 243, 247, 248, 257, 274, 277, 278, 284, 297, 309
  logic of, 278
  originary, 243
  real state of, 92, 93, 157
  and rule, 33, 165, 248, 253
  sovereign, 89, 275, 296
  state of, 20, 33, 53, 88, 89, 92, 156, 157, 162, 165, 166, 167, 168, 170n, 194, 199n, 234, 238, 239, 244, 245, 246–7, 254, 256, 259, 278, 288, 306
exclusion, 17, 69, 73, 95, 104, 106, 107, 148, 176, 181, 191, 244, 254, 255, 279, 298, 309
  inclusive/inclusionary, 3, 89, 95, 96, 106
  zone of, 105
experience, 3, 30, 44, 66, 68, 112, 125–6, 139, 142, 163, 164–5
  aesthetic, 126
  destruction of, 3
  ecstatic, 112, 113
  of history, 30, 91, 312
  inner, 113, 114
  intellectual, 128
  of language/speech, 8, 30, 43, 117–19, 122, 127, 140, 141, 174, 258, 304
  loss of, 3
  original, 164, 165
  pure, 165
  sensible, 128
experimentum linguae, 44, 118

facticity, 63, 72, 224
feast/festival, 242, 267
fetishism, 242, 252
  commodity, 30, 42
Feuerbach, Ludwig, 9–11, 35, 280n
finitude, 63, 67
force, 293–6, 297
  of the law, 156
  weak messianic, 103, 221, 225
  without significance, 32, 92, 156, 157, 158, 278

form-of-life, 12, 15, 21, 23, 51, 58, 60, 73, 79, 95, 96, 128, 129, 140, 175, 179, 195, 235, 259, 298, 299, 308, 310
Foucault, Michel, 10, 23, 33, 50n, 51–62, 69, 87, 88, 90, 103, 109, 110, 112, 113, 123, 171, 174, 175, 176, 195, 212, 231, 232, 239n, 242, 253, 273, 303, 306, 307
foundation, 3, 7, 15, 66, 69, 167, 180, 309
  ineffable, 3, 141, 258
  mystical, 239, 259
  negative, 68, 72, 95, 139, 140, 141, 142, 254, 257, 258
Francis of Assisi, 151
Franciscanism, 21, 81, 108n, 168, 278
Freud, Sigmund, 117, 242–51
future, 55, 82, 83, 106, 283, 288, 290
  anterior, 55, 275

genealogy, 2, 51, 55, 56, 57, 61n, 69, 70, 197, 272, 296, 307, 308
gesture, 35, 43, 158, 159, 212, 213
Ghirlandaio, Domenico, 210
Giacometti, Alberto, 10, 12n
glory, 86, 94, 95
God/gods, 20, 53, 57, 61n, 73, 80, 81, 91, 93, 94, 113, 116, 133, 134, 137, 143, 149, 150, 154, 155, 159, 167, 174, 190, 191, 203, 243, 247, 249, 265, 282, 284, 285, 289, 293, 294, 295, 296, 297, 298, 299, 308
Godard, Jean-Luc, 49n
Gould, Glenn, 259
governance, 52, 90, 95, 104
government, 21, 52, 57, 61n, 62n, 70, 87, 89, 93, 94, 159, 276
  pastoral, 56
governmentality, 51, 52, 56, 57, 58, 69, 70
Gregory of Nazianzus, 57
Gregory of Nyssa, 85
Guantanamo, 90
Guattari, Félix, 118, 131, 132, 135, 136, 250n
Guillaume, Gustave, 117
guilt, 127, 157–8, 242

habit, 18, 22–3, 96, 129, 263
habitus, 127, 128

Hadot, Pierre, 58, 59
happiness, 35, 139, 282, 283, 286–7
Hardt, Michael, 276
Hegel, Georg Wilhelm Friedrich, 64–5, 66, 67, 110, 115, 138–45, 197, 221, 231, 232, 233, 240n, 243, 244, 258, 265
Hegelianism, 110, 138, 139, 140
Heidegger, Martin, 2, 10, 15, 18, 19, 22, 23, 25n, 27, 30, 33, 34, 36n, 37n, 38n, 39, 59, 63–75, 77, 81, 83, 85, 87, 109, 112, 117, 118, 119, 123, 123n, 135, 146, 147–8, 149, 150, 151, 152, 152n, 153n, 172, 173, 176, 185n, 202, 206, 224, 231, 232, 240n, 243, 244, 250n, 253, 256, 258, 260n, 303
Heinle, Christoph Friedrich, 28
Heller, Hermann, 274
Henrich, Dieter, 147
Heraclitus of Ephesus, 24n, 64, 65, 147
hexis, 18, 21–4
Hierocles, 237
history, 31, 34, 44, 54, 55, 57, 70, 81, 133, 147, 156, 174, 208, 213, 214, 221, 283, 285, 290
  angel of, 29, 282, 286
  of being, 67, 69, 70, 71, 73
  bourgeois, 275
  as catastrophe, 30, 224
  end of, 110, 142–3, 268, 283, 287
  experience of, 30
  human / of humanity, 67, 72
  of philosophy, 128, 132, 133, 135, 227
  philosophy of, 29, 47, 159, 276, 283
  post-, 142, 143
Hjelmslev, Louis, 118
Hobbes, Thomas, 11, 12, 83, 92, 93, 104, 112, 238, 247, 248
Hölderlin, Friedrich, 12, 34, 38n, 103, 139, 146–53
homo sacer (concept), 3, 52, 53, 54, 89, 90, 95, 114, 123, 132, 133, 195, 211, 220, 243, 297, 298, 306, 310
Homo Sacer (project/series), 10, 15, 21, 24, 31, 32, 34, 35, 41, 51, 52, 55, 58, 63, 65, 68, 69, 80, 81, 87, 93, 97, 109, 122, 186, 193, 196, 205, 224, 227, 238, 247, 262,

283, 306, 307, 308, 309, 310, 311
Horkheimer, Max, 193, 199n
Husserl, Edmund, 232, 234, 236, 237, 238, 240n, 241n, 253
hypostasis, 186, 188, 189, 238

I
　empirical, 163, 167, 168
　transcendental, 163, 167
image, 42–3, 49n, 126, 182, 208, 210, 212–13, 214, 258
　dialectical, 9, 307
imagination, 125, 126, 128, 213
immanence, 132, 133–4, 135, 136, 202, 203, 204, 274
　absolute, 273
　philosophy of, 106, 135, 253
impotentiality, 189, 253, 259, 273, 278, 279, 299
inclusion, 53, 73, 88, 95
　exclusive, 17
　political, 104
indistinction/indifference, 43, 96, 134, 136, 144, 205, 247, 260n, 265, 278, 286, 299
　zone of, 53, 186, 203, 232, 234, 246, 265
infancy, 3, 30, 118, 162, 165, 168, 168, 209, 231
inoperativity, 5, 34, 63, 64, 68, 73, 92, 93, 95, 132, 142, 168, 201, 205–7, 262, 267, 269, 278, 280, 298–9, 308, 310
intellect, 186, 187, 190, 204
　active, 128–9
　potential, 128–9
　universal, 128
intelligibility, 184, 219
interruption, 30, 32, 225, 305
inversion/reversal,
　messianic, 6, 34, 38n, 289

Jakobson, Roman, 118, 122
Jellinek, Georg, 274
Jesi, Furio, 11
Jesus, 79, 294, 295; *see also* Christ
jouissance, 253, 254, 255, 256, 259, 260n
Judaism, 5, 77, 85, 284, 285, 289
judgment, 79
　aesthetic, 65, 164
　divine, 289
Jung, Carl Gustav, 249n, 250n

justice, 7, 42, 43, 78, 79, 158, 233, 289–90
　natural, 179
iustitium, 245

Kabbalah, 282, 286, 288
Kafka, Franz, 6, 7, 32, 34, 35, 38n, 77, 154–61, 254, 288
kairos, 9, 82–3, 84, 260, 275, 281n
Kant, Immanuel, 30, 118, 138, 139, 148, 162–70, 173, 193, 236, 253
katargesis, 23, 34, 78, 80, 92, 143
katechon, 77, 83–4, 87, 90–3, 284, 285, 289
Kelsen, Hans, 170n, 274
Kingdom, 94
　of God, 93
　Messianic, 93, 256, 259, 312
Klee, Paul, 282, 286
Kleist, Heinrich von, 197
Klossowski, Pierre, 111, 193
Kojève, Alexandre, 109, 110, 139, 140, 142, 143
Kommerell, Max, 11
Kraus, Karl, 42

labour, 22, 115, 144, 266–7, 268, 269, 280
　division of, 268–9
Lacan, Jacques, 117, 118, 122, 124n, 147, 193, 252–61
Laclau, Ernesto, 250n
Lacoue-Labarthe, Philippe, 147
language, 3, 4, 29, 30, 31, 41–4, 47, 49n, 65–6, 68, 69, 72, 86, 89, 120, 121, 123, 126, 131, 132, 134, 135, 136, 137, 138, 139, 140, 141, 143, 174, 178, 180–2, 183–4, 202, 207, 230, 237, 253, 259, 279, 304, 305, 307, 309, 313
　being-in-, 48
　experience of, 8, 30, 117–19, 122, 127, 141, 174, 258
　fact of, 277, 304, 311
　limits of, 118
　philosophy of, 29, 30, 159
　place of, 118, 120, 140, 279
　pure, 165
　question of, 30, 118, 183
Lassalle, Ferdinand, 274
law, 1, 7, 21, 52, 60n, 61n, 64, 77–80, 81, 89, 90, 94, 95, 96, 104, 111, 133, 134, 136, 143, 155–9, 165, 166, 167, 168, 225, 239, 245,

law (cont.)
    247, 248, 253–4, 255, 256, 257,
        259, 261n, 273, 274, 275, 276,
        277, 278, 286, 287, 288, 289,
        305
    absence of, 92
    constitutional, 238, 284
    consummation/fulfilling of, 77, 78,
        79, 157
    deactivation/deposition of, 7, 78–9,
        80, 81, 83, 143, 158
    divine, 167
    door of, 157, 254
    -of-the-Father, 256
    force of, 156
    historical / of history, 102
    international, 90, 104, 112
    and order, 92
    origin of, 242, 244, 248
    play with, 157, 158, 261n, 312
    positive, 88, 113
    Roman, 53, 89, 280, 298
    sovereign, 243, 244, 249
    study of, 7, 78, 158
    suspension of, 92, 111, 156, 194,
        245, 253
    violence and, 29, 32, 78, 79, 179
    see also norm; rule
lawlessness, 83, 84, 92, 136
Le Thor, seminars, 39, 64, 66, 67, 70,
    72, 147, 150, 151
Lebovici, Gérard, 48n
legislation, 105, 245, 247
    security, 107
legitimacy, 6, 305
    crisis of, 273
    political, 104
Leibniz, Gottfried Wilhelm, 9, 203
Leopardi, Giacomo, 140
Levi, Primo, 119, 236
Lévi-Strauss, Claude, 11, 117
Levinas, Emmanuel, 11, 224, 236,
    241n, 253
liberalism, 170n, 284–5
life, 18, 51, 52, 56, 58, 68, 72, 89, 90,
    104, 134, 136–7, 142, 175, 187,
    189, 190, 191, 192, 201, 209,
    238, 254, 259, 273, 285, 288
    active, 290
    animal, 24n, 293, 296
    bare, 3, 17, 24, 32, 33, 37n, 53, 54,
        55, 63, 69, 73, 88, 89, 95, 104,
        105, 106, 114, 123, 132, 133,
        134, 135, 153n, 159, 165, 175,
        195, 211, 232, 238, 253, 254,
        256, 257, 258, 259, 260, 277,
        280, 292, 293, 296–9, 300n
    biological, 52, 268
    civil, 104
    community of, 144
    contemplative, 16, 205–6
    creaturely, 167, 292, 293–6, 297,
        298, 299
    eternal, 190, 191
    everyday, 44, 107, 112, 127
    finite, 190
    form of see form-of-life
    Greek definitions of, 15, 53, 233
    human, 4, 16, 17, 23, 80, 93, 135,
        137, 168, 195, 199n, 205, 213,
        226, 243, 298
    language and, 41–4, 47, 49n
    law and, 21, 89, 156, 167, 168
    mere, 32, 133, 296
    messianic, 144
    mode of, 15, 16, 24, 25n, 175,
        179
    monastic, 196
    naked, 37n, 115, 140, 281n, 298
    natural, 69, 181, 244, 259, 277
    organic, 136, 191
    philosophical, 59, 173
    physiological, 195
    political, 15, 16, 95, 128, 190, 235,
        238, 259
    power over, 53, 58, 243, 244, 293,
        294, 297
    private, 41, 42, 248
    sacred, 32
    true, 59
    unqualified, 95
    vegetative, 17
    worthy of being lived, 105
linguistics, 29, 31, 65, 117, 118, 119,
    120, 121, 122–3, 249n
liturgy, 71, 72, 210, 308
Locke, John, 9
logos, 17, 22, 64, 144, 166, 181, 182,
    183, 184n, 263, 279
Lohmann, Johannes, 117
Loraux, Nicole, 11, 240n, 246, 247
love, 79, 130n, 142, 178, 194, 253,
    254, 255, 258–9, 260n, 293, 294,
    295
    courtly, 126–7, 197
    of one's neighbour, 79
    of the world, 106
Löwith, Karl, 173, 177n

Lucretius (Titus Lucretius Carus), 234, 237
Lumpenproletariat, 115
Luther, Martin, 143

Machiavelli, Niccolò, 201
machine
  anthropological, 85, 176
  biopolitical, 73
  cultural, 6, 7
  governmental, 70, 94
  metaphysical, 72, 73
  providential, 57
  redemptive, 85
Magritte, René, 193, 198n
Man Ray, 193
Marx, Karl, 115, 138, 142, 262–71
Marxism, 78, 115, 138, 220, 221, 223
  Italian, 280n
materialism
  base, 114, 115
  historical, 33
Mauss, Marcel, 109, 110, 115
means
  pure, 34–5, 144
  without end, 34, 161
mediality, 35, 125, 212, 213
melancholy, 6, 30, 252, 283, 286
Melville, Herman, 6, 21, 260n
Messiah, 23, 34, 77, 80, 82, 83, 84, 143, 156, 157, 159, 233, 275, 276, 283, 285, 288, 313
messianicity, without messianism, 233
messianism, 5, 8, 34, 106, 233, 253, 285, 287, 288, 305
  Christian, 285
  Jewish, 38n, 284, 285, 288
  thwarted, 233
  weak, 289
metaphysics, 2, 65, 66, 67, 71, 75n, 139, 140, 151, 226, 231, 258, 272
  of the body, 197
  critique of, 63, 68, 69, 73
  end of, 138
  overcoming of, 4, 64
  of subjectivity, 73
  Western, 2, 3, 50n, 63, 66, 68, 69, 70, 72, 138, 148, 184n, 186, 189
  of the will, 173, 187
middle voice *see* voice
Mommsen, Theodor, 6
monasticism, 308
  Franciscan, 168
Morante, Elsa, 12, 204, 299n

multitude, 64, 128, 129, 274, 275, 276
Muselmann, 17, 102, 105, 165, 166, 220, 236, 238, 306

Nancy, Jean-Luc, 89, 111, 184
nature, 104, 164, 173–4, 203, 205, 210, 211, 251n, 269
  corrupt, 256
  and culture, 221
  human, 102, 105, 128, 256, 268
  order of, 20
  state of, 92
Nazism, 17, 32, 56, 90, 195, 198, 199n, 219
necessity, 72, 171, 268
  natural, 169n
negation, 78, 88, 97, 113, 139, 140, 142, 148, 240n, 264
  of negation, 224, 225, 226
  self-, 164, 168, 264
negativity, 3, 66, 67, 68, 69, 110, 139, 140, 141, 142, 174, 231, 232, 233, 236, 240n, 253, 258–9, 299
  a-relational, 110
  disengaged, 110, 140
  unemployed/without employ (*sans emploi*), 110, 111, 299
Negri, Antonio, 138, 204, 272–81
Neoplatonism, 137, 183, 188
Newton, Isaac, 203
Nietzsche, Friedrich, 18, 54, 55, 58, 123, 164, 171–7, 206, 212, 232, 233, 243, 244, 253, 307
nihilism, 2, 43, 47, 65, 66, 67, 68, 69, 73, 74, 171, 173, 258, 286
  imperfect, 156, 157
  perfect, 157
9/11, 87, 90, 107
Nougé, Paul, 198n
norm, 1, 2, 23, 88, 89, 90, 96, 97, 104, 166, 167, 168, 273
  constitutional, 88
  juridical, 166
  see also law; rule
noumenon, 163, 166, 167
now-time *see* time: now-
nuda vita, 31, 292, 296; *see also* life
nudity, 224, 255, 256, 259, 260

oath, 79, 80, 178, 305, 307, 308
objet a, 255, 256
Oedipus, 174, 244, 250n
office, 21, 84, 167, 185, 187, 251n, 265–6; *see also* duty; *officium*

officium, 186; *see also* duty; office
oikonomia, 6, 57, 61n, 70, 71, 94, 167, 280
oikos, 53, 243, 244, 246, 248
ontology, 4, 18, 58, 59, 63, 70, 71, 72, 87, 90, 129, 134, 138, 180, 181, 188, 189, 190, 203, 276, 280, 307, 309
   of actuality, 207
   Christian, 186
   classical, 186
   of command, 162, 167, 168
   of habit, 23
   in the middle voice, 203
   modal, 23, 72, 95, 96, 97, 136
   modern, 186
   of nudity, 256
   of operativity, 167
   political, 15
   of potentiality, 18, 21, 206, 207
   presuppositional, 97
   of style, 59, 128, 175
   of substance, 162, 167
   of transformation, 290
   Western, 94
ontotheology, 66, 67
Open, the, 259
operativity, 72, 167, 186, 187–8, 189, 190, 191, 192, 276, 279, 286
opposition, binary, 127, 231, 232
order, 91–2, 96, 104, 132, 275
   biological, 191
   biopolitical, 191
   feudal, 265
   Franciscan, 278
   historical, 283, 286
   juridical, 111, 167
   juridico-political, 88, 244, 277
   legal, 88, 277, 286
   natural/of nature, 20, 264
   normative, 89
   political, 89, 194, 227, 243
   social, 89, 219
   Symbolic, 253, 254, 257
   theological, 264
origin, 4, 15, 55, 69, 121, 174, 212–13, 237, 242, 248, 286, 289
Overbeck, Franz, 174

paradigm, 4, 20, 22, 51, 53, 54–5, 29, 69, 70, 71, 72, 88, 89, 94, 96, 121, 132, 133, 134, 136, 140, 148, 163, 165, 166, 167, 168, 179, 181, 187, 188, 190, 191, 192, 212–13, 252, 255, 256, 272, 273, 274, 288, 298, 306, 312
Parmenides of Elea, 64
parody, 197, 200n
parousia, 5, 82, 83, 91, 257
Pasquali, Giorgio, 6
Pasolini, Pier Paolo, 12
passivity, 6, 202, 209, 235–6, 281n
pathos formula (*Pathosformel*), 209–10, 211, 213, 214n
Patriot Act, 90
Paul the Apostle, 8–9, 23, 34, 38n, 76–86, 91, 92, 111, 117, 143–4, 198, 221, 223, 224, 233, 264, 284, 285, 286, 288, 289, 312
Peckham, John, 126
Peterson, Erik, 11, 94, 191
phantasm, 126, 128, 152, 172, 178, 197, 242, 252
phenomenology
Philo of Byblos, 24
philology, 118, 305
philosophy, 1–2, 5, 8, 9, 10–11, 27, 29, 64, 65, 132–3, 139–40, 141, 143, 146, 147, 151, 201, 212, 222–3, 226, 304, 305, 313
   coming, 3, 7, 119, 183
   end of, 172, 174
   first, 59
   Greek, 58
   history of, 132, 135, 227
   of history, 29, 47, 276, 283
   of language, 30
   modern, 71, 164, 236
   moral, 167
   political, 63, 76, 88, 127, 159, 195, 196
   Western, 128, 162, 164, 165, 157, 181, 203, 258
Plato, 24n, 75n, 96, 131, 132, 134, 144, 178–85, 252, 304, 305
play, 35, 142, 157, 158, 252, 251n, 261, 312, 313
Pliny the Elder, 28
Plotinus, 25n, 186–92, 236
poetry, 2, 8, 10, 30, 83, 118, 126, 127, 139, 140, 143, 146, 147, 148, 150, 151, 178, 207, 220, 260n, 305, 311
poiesis, 19, 22, 280
police, 56, 94, 104, 159, 284
polis, 4, 17, 53, 64, 69, 89, 102, 148, 153n, 191, 235, 244, 246, 248, 256, 268

political theology *see* theology: political
politics, 1, 4, 29, 33, 34, 35, 41, 52, 59, 69, 74, 90, 94, 95, 102, 103, 104, 106, 108, 127, 129, 171, 175, 176, 178, 191, 206-7, 245, 246, 247, 252, 263, 276, 279, 285, 290, 297, 307, 309
 classical, 190, 298
 coming, 224
 contemporary, 50n, 201
 democratic, 103, 105, 107
 of inoperativity, 73
 liberal, 105, 107
 messianic, 76, 86
 modern, 53, 54, 104, 105, 235
 ontic, 71
 pastoral, 56
 radical, 194
 republican, 103
 spectacular, 44-8
 totalitarian, 104, 235
 Western, 16, 33, 68, 70, 90, 106, 268
 world, 273, 286
pornography, 197
Porphyry of Tyre, 24n
post-history, 142, 143
potential, 6, 10, 15, 18-21, 22, 23, 104, 106, 129, 182, 186, 187, 205, 206, 207, 266
 destituent, 21, 96, 162, 168, 169, 179, 239, 273, 278-80, 310
 not-to, 20, 236, 259, 279, 299
potentiality, 5, 10, 17, 18, 20, 21, 26n, 68, 96, 103, 125, 127, 128, 129, 135, 136, 142, 144, 168, 171, 172, 187, 189, 206, 207, 209, 220, 235, 253, 259, 261n, 263, 265, 266, 269, 273, 278-80, 280n, 288, 289, 292, 299
 pure, 6, 190, 220
potestas, 243, 244, 245, 273
 vitae necisque, 243, 244
power, 18, 43, 50n, 51, 60n, 61n, 80, 81, 83, 86, 89, 90, 92, 93, 96, 97, 103, 104, 111, 112, 135, 154, 158, 159, 191, 206, 223, 247, 253, 263, 265, 273, 284, 289, 294, 297
 absolute, 20, 26n, 94, 102
 angelic, 80
 bio-, 52, 53, 276
 constituent, 18, 20, 21, 59, 102, 168, 239, 273-6, 277, 278, 280, 280n
 constituted, 18, 20, 59, 84, 92, 168, 169, 273-6, 278
 constituting *see* power: constituent
 destituent, 21
 disciplinary, 53
 divine, 20
 emergency, 107
 executive, 289, 290
 of the father over the son, 243, 244, 245
 governmental, 94
 heavenly, 80
 juridical, 166
 labour, 266, 267
 messianic, 90, 92
 mundane, 80
 ordained, 20, 23, 26n
 over life and death, 53, 58
 pastoral, 56, 57
 political, 43, 58, 86, 243, 248, 285
 presuppositional, 144, 181, 183
 profane, 80, 92
 religious, 86
 sovereign, 18, 52, 53, 54, 61n, 69, 73, 87, 88, 89, 91, 93, 103, 107, 159, 165, 166, 195, 243, 245, 274, 277, 292, 293, 294, 295, 296, 297, 298, 299
 State, 53, 92
 will to, 173
praxis, 3, 19, 22, 94, 96, 128, 142, 144, 166, 167, 186, 192, 206, 211, 221, 261n, 266, 274, 275, 278, 279, 280
 administrative, 167, 168
 animal, 142
 human, 73, 86, 93, 141, 144, 167, 168, 262
 political, 73, 222
 social, 141
presupposition, 44, 73, 94, 95, 96, 139, 140, 141, 142, 144, 178, 181-2, 183
priest, 187, 249, 265, 266, 308
productivity, 74, 273, 279, 280
profanation, 35, 86, 144, 227, 228n
profane, the, 35, 93, 112, 159, 287, 297
proletariat, 115, 191, 264, 266
prophecy, 285, 289
Protogenes, 29
Proust, Marcel, 132

providence, 57, 70
psychoanalysis, 252, 257, 260n, 261n, 308
psychology, 213, 245, 249n
purity, 232, 236

Queneau, Raymond, 142

Rabelais, François, 196
racism, 52, 199n
Rawls, John, 274
redemption, 5, 34, 45, 79, 85, 86, 91, 93, 127, 133, 136, 156, 159, 222, 223, 224, 253, 257, 264, 283, 285, 286, 287, 288, 289, 290, 296, 299, 312
refugee, 105, 107
repressed, return of, 249
repression, 242
revelation, 66, 156, 255, 299
  Nothing of, 156, 287
reversal/inversion, messianic, 6, 34, 38n, 289
revolution, 78, 264, 267
  French, 193
right, 143, 204, 265
  divine, 194
  human, 104–5
  over life and death, 243
Rilke, Rainer Maria, 11, 12
Robertson Smith, William, 115
Rousseau, Jean-Jacques, 61n, 62n, 263–4
rule, 69, 88, 89, 165, 167, 186, 196, 197, 249n, 277
  authoritarian, 90
  and exception, 33, 88, 111, 156, 248, 253
  of law, 287
  majority, 104
  monastic, 196
  positive, 105
  see also law; norm
rupture, 4, 82, 258
  historical, 2, 101
  moments of, 101

Sabbath, 85, 256, 257
sacer, 3, 116, 235, 242, 243, 250n
  esto, 244
  and taboo, 243
sacrament, 65
sacratio, 243
sacred, the, 109, 112, 114, 116, 142, 150, 159, 228n, 242, 287, 297, 307
  ambivalence of, 115, 116, 249n
sacredness, 32
sacrifice, 3, 89, 109, 110, 114, 258, 259
Sade, Marquis de, 193–200
sadomasochism, 194, 195, 199n
salvation, 5, 71, 85, 93, 105, 257, 286, 288, 312
Saussure, Ferdinand de, 117, 118, 119, 120, 122, 124n
Saxl, Fritz, 210
Schelling, Friedrich Wilhelm Joseph, 18, 206, 242, 243
Schmitt, Carl, 11, 12, 32–3, 38n, 53, 76, 83, 86, 87–98, 105, 107, 109, 111, 152n, 170n, 198, 232, 233, 240n, 247, 248, 253, 274, 277, 284–5, 287, 288, 296
Scholem, Gershom, 7, 32, 38n, 156, 282–91
secularism, 312
secularisation, 57, 86, 91, 143, 307
self-reference/self-referentiality, 165, 166, 167, 231, 234–5, 237, 238
  paradox of, 234, 235
semiology, 2, 120
shame, 159, 236, 241n
Shekhinah, 42, 44, 45, 47, 286, 290
sigetics, 258
signature, 54, 61n, 133, 209, 210, 211, 212, 213, 256, 307, 308, 312
singularity, 58, 73, 95, 175, 212
  whatever, 48, 60n, 259
Situationist International, 40
slave, 17, 22, 72, 81, 144, 268, 269, 280, 295
  and master, 110, 140, 144
slavery, 144, 195, 294, 298
Smith, Adam, 57
society, 31, 50n, 115, 267
  classless, 262, 263, 267–70
  democratic, 106
  post-democratic, 104
  spectacular / of the spectacle, 40, 41, 42, 43–4, 45, 46, 47, 48, 104
  totalitarian, 104
sociology, 90
  of religion, 242
Socrates, 24n, 178, 179, 184n
Sophocles, 147, 148, 152n, 153n
soteriology, 5, 6, 32, 34

sovereign, 88, 89, 92, 94, 96, 105, 111, 112, 159, 167, 194, 195, 243, 244, 247, 248, 249, 265, 297
  absolute, 112
sovereignty, 32, 33, 42, 51, 53, 57, 61n, 62n, 69, 70, 88, 93, 94, 96, 102–3, 106, 107, 109, 111, 112, 114, 115, 134, 143, 158, 159, 171, 179, 230, 231, 238, 243, 247, 251n, 253, 254, 256, 257, 258, 260, 160n, 261n, 274, 275, 276, 277, 278, 284, 298
  aporias of, 18
  baroque, 97
  logic of, 21, 89, 94, 95, 97
  paradox of, 111, 112
  theory of, 32, 53, 87, 88, 89, 90, 254
Spinoza, Baruch, 18, 76, 95, 131, 135, 201–7, 253, 272–3, 280n
stasis, 178, 238, 244, 246–7, 248
state, 44, 47, 48, 61, 68, 78, 80, 83, 84, 91, 104, 112, 143, 167, 191, 192, 225, 250n, 273, 274, 275
  biopolitical, 56
  modern, 52, 56, 94
  nation, 104, 105
  Nazi, 53
  police, 104
  security, 107
  totalitarian, 52, 162
state of emergency *see* exception
state of exception *see* exception
state of nature *see* nature
Statius, Publius Papinius, 128
stil novo see dolce stil novo
Stoa, 22, 24n, 234, 237
structuralism, 117
study, 1, 4–7, 35, 38n, 79, 157, 158, 305, 312, 313
style
  of life, 58, 96, 128, 175
  ontology of, 59, 128, 175
subject, 4, 8, 23, 56, 58–9, 61n, 112, 114, 122, 136, 142, 150, 167, 176, 181, 183, 187, 188, 189, 190, 202, 213, 223, 225, 236, 245, 252, 253, 254, 255, 262, 264, 272
  free, 59
  Kantian, 139, 166, 168
  Lacanian, 252–60
  of law, 133
  messianic, 264

and object, 65, 126, 127, 129, 134, 202, 237
  political, 85, 115
  of religion, 257
  transcendental, 139, 164, 165, 166, 168, 169
subjectification, 59, 61n, 236, 237, 238
subjectivity, 65, 73, 165, 166, 189, 236, 237, 253, 262
  transcendental, 163, 165
sublation, 65, 110; *see also Aufhebung*
sublime, 164, 165, 167, 169
substance, 23, 95, 107, 164, 183, 188, 190, 203–5, 265, 266
  ontology of, 162, 167
superstructure, 115, 221
Surrealism, 198n
suspension, 81, 88, 89, 127, 129, 164, 165, 166, 233–4, 242, 248, 256, 267, 278
  messianic, 221, 223
  of the law, 92, 156, 194, 245, 277
Szondi, Peter, 147

taboo, 245, 247, 248–9, 251n
  incest, 253
  and *sacer*, 243–4
Talmud, 5, 7
Taubes, Jacob, 11, 12, 222, 284–7, 288, 289
temporality, 67, 275, 276, 281n, 304
  political, 276
Tertullian, 83, 91
testimony, 8, 59, 119
theology, 29, 34, 38n, 53, 94, 113, 134, 167, 292, 312
  Christian, 56, 57, 143
  economic, 94
  negative, 113
  political, 76, 87, 91, 94, 272, 276
  positive, 113
thing itself, 125, 126, 144, 180, 181, 182, 183, 184, 223
Third Reich, 195
Thomas, Yan, 11, 25:n
Thompson, E. P. (Edward Palmer), 263–4
threshold, 22, 32, 109, 119, 120, 122, 126, 132, 133, 134, 135, 219, 232, 247
time, 25n, 30, 43–4, 55, 139, 159, 178, 208, 236, 241n, 276
  apocalyptic, 256, 257
  chronological, 257, 288

time *(cont.)*
  cyclical, 43
  end of, 82, 93, 142, 156, 284
  eschatological, 82
  hitorical, 283, 288
  irreversible, 43, 44
  kairotic, 284, 288
  linear, 221, 276
  messianic, 23, 82–3, 85, 92, 117, 143, 221, 257, 288, 289
  now-, 82–3, 84, 85, 283, 287, 288
  operational, 117, 288
Titian (Tiziano Vecellio), 132
Torah, 143, 155, 287, 288, 290
totalitarianism, 101, 102, 104
trace, 231–2, 233, 234–5, 236, 237, 238, 239
tradition, 1, 2–4, 5, 6, 7, 8, 57, 63, 66, 79, 101, 151, 212, 305
  Christian, 190
  crisis of, 2, 3
  critique of, 2, 230
  democratic, 107
  Judaeo-Christian, 34
  metaphysical, 69, 142, 165, 230
  ontological, 258
  political, 32, 104, 106, 175
  republican, 106
  theological-political, 105
  Western, 3, 4, 6, 29, 78, 90, 101, 102, 183, 306, 311
transcendence, 171, 235, 253, 275, 283, 285
transcendentalism, 163
transmissibility, 2, 5, 34, 159
Trinity, 57
Trump, Donald, 251n
typos, 9, 82

ultrahistory, 312
unconscious, 122, 212, 213, 242, 246, 249, 251n, 252, 260n
undecidability, 144, 164
Unheimlich, 242, 244, 247, 250n
unknowable, 164, 227
unsayable, 182, 184n
unthought, 219–20, 227
Urphänomen, 213
use, 1, 2, 21–4, 34, 72, 138, 143–4, 150, 188, 189, 190, 192, 235, 242, 248, 249, 272, 279, 310
  another/new, 4, 6, 7, 80, 81, 143, 144, 158, 192, 261n, 261, 269, 280

  of the body, 22, 60, 144, 234, 237, 238, 248, 273, 280
  common, 86, 248, 261n
  free, 143, 144, 149, 150, 151
  messianic, 81
  of the proper, 150
  of the self/oneself, 22–3, 144, 149, 151, 188–9, 234, 238, 239, 273
utilitarianism, 102
utopia/utopianism, 106, 225, 226–7, 267–8, 269, 283, 287

value, 30, 210, 232
  exchange, 42
  truth, 8
  use, 42
violence, 31, 69, 79, 83, 95, 102, 103, 104, 198, 206, 243, 253, 258, 264, 293
  aestheticisation of, 114
  divine, 32, 92
  governmental, 83
  and law, 29, 32, 78, 158, 167, 179
  law-positing, 32
  law-preserving, 32
  political, 297
  pure, 32, 34
  sovereign, 73
Virgil (Publius Vergilius Maro), 127
Virno, Paolo, 49n
vocation, 64, 68, 144, 184n, 263, 264, 265, 268, 269, 280
  biological, 23
  messianic, 77, 84, 143, 223, 264
  revolutionary, 264
voice, 66, 138, 140, 141, 142, 174, 184n, 231
  animal, 140
  medial/middle, 22, 202–5, 237, 272
  passive, 22

Waiblinger, Wilhelm, 148
Walser, Robert, 6
war, civil, 178, 242, 246, 247, 284
Warburg, Aby, 121, 208–15
Weber, Max, 108
Weil, Simone, 292–301
whatever
  being, 136, 227
  singularity, 48, 60n, 259
will, 23, 104, 163, 175, 187–8, 189, 235, 266, 269
  democratic, 274, 275
  divine, 20, 102, 265

free, 164, 167, 187
  metaphysics of, 173, 187
  of the people, 107
  political, 107
  to power, 173
  utopian, 106
witness, 119–20, 165, 166, 236, 238
  complete, 166, 167
Wittgenstein, Ludwig, 11, 12
Wölfflin, Heinrich, 214n
work, 6, 10, 18, 21, 22, 23, 24n, 78, 104, 142, 186, 187–8, 205, 206–7, 209, 257, 262–3, 267, 269, 273, 279
  absence of, 142, 206, 267
  of art, 33, 35, 58, 172, 173–6, 208, 209
  of man, 159, 262–3, 279, 280
  see also ergon

Yates, Frances, 214

Žižek, Slavoj, 32, 225, 228n, 229n, 257
zoè, 15, 16–18, 21, 24, 24n, 53, 68, 69, 70, 73, 75n, 95, 122, 127, 175, 179, 181, 184, 190, 192n, 224, 232, 244, 255, 259, 297

EU representative:
Easy Access System Europe
Mustamäe tee 50, 10621 Tallinn, Estonia
Gpsr.requests@easproject.com

www.ingramcontent.com/pod-product-compliance
Lightning Source LLC
Chambersburg PA
CBHW061706300426
44115CB00014B/2579